University of the
West of England
BRISTOL

ST. MATTHIAS
LIBRARY

This book should be returned by the last date
stamped below.

UWE, BRISTOL        B1087 6.93
Printing & Stationery Services

# A DIFFERENT WORLD
## FOR WOMEN

*Millicent Garrett Fawcett, 1890.*

# A DIFFERENT WORLD
# FOR WOMEN

## The Life of Millicent
## Garrett Fawcett

—————— • ——————

# DAVID RUBINSTEIN

 HARVESTER
WHEATSHEAF

NEW YORK   LONDON   TORONTO   SYDNEY   TOKYO   SINGAPORE

First published 1991 by
Harvester Wheatsheaf
66 Wood Lane End, Hemel Hempstead
Hertfordshire HP2 4RG
A division of
Simon & Schuster International Group

Typeset in 10½/12 pt Bembo
by Inforum Typesetting, Portsmouth

Printed and bound in Great Britain by
BPCC Wheatons Ltd
Exeter

British Library Cataloguing in Publication Data

Rubinstein, David
A different world for women: the life of Millicent
Garrett Fawcett.
I. Title
305.42092

ISBN 0-7108-1104-7

1 2 3 4 5   95 94 93 92 91

To
Claude and Pierre Pujol
with love and thanks

# CONTENTS

viii                          *Contents*

# LIST OF ILLUSTRATIONS

# PREFACE

The idea of writing a biography of Millicent Garrett Fawcett occurred to me
when I was working on *Before the Suffragettes* (1986). Somewhat to my
surprise I discovered that she had become one of the leading figures in that
book, her interests stretching over the whole gamut of the women's movement and her writing being informed by a lucid, compelling common sense.
There has been no full biography of her apart from Ray Strachey's, published two years after her death in 1929, and while that book contains a great
deal of essential information including letters unavailable elsewhere, it is
marked by a reticence remarkable even at that date and by the implicit
assumption that everything Mrs Fawcett did was right. I have often disagreed with her, sometimes strongly, but I hope that she emerges as a
woman of exceptional talents and achievements, and as the principal leader
of one of the most important movements of modern times. This is the more
important as she is so often known to non-specialists, even in her own
birthplace, as a sister and wife rather than in her own right.[1]
   As a biographer I have faced three problems easier to specify than to
resolve. Mrs Fawcett's political convictions and actions emerge from this
account more clearly than the details of her personality and private life. That
this is so is dictated by the nature of the available evidence, for she assiduously guarded her dignity and privacy. Second, during the most intense
years of the suffrage struggle and later, her public statements were often
drafted collectively rather than personally. Although they undoubtedly represented her convictions, her personality for crucial periods was partly sub-
merged in the organizations which she led or represented. Finally, during
the same period, when she was the public voice of constitutional suffragists,
she was often written and spoken about in terms of adulation. The praise she
received was sincere as well as a boost to morale, but further evidence of
disagreement with her attitudes and methods would have helped to produce
a more rounded picture.
   My heavy debt to the Strachey biography, to Leslie Stephen's life of
Henry Fawcett and Jo Manton's life of Elizabeth Garrett Anderson will be
obvious. It will also be obvious that it would have been very much more

difficult to have written this book without the published and unpublished work of many contributors to the 'new wave' of women's history which has done so much to reshape our views of the past. These include Johanna Alberti, Rosamund Billington, Patricia Hollis, Sandra Stanley Holton, Leslie Parker Hume, Susan Kingsley Kent, Rita McWilliams–Tullberg, Andrew Rosen, Constance Rover, Jo Vellacott and Ann Wiltsher. I am also heavily indebted to Brian Harrison and Martin Pugh, from whose writings I have greatly benefited, perhaps not least because my sympathies often differ from theirs. I have also been assisted by short and perceptive biographies of Mrs Fawcett by Barbara Caine, Ann Oakley and Dale Spender.

My personal obligations have also been heavy. The first and most enduring has been to Gail Malmgreen, who, without wholly concealing her doubts about the appropriateness of a man writing women's history, has provided 'Millie' letters and references from numerous archives in Britain and the United States, and consistent encouragement during busy and fraught years. She has also read the manuscript of this book and vigorously suggested numerous improvements and corrections to my great benefit. The manuscript has also been read by Graham Johnson and David Martin at a time when they were heavily preoccupied by pressing, complementary academic matters. I hope that they will find some recompense for their labours in the fact that I have adopted almost all of their suggestions. I have also been assisted by many other scholars, all of whom have displayed heartening interest in my work and suggested many essential sources. I have benefited in particular from a long and fruitful correspondence with Leah Leneman, who has generously offered advice and provided valuable material, particularly relating to Scotland. Other assistance has been provided by Joyce Bellamy, Barbara Caine, Sheila Fletcher, Lawrence Goldman (to whom I am grateful for an opportunity to publish an article on the Fawcett marriage), June Hannam, Brian Harrison, Patricia Hollis, Joan Huffman, Philippa Levine, Jane Lewis and Jo Manton. I hope that they will forgive me for omitting, for reasons of space, acknowledgement of each of their references and suggestions. I have also been guided through the arcane mysteries of the Public Record Office by Susan Sutton and the Bertrand Russell Papers by Sheila Turcon.

One of the delights of research is the opportunity which it offers to the mendicant scholar to meet friendly, interesting and hospitable people. I am particularly indebted in this context to Catriona Williams, great grand-daughter of Elizabeth Garrett Anderson, and to her husband John for making access to the Anderson Papers in their custody such an enjoyable and memorable experience. I am also indebted to Christopher Wood, another Fawcett great grand-nephew, for sharing his knowledge of Aldeburgh and Garrett family history; to Barbara Strachey Halpern for making available to me the wealth of family files then in her custody and reminiscences of her mother, Ray Strachey; to Barbara Brook, Owen Justice, Catherine and Ian Russell and John and Lucy Tabor.

The libraries and other archives in which I have worked, too numerous to list here, are indicated in the bibliography. I have been particularly assisted by David Doughan, Susan Cross and Penny Baker at the Fawcett Library, and Jean Ayton and her colleagues in the archives of Manchester Public Library, all of whom displayed greater forbearance and interest than I expected or deserved. Annette Mevis of the International Information Centre and Archives of the Women's Movement, Amsterdam, came to my rescue at a critical stage by sending me copies of Mrs Fawcett's letters to Helena Auerbach. I am also much indebted to John Pinfold, Angela Raspin and their colleagues at the British Library of Political and Economic Science, Ann Phillips of Newnham College, Kate Perry of Girton College, and Sandra Raban and Jonathan Steinberg of Trinity Hall, Cambridge, June Norman and David Bones of the National Council of Women, Soudi Janssens of the State Historical Society of Iowa, and staff of the University of Hull Library, the magnificent John Rylands Library, Manchester, the International Institute of Social History, Amsterdam, and the Suffolk and Cumbria Record Offices, at Lowestoft, Bury St Edmunds and Carlisle. Although I have seldom been able to emancipate myself from using titles when writing about the women of a period when the use of titles was universal, I hope that the people mentioned here will accept the assurance that no offence is intended by their omission in the more informal conditions of the 1990s. My visits to archives have been made possible by generous and repeated financial assistance from the Nuffield Foundation, to which I owe, and here offer, warmest thanks.

After my retirement from the University of Hull in 1988 I was enabled to write in calm and friendly conditions during an eighteen-month period as visiting professor at the University of Tours. I am grateful for the support and interest which my colleagues there displayed across the boundaries of nationality and discipline. Finally I am grateful to Ann Holt above all others. She has coped with the intrusive 'Millie' as a ghost in her home for a prolonged period, assisted with research, read drafts, adjudicated over matters of English style and generally been of as much assistance and support as one writer and spouse can be to another. Words are an inadequate means of indicating, let alone repaying my debt.

David Rubinstein
London, July 1990

NOTE

1. Ronald Blythe, guide to Aldeburgh parish church, 1988 edn, p. 13.

# ACKNOWLEDGEMENTS

The author and publisher are grateful to the following individuals and institutions for permission to publish copyright material: the Right Hon. Earl of Balfour (A.J. Balfour Papers, Lady Frances Balfour Papers; Fawcett Library, Scottish Record Office); the Mistress and Fellows, Girton College, Cambridge (Girton Archives); the Principal and Fellows, Newnham College, Cambridge (Newnham Archives); the Master and Fellows, Trinity College, Cambridge (Pethick-Lawrence Papers); Trinity Hall, Cambridge (Leslie Stephen manuscript biography of Henry Fawcett); Corporation of London, Greater London Record Office (W.H. Dickinson Papers, Women's Local Government Society Papers); Cumbria Record Office and Frank Marshall (Catherine Marshall Papers); James Fawcett (Millicent Garrett Fawcett Papers; Fawcett Library and other archives); Josephine Butler Society (Josephine Butler Papers; Fawcett Library), Jill Liddington (Selina Cooper Papers; Lancashire Record Office); McMaster University, Russell Permissions Committee (Bertrand Russell Papers); Macmillan Publishers Ltd and the University of Reading (Macmillan Archive); City of Manchester Leisure Services Committee (Manchester Society for Women's Suffrage Papers, Millicent Garrett Fawcett Papers); John Rylands University Library of Manchester (C.P. Scott Papers, Women's Suffrage Collections); Bodleian Library, Oxford (H.A.L. Fisher Papers, Sidney Lee Correspondence, C.H. Pearson Papers); Sidgwick & Jackson (Sidgwick & Jackson letter-book); W.K. Stead (W.T. Stead Papers; Churchill College, Cambridge, and Manchester Public Library). The author and publisher ask the indulgence of any other copyright holders whom they have been unable to locate in advance of publication.

The illustrations are reproduced by permission of the following copyright holders: British Library, frontispiece, 3, 13; the Principal and Fellows, Newnham College, Cambridge, 5; Fawcett Library, 14; *Illustrated London News*, 6, 7, 12; City of Manchester Leisure Services Committee, 8, 9, 11; *Punch*, 4; Catriona and John Williams, 1, 2.

# ABBREVIATIONS

I have tried to present the notes as concisely as possible consistent with clarity. Where a single name is indicated in a note, fuller details are provided in the bibliography.

The principal abbreviations used in the text and notes are the following:

| | |
|---|---|
| BL Add. Mss | British Library Additional Manuscripts |
| BLPES | British Library of Political and Economic Science (London School of Economics) |
| CC | *Common Cause* |
| CNSWS | Central National Society for Women's Suffrage |
| D/Mar/3 | Catherine Marshall Papers, Cumbria Record Office |
| EFF | Election Fighting Fund |
| ER | *Englishwoman's Review* |
| FLA | Fawcett Library Archives |
| FLALC | Fawcett Library Autograph Letter Collection |
| GLRO | Greater London Record Office |
| IIAV | International Information Centre and Archives for the Women's Movement, Amsterdam |
| IWSA | International Woman Suffrage Association |
| JRL | John Rylands Library, Manchester |
| LNSWS | London National Society for Women's Suffrage |
| LNU | League of Nations Union |
| LSWS | London Society for Women's Suffrage |
| M50/1 | Manchester Society for Women's Suffrage Papers, Manchester Public Library |
| M50/2–8 | Millicent Garrett Fawcett Papers, Manchester Public Library |
| MAS | Maud Arncliffe-Sennett Collection, British Library |
| MG | *Manchester Guardian* |
| MGF | Millicent Garrett Fawcett |
| MGF | Ray Strachey, *Millicent Garrett Fawcett* (1931) |
| NSWS | National Society for Women's Suffrage |

| | |
|---|---|
| NVA | National Vigilance Association |
| NUSEC | National Union of Societies for Equal Citizenship |
| NUWSS | National Union of Women's Suffrage Societies |
| NUWW | National Union of Women Workers |
| PP | Parliamentary Papers |
| PRO | Public Record Office |
| TAS | Travellers' Aid Society |
| *WIR* | Millicent Garrett Fawcett, *What I Remember* (1924) |
| *WL* | *Woman's Leader* |
| WLF | Women's Liberal Federation |
| WLUA | Women's Liberal Unionist Association |
| WLGS | Women's Local Government Society |
| *WSJ* | *Women's Suffrage Journal* |
| WSPU | Women's Social and Political Union |

# PART I

# YOUTH AND MARRIAGE 1847–84

# CHAPTER 1

## THE MAKING OF A FEMINIST 1847–67

The family of Newson Garrett (1812–93) and Louisa Dunnell (1813–1903) was one of the most remarkable in the history of British feminism. Three of their six daughters were important pioneers. Elizabeth (1836–1917) was the first British woman doctor and remains the best-known member of the family. Her struggle against institutional and personal prejudice was a classic case of confronting the male establishment and emerging victorious. Agnes (1845–1935) contributed to opening the professions to women by becoming one of the first women 'house decorators'; she worked in partnership with her cousin Rhoda Garrett and remained in business long after Rhoda's death in 1882. The problems which they were warned that they would face, especially the supposed need to swear at workmen and mount ladders,[1] did not stand in their way. Millicent (1847–1929), the subject of this book, is best known for her work in the women's suffrage movement, but she was active in almost every aspect of women's emancipation. She was also involved in campaigns affecting children, notably their employment in theatres, and their early marriage in India. In most of her activities she became a leader, and she was always a respected and formidable figure.

The other daughters were less prominent. Louisa (1835–67), the eldest, was briefly the secretary of the first London women's suffrage organization and but for her early death might have become more active than her status as 'Hon. Sec. pro tem' implied. Alice (1842–1925), after living for nearly ten years in India with her lawyer husband, served somewhat inconspicuously on the London School Board from 1873 to 1876. Josephine (1853–1925), the youngest, was the only sister who took no public part in working for the emancipation of her sex.

The four Garrett sons (a fifth died in infancy in 1838) were less in the public eye than the daughters, concentrating on earning the living with which most of their sisters did not have to concern themselves. Newson (1839–1917) became an army officer and black sheep, while Edmund (1840–1914) and George (1854–1929) went into the family business. Only Sam (1850–1923), Millicent's immediate junior and favourite brother, played an active part in promoting the emancipation of women. He was a

3

prominent London solicitor and a strong and effective advocate of women's entry into the legal profession. Two of the sons took part in local government, like their father and their brother-in-law Skelton Anderson. George and Sam became mayors of Aldeburgh, but only Elizabeth, in 1908, achieved renown as the first woman mayor of an English borough.[2]

Even without their famous daughters the Garretts of Aldeburgh were an unusual family. At first glance, however, they were not so exceptional as to produce three leading pioneers of women's rights. Why this should have happened is a fascinating question to which no conclusive answer can be given.

Jo Manton's biography of Elizabeth Garrett Anderson provides a vivid description of the Garrett family background. Both parents were by origin from Suffolk. Newson, who was named after his maternal grandmother, Elizabeth Newson, belonged to a family of agricultural machinery makers in Leiston which long remained prominent.[3] Louisa's family appear to have been smallholders from Dunwich. By the late 1820s her parents John and Elizabeth Dunnell were keeping a public house in London, where her sister Elizabeth married Newson's eldest brother Richard in 1828. Newson himself went at an unspecified date to live in London and married Louisa in 1834 at the same church, St Mary Bryanston Square. After their marriage they moved to Whitechapel and took charge of a pawnbroker's shop belonging to John Dunnell. Newson Garrett was to continue in this occupation for about six years, though he later moved to a site close to Trafalgar Square and was described as 'pawnbroker and silversmith'.[4] It is noteworthy that the wealth of the Garrett family, a secure base from which the sisters could struggle for the emancipation of their sex, should have owed so much to the public house and the pawnbroker's shop.

In 1840 or 1841 Newson Garrett was able, through combining money from his wife and her family, his own savings and a small inheritance from his father Richard of Leiston, to buy a corn and coal warehouse at Snape Bridge near Aldeburgh.[5] It was, in the hindsight of his granddaughter Louisa Garrett Anderson, 'a queer place for an ambitious man to choose for founding a business and a family'.[6] It must have seemed so at the time. An account of Aldeburgh published in 1844, three years before Millicent Garrett's birth, noted that its population, 1,557 in the 1841 census, was heavily dependent upon tourism. There were over fifty houses where lodgings could be obtained, and two inns. It had long been popular with invalids for its pure air, its open coastline and its quiet situation. The anonymous author added, perhaps with a touch of exaggeration: 'To Aldeburgh flock the gay, the fashionable, the healthful', to enjoy 'its convenient beach, and . . . its pleasant neighbourhood.'[7] Millicent herself, writing about Aldeburgh as 'Norborough' in *Janet Doncaster*, her only acknowledged novel, remembered it in a less kindly light: 'Its non-distinctive features were its long rambling street of nearly a mile from end to end, breaking out fitfully now and then into little dreary patches of common, ornamented with clothes-lines and fishermen's nets . . . Norborough was not a lively place.'[8] To most of its inhabitants its main claims to fame, its sixteenth-century Moot Hall and the fact that it was the birthplace of the poet George Crabbe (in 1754) must have held little significance.

Writing when Millicent was 15, Wilkie Collins, one of several nineteenth-century writers attracted by Aldeburgh, commented on the havoc wrought by prolonged coastal erosion, which had swept away Crabbe's house and left only 'one straggling street [to] this curious little outpost on the shores of England'.[9] In 1880 its 'principal charm' was said to be that it was 'retired and quiet', and as late as 1906 it was described as 'still much the same . . . as it was 150 years ago'.[10] None the less, Aldeburgh, now an attractive and popular festival centre, quickly enabled Newson Garrett to become a dominant local figure, and it was a home for which most of the Garrett children felt a lifelong affection. The fact that it was a sleepy backwater when Newson Garrett arrived there was part of the reason for his success. Millicent wrote in her novel that 'there was curious stillness and stagnation in the little place'. 'Mr Ralph', who represented her father, was regarded as 'a prodigy of activity and business capacity' because he went to London twice a month in connection with his business as a corn merchant.[11] Newson did not hesitate to seize the opportunity which time and place offered him, however unchanging Aldeburgh might have appeared to the visitor. As his granddaughter Louisa wrote: 'He became the active man for all business in Aldeburgh and the surrounding district.' The basis of his prosperity was the maltings at Snape, a few miles away, but he also owned sailing barges, founded a gas works, and was owner or partner of a brickyard, brewery, whiting works and shipyard. His merchant trade included corn, coal and lime, and he was instrumental in bringing a branch line of the East Suffolk Railway to Aldeburgh in 1860.[12]

In or soon after 1850 the family were able to move from the Uplands, the Georgian house which was their first home in Aldeburgh, to a new home and estate at Alde House. Later they had another house in Snape, where they spent the winters after the arrival of the railway.[13] By the time that Millicent, who was born at the Uplands on 11 June 1847, was aware of the world her family had a wealthy, assured position in East Suffolk, from which she and her sisters could move with confidence into the wider world of affairs. It was an achievement of considerable magnitude for a self-made man whose ability to write has been questioned.[14] Though Aldeburgh was riven by petty snobberies and social distinctions it lacked a resident aristocracy. This not only gave Newson Garrett, the former pawnbroker, a leading social position,[15] but meant that he was in no danger of dissipating any of his formidable energy in quarrelling with the local gentry.

The first part of a suggested explanation of the Garrett sisters' early adoption of feminism lies in their comfortable family background. The second must lie in their parents themselves. Louisa Garrett is at first sight a less likely source of feminist inspiration than her husband. She was a deeply religious woman of a strict evangelical type.[16] In most matters she was strongly conventional, and her religious convictions encouraged the belief that women should not challenge their accepted position in society. She was horrified by Elizabeth's determination to become a doctor and insisted that it would be 'a source of life-long pain to her, . . . a living death', Elizabeth reported to Emily Davies, her close friend and mentor, in August 1860.[17] She was opposed to Millicent's launching into a career of public speaking and anguished by her profaning the Sabbath in doing so.[18] None the less, she indirectly encouraged her daughters in three ways.

The first was the provision of a secure family background, which was a source of enormous strength. Millicent was deeply attached to most of her sisters, her brother Sam, the family home and both her parents. They provided her with a base which might, as in so many Victorian families, have been stifling but which proved to be the reverse. There is every reason to accept at face value her letter to her mother returning thanks for birthday wishes received when she was 49: 'I am more and more thankful for the close tender love of one's family. Those who miss it, miss one of the best things in life.' Elizabeth obviously felt the same. Writing soon after her mother's death she told her husband's cousin Adelaide Anderson: 'It is not given to many people to be able to get so near their fellow creatures' hearts as my dear mother did.'[19] The second was the example which Mrs Garrett provided in looking after her large family, her household provisions and accounts and not least the important part which she played in her husband's affairs. She wrote and sometimes composed letters for him, and in Millicent's view would have made 'a very capable organiser of a big business'.[20]

The third manner in which Louisa Garrett may have influenced her daughters to think for themselves lay paradoxically in her narrow and tenacious evangelicalism. The inspiration of the evangelical came from within, and religious faith was a matter of unshakeable conviction. Neither Millicent nor her sisters shared their mother's religion, but she had the evangelical's commitment and adherence to morality as she understood it. In 1910, when she was over 60 Alice Cowell wrote to her after a speech: 'I felt, dear sister, that the [women's suffrage] cause is to you what religion was to dear mother.'[21] It is not fanciful to suppose that at a time when individual conscience was turning from religious to social expression Louisa Garrett's faith passed transformed to more than one of her daughters. It is also worth noting that in Millicent's view her normally gentle mother was a stronger personality than her violently forceful father.[22]

Newson Garrett's influence on his daughters in their espousal of feminism is easier to understand than that of his wife. He was all the things that the Victorian lady could not be: impetuous, single-minded, impassioned in secular affairs, quarrelsome. The nature and number of his quarrels have been lovingly delineated by Millicent and the family biographers.[23] There is no doubt that his forcefulness encouraged his daughters to assert their wills in a manner which stretched the accepted behaviour of middle-class women to its limits. There is also no doubt that they realized this. In a letter to her friend Harriet Cook in 1864 Elizabeth reflected:

> No! I am *not* uncommon . . . I am sure even in my small circle I know several women who wd cut me *all to nothing* if they would but try. My strength lies in the extra amount of daring wh. I have as a family endowment. All Garretts have it & I am a typical member of the race & so can't help it any more than I can help being like them in face & physique. There's a deal in blood I think.[24]

Whether Newson's combative nature passed to his daughters by 'blood' or through family life, their 'daring' is certainly not in doubt.

Their formal education, competent within its brisk and brief limits, probably did relatively little for them. All the girls except Josephine, the youngest, attended the Boarding School for Ladies at Blackheath, South London, and Millicent wrote of it appreciatively in old age. She left school before she was 16, however, during a temporary crisis in her father's business affairs. Lessons were conducted in French, and a glimpse of the effectiveness of its formal instruction may be obtained from a letter which Millicent wrote to her mother in later life during a visit to Avignon with her sister, niece and daughter: 'Alice and Marion so far cannot be induced to talk French. Philippa and I are more courageous and plunge boldly on in genuine British French, saying all we know and more too.'[25] What they may have learned in Blackheath, however, was lucid English. Millicent's prose style was a major asset in public life, Alice's letters home from India were sparkling and vivid and Elizabeth also wrote 'straightforward, vigorous English'. They also learned a ladylike manner which tended to disarm the opposition they faced in later life and to shield their uncompromising beliefs and actions.[26]

What they learned at school, however, was much less important than what they learned at home. It may be surmised that Newson Garrett had no interest in feminism for its own sake; certainly he needed vigorous pushing before he agreed to support Elizabeth's choice of the medical profession against opposition inside and outside the family.[27] The liberality of his behaviour towards his daughters probably sprang from family pride and solidarity, though he was not the only father among his contemporaries to value his daughters' education.[28] In any case, as Agnes Garrett recalled in an interview in 1890 no distinction was made between the boys and girls in her home; both had equal privileges. The daughters were brought up to think for themselves and encouraged by their father to express their views:

> Miss Garrett says she shall never forget their surprise as children at the evident astonishment and amusement of a gentleman who was calling, and who expressed to their father his feelings on hearing them give forth their ideas and opinions with such thorough confidence, it was so much a matter of course to them to say what they thought that they could not understand it seeming strange to anyone else.[29]

For children to become involved with the world around them encouragement to express themselves was insufficient; there had to be something to think and talk about. The atmosphere of the Garrett family home was strongly political and receptive to ideas and opinions. Millicent recalled that she began to hear about public events at an early age and retained vivid memories of the Crimean war which began when she was 7. Her father's delight over the taking of Sebastopol is significant in view of the strong patriotism which was so marked a feature of her own life. While Elizabeth was still a daughter at home in the later 1850s she held weekly 'talks on things in general' with the younger children, at which the major national and international developments of the day were discussed as well as publications by such authors as Carlyle and Macaulay. It is hardly surprising that Millicent, given this family environment, should have become, as she later wrote, a suffragist from her cradle.[30] Both she and Agnes recalled long hours of uninterrupted reading as girls, and according to a profile written of Millicent in 1898 they were reading *Othello* aloud and darning when Henry Fawcett first visited the Garrett home in Aldeburgh.[31] Indeed, one account credited her and her 'clever sisters' with having converted Newson Garrett from Conservatism to Liberalism.[32]

The final link in the chain which bound Millicent Garrett to a feminist outlook by the time of her marriage in 1867 was the example set before the younger Garrett girls by the struggle of their sister Elizabeth to become a doctor. It is worth emphasizing how early in the history of English feminism that struggle began. The *Englishwoman's Journal* was established only in 1858, the Society for Promoting the Employment of Women in 1859. Though both were in their infancy they were to be of material assistance to Elizabeth.[33] By the late 1850s the ideas for which they stood represented the views of a not inconsiderable number of young middle-class women, but it was Elizabeth Garrett who set about putting them into practice. In June 1860 she wrote to Emily Davies that she had told her father: 'I could not live without some real work.' A month later she wrote to her aunt Elizabeth Garrett: 'I think you will not be surprised that I should feel this longing, for it is indeed far more wonderful that a healthy woman should spend a long life in comparative idleness, than that she should wish for some suitable work.'[34] It was natural that Millicent should have found inspiration in her sister's struggle, and that her interest should ripen into commitment during her visits to Elizabeth and her eldest sister Louisa in London in the 1860s. The fact that 'Louie' took her to hear such a stimulating and unconventional preacher as F.D. Maurice and to one of John Stuart Mill's election meetings in 1865 marked a further stage in her social and political education.[35]

From the glimpses which Millicent afforded of herself in her autobiography and those contained in the Anderson papers one sees her childhood as happy, secure and free of drama. Elizabeth wrote a revealing letter about her sisters in January 1861 to Emily Davies. She was 'not satisfied with

*Elizabeth Garrett, would-be medical student, St Andrews University, 1862.*

[Millicent's] physical progress, she is too quiet and dreamy for health. If she grows into a strong woman she would make a capital worker in some line.' She suggested that 'Millie' might follow her as a doctor, but doubted that she possessed the 'quiet unexcitability necessary for doctors'. Millicent did grow into a strong woman and a capital worker, and quiet unexcitability was regarded both by friends and opponents as one of her chief characteristics. But even the Garrett girls could be limited by family pressures. Emily had suggested that Alice, then aged 18 and her mother's companion, should take the civil service examinations. As there were no women employees in the civil service at this time Emily presumably had in mind another epic Garrett struggle. Alice had replied that their mother 'would be in a great fright at the sound of anything that would take [her] away'. Agnes, in Alice's view, would marry young (in fact she never married) and as Millicent was only 13 her own place would be with her mother for some years to come.[36]

Two letters from Millicent to her mother survive from a visit which she and Agnes paid to Oxford in 1864, shortly before her eighteenth birthday. They watched cricket and rowing and she mentioned some of the famous men who had attended the colleges which she visited. The letters are full and affectionate and contain some characteristic phrases: the cricket players included 'some of the most celebrated players in England and therefore in the world', and they overflowed with good wishes for her mother's fifty-second birthday, when they would be separated 'for almost the first time . . . we shall be together in the spirit, if not in the body'.[37]

Elizabeth continued to employ her formidable talents and energy on behalf of her younger sisters. In an 1864 letter she commented that she was pleased that Agnes had begun to learn Italian and encouraged her and Millicent in their German lessons.[38] Two years later she wrote to their father strongly supporting Agnes's desire 'to do something . . . I do feel very strongly that both she & Milly ought to prepare for supporting themselves and not blind themselves to the possible necessity for doing so entirely at no very distant date. They would be all the happier for doing something.' In her next letter she urged that careers would be good for them 'now and afterwards' and would not affect their prospects of marriage other than to improve them: 'They would see very many more people whom they could marry, and my experience is that men like women all the better for showing that they are not _waiting_ for marriage as the only object in life.' By now experienced at coping with her father's hesitations, she tactfully brushed them aside in a further letter written three days later.[39] Elizabeth's letters also referred to Millicent's other interests and accomplishments. These included her love of dancing and her competence as a musician, presumably at the piano since the same sentence favourably mentioned Agnes's singing. She commented in an 1864 letter on their appearance: 'The girls are so pretty and nice, it is quite an enjoyment to look at them.' In about 1866 Elizabeth attended a dinner party where she met George Du Maurier, the *Punch* cartoonist: 'I thought of Milly & wished she had been in my place, as I have no doubt she knows him more intimately than I do.'[40] Not yet 19, Millicent was clearly an intelligent, well-educated and accomplished young woman.

Influenced by Elizabeth she warmly espoused the cause of the North in the American Civil War, which began when she was 13. Four years later, in 1865, Abraham Lincoln was assassinated. Attending a party in London soon afterwards she remarked confidently that his death was a greater tragedy than would be the death of any European crowned head. As she wrote later, there was nothing exceptionally perspicacious about this comment, but one can well imagine that it must have caused a stir for so young a woman to utter such a radical sentiment. In any event the observation seems to have caught the attention of Henry Fawcett, who was attending the same party. He asked his hostess, the suffragist Mentia Taylor, to introduce him to the speaker.[41] The next year he accepted an invitation from Newson Garrett to visit Aldeburgh. There he again met Millicent and in October 1866 they became engaged.[42]

NOTES

1. Moncure Daniel Conway, *Autobiography*, vol. 1 (Cassell [1904]), p. 403; Millicent Vince, 'Agnes Garrett: pioneer of women house decorators', *Woman's Leader*, 11 September 1925, pp. 259–60.
2. The foregoing owes much to Jo Manton's biography of *Elizabeth Garrett Anderson* (1965) and Ray Strachey's *Millicent Garrett Fawcett* (1931).
3. It was, as Leonore Davidoff and Catherine Hall point out, common in marriages which united rising middle-class families to give a younger son his mother's or grandmother's maiden name *(Family Fortunes*, 1987), p. 222. Newson Garrett's elder brother Balls was named after his mother Sarah Balls. Newson and Louisa Garrett gave their first son (who died in infancy) the name Dunnell Newson, their second Newson Dunnell. See also J.H. Clapham, *An Economic History of Modern Britain*, vol. 1 (Cambridge: Cambridge University Press, 1930 edn), p. 462.
4. Manton, ch. 1.
5. Manton, pp. 17, 25, says 1841; Louisa Garrett Anderson (*Elizabeth Garrett Anderson 1836–1917* (1939), pp. 26–7) suggests 1840.
6. Anderson, p. 27.
7. *Aldborough and its Vicinity* (Ipswich: Pawsey, 1844), pp. 18–21. The spelling of the town's name still varied, even (as here) in the same book. Although the population of Aldeburgh grew steadily from only 804 in the first census, 1801, by 1871, when Millicent had married and left Suffolk it had not reached 2,000 (*Population Tables*, P.P. 1852–3, vol. LXXXV [1631], p. 36; 1872, vol. LXVI–I [C. 676], p. 366).
8. MGF, *Janet Doncaster* (1875), pp. 1–2.
9. Wilkie Collins, *No Name*, vol. 2 (Sampson, Low, 1862), pp. 141–3.
10. Norman Scarfe, *The Growth of Aldeburgh* (Felixstowe: East Anglian Bookshop, 1951), p. 20; [Anon.], *Notes on Aldeburgh* (Watford: Peacock 1906), p. 3.
11. MGF, *Janet Doncaster*, p. 10; 'Millicent Garrett Fawcett & her daughter', *Review of Reviews*, July 1890, p. 19.
12. Anderson, pp. 29–30; Manton, pp. 28, 43; [Edward Clodd] *A Guide to Aldeburgh* (Aldeburgh: Buck, 1861), pp. 74, 81, 89; *WIR*, p. 30. According to Clodd (p. 81) half of the twenty-four merchant ships in Aldeburgh harbour belonged to Newson Garrett.
13. Anderson, p. 35; Manton, pp. 26, 37, 43; *WIR*, p. 31. The population of Snape first exceeded 500 in 1821. By 1871 it was still below 600 (P.P. 1852–3, vol. LXXXV, p. 36; 1872, vol. LXVI–I, p. 369).
14. Anderson, p. 29; Manton, pp. 18, 20. Manton concludes that Louisa Dunnell

signed her husband's name in the marriage register, but inspection of the microfilm register in the Greater London Record Office suggests that she is in error.

15. *WIR*, p. 16; Davidoff and Hall, p. 243.

16. *WIR*, pp. 34–5.

17. Anderson, p. 61; also pp. 47, 50 and *WIR*, p. 33. The letter was dated 17 August 1860.

18. Alice Cowell, Millicent's elder sister, wrote to her mother on 20 April 1870, sharing her regret at Millicent's public speaking, and on 4 April 1872 'feeling so sorry for your sorrow – but . . . is not that Sunday question one above all others to be left to people's own consciences' (Anderson Papers, St Brelade).

19. MGF to Louisa Garrett, 11 June 1896; Elizabeth Garrett Anderson to Adelaide Anderson, 23 January 1903 (*ibid.*).

20. Anderson, pp. 27–9; *WIR*, p. 36.

21. *MGF*, p. 230.

22. *WIR*, p. 35.

23. In the early pages of *ibid.*, *MGF*, Anderson and Manton.

24. Elizabeth Garrett to Harriet Cook, 12 April [1864] (Anderson Papers). Many of the letters in these papers are dated only by day and month and a small number are wholly undated. Dates have been added in most cases by an unknown hand and must be treated with caution.

25. *WIR*, pp. 38–9, 50; Anderson, pp. 32–3; Manton, pp. 33–6; MGF to Louisa Garrett, 22 December [1895] (Anderson Papers).

26. Alice's letters are in the Anderson Papers; Manton, pp. 35–6.

27. Anderson, pp. 43–6, 50; Manton, pp. 73–5.

28. Anderson, p. 40; Davidoff and Hall, p. 332.

29. *Women's Penny Paper*, 18 January 1890, p. 145.

30. *WIR*, pp. 9–10, 41–2, 52.

31. *ibid.*, p. 51; *Women's Penny Paper*, 18 January 1890, p. 145; *Review of Reviews*, July 1890, p. 19; Sarah A. Tooley, 'Notable women of the day', *The Woman at Home*, December 1898, p. 213; Jennie Chappell, *Noble Work by Noble Women* (Partridge [1900]), p. 114.

32. John F. Rolph, 'Mrs Fawcett at home', *Woman's World*, October 1890, p. 620.

33. Manton, pp. 44–52, which also deals with the inspiration which Elizabeth drew from the American career of the English-born Elizabeth Blackwell.

34. 15 June and 13 July; quoted in Anderson, pp. 46, 57.

35. *WIR*, pp. 42–3, 51–2. Elizabeth discussed Millicent's visits in 1864–6 in letters to their parents. Agnes told her mother on 11 July 1865 that she and Millicent had attended an election meeting in Mill's support which had been punctuated by 'unearthly yells and noises' (Anderson Papers).

36. Elizabeth Garrett to Emily Davies, January 1861 (*ibid.*). Alice was married two years later.

37. Millicent Garrett to Louisa Garrett [25 May 1865] and 26 May 1865 (*ibid.*).

38. Elizabeth Garrett to Agnes Garrett, 6 February [1864] (*ibid.*).

39. Elizabeth Garrett to Newson Garrett, 3 February 1866, 5 and 8 February [1866] (*ibid.*).

40. Elizabeth Garrett to Louisa Garrett, 6 June 1864, 16 January [1866], 7 April [?1866] (*ibid.*).

41. So she was told many years later (*WIR*, p. 54). In any event their first meeting did take place at a party at the Taylor home (Mentia Taylor to Elizabeth Garrett, 1 November 1866, *ibid.*).

42. *WIR*, pp. 52–4.

# CHAPTER 2

## THE FAWCETT MARRIAGE 1867–84

The career of Henry Fawcett, the blind professor of political economy and government minister, is almost as remarkable an example of struggling against apparently insuperable odds as that of Elizabeth Garrett. He was born on 26 August 1833, the son of William Fawcett, a Westmorland man who had moved to Salisbury and prospered in commerce there, and Mary Cooper, daughter of a local solicitor. Henry, or Harry as he was known to his intimates, was born into a strongly Liberal family and remained a troublesomely independent radical all his life.

Graduating from Trinity Hall, Cambridge, in 1856, he was awarded a fellowship by his college in the same year. It was early in 1857 that he began to suffer from eye trouble. He was told that he must rest his eyes for a full year and abstain from reading during that period. He wrote to a friend that his sister Maria, to whom he was strongly attached, would 'resign her needle with great composure to devote herself to reading to me',[1] a revealing comment about Fawcett himself, his relationship with his sister, and the position of unmarried daughter and sister which Elizabeth Garrett was so determined to escape. He also sought work which would take him abroad, and a letter survives from Sidney Herbert, a prominent political figure and Wiltshire neighbour, saying that he would as requested recommend Fawcett as a travelling tutor or companion to his friends' sons.[2]

To what extent his eyes recovered in the eighteen months after the above letter was written his friend and biographer Leslie Stephen does not say. But any recovery was short-lived. In September 1858 Fawcett was shooting near Salisbury with his father, who was suffering from incipient cataract in one eye. Stray pellets from his father's gun entered his eyes and, according to Stephen, he was instantly blinded.[3] Elizabeth Garrett, however, wrote after her first meeting with him early in 1865, that one eye had been blinded at once, the other subsequently from 'sympathetic inflammation'.[4]

From this catastrophe he made an heroic recovery. Only a year after the accident he presented two papers to the Social Science Association at Bradford. There he met Thomas Hare, apostle of proportional representation. Hare was a friend of John Stuart Mill and his description of Fawcett was

13

received sympathetically by Mill. Fawcett soon became one of Mill's leading disciples. His large *Manual of Political Economy*, published in 1863, was strongly influenced by Mill, who supported his successful effort in the same year to be elected professor of political economy at Cambridge. In the meantime his political ambitions remained as firm as his academic ones. An abortive contest at Southwark in 1860 was followed by defeats at Cambridge and Brighton, before he was returned for Brighton in the general election of 1865. Not yet 32, and blind for nearly seven years, he was a Cambridge professor and a Liberal Member of Parliament.[5] As *Vanity Fair* commented a few years later, he was a self-made man who was born into a family 'possessing neither influence nor fortune' and had so far overcome his blindness that 'it seems scarcely to exist'.[6]

Certainly Fawcett's attempts to live normally were remarkable. Long afterwards a parliamentary journalist recalled his pleasure in life, his enjoyment of the changing sounds and 'feel' of the countryside on a rural drive.[7] Leslie Stephen and Edward Carpenter, another early friend, wrote vividly about his activities as a sportsman, including walking, fishing, skating, rowing and riding. When Stephen accompanied him on his first skating expedition after his accident, 'the only difficulty was to keep his pace down to mine'.[8] According to Carpenter, 'Fawcett's pluck and vitality were however sometimes a trial to his friends. I have a rather *too* vivid recollection of riding with him, over the Brighton Downs or along the green lanes of Cambridgeshire.'[9] When she first met him Elizabeth Garrett commented: 'He keeps up wonderfully with the latest news in almost every direction, by being read to almost incessantly.' 'But' she added, 'it was a sad sight to see a tall athletic man in the early prime of life in many ways so dependant and so cut off from many of the greatest sources of happiness.'[10]

If the blind Fawcett feared that he would never be accepted as a marriage partner it would be difficult to blame him. Certainly he seems to have made a habit of proposing to women of independent mind and achievements. This was undoubtedly the result of his search for intellectual companionship and his general political convictions, as well, one may suppose, as the fact that ordinary forms of courtship with conventional young women presented obvious difficulties to him.

It was probably at the end of 1859 that he proposed to Bessie Rayner Parkes, who had been instrumental in establishing the *Englishwoman's Journal*. She rejected him, and writing later to her friend Barbara Bodichon about his marriage she commented: 'I don't think *we* should ever have done together. He is strong & heroic, but cut off by nature & by his sad calamity from the sort of things I care about'.[11] In 1864 he became engaged to Eleanor Eden, daughter of the Bishop of Bath and Wells and author or editor of several books. The existence of a letter from Fawcett to her aunt Emily Eden suggests that the two families were friendly. He wrote about his engagement to his friend Fanny Hertz, a pioneer of women's education in

Bradford, and it was officially announced in the *Bath Chronicle*; but it was subsequently broken off and Eleanor Eden did not marry.[12] Then, in February 1865, he met Elizabeth Garrett while visiting her friend Jane Crow, who had on several occasions stayed with the Fawcett family in Salisbury.[13]

The friendship quickly ripened, encouraged no doubt by a visit from Maria Fawcett in late March.[14] On 8 May 1865 Elizabeth wrote a momentous letter to her parents: 'Mr Fawcett came up from Cambridge to ask me to be his wife.' She told them that she had declined, saying that her work would make marriage impossible. She had also declined his offer to wait for three or four years until she had become established in the medical profession. None the less, she may have had a twinge of regret: 'I have not the least doubt about having been right in decidedly refusing though at the same time I know of few lives I should have liked better than being eyes & hands to a Cambridge professor & an M.P.' Curiously, in view of subsequent events, she added: 'I wish though that it had been Agnes.'[15]

She could not have known that her next letters would be full of accurate predictions about Millicent's future. Her father, notwithstanding his alleged writing problems, sent an affectionate and immediate reply and on 10 May she wrote to him:

> The more I think of it the more sure I am that it was far better to decide completely about it at once. You see marrying him would involve *completely* giving up my profession . . . Mr Fawcett's wife wd also have to give up her time to his pursuits even more than most people's need do. Anything like independent work in a completely different life would be impossible.

She told her mother on the 13th: 'I see that his wife – if she really entered into his work not because it was *his* but because she had a keen interest in the subject originally – would probably have a better position than many wives have.' She added that she had no desire to give up her profession, but that if she had not been tied by it and if she had liked Fawcett sufficiently his blindness would not have prevented her from marrying him.[16]

Elizabeth's first letter enjoined her parents to secrecy and there is no means of knowing whether Millicent ever knew of the proposal. But Elizabeth referred to it obliquely but unmistakably in a letter the next year to her friend Harriet Cook,[17] and it is possible that the secret was extended to other intimates and her immediate family circle. In any event it became known to only a handful of people.[18]

In October 1866 Millicent, now aged 19, was asked by Henry Fawcett to marry him and accepted. One of the last acts of her sister 'Louie' before her untimely death the following February was to argue Millicent's case to Elizabeth and her mother. Although Fawcett had been an MP for little more than a year Louie commented: 'I should not think there can be any question as to his being a rising man in Parliament.' As for her sister:

> I do think Milly is admirably fitted to be happy as the wife of a man who is intensely interested in public work – to enjoy the society which this state of

things will bring her into – and to make her husband very happy and proud too.[19]

Elizabeth was soon won round. Her letter to Harriet Cook admitted that initially she had regretted the match and added that Fawcett had minor faults intensified by his blindness and the indulgence he had consequently received, but that he also had good qualities and was unlikely to be 'too exacting a husband'. He would show himself at his best 'under a good wife's influence'. As for her sister:

> Millicent is rather young in years, but practically she is as old as many people 10 years older. She has never been unwise or flighty, and she is heartily in love with him so that she will not feel the service a burden. I have liked him much better than I ever did before since the engagement . . . Mr Fawcett says frankly that Millicent is extremely like me & that that is how he first thought of her, & I dare say it is so. As a matter of fact she & I are more alike in every way than any of the others.[20]

Her biographer suggests that Elizabeth's initial opposition stemmed from wounded pride,[21] but however accurate the suggestion it is unlikely that her final comment was motivated simply by rationalization. In any case Henry Fawcett echoed it when he wrote the next day to Lady Amberley about his fiancée: 'In her whole character, she bears a remarkable resemblance to Miss [Elizabeth] Garrett, and I quite acknowledge with you that this is paying her a very high compliment.'[22] After his previous history of rejections and a broken engagement he must have been a happy man.

Although Newson Garrett had often quarrelled with Henry Dowler, vicar of Aldeburgh, it was Dowler who performed the marriage ceremony on 23 April 1867 and Newson signed his name as a witness with a flourish. Less than twenty years earlier Dowler had baptized Millicent in the same church.[23] Though planned as a quiet wedding in view of Louie's recent death, Alice Cowell, then in India, was told that it 'went off cheerfully & pleasantly'. 'Millicent must have looked very sweet & pretty & nice', Alice commented after studying the photograph.[24] A local paper described her as looking 'very lovely' in her white satin dress, wreath of orange blossoms and tulle veil. The marriage was a considerable event, and although the festivities were relatively restrained, there was much rejoicing and flags were flown by the townspeople 'in all directions', another paper commented. The presents were 'numerous and costly', and included silver, china, glass and books specially illuminated or bound.[25] There is no indication that Millicent, still only 19, omitted the promise to 'obey' her husband as Elizabeth was to do four years later, but she preceded Elizabeth in continuing to use her family name. As an author she was from the first known as Millicent Garrett Fawcett.[26]

Although Henry Fawcett had a permanent disability which required constant attention from his wife one may speculate that she expected and exacted more from marriage than he did. The puritan morality which was to

*Henry Fawcett, probably around the time of his marriage, 1867.*

be so important a feature of her life was probably a product of her childhood rather than her marriage. In the absence of direct information about the intimate relations of the couple it is legitimate to consider the picture of marriage given in *Janet Doncaster*, her only surviving novel, published in 1875.[27] The book is characterized not only by a strong moral sense and pronounced feminism, but also by the marked wit for which she became known, and dislike both of upper-class pretensions and religious cant. Janet, clearly the author's *alter ego*, lives in modest middle-class comfort with her widowed mother, and is inveigled into marriage with a member of the landed class whom she does not love through various pressures which she feels unable to resist. The fact that she does not know 'any married people who seem very rapturously in love with each other' weakens her resistance to the marriage. 'And if the enthusiasm lasts such a little time', she tells herself, surely it was unnecessary to 'make a great point of starting with it'.[28]

The reader knows, though Janet does not, that her husband is an hereditary drunkard, a state then often assumed to be incurable. 'If it had not been for this misfortune Lady Ann would as soon have thought of marrying him to a housemaid as to Miss Doncaster.'[29] He is coaxed into abstention before his marriage, but soon afterwards he drinks himself into a stupor, 'stupidly (not violently) drunk' as a reader, shocked by her behaviour, pointed out.[30] Janet leaves him at once, telling an acquaintance that if she returned to him she would be worse than a prostitute. As Ray Strachey pointed out, Janet, like her creator, was immovable, followed her own judgement and was passionately devoted to moral principle.[31]

Though *The Times* gave the book a long and sympathetic review, Janet's departure from her marital home, her successful efforts to earn her own living as a translator and her acknowledged love for another man while her husband was still living were distasteful to some readers.[32] The book may seem to modern readers a morality tale with a rather priggish heroine, but as *The Examiner* pointed out, it protested effectively 'against the injustice of treating a woman as if her mission in life was amply fulfilled by her being employed to redeem an uninteresting man from drunkenness'.[33] If Henry Fawcett was a more sensitive man than his contemporaries suspected, he must have listened to his wife's strictures on the duties of a husband with some unease.

Despite Janet's sceptical view of the married state there is no reason to assume that the Fawcett marriage was other than a success. Ray Strachey, a competent though cloying biographer, quotes a number of incidents attesting to their happiness and pleasure in each other's company.[34] One of Elizabeth's letters contains a delightful picture of Millicent, 21-years-old and a mother, being mistaken on a train for a schoolgirl. This kind of incident caused great hilarity. 'You can imagine how Harry roared over the joke when Milly told it', she commented.[35] Much of the success of the marriage was due to Millicent's competence and her desire to make life as easy as possible for her husband.

When the couple first married money was short, although Harry had told her father that his total income was £800 per annum, a surprisingly high figure. She was, she wrote, 'a dragon over every unnecessary expenditure' and with homes to maintain in both London and Cambridge some economy was undoubtedly necessary. After a number of years their finances became somewhat less stringent, and in 1874 they were able to move to permanent homes in Vauxhall, Lambeth, an unfashionable but convenient part of south London, and 18 Brookside, Cambridge. In both places Millicent's taste as a home furnisher and decorator, aided by Agnes and Rhoda Garrett, was admired by their visitors.[36] A letter probably dating from about 1876, in which Millicent asked the help of an acquaintance in finding 'a promising young girl' for the position of kitchen maid in her Vauxhall home suggests a moderate but definite degree of prosperity.

> We keep no man or boy, therefore the little maid would have to do a good deal of rough work, clean boots, scrub steps, fill coal scuttles etc. Sound health is accordingly indispensable. After doing this sort of thing daily her work would be to help the housemaid in the morning & the cook in the afternoon.[37]

Millicent at once became the blind man's eyes and hands, the necessary function foreseen by her sister Elizabeth. She was initially his secretary, reading to him and writing his letters until a paid secretary, J.F. Dryhurst, was appointed in 1871.[38] She was also a familiar figure in the role of guide to the blind MP, as a well-intentioned description published early in 1875 attests.

> The visitor to the House of Commons . . . will no doubt have his eye particularly arrested by a tall, fair-haired young man, evidently blind, led up to the door by a youthful *petite* lady with sparkling eyes and blooming cheeks. She will reluctantly leave him at the door . . . As she turns away many a friendly face will smile, and many a pleasant word attend her as she trips lightly up the stairway leading to the Ladies' Cage . . . Not the daintiest live doll moving about London drawing-rooms surpasses her in the care of her household, her husband and her child.[39]

The attention given to her appearance is significant. It was important to a blind but ambitious politician of unorthodox views and unreliable party loyalty that his wife should appear attractive and pleasant to the important and influential. A younger contemporary recalled Millicent in her married years as small and fair, with masses of beautiful amber hair.[40] Edward Hamilton, Gladstone's private secretary, dined with the Fawcetts in their 'nice little house' in Vauxhall in June 1882 and wrote in his diary: 'She is a very nice attractive ladylike little person and bears no trace of the "strong-minded female" about her.'[41] Such a reaction benefited not only Harry but also Millicent herself as a leader of the women's movement. It was highly desirable that 'advanced' women should appear attractive and ladylike, and that they should perform domestic 'duties' at least as well as other women.[42]

In November 1867, seven months after the wedding, Elizabeth Garrett wrote to her mother after talking to Harry's sister Maria, who had been visiting the Fawcetts in Cambridge:

> She gives a very nice account of Millicent in every way. She thinks she is filling her place at Cambridge most satisfactorily, managing the house well, doing all that Harry wants done, & at the same time keeping up her own interest in things independently of him.[43]

By this time she was already pregnant with her only child, who was born the following April. She was called Philippa, 'a good fighting name', her mother told enquirers.[44] Alice Cowell's letters reflect a picture of Millicent recovering slowly from the birth of Philippa, the tiny baby of a mother unable to nurse her, and of Philippa being unwell in infancy. She was also given to prolonged screaming fits, which may have resulted from ill health.[45]. But by December 1869 Millicent was able to report to her mother that Philippa had been found 'much improved' by her aunt Maria Fawcett since the autumn, and a fortnight later that she was 'wonderfully well' and joining energetically and precociously in the games which Maria taught her such as 'round and round the mulberry tree'. Harry, sending Christmas greetings to his mother-in-law, also wrote about Philippa's improved health, and commented: 'Each recurring year I seem to have more to be thankful for. The longer I live with Millicent the more I become impressed that she is all that a wife can be.'[46] A similar comment had been made the previous year in a letter written by his publisher: 'Fawcett . . . looks wonderfully happy with his charming and clever little wife, and the little girl, their baby.'[47]

Although Philippa was boarded with a family in Worcester Park during some of the periods when her parents were in Cambridge, giving rise to a degree of malicious gossip, Millicent was a loving and conscientious mother, who knitted her baby clothes and cared for her health.[48] But there were no more children. The Fawcetts believed in Malthusian theories of population; it is reasonable to suppose that they practised some form of birth control, and by the late 1880s Millicent's sister advised it to at least one of her patients.[49] There were, however, in the Fawcetts' view limits to the public discussion of the subject. Though an attempt was made to subpoena them, they refused to give evidence for the defence in the famous Bradlaugh-Besant birth control trial in 1877, where their works were cited by both defendants. If Bradlaugh's daughter is to be believed, Harry went so far as to declare that he would send Millicent abroad if necessary so that she would not have to give evidence.[50] Her reaction to such a striking example of the dominant male is not recorded, but she strongly agreed that Bradlaugh had been unwise to reprint a pamphlet on birth control in conditions designed to secure maximum publicity.[51] The author of *Janet Doncaster* could be counted on to oppose any attempt to strike at accepted standards of public morality. But whatever the means, freedom from regular pregnancies and child-bearing must have done much to enable her to begin and develop her career as speaker and writer.

Though her marriage was to take her into worlds about which she had known nothing, Millicent appears to have coped with the situations she met without losing her composure or her sense of humour. In February 1884, when Harry was Postmaster-General, they attended a dinner given by the Prince and Princess of Wales at Marlborough House. Millicent wrote to her mother-in-law about the occasion, a letter sent on to Mrs Garrett with the covering note: 'Whoever would have thought <u>our</u> children, would have been in such grand company.' The guests processed in to the dinner behind their hosts in order of importance, 'the greatest swells in order of swelldom & the small fry to bring up the rear . . . Everything at dinner was very gorgeous.' She referred to 'the frightful daubs' on the walls, 'things no better than you might see on the walls of a country inn – quite inconceivably bad'. The princess wore three diamond necklaces and emerald pendants, while Millicent wore a deep cream frock given her by her father, with roses in her hair. 'I presented a most elegant appearance & looked quite the Postmistress.'[52]

Anchored in Harry's dependence and devotion, Millicent's dedication and loyalty, and the support of both families the Fawcett marriage was also sustained by the similar personalities of the partners. Harry was less reticent than Millicent and expressed himself with less concern for the feelings of others.[53] But both were single-minded to an unusual degree in political figures, even when they suffered in consequence. For both of them life was a question of following right and rejecting wrong in a straightforward, uncomplicated way. *Punch* was more perceptive than it realized when it jested that a process of 'natural selection' had brought them together.[54] Their belief in their causes and in themselves made them work without faltering and without discouragement when they were on the losing side. It was this gift for seeing the complications of life in terms of simple right and wrong which made them happy warriors who rejoiced in struggle. It was also this identity of outlook which helped them to live together successfully through seventeen crowded years of personal and political life.

### NOTES

1. Leslie Stephen's *Life of Henry Fawcett* (1885) remains the indispensable source. The above passage is drawn from his first chapter, the quotation from p. 41.
2. Sidney Herbert to Henry Fawcett, 25 June 1857 (FLALC, vol. 8a); also Stephen, p. 36.
3. Stephen, pp. 43–4.
4. Elizabeth Garrett to Louisa Garrett, 11 February 1865 (Anderson Papers, St Brelade).
5. This paragraph draws on Stephen, chs 3–5; Francis E. Mineka and Dwight N. Lindley (eds), *The Later Letters of John Stuart Mill 1849–1873*, vol. 2 (1972), pp. 642 & n., 859–60, 906; L.L. Price, *A Short History of Political Economy in England* (13th edn, Methuen, 1927), pp. 117, 179; chapters by Stefan Collini, Giacomo Beccatini and Lawrence Goldman in Lawrence Goldman (ed.), *The Blind Victorian: Henry Fawcett and British Liberalism* (1989), esp. pp. 45–8, 134–5, 152.
6. *Vanity Fair*, 21 December 1872.
7. Bernard Bussy quoted in *Review of Reviews* (August 1908), p. 171.
8. Stephen, pp. 56–67. The quotation is from p. 61.
9. Edward Carpenter, *My Days and Dreams* (Allen & Unwin, 1916), p. 214.
10. Elizabeth Garrett to Louisa Garrett (note 4 above).

11. The evidence in the Bessie Rayner Parkes Papers (Girton College Archives, Cambridge) is circumstantial but strong; Henry Fawcett to Bessie Rayner Parkes, 23 October 1859, a fragment of an undated letter from Parkes to Barbara Bodichon and a typescript article on Fawcett by Parkes's granddaughter Elizabeth Countess of Iddesleigh (n.d. but probably 1960s).

12. *Bath Chronicle*, 25 August and 20 October 1864. Lawrence Goldman quotes Henry Fawcett's letter to Fanny Hertz, dated 3 September 1864 (Goldman (ed.), p. 11 & n.). For Eleanor Eden see Frederic Boase, *Modern English Biography; Supplement to vol. 2* (Cass, 1965 edn), p. 195. For a likely Fawcett–Eden family friendship see Henry Fawcett to Emily Eden, 1 June 1860 (Auckland Papers, BL Add. Mss).

13. See note 4 above.

14. Elizabeth Garrett to Louisa Garrett, 25 March, 1 and 29 April, 6 May 1865 (Anderson Papers).

15. Elizabeth Garrett to Louisa and Newson Garrett, 8 May 1865. Henry Fawcett was not elected to Parliament until the following July. As Abraham Lincoln was shot on 14 April, if Millicent's comment on his death had a romantic effect on Fawcett (see pages 10–11 and note 41) it could only have been to encourage him to propose to Elizabeth, not to her.

16. Elizabeth Garrett to Newson Garrett, 10 May 1865; to Louisa Garrett, 13 May 1865 (Anderson Papers).

17. 'My sister Millicent is going to be married to Mr Fawcett. Is it not funny altogether?' (Elizabeth Garrett to Harriet Cook, 6 November [1866], Anderson Papers).

18. There is an incomplete account in Jo Manton, *Elizabeth Garrett Anderson* (1965), pp. 156–7.

19. Louisa Smith to Louisa Garrett (Anderson Papers). This undated letter has been dated 23 July 1866 by another hand, but all other accounts agree that the engagement was concluded the following October. Millicent's letter to Louisa Smith, apparently in consequence and dated 24 October 1866, is printed in *MGF*, pp. 26–8.

20. As note 17 above.

21. Manton, p. 181.

22. Henry Fawcett to Lady Amberley, 7 November 1866 (Bertrand Russell Papers, McMaster University).

23. Microfilm Aldeburgh Marriage Register, Suffolk Record Office, Lowestoft; *WIR*, p. 30.

24. Elizabeth Garrett to Louisa and Newson Garrett, 20 February 1867; Alice Cowell to *idem*, 31 May [1867], to Louisa Garrett, 15 June 1867 (Anderson Papers).

25. *Ipswich Journal, Suffolk Mercury*, 27 April 1867.

26. She usually signed her letters 'M.G. Fawcett'. Press reports referred to her as 'Mrs Henry Fawcett' and she never adopted the style 'Garrett Fawcett'.

27. She wrote another novel under a pseudonym which has not been traced; *MGF*, pp. 55–6.

28. *Janet Doncaster*, p. 168.

29. *ibid.*, p. 99.

30. Evelyn Stanhope to Lord Stanhope, 8 July 1875 (Stanhope Mss, Kent County Record Office), partly quoted in Pat Jalland, *Women, Marriage and Politics* (1986), p. 212.

31. *Janet Doncaster*, p. 228; *MGF*, p. 55.

32. *The Times*, 25 June 1875; Stanhope letter (note 30 above); *Saturday Review*, 12 June 1875, pp. 761–2; *The Examiner*, 22 May 1875.

33. *The Examiner*, 22 May 1875.
34. *MGF*, pp. 60–8 and *passim*.
35. Elizabeth Garrett to Harriet Cook, 24 December 1868 (Anderson Papers).
36. *MGF*, pp. 28, 36, 69; Ethel Sidgwick, *Mrs Henry Sidgwick* (Sidgwick & Jackson, 1938), p. 52; *WIR*, p. 55; Stephen, pp. 128–9. Fawcett's stipend from his university chair was £300 per annum (*ibid.*, p. 117). He received generous royalties (FLALC, vol. 8b, contract with Macmillan & Co., 18 April 1876) and an allowance from his father (*MGF*, p. 68).
37. MGF to Miss Dew, 11 February [?1876], FLALC, vol. 8b. The kitchen maid was to be paid a minimum wage of £6 per annum in addition to board and lodging.
38. *WIR*, pp. 55–7, 64. Dryhurst became a trusted and lifelong friend.
39. [Moncure Conway], 'Professor Fawcett', *Harper's New Monthly Magazine* (New York, February 1875), p. 352.
40. Margaret Heitland, obituary in Newnham College Roll *Letter*, January 1930, p. 19.
41. Quoted in Rosamund Billington, 'The women's education and suffrage movements, 1850–1914' (1976), p. 498.
42. *ibid.*, p. 495. See also Lisa Tickner, *The Spectacle of Women* (1987), ch. 4.
43. Elizabeth Garrett to Louisa Garrett, 26 November 1867 (Anderson Papers).
44. *CC*, 8 June 1917, p. 100.
45. Alice Cowell to Louisa Garrett, 14 May [1868], 12 April, 16 May, 1 July, 23 July 1869, 7 March 1870; Katie Garrett to *idem*, 22 May [1868] (Anderson Papers); *MGF*, p. 40.
46. MGF to Louisa Garrett, 3 and 17 December [1869]; Henry Fawcett to *idem*, 24 December 1869 (Anderson Papers).
47. Alexander Macmillan to C.B. Clarke, 16 December 1869, in George A. Macmillan (ed.), *Letters of Alexander Macmillan* (priv. print 1908), p. 259.
48. *MGF*, pp. 39, 62, 74; Stephen Siklos, *Philippa Fawcett and the Mathematical Tripos* (Cambridge: Newnham College, 1990), p. 21.
49. Barbara Strachey, *Remarkable Relations* (Gollancz, 1980), p. 103. Elizabeth Garrett Anderson remained silent on the subject in public (Manton, p. 284).
50. *In the High Court of Justice: the Queen v. Charles Bradlaugh and Annie Besant* (Freethought Publishing, [1877]), pp. 70, 92–5, 113, 163; Hypatia Bradlaugh Bonner, *Charles Bradlaugh*, vol. 2 (T. Fisher Unwin, 1895), p. 23.
51. *MGF*, p. 89.
52. MGF to Mary Fawcett, 24 February 1884; Mary Fawcett to Louisa Garrett, 26 February 1884 (Anderson Papers). See also Winifred Holt, *A Beacon for the Blind* (Constable, 1915), pp. 292–4, and *WIR*, p. 108.
53. After meeting Fitzjames Stephen at a dinner party in India in 1872 Alice Cowell wrote to her father: 'He told me of Harry having skated from Cambridge to Ely soon after his blindness with his brother Leslie Stephen and seemed to think the fearless way in which he went ahead regardless of holes & other people's toes typical of his whole career' (Alice Cowell to Newson Garrett, 10 April 1872, Anderson Papers).
54. *Punch*, 16 April 1870, p. 155.

# CHAPTER 3

---- · ----

# INTO THE LIMELIGHT 1868-74:
# EDUCATION AND ECONOMICS

Millicent Garrett Fawcett was more talented than her husband, but at the start of their marriage she had more to gain intellectually than he. Not yet 20, and having lived her life in 'the quietest of quiet country life'[1] she was suddenly plunged into prominent radical-Liberal circles in London and among leading university figures in Cambridge. As her comment about Abraham Lincoln had shown, she held strong political views when very young. Her sister Alice wrote home from India when the reform bill was under discussion: 'Agnes and Millie pitch into me so now for being "un-Liberal" that I am half frightened.'[2] Six months later Harry told Lady Amberley: 'She is very clever, is a thorough Liberal, and takes the keenest interest in politics. Between us, there is such perfect intellectual sympathy that I am convinced we shall enjoy the most complete happiness.'[3] Now she had the opportunity to expand her knowledge, interests and participation. Reading newspapers and political reports to Harry and attending parliamentary debates at his instance introduced her to political life,[4] but she took care to be more than a passive observer. After talking to Maria Fawcett in November 1867 Elizabeth wrote that Millicent was

> attending two courses of lectures & Maria said she was quite astonished with the ability she showed in discussing their subjects afterwards. Of course Maria is easily astonished but I have no doubt Milly will develope [sic] quite unusual brain power if she can keep herself from being absorbed & distracted by the interruptions of life.

It was 'so important', she wrote, that Millicent should continue to develop mentally. Her concern was for Harry and her children (Philippa was not yet born): 'It wd be ruinous to Harry if she fell out of an independent interest in his subjects.'[5]

With Harry's active encouragement Millicent began to write. Her first article, which appeared in *Macmillan's Magazine* in April 1868, the month of Philippa's birth, was entitled 'The education of women of the middle and upper classes'. It paid her £7, which she promptly gave to J.S. Mill's unsuccessful campaign for re-election,[6] and thus began a writing career which was to take her into an enormous number and variety of journals.

24

The background to the article was the movement for the higher education of women, which had been gathering support since the mid-century. Its focus was Cambridge. Spearheaded by Emily Davies and assisted by a number of leading academics including Henry Fawcett, the movement had succeeded in opening the Cambridge local examinations to women, thus preparing them for university entrance.[7] Moreover, a number of professors had opened their lectures to women,[8] and it was presumably these that Millicent had been attending.

Although she was not yet 21, the article was characterized by the blend of knowledge of her subject, persuasive common sense, independence of thought and lucidity which she was to make her own. Her thinking had been influenced by her sister Elizabeth, Emily Davies, Harry and others, but she made no overt acknowledgement of her indebtedness. Drawing no doubt on her own experience she asserted that girls' formal education was grossly inadequate, being designed not as education but as 'accomplishments' in such fields as music and French. In consequence of their inferior education it was asserted that women's minds were inferior, a charge unsupported by evidence except in so far as their education caused deterioration in their intellects. Unmarried girls at home were expected to spend their time enjoying themselves or acting as poor substitutes for the curate, the nurse or the cook. A great range of women had nothing to do with their time: 'It is not too much to say that one of the great curses of society is the enforced idleness of such a large proportion of its members as is formed by the women who have nothing to do.'

Her solutions were as forthright as her diagnosis. Endowments which had been founded for both sexes like Christ's Hospital, then educating over a thousand boys, should be restored to their original purpose. Equal educational opportunities should be provided for the two sexes. Women should be allowed to study at Cambridge and, 'with perfect propriety, become graduates of the University'. All professions should be thrown open to women. For the good not of women alone but of society at large, she concluded, there must follow 'the extension to women of those legal, social, and political rights, the withholding of which is felt, by a daily increasing number of men and women, to be unworthy of the civilisation of the nineteenth century'.[9]

The article attracted a good deal of attention. When Helen Taylor, Mill's step-daughter, was asked the same month by John Chapman, proprietor and editor of the *Westminster Review*, to contribute an article to the journal, Mill replied that in Taylor's view Mrs Fawcett would be 'a more capable person for the work'.[10] She did not write for the *Westminster*, but the following November her article on 'The medical and general education of women' appeared in the *Fortnightly Review*, edited by Harry's associate and political ally John Morley. The article was read and approved by both Mill and Taylor before publication.[11]

Like the earlier article it was well prepared and informed, and like it there was no overt indication that her views had been influenced by others. She urged that girls' education should be greatly improved and stressed that the choice of women's occupations was very narrow for the educated. Women who were interested in mental activity tended to be dismissed as 'blue stockings' or 'strong-minded'. Parents were prepared to give their sons a good education because it was financially profitable for them to do so, but not their daughters because it was not. It was 'vastly important for national welfare that . . . mothers of children should be persons of large, liberal and cultured minds', but in the popular view little importance was attached to the role of the mother in educating the next generation. In the future, she concluded hopefully, the restrictions placed on women in all spheres 'will be looked upon as the production of a coarser age'.[12] As with so much that she wrote and said in the next sixty years her arguments now seem the most moderate common sense, but it would be necessary to repeat them over and over again before they found even nominal acceptance.

The articles quickly won an audience both for the author and the subject. Writing to her mother from India in March 1869 Alice Cowell commented: 'Milly's fame as a "terrible little Radical" has spread to the Cambridge men here.'[13] Undaunted by the gossip she had aroused she became a member of the small group of dons and their wives and daughters which established formal lectures for women at Cambridge as the precursor of Newnham Hall, later College. Nor did fears for her reputation discourage the initial meeting which preceded the lectures from being held in December 1869 in the Fawcetts' Cambridge home. She modestly recalled that the location of the meeting had been chosen because their rented furnished house had a sufficiently large drawing room: 'Nevertheless, such is human folly, I go on being proud and pleased about it.'[14]

Millicent's own desire was to admit women to membership of the university itself, a preference she had made perfectly clear in her articles published the previous year. In her *Fortnightly Review* contribution she had been unenthusiastic about a women's college, regarding it only as a pragmatic measure less likely to fall foul of parental opinion than admitting women to the universities.[15] But even a women's college was controversial, as was quickly shown when detailed planning for the higher education of women at Cambridge began. Over twenty-five years later she wrote that in convening the initial meeting it had been necessary to follow the line of least resistance, being careful not to frighten any potential supporter. Therefore the residential aspect of the scheme was hardly mentioned.

> I ask those who would point the finger of scorn at us to remember that if we had said we wished to establish a College for women at Cambridge we might as well have said that we wished to establish a College for women in Saturn. It was an absolute necessity to proceed with great caution.[16]

She consoled the more ardent spirits by pointing out that if scholarships were provided for students from outside Cambridge the question of residence would inevitably be raised.[17] Writing to Helen Taylor on 4 December 1869, apparently six days before the initial meeting, she made her intentions clear:

> All the promoters of this scheme feel that it will probably be the means of ultimately admitting women to the University. They do not urge this publicly in favour of their scheme, because it would frighten so many excellent people who are now willing to help us.[18]

Her role as one of the principal founders and supporters of Newnham College, at an age when she could easily have been a student herself, does not rest on the provision of a drawing room for an initial meeting. She was closely involved in organizing lectures and raising money and in attracting serious students, as opposed to those 'ladies of all ages and occupations', she told Taylor, 'who will go just for amusement, & with no idea of going through an examination or really of learning much at all'.[19] Writing to her mother on 17 December she expressed delight that the scheme was progressing 'capitally', with the lecturers and subjects decided and the prospectus published.[20] Harry played an uncharacteristically minor role in the venture, but his support was clear. In October 1868 he had publicly expressed the belief that women should share in the advantages of residing and studying at Cambridge and Oxford.[21] Now he wrote to his mother-in-law, whose interest and sympathy may be supposed to have been less than his own, saying that 'the scheme for giving lectures to ladies at Cambridge . . . seems to me one of the most sensible and practically useful plans which has been started for promoting the education of women.'[22]

Millicent continued her efforts in the most practical manner. She secured a subscription of £40 a year from J.S. Mill and Helen Taylor, and acted as one of the chief lieutenants of Henry Sidgwick, the philosopher and political economist who was the main driving force among Cambridge academics behind the Newnham scheme.[23] She remained an active member of the scheme's executive committee and, over the years, gave substantial sums of money.[24] She also helped to recruit and retain students for the college, and when the residential element was introduced became the friend of a number of them. According to Mary Paley, one of the first students and later married to Alfred Marshall, she escorted them to the Cambridge town gymnasium where she was the best climber on the high rope.[25] As she shared Harry's love of the outdoor life and was an enthusiastic mountaineer, walker, rider and skater,[26] her proficiency is not surprising.

The young wife, spending much of each year in rarefied intellectual circles at Cambridge and conscious of her own limited educational opportunities, was a natural recruit to the movement for the higher education of women. Unlike her sister Elizabeth she was not a participant in Emily Davies's simultaneous and more ambitious effort to establish a college, the future Girton, seeking equal conditions with men and degrees for women. To some extent this was the result of circumstances, including the Fawcetts' academic and personal contacts and Millicent's reluctance to work with the domineering Davies. But this first venture into political possibilism showed many of the characteristics of the mature woman, seeking to marshal maximum support for far-reaching ends without frightening the faint-hearted. What could not have been predicted is that at the age of 22 she should have been capable of wielding so competent and influential a pen and showing unmistakable signs of political leadership.

Her Liberal background, the dogmatic though contrasting beliefs and behaviour of her parents and her early marriage to a leading Liberal political economist helped to ensure that she was a pupil ready to absorb what would soon be widely regarded as old-fashioned individualism. Though his adherence to non-interventionist principles was limited by the pragmatic outlook of the politician, Henry Fawcett's prominence and the uncompromising manner in which he expressed himself meant that he was widely regarded as an unbending exponent of *laissez-faire*.[27] His gift was for popularizing received opinion, not for modifying his views with the passage of time or publishing new interpretations of social developments.[28] Millicent possessed a more open and subtle mind, but as with Harry's encouragement she turned to write about economic questions, she accepted most of his convictions at a time when many other Liberals were in the course of modifying or abandoning them. In her case there was an additional reason to accept the individualist case, for it seemed to almost all early feminists to offer wider opportunities for the employment of women than the double-edged protection afforded by the Factory Acts.[29] That women's employment was not the source of her commitment to individualism, however, is suggested by the fact that her two early books, *Political Economy for Beginners* and *Tales in Political Economy*, published in 1870 and 1874, do not deal with the question.

The first book, whose financial rights as the law then stood belonged to Harry,[30] was conceived when she was helping him to prepare the third edition of his *Manual of Political Economy*. The thought occurred to both of them, she explained, that a book on political economy for those new to the subject, especially schoolchildren, was desirable.[31] The book was hugely successful. It was published in ten editions and was still in demand when its author's autobiography appeared in 1924. The sixth edition, published in 1884, consisted of 15,000 copies. It was translated into Italian and German, and translations were authorized into Arabic and several Indian languages.[32] It was used in their youth by such prominent figures as J.A. Hobson and Philip Snowden, and its appearance as a set book in political economy in the first prospectus of the University College of Bristol in 1876 was undoubtedly typical.[33]

Examination of the book suggests why the kind of liberal economics refined by Mill and preached by such influential disciples as the Fawcetts could appeal to an early generation of skilled working men, despite the fact that it offered them a relatively minor role in a structure devised in the interests of the entrepreneurial and commercial middle class. Its primary aim was to advocate the virtues of uninhibited competition and free trade. It opposed the attempts of both trade unions and professional associations to manipulate the labour market and insisted that, at least in the short term, the 'law' of the wages fund decreed that wages could not rise in one industry without falling in another. The bleak solution of limiting family size was offered with the observation that a lower birth rate among the poor was an indication of advancing civilization. It argued the case for profit and condemned in forthright terms the trade union violence which had received much public attention in recent years.[34]

On the other hand the book displayed scant sympathy with landlords, the object of the special (if anomalous) antagonism of trade unionists, and advocated a tax on their rents. It strongly defended the right of workmen (women were absent from the book), to combine, despite the abuses committed by some of their number. Its appeal to the respectable working class was enhanced by the assertion that labour productivity was affected by the worker's skill, intelligence and morality, and that intemperance, which Millicent Garrett Fawcett deplored, often resulted from the low standard of popular education. The book praised the principle of both producer and retail co-operation also associated with the skilled workers and their families, picking out the Rochdale Pioneers for special mention. Although it opposed communism, usually understood in 1870 as a type of rural community in past times or the contemporary United States, for allegedly discouraging work or thrift, it did not do so without qualification: 'The present system does not work so well as to be absolutely incapable of improvement; and we ought to be ready to admit that some improvement is necessary in a community of which five per cent. are paupers.'[35]

The book was carefully kept up to date in successive editions, the most significant additions being fuller discussion of socialism in the light of its increasing popularity. Its reception by professionals was naturally less enthusiastic than by those for whose special benefit it had been written. The economist J.E. Cairnes, a friend of both the Fawcetts, called it 'useful' and sent the author detailed criticisms. E.E. Bowen, the Harrow master, wrote in more appreciative terms, calling the book 'admirably simple' and suggesting 'little puzzles' to supplement the questions which she had appended to the ends of the chapters.[36] Harry repeatedly referred to it as 'my wife's little book' in writing to their publisher, but in 1876 he attempted to secure a large new edition at an increased royalty. He added that Edward Hermon, Conservative MP for Preston and a cotton manufacturer, was so favourably impresssed and anxious for the Lancashire operatives to read it that he had vainly asked for copies at fifty railway station bookstalls.[37]

The success of Millicent's first book was not repeated. A paper on Fox which Anthony Trollope agreed to read with a view to publication in *St Paul's Magazine* did not appear.[38] Her *Tales in Political Economy*, sermons on free trade, the division of labour, money and credit, sugar-coated in the form of stories, did not sell well enough to be reprinted, though Marathi and Swedish translations were being prepared in 1882.[39] But on 14 December 1870 her lengthy letter on free education was published across three closely printed columns of *The Times*. Reprinted two years later in a book of essays by Harry and herself and published by the faithful Macmillan, it was a widely noticed expression of her chillingly inflexible views applicable to a whole range of social reforms.[40]

The principal theme of the letter was that free education like the poor law would teach the poor that there was no need for self-restraint, for self-indulgence would have no adverse consequences. 'Free' education, she argued, was not really free, but an extravagant manner of paying for education, since there would be no motive to exercise economy. Early marriages and large families would be encouraged; profits and wages likely to suffer. 'The best and most independent of the working classes' had formed benefit societies, trade unions and sickness clubs, but free education would militate against this type of thrift and also against temperance, since many fathers resisted the temptations of drink in order to pay for their children's education. Free education, conceived of as a benefit to the working classes, would in fact tend to pauperize them.[41]

Her letter was bound to dismay many fellow Liberals at a time when elementary education was one of the most controversial and topical subjects of political debate and many middle-class radicals and working-class trade unionists were demanding free schools. One of her critics was Sir Charles Dilke, the radical MP and associate of Henry Fawcett. In a private letter he told her: 'There are parts in yr letter on Free Schools with which I can't in the least agree.' Undaunted, she wrote a spirited and formidable reply, arguing her case at least as effectively as Dilke had put his. On one point she was more perspicacious than Dilke, who had mentioned favourably the common schools catering for all social classes existing in the American state of Massachusetts. She replied that she did not believe that such schools could flourish in England, where 'nothing is strong enough to destroy caste.'

At the end of her letter she wrote, in a reference to Harry: 'You will, I hope, at the Political Economy Club on Friday meet a more able opponent of the Free School system than I am.'[42] In fact had Dilke had his way he might have met Millicent too. A few days earlier he had written to John Stuart Mill to recommend her election to the club, a prestigious group of Liberal economists and men of affairs founded in 1821. He cited in her support her 'little book' (*Political Economy for Beginners*), many articles 'both signed and anonymous', and the very *Times* letter about which he was to write to her reproachfully only a few days later. Dilke pointed out that he was too junior a member to propose her and suggested that Mill might be willing to do so.[43] Mill, who had been elected in 1836, lacked neither seniority nor prestige, but, on this occasion, courage and good will. Although acknowledging that 'Mrs Fawcett has far better claims to be a member of the Political Economy Club than many of its present members', he refused to propose her, allegedly because he was known as an advocate of the rights of women. She was not elected, nor was any women at least until after 1920,[44] but the incident does suggest that her standing as an economist was generally accepted in radical circles.

She was, however, an active member of the Radical Club, a group founded by Henry Fawcett and others at some point after his election to Parliament in 1865.[45] It contained many of the same members as the Political Economy Club, as well as a small number of women. In February 1871 one of them, Helen Taylor, announced her decision to resign, apparently on grounds of ill health. Millicent's letter, urging her to reconsider, demonstrated her own keen interest in the club, particularly that 'the female element' should not be weakened.[46] Her letters to Dilke, the secretary, also indicate her interest and competence, both in the subjects discussed and in collecting names and subscriptions.[47] A third club in which she may have been involved was the Republican Club, founded in 1870 by a small group of Cambridge men among whom Harry was prominent. At Millicent's insistence it had proclaimed among its objects its opposition to denying 'social and political privileges' on grounds of sex. She wrote in some perplexity to Helen Taylor in November 1870 asking her advice on whether to join. She made explicit her opposition to an hereditary monarchy and aristocracy, but added that she hesitated to join for fear of harming the women's cause. 'If I do not, I suspect myself of want of courage & of letting the fear of Mrs Grundy outweigh the desire of acting up to my principles.'[48] Taylor's reply, counselling against membership, observed: 'I am sure there never can be any danger of your showing want of courage',[49] a comment amply justified by subsequent events.

The Fawcetts' *Essays and Lectures*, published in 1872, contained six by Harry and eight by Millicent, two of them previously unpublished. Five years after her marriage they represented fairly the range of her interests. Two dealt with women's education, two with women's suffrage, two with representative government – especially proportional representation, in which she and Harry enthusiastically followed the lead of John Stuart Mill. The seventh was her letter to *The Times* on free education and the eighth, reprinted from *Macmillan's Magazine* in January 1872, concerned 'National debt and national prosperity'. As might be expected she opposed national debt, especially when, as in the case of contemporary Britain and France, it had resulted from fighting foreign wars, expenditure on the poor law and uncontrolled population increase: 'Nothing will permanently affect pauperism while the present reckless increase of population continues.' The article also contains a straightforward attack on upper-class idleness typical of the middle-class radicalism of the period. One class, she observed, passed through life 'surfeited with leisure' and principally concerned with 'seeking means of killing time', while another worked unceasingly, 'reduced into mere human machines'.[50] This type of onslaught suggests why the austere philosophy of individualism, also embodied in her *Political Economy for Beginners*, held so marked an appeal to the trade-union elite of the period.

She had not yet begun to write for the daily or weekly press in this early period, apart from *The Examiner*, a Sunday paper purchased by H.R. Fox Bourne in 1870 and which remained in Liberal–radical hands until its demise in 1881. She became, Bourne wrote, a frequent contributor, and in view of the fact that most of the articles were anonymous and now untraceable the assertion can only be accepted on trust. Such of her articles as can be identified deal with economic or political subjects, and she was the only woman who contributed to the twelve obituary notices of Mill published in 1873.[51]

If her economic training came from Harry she proved herself an apt pupil. As Leslie Stephen wrote, the Fawcetts' book of essays showed 'the agreement of independent minds, not the relation of teacher and disciple'.[52] The fact that she revised her own 'little book' so many times and her close collaboration with Harry on revisions of the *Manual*, which she kept up to date after his death, shows that her interest in economics was not exhausted after the early 1870s. Further evidence is provided by her later activity as a lecturer in economics.[53] But even in these early years, when she came to the attention of the public in so many different spheres, her main interest lay in women's suffrage, the subject to which she was to devote her life.

## NOTES

1. *WIR*, p. 55.
2. Alice Cowell to Newson Garrett, 6 May 1866 (Anderson Papers, St Brelade).
3. Henry Fawcett to Lady Amberley, 7 November 1866 (ch. 2, note 22 above).
4. *WIR*, p. 64.
5. Elizabeth Garrett to Louisa Garrett, 26 November 1867 (Anderson Papers).
6. *WIR*, pp. 85–6. Ray Strachey points out that by law the money was her husband's (*MGF*, p. 53).
7. Rita McWilliams-Tullberg, *Women at Cambridge (1975)*, ch. 2; Leslie Stephen, *Life of Henry Fawcett* (1885) pp. 173–4; Arthur Sidgwick and Eleanor Mildred Sidgwick, *Henry Sidgwick* (1906), chs 3–4; Barbara Stephen, *Emily Davies and Girton College* (1927), chs. 9–10, 12–13.
8. MGF, 'The education of women of the middle and upper classes', *Macmillan's Magazine* (April 1868), p. 514.
9. *ibid.*, pp. 511–17. The quotations are from pp. 514 and 517.
10. Mill to Chapman, 23 April 1868; Francis E. Mineka and Dwight N. Lindley (eds), *The Later Lectures of John Stuart Mill 1849–1873* (1972), vol. 3, p. 1390.
11. Mineka and Lindley (eds), pp. 1417–18, 1512.

12. MGF, 'The medical and general education of women', *Fortnightly Review* (November 1868), pp. 554–71; reprinted in revised form in Henry Fawcett and Millicent Garrett Fawcett, *Essays and Lectures on Social and Political Subjects* (1872), pp. 185–205.
13. Alice Cowell to Louisa Garrett, 28 March 1869 (Anderson Papers).
14. *WIR*, p. 73; McWilliams-Tullberg, p. 56.
15. *Fortnightly Review* (note 12 above), pp. 570–1.
16. MGF, 'The story of the opening of university education to women', *Cheltenham Ladies' College Magazine* (spring 1894), p. 16. She sent her mother on 3 December 1869 a handwritten notice entitled 'Lectures for women' which explained that if women should come to Cambridge to attend the lectures 'they would be required to reside either with their friends, or in some lodging or hall which had received a certificate from the committee of management' (Anderson Papers).
17. Eleanor Mildred Sidgwick, letter in *CC*, 8 June 1917, p. 100.
18. MGF to Helen Taylor, 4 December [1869] (J.S. Mill Letters, Johns Hopkins University).
19. *ibid.*
20. MGF to Louisa Garrett, 17 December [1869] (Anderson Papers).
21. *The Times*, 5 October 1868; *ER* January 1869, p. 79. The occasion was an intervention at the annual congress of the Social Science Association.
22. Henry Fawcett to Louisa Garrett, 24 December 1869 (Anderson Papers).
23. MGF to Helen Taylor, 4 March [1870] (J.S. Mill Letters), 14 and 27 December [1873] (Mill Papers, Yale University Library); Helen Taylor to MGF, 19 December 1873 (FLALC, vol. 4a); Sidgwick and Sidgwick, p. 206.
24. *Reports* of the Association for Promoting the Higher Education of Women in Cambridge; *Record of Benefactors* (1921) (Newnham College Archives, Cambridge).
25. *MGF*, pp. 65, 75–80; Kathleen McCrone, *Playing the Game* (1988), p. 55.
26. Rolph interview (ch. 1, note 32), p. 621. See also below, ch. 7.
27. Lawrence Goldman (ed.), *The Blind Victorian* (1989), esp. pp. 15, 50–1, 56–7, 100–3, 115; Leslie Stephen, ch. 4 and pp. 262–7.
28. [James Bryce] 'The late Mr Fawcett', *The Nation* (New York), 27 November 1884, pp. 457–8; Leslie Stephen, *Some Early Impressions* (Hogarth Press, 1924), pp. 75–6 (first published as articles in 1903).
29. See Rosemary Feurer, 'The meaning of "Sisterhood" ', *Victorian Studies* (vol. 31, 1988), pp. 233–60.
30. *WSJ*, 1 June 1880, p. 108. The first Married Women's Property Act was passed later the same summer.
31. MGF, *Political Economy for Beginners* (1870), Preface.
32. *WIR*, p. 87; MGF to Macmillan, 6 July 1887, 12 October 1888, 16 August (n.d.) (Macmillan Archive, University of Reading); *WSJ*, 1 April 1882, p. 50.
33. J.A. Hobson, *Confessions of an Economic Heretic* (Allen & Unwin, 1938), p. 23; Philip Snowden to MGF, 13 July 1928 (FLALC, vol. 1m); E.C. Wright, Registrar and Secretary, University of Bristol to author, 3 April 1987.
34. *Political Economy for Beginners*, pp. 98–101, 109, 114, 123, 130–2, 142–3.
35. *ibid.*, pp. 17–18, 35–8, 87–9, 128–30, 133–8, 193. The quotation is from p. 37.
36. J.E. Cairnes to MGF, 31 May 1871; E.E. Bowen to MGF, 1 November [?1871] (FLALC, vol. 8a). The author had presented copies of her book to both men.
37. The Macmillan Archive in the British Library Add. Mss includes letters from both of the Fawcetts. The letter cited was written by Henry Fawcett to Alexander Macmillan on 20 February 1876.
38. Anthony Trollope to Henry Fawcett, 4 February 1869 (FLALC, vol. 7a). Which Fox was the subject of the essay was not specified, but it is more likely to

have been the minister, MP and free-trader William Johnson Fox (1786–1864) than the more celebrated Charles James Fox (1749–1806).

39. *WSJ*, 1 April 1882, p. 50.
40. *MGF*, p. 51. The letter was again reprinted with an extract from one of Harry's works when the subject became topical in 1890. An act to encourage free elementary education was passed in 1891.
41. MGF, 'Free education in its economic aspects (with a postscript)' in Fawcett and Fawcett, *Essays and Lectures* (1872), pp. 50–67.
42. Dilke to MGF [copy, 24 January 1871], MGF to Dilke, 27 January 1871 (Dilke Papers, BL Add. Mss).
43. Dilke to Mill, 16 January 1871 (Mill Papers).
44. Mill to Dilke, 17 January 1871; Mineka and Lindley (eds), vol 4, p. 1797 & n. A list of the members in 1873 with details of dates of election is included in the Mill Papers at Yale.
45. Leslie Stephen, p. 286; Stephen Gwynn and Gertrude M. Tuckwell, *The Life of Sir Charles W. Dilke*, vol. 1 (1917), p. 100 & n.; Christopher Harvie, *The Lights of Liberalism* (1976), p. 187.
46. MGF to Helen Taylor, 24 February [1871] (Mill Papers).
47. MGF to Dilke, 12 February [1871] and [February 1872] (Dilke Papers). For further clubs involving Henry Fawcett, Mill, Dilke and others see Frederic Harrison, *Realities and Ideals* (Macmillan, 1908), pp. 369–77; *idem, Autobiographic Memoirs*, vol. 2 (Macmillan, 1911), p. 83.
48. MGF to Helen Taylor, 8 November [1870] (Mill Letters; club rules enclosed).
49. Taylor to MGF, 9 November 1870 (FLA, box 89 vol. 1).
50. Fawcett and Fawcett, pp. 125–53. Quotations are from pp. 149, 152.
51. H.R. Fox Bourne, *English Newspapers*, vol. 2 (Chatto & Windus, 1887), pp. 289–91. The only articles of hers which I have traced are a review of a book by Thomas Hare (15 March 1873, p. 281); 'The Government and the Bank Act' (5 April 1873), p. 351); '[John Stuart Mill's] influence as a practical politician' (17 May 1873), pp. 515–17); and an unsigned obituary of the economist J.E. Cairnes (10 July 1875, identified in a letter from Harry to E. Spender, 10 July 1875, FLALC, vol. 8b), pp. 769–70.
52. Leslie Stephen, p. 127.
53. See below, pages 50, 106.

# CHAPTER 4

## INTO THE LIMELIGHT 1869–73:
## WOMEN'S SUFFRAGE

The women's suffrage movement was of recent vintage when Millicent Garrett Fawcett made her first speech in 1869. The late nineteenth century was a period of growth and achievement for women's rights in several fields, and her concentration on an aspect in which no progress was made may strike modern readers as mistaken. Barbara Caine, at the end of a stimulating reassessment of John Stuart Mill and the women's movement, questions his belief that the parliamentary vote was the key to success in all other aspects of the movement.[1] But if this assumption was a misapprehension, it was one shared by most of the feminists of his day and long afterwards. Voting was regarded by supporters and opponents alike as the symbol of women's inferiority to man.[2] It could hardly have been guessed that it would take over five decades and a great war to achieve the modest demand to enfranchise women householders which was first put forward in the 1860s. It was not unreasonable for suffragists in the later 1860s to think that the demand might be realized with relatively little difficulty at a time of significant institutional change when their male relatives and friends were unprecedentedly influential in press and Parliament.[3] Only with the perspective of history can it be seen in the Victorian context as a cause lost because its support was insubstantial or evanescent.

Demands for the emancipation of women began long before the mid-1860s or the establishment of the *Englishwoman's Journal* in 1858. It was, however, in 1865–6 that a discernible women's suffrage movement arose from the activities of groups of women based in Langham Place and Kensington and initially concerned with employment and education. Mill included the demand for the suffrage in his election programme in 1865, and it was with his support that Emily Davies and Elizabeth Garrett took to the House of Commons in June 1866 the famous petition signed by 1,499 women in support of the case for enfranchising women householders.[4] If Mill and Helen Taylor were subsequently vain, autocratic and divisive forces within the women's movement, as recent writers have argued persuasively,[5] Mill's work in Parliament and the seminal *Subjection of Women*, published in 1869, showed him at his best. He was a uniquely inspiring force, except when compelled to work with others. Certainly Millicent Garrett Fawcett, though she was to be denigrated and traduced by Mill, did not doubt that his influence inaugurated 'an epoch in the history of the women's movement'.[6]

Among those who owed their political creeds to Mill was Henry Fawcett, as he proclaimed to the House of Commons in a speech supporting women's suffrage in 1867.[7] He demonstrated his support in practical fashion in 1866 by advising the petition's organizers, coming to their rescue when they arrived at Westminster uncertain of where to bestow their unwieldy parcel of signatures and joining Mill in presenting the petition to the House of Commons.[8] It did not include the name of Millicent Garrett since she was on the verge of her nineteenth birthday and apparently regarded as too young to sign.[9]

Later in the year her engagement to Henry Fawcett was announced. Emily Davies viewed the engagement with a hint of cynicism which the movement could profitably have retained in its subsequent dealing with politicians. Writing to Helen Taylor she commented: 'So we may now rely upon his being kept in the path of duty.' 'Miss M. Garrett is rather young (only nineteen)', she added. 'In other respects they seem likely to suit very well.'[10] One hopes that Davies was pleased with the accuracy of her predictions.

Writing a few weeks later to Lydia Becker, the Manchester-based suffrage leader, Davies observed: 'Mr Fawcett is strongly in our favour.' He had suggested to her that Mill should bring the subject before the House of Commons 'in some way or other' and thus demonstrate that women's suffrage was more popular than was commonly thought.[11] When Mill did so the following May Fawcett, now a married man, spoke in support of the demand of votes for qualified women. Following events from India, Millicent's sister Alice Cowell told their mother that she had read 'comments innumerable' on the debate. 'Mr Fawcett is generally treated to mild chaff upon the "lover-like ardour" with which he took up the question.'[12] By this time Millicent had become involved in the movement. When the London National Society for Woman (subsequently Women's) Suffrage was formed in July 1867 she was elected to its executive committee.[13] As with her educational work at Cambridge she proved to have a gift for suggesting generally acceptable policies.[14] She also showed an early talent for meticulous organization, beginning her career as a parliamentary lobbyist by carefully preparing a division list of members and recording their votes on Mill's amendment.[15] There was no further division until May 1870, but challenges were mounted from various quarters to women's exclusion from voters' lists, and in spring 1868 the first women's suffrage meetings were held in Manchester and Birmingham. Lydia Becker and Annie Robertson of Dublin were among the speakers at both meetings.[16] Soon afterwards Millicent became the treasurer of a 'Ladies' Association for Collecting Funds for Mr

Mill's Election for Westminster', a body which failed to prevent his defeat at the hands of W.H. Smith.[17]

The first women's suffrage meeting in London did not take place until 17 July 1869. On Mill's motion Mentia Taylor, one of the leaders of the movement and also married to a radical Member of Parliament, took the chair. Millicent was the only other woman speaker.[18] Although she was barely 22 it was not her introduction to a public platform. The previous October she had read to the Social Science Association Harry's paper on economy and trade. *The Times* primly recorded that she had done so 'with remarkable propriety' and the president, the Earl of Carnarvon, referred amidst cheers to 'the singular clearness of enunciation with which she had done justice to the paper'.[19] The fact that the newspaper comment was looked upon as amusingly old-fashioned just over twenty years later suggests that, although women's suffrage was still far distant, the movement had succeeded in modifying the public standard of acceptable female behaviour, an achievement of some significance.[20] Carnarvon's comment is also worth noting, for clarity of thought and enunciation were always to be associated with her public career.

There is no reason to doubt Millicent's recollection that she was 'terrified'[21] by the prospect of a short speech, given in the company of Harry and a galaxy of radical stars including Mill, Dilke, Lord Houghton, James Stansfeld, John Morley, Charles Kingsley and others. The most important part of her speech was the section in which she warned that the supporters of women's suffrage were a small minority, inclined by their intellectual and personal associations to underestimate the strength of the opposition and indulge in unrealistic self-congratulation. A proper understanding of the task confronting them, she pointed out, 'should be our strongest incentive to increased exertion'.[22] It was a sombre and timely warning which her subsequent speeches did not often repeat, and bold advice from a novice female speaker to her august colleagues that they should attempt to understand the nature of the world they lived in.

The meeting was widely reported (although ignored by *The Times*), but there was little editorial comment. *The Daily Telegraph*, however, pointed to the existence of a problem which was to bedevil the movement for fifty years. Although women's suffrage, it commented, had now entered the political arena, its advocates were divided about which women to enfranchise and whether to seek a limited reform or the removal of all the legal and social disabilities to which women were subjected. 'Between the two objects there is a wide distinction.'[23] There was no press comment about Millicent's speech or the propriety of her making it, but privately there was much gossip. Alice wrote from India after seeing a press report, asked if their father had attended the meeting and added: 'It is very difficult not to talk.'[24] It was a difficulty not resisted by H.C. Raikes, the Conservative member for Chester, who according to Millicent's recollection told the

House of Commons a few days later that she and Mrs Taylor had 'disgraced themselves'.[25]

Her speaking career was now launched. She was to insist over the years that she was an unwilling public speaker,[26] but her dislike, like her apprehension about her initial appearance, must be set against the forthright content of her speeches and a subsequent platform career which lasted until shortly before her death sixty years later. It seems more likely that she felt the combination of attraction and repugnance familiar to most people who have addressed large audiences on controversial subjects. Being photographed she also regarded as 'a penance',[27] but it was a penance to which she repeatedly subjected herself.

Her initial speech made sufficient impression on Mill for him to suggest her name a few weeks later for a proposed meeting in Stoke-on-Trent. In recommending her he wrote: 'The cause of Women's Suffrage has no more active, judicious and useful friends than Mr and Mrs Fawcett.'[28] In October 1869 she attended a meeting in Warwick with Harry, where she spoke briefly, supporting demands for working-class MPs and advocating 'the extension of the franchise to the ladies'.[29] Harry reported on the meeting to Mill, stressing Millicent's favourable reception and her intention to prepare a lecture on the subject. Mill was delighted: 'What she has already written is a guarantee for its being excellent both in matter and stile, and her person and manner will dispel prejudice and attract adherents wherever she delivers it.'[30] In February 1870 she and Harry, in a practical demonstration of support for trade unionism across class lines and party allegiance, spoke on behalf of George Odger, the independent union candidate at a Southwark by-election. They followed up their speeches by practical election work.[31] After her death nearly sixty years later her involvement was recalled by a member of her audience: 'Her voice, her manner, her command of speech, her self-possession and her lady-like modesty were simply faultless.'[32]

In March 1870 she delivered her first substantial speech, a lecture on women's suffrage to Harry's Brighton Liberal constituents. The Conservative *Brighton Gazette* observed sniffily: 'Female political orators we must regard as altogether intolerable', but the *Brighton Daily News*, described by Harry as 'by far the most important paper in Brighton', treated the speech as the sensational success it obviously was, spreading its report across three pages. The town hall was filled to capacity and several hundred people were turned away. A third paper, the *Brighton Herald*, commented: 'She is a lady of small stature, and of fragile but very pleasing appearance; perfectly collected in her manner, and with a very clear, distinct, emphatic delivery, not at times without a touch of humour.'[33] Doubt about her stated antipathy to the public platform and perhaps also about Harry's support for her speaking career may be derived from his remark to the audience that she knew that 'some persons' would find her speaking 'a strange and somewhat irregular proceeding . . . But my wife felt she ought to deliver the lecture.'[34]

After speeches at meetings in Hanover Square and Greenwich she and Harry visited Dublin in April, where her large audience included the parents of Oscar Wilde.[35] Her speech was a triumph. As the faithful Alice wrote to their mother,[36] the *Irish Times* was overwhelmed. Its leading article was rapturous about her poise, knowledge and appearance:

> Mrs FAWCETT's extensive reading, her speculative power, her close reasoning, her evident aptitude for social and political discussions, do not appear to have robbed her of one natural grace, nor interfered with an exquisite feminine culture except to enhance it.

The most conclusive of her arguments for women's suffrage, it asserted, was 'her own appearance at the reading-desk'.[37]

She had quickly become one of the very few women to make regular appearances on the platform. In March 1871, less than two years after her initial speech, she undertook a tour of the West Country, speaking at Frome, Bath, Bristol, Taunton, Tavistock, Plymouth and Exeter to large and enthusiastic audiences.[38] Harry did not accompany her, adding to the adventurous quality of the tour. Her speech at Plymouth, which took over ninety minutes to deliver, was described by the *Western Daily Mercury* as 'convincing, clear and trenchant'. It was impressed by her 'rich, full voice', as was the *Bristol Times and Mirror*, which referred to it as 'clear, silvery, and expressive'. It also mentioned her 'extremely youthful appearance',[39] a point later stressed by her friend and colleague Lilias Ashworth Hallett, who recalled her 'girlish figure' and the cheers given at several meetings for Harry, who despite his affliction had generously spared her 'to go forth and plead for this new gospel'.[40]

By this time she had obviously become an accomplished speaker. Her wit, detailed argument, youth and eloquence were compelling attractions to contemporary audiences. The first two attributes remained with her throughout her speaking career, and she was described as youthful in appearance into her seventies.[41] The frequent descriptions of her speaking as eloquent were contradicted by later reports of her factually-based appeals to reason, for speaking 'to the head and not to the heart', as one of her colleagues wrote in 1909.[42] The explanation may lie in the unfamiliar experience of a young woman speaking in public and the novelty of women's suffrage to mid-Victorian audiences, combined with the deep sincerity which she obviously felt for her subject. In any event there is no doubt that her early audiences were not only impressed and respectful, but often emotionally moved.

It is now time to turn to the content of her speeches. They pose a problem to the modern reader, for however ingrained the assumption of women's inferiority remains in contemporary society the right of women to vote is now as uncontentious and uninteresting as its Victorian advocates predicted that it would become. It is necessary to remember that when the young Millicent began her speaking career not only women but the majority of men were denied the parliamentary vote. The subject and the speaker had a freshness which is now impossible to recapture.

Her early speeches were fully reported and in some cases reprinted verbatim. This was the case with 'The electoral disabilities of women', which she delivered in various forms in Brighton, Dublin, the West Country and London.[43] It was the classic expression of her early views, a list of up to sixteen objections to women's suffrage, each of which was then demolished. Women with votes would not neglect their families; they would be better wives and mothers because of their knowledge of the world. Women's intellectual inferiority was unproven and if true did not apply to all women. As to their physical inferiority, it had not been suggested that a Cabinet should be composed of prize fighters and acrobats. In reply to the assertion that women were superior beings to males who should not sully their purity by voting, she queried the logic which would reserve the vote to the inferior sex. She ridiculed the argument that petty courtesies like having doors opened and seats reserved were preferable to the vote and also the allegation that women were natural Conservatives. She doubted that it would be claimed that all Conservatives should be disenfranchised, and as for the courtesies, she declared, 'she chose freedom rather than favour' and looked forward with perfect equanimity to opening doors for herself. Women, she asserted, should insist that they would 'no longer forego their claims to equality for toys and sugar-plums'. She did not fear boisterous elections, she said, which should become more decorous when a secret ballot was introduced. In any case she had visited a polling booth during a contested election and found it less unpleasant than 'the staircases of great London houses after a reception'.[44]

She made fun of the argument deployed by a Member of Parliament that votes for women would obliterate the distinction of sex. She told her West Country audience 'amidst much merriment' that women were neither made nor unmade by Acts of Parliament.[45] It was said that women did not want the vote, and though this was true of some, an increasing number did want it; those who did not need not use it. As for biblical support for the subjection of women, she made plain her view that the Bible was not an adequate guide to modern political behaviour. In any event the ideal of the New Testament was human equality; there should be 'neither Jew nor Greek, male nor female, bond nor free'.

A speech which she delivered in Birmingham town hall in December 1872 appealed to the idealism of her audience. She said that after a previous speech there a year before two women had thanked her for having made them 'feel two inches taller'. That 'homely metaphor', she declared, should summarize the aim of the women's movement. Women's position in England had improved in the past thirty years and would improve even more in the next thirty. It was idle to say that the progress of the nation must now come to an end.[46] Each generation should exert itself for the benefit of the next. She concluded:

To promote the improvement of the condition of women is a great and noble cause to devote one's life to. Success in such a cause is a goal worthy of the noblest ambition; and failure in such a cause is a better thing than success in any meaner or pettier object.[47]

She did not attempt to deceive her audience into thinking that women should be granted the vote simply because voting was a noble ideal and the arguments of the opposition frivolous. Women, especially married women, suffered from explicit wrongs which she believed that the possession of the vote would do much to put right. 'We could hardly take up a newspaper without seeing some case of misery which could be traced to the position of serfdom in which the law places married women', she declared roundly. Drunken, violent husbands could with impunity forbid their wives from access to their children.[48] A case like that of Martha Torpey, acquitted in 1871 of a jointly planned and executed diamond theft on grounds that she had acted at the bidding of her escaped husband was a further argument for reforming the law.[49] The right of married women to their earnings was absurdly inadequate, despite the passage of the first Married Women's Property Act in 1870.

She had learned at an early age to put little faith in male declarations of belief in freedom and liberty, for the belief too seldom extended to the domestic hearth.[50] As early as 1865 when she was barely 18, she told a Bedford meeting in 1873, she had asked a number of prominent Suffolk Liberals attending a meeting with her father to sign a petition in support of married women's property rights. 'Alas,' the Liberal MP's wife told the meeting, 'I was very inexperienced then, and I did not know that Liberalism, like beauty, is only skin deep.' Though the men to whom she had presented the petition expressed pleasure at the prospect of being freed from responsibility for their wives' debts, they were adamant when one found that if his wife inherited money he would have no control over it. 'That gentleman strutted to the end of the room, and they all raised a kind of chorus, saying "We won't sign it"; and not a single signature did I get to that unfortunate petition.'[51]

She also learned when still young to regard with some cynicism the attention devoted to her appearance on the platform. She denounced as frivolous the concentration on a woman's dress, voice and manners. Imagine, she asked a Royston audience in 1873, a man being treated in the same fashion:

He was quietly but richly dressed in a coat of dark blue cloth, with trousers of a lighter colour. It may interest our readers to learn that his hair is raven black and that he wears a beard and moustache. His voice is clear and musical, and although he spoke with considerable self-possession and fluency, there is nothing unmasculine in his appearance.[52]

By this time she had become a respected, even a formidable figure. When she visited a reading room in Westminster and was turned away because she was a woman she wrote to the library commissioners and was assured that women had the right of entry.[53] She was undeterred by public rebuke, and by private remonstrance that '*no Christian Woman*' should take part in politics or speak on the platform.[54] She was openly spoken of as a future Member of Parliament, not only in jest but in a serious political profile which observed that it was 'hardly possible to think of her except as an absentee member of the House'.[55]

At the same time it had become evident by 1873 if not earlier that if there had ever been a realistic hope of a speedy passage of a women's suffrage bill the moment had definitively passed. John Stuart Mill, whose moral stature and authority as a champion of women's suffrage were irreplaceable, died in that year and by the time of his death the cause had suffered five defeats in Parliament.[56] An irrefutable case for adding women to the voters' registers had long since been made, but the parliamentary indifference and chicanery which were to afflict the movement for so long were already apparent. The days of initial glory were over and the long haul had begun.

## NOTES

1. Barbara Caine, 'John Stuart Mill and the English women's movement', *Historical Studies* (vol. 18, 1978), p. 67.
2. Philippa Levine, *Victorian Feminism 1850–1900* (1987), pp. 58–9.
3. Andrew Rosen, 'Emily Davies and the women's movement, 1862–1867', *Journal of British Studies* (vol. 19, 1979), pp. 111–12; Leslie Parker Hume, *The National Union of Women's Suffrage Societies* (1982), pp. 13–14.
4. I have followed the accounts by Rosen, pp. 107–9, and A.P.W. Robson, 'The founding of the National Society for Women's Suffrage 1866–1867', *Canadian Journal of History* (vol. 8, 1973), pp. 2–8.
5. Caine, Rosen and Robson.
6. MGF, 'The women's suffrage movement' in Theodore Stanton (ed.), *The Woman Question in Europe* (1884), p. 4; also her *Women's Suffrage* [1912], pp. 16–19, and *WIR*, pp. 51–2, 60–1, 64–5, 87.
7. *Parl. Deb.*, 3rd ser., 187, col. 835 (20 May 1867).
8. Henry Fawcett to Elizabeth Garrett, 30 May 1866 (Mill–Taylor Collection, BLPES); Helen Blackburn, *Women's Suffrage* (1902), pp. 55–7; Constance Rover, *Women's Suffrage and Party Politics in Britain 1866–1914* (1967), p. 5.
9. *MGF*, p. 42. Her mother, two sisters, a sister-in-law and her future mother-in-law were among the signatories (copy of petition in Fawcett Library).
10. Davies to Taylor, 15 December 1866 (Mill–Taylor Collection).
11. Davies to Becker, 9 February 1867 (M50/1/2/8).
12. Alice Cowell to Louisa Garrett, 27 June [1867] (Anderson Papers, St Brelade). 'I wonder whether universal suffrage will come in our time', she mused.
13. Robson, pp. 18–21.
14. A letter from Priscilla Bright McLaren to MGF recollecting this gift (22 November 1895, FLALC, vol. 1b) is quoted in *MGF*, pp. 43–4.
15. Her analysis of twelve division lists from 1867 to 1883 is in M50/2/3/1 and 2.
16. MGF in Stanton (ed.), pp. 10–12. Reports of the meetings from the *Manchester Examiner and Times* (15 April 1868), the *Birmingham Gazette* and *Birmingham Daily Post* (both of 9 May 1868) are filed at M50/1/9/1.

17. An undated letter from Caroline A. Biggs to an unspecified newspaper giving the association's name is at *ibid.* See also *ER*, July 1868, p. 534.
18. *Report of a Meeting* of the London National Society for Women's Suffrage, 17 July 1869 (Fawcett Library).
19. *The Times*, 7 October 1868.
20. Rolph interview (ch. 1, note 32 above), p. 620. Mrs Fawcett noted as early as 1884 the change in public opinion about 'the propriety of women speaking on the platform' (Stanton (ed.), p. 10n.).
21. *WIR*, p. 87.
22. *Report of a Meeting* (note 18 above), p. 20.
23. *The Daily Telegraph*, 19 July 1869.
24. Alice Cowell to Louisa Garrett, 20 August 1869 (Anderson Papers).
25. The incident and its aftermath are amusingly described in *WIR*, pp. 87–8, but the official report (*Parl. Deb.*, 3rd ser., 198, col. 403, 21 July 1869) is disappointingly colourless.
26. E[dith] P[alliser], *CC*, 22 April 1909, p. 23; *MGF*, pp. 100, 131; Brian Harrison, *Prudent Revolutionaries* (1987), p. 24.
27. MGF to W.T. Stead, 17 August [1890] (Stead Papers, Churchill College, Cambridge).
28. Mill to William Wood, 30 August 1869 (Mineka and Lindley (eds), vol. 4, p. 1636). I have been unable to discover any evidence of this proposed meeting.
29. *Warwick and Leamington Times*, 16 October 1869.
30. Mill to Fawcett, 24 October 1869 (Mineka and Lindley (eds), vol. 4, pp. 1657–8).
31. *The Times*, 15 February 1870; F.W. Soutter, *Recollections of a Labour Pioneer* (T. Fisher Unwin, 1923), pp. 49–50.
32. Sir George Young, *The Times*, 9 August 1929.
33. *Brighton Gazette*, 24 March 1870; *Brighton Daily News*, 24 March 1870; *Brighton Herald*, 26 March 1870; Henry Fawcett to Alexander Macmillan, 4 April 1872 (Macmillan Archive, BL).
34. *Brighton Daily News*, 24 March 1870. Ray Strachey's statement (*MGF*, p. 47) that the meeting thanked Henry Fawcett for allowing his wife to speak seems to be a misunderstanding of the vote of thanks reported in the *News*.
35. *The Times*, 28 March 1870; *WSJ*, 2 May 1870, pp. 21, 23–4; *Daily Express* (Dublin), 19 April 1870.
36. Alice Cowell to Louisa Garrett, 3 June 1870 (Anderson Papers).
37. *Irish Times*, 19 April 1870.
38. *The Times*, 18 March 1871.
39. *Western Daily Mercury* (Plymouth), 15 March 1871, *Bristol Times and Mirror*, 9 March 1871. Cuttings from both papers are filed at M50/1/9/3.
40. Quoted in Blackburn, pp. 109–10.
41. See, e.g, Harrison, p. 17.
42. Edith Palliser (note 26 above).
43. For printed versions see MGF, 'The electoral disabilities of women', *Fortnightly Review*, May 1870, pp. 622–32; lecture delivered at Tavistock, 11 March 1871, reprinted in Jane Lewis (ed.), *Before the Vote was Won* (1987), pp. 100–17; Fawcett and Fawcett, pp. 230–61, from which the next two paragraphs (apart from notes 44 and 45) are drawn.
44. Unidentified Bath paper, 9 March 1871 (M50/1/9/3).
45. *Western Daily Mercury*, 15 March 1871 (*ibid.*).
46. 'No man has a right to fix the boundary of the march of a nation', Charles Stewart Parnell was to declare in Cork in 1885. Mrs Fawcett was to be one of his most determined opponents.

47. *Mrs Fawcett on Women's Suffrage* [?1872]; (BLPES).
48. Unidentified Bath paper (note 44 above).
49. *The Times*, 4 and 9 March 1871.
50. Fawcett and Fawcett, *Essays and Lectures* (1872), pp. 270–4, 281.
51. *WSJ*, 1 February 1873, pp. 18–19. The story was a favourite of hers, often repeated.
52. *The Times*, 15 December 1873.
53. *ibid.*, 19 May 1873. Not many women felt able to exercise the right, and in 1883 a Ladies' Reading Room was opened (*Women's Union Journal*, December 1883, p. 101).
54. 'A follower of Christ and of Paul his Apostle' to MGF, 11 May 1872 (M50/2/1/6).
55. *Punch*, 16 April 1870, p. 155; 'Henry Holbeach' (William Brighty Rands), 'Literary legislators. No. V – Mr and Mrs Fawcett', *St Paul's Magazine*, July 1872, p. 78. Moncure Conway made the same point (ch. 2, note 39 above).
56. Useful tables of parliamentary divisions may be found in Rover, pp. 218–23, and Brian Harrison, *Separate Spheres* (1978), pp. 28–9. The 1870 bill passed its second reading by a majority of 33 but was defeated in committee a week later by 126 votes.

# CHAPTER 5

## QUIET YEARS 1874–83

After the excitement of her first few years of married life the subsequent decade was a relatively quiet one for Millicent Garrett Fawcett. Between 1867 and 1874 she had married, become a mother, written two economics books, much of a third and many articles, been heavily involved in opening higher education at Cambridge to women and carved out for herself a novel and controversial role as a public speaker on women's suffrage. This was in addition to her marriage to a blind man with whom she shared an active social life as well as many of his political and intellectual activities, while maintaining her own circle of friends, her Garrett family links and two homes. It is true, as Mary Stott has pointed out, that she did not have to earn a salary, live on a small income, keep house or care for Philippa without domestic assistance.[1] Yet even with such advantages her first six or seven years of married life would seem sufficient for several people. Perhaps their unbroken activity helps to explain why she published no more books after *Janet Doncaster* (1875), apart from a second novel published under a pseudonym, until her short biographies of eminent women were published in a collected version in 1889.[2] She also became less prominent in the women's suffrage movement. Her speaking engagements were less numerous, and she was no longer a certain speaker on major occasions.

The beginning and end of the period are relatively easy to understand. In December 1873 she was nursing a sick or dying friend and early the next year a bad fall from a horse caused her to cancel some engagements, though probably not for a prolonged period. Harry thought that she had been killed, and his biographer wrote of 'the pathetic weeping of the strong man'.[3] At the end of the period Harry's rise to ministerial status as Postmaster-General and the consequent round of social functions were inhibiting factors, and his dangerous illness in the autumn of 1882 and prolonged recuperation would have prevented her from carrying out a heavy programme of engagements. Yet these considerations do not explain her reduced level of activity after 1874, and they did not prevent her from undertaking a flurry of suffrage work in 1884, the year of Harry's death.

Certainly there was no reduction in the range of her interests. Women's suffrage and education remained central to her life and she was more involved than previously with encouraging the employment of working-class women. It is difficult to believe that one of so sanguine a temperament became less active because of the unbroken line of defeats of women's suffrage bills in the House of Commons. It is more likely that having partially withdrawn from the movement because of internal dissension, she was for a period unable or unwilling to resume all her former activities.

By the mid-1870s women's suffrage societies existed in several of the larger cities. It could hardly have been expected that organizations demanding so new and controversial a measure as women's suffrage, staffed mostly by novices to political agitation, should have worked together without friction. In the initial 'heroic' years when the first speeches and parliamentary divisions were taking place a reasonable degree of unity might be expected to prevail. But when an issue of substance arose with potential for sharply contrasting convictions, it was inevitable that harmony would be endangered.

The suffrage movement was in any case hindered by the fact that its unchallenged leaders, John Stuart Mill and Helen Taylor, were often abroad, conscious of their own superiority and unwilling to modify their views or listen to argument.[4] This was notably the case in 1869 when Josephine Butler founded the Ladies' National Association dedicated to the abolition of the Contagious Diseases Acts. The acts, passed in and after 1864, were intended to combat diseases associated with prostitution, but their operation threatened all working-class women in certain garrison and naval towns with forcible inspection for venereal disease and subsequent treatment in special 'lock' hospitals.[5] Almost all feminists opposed the acts, although Elizabeth Garrett, a medical practitioner, was a prominent and vocal exception. On the other side many suffragists, including the Garrett cousin Rhoda, probably the outstanding speaker in the movement, strongly supported the work for abolition and felt no conflict between it and their suffrage work.

Millicent felt strongly about the contagious diseases question, as she was to do about moral issues throughout her life, with a passion which women's suffrage never aroused in her. But she also felt strongly that the two issues should not be confused and that suffrage work would be disastrously affected it if were associated in the public mind with issues arising from prostitution.[6] She took this line from the start of the controversy, and Mill, though defending the women's agitation against the Contagious Diseases Acts and giving evidence against the acts to a parliamentary committee in 1871,[7] took the same view. During the course of 1871, however, he adopted a position of suspicion towards her which hardened into hostility in the next year. Her doctrinaire economic views irritated him, and the fact that she thought for herself and was unwilling to shape her convictions to the bidding of others is unlikely to have ameliorated his feelings.[8] Unlike him, she was anxious to prevent an irrevocable public demonstration of the discord between the differing groups within the suffrage movement.

The steps taken in November 1871 by the Manchester suffragists and their allies to create the central committee of the National Society for Women's Suffrage, though ostensibly intended as a step towards unifying the various local suffrage societies,[9] increased the strains within the move-Ment. No letters survive which explain Millicent's point of view, but it must have been an unhappy period for her. She did not join the new central committee, which favoured working for both the suffrage and the repeal of the acts, though both Agnes and Rhoda Garrett did so and Agnes was for a period one of its honorary secretaries.[10]

But she did not escape the censure of Mill, busily spinning webs in Avignon. He and his faction decided in the autumn of 1872 to express their personal and political dissatisfaction with the Central Committee. Their principal targets were the Manchester-based Lydia Becker, editor of the *Women's Suffrage Journal*, and Jacob Bright, its parliamentary chief, who had done much to identify women's suffrage with the repeal movement. The means chosen was an address calculated to deepen the division between the two groups. Millicent, evidently still attempting to minimize dissension within suffrage ranks, refused to be associated with the address. Mill then wrote to his disciple George Croom Robertson that if the committee of the London National Society for Women's Suffrage were to be guided by her he would leave it. The society was, he took care to point out, held together mainly by his name. Millicent was too prone to self-confidence and apt in consequence to plunge into error. 'She has neither a speculative nor an organising intelligence, and therefore, even supposing that she were twice her present age, she is quite unfit to be a leader, though an excellent guerilla partisan.'[11]

Mill's judgement was not so obviously inaccurate as previous writers have assumed.[12] Millicent was notably prone to rely on her own judgement. A philosopher might well think that she lacked a speculative intelligence, though she was better able to grapple with theoretical issues than most political figures. Organization was not her particular skill, and she did not become the undisputed leader of a women's suffrage organization for nearly thirty-five years, though she remained, as in 1872, one of the leading figures in the movement throughout the period. The episode shows her in what was becoming a familiar role as would-be peacemaker and Mill as vain and malicious, but it does not demonstrate that his judgement was self-evidently false.

The quarrel is too little documented, particularly from Millicent's side, to write of it with much confidence. She did not immediately leave the LNSWS, remained on reasonably good terms with Helen Taylor, wrote a glowing obituary of Mill in *The Examiner*, and with Charlotte Burbury, whom Mill had also denigrated, was one of two women members of a committee of fifteen established to devise a memorial in his memory.[13] However, the dissension which Mill had done much to inspire continued to divide suffragists. Following an exchange of letters between the LNSWS and the Central Committee of the NSWS in February 1874, in which Helen Taylor showed herself to be as petulant and uncompromising as her step-father, Millicent resigned from the former and gradually became more active in the affairs of the latter.[14] The two societies were reconciled in 1877–8 and she joined the executive in 1878, but she appears not to have taken a leading role for another decade when, ironically, she was a key figure in another split. By 1880 she had retired from the leadership of the movement sufficiently not to figure as an advertised speaker in hugely successful mass meetings held in 1880–2 in Manchester, London (where she did address an overflow meeting), Bristol, Nottingham, Birmingham, Bradford, Sheffield and Glasgow.[15] But she remained a name to conjure with, well known to the public as a compelling and still youthful speaker, her attraction enhanced by her marriage to the blind MP who in 1880 became Postmaster-General.

Her relatively few appearances and articles on the suffrage question gave her ample opportunity to articulate her distinctive approach to the issues, in speeches laced with quotations from contemporary writers among whom George Eliot was prominent. She was fond of quoting *Adam Bede* (1859): 'I'm not denyin' the women are foolish. God Almighty made 'em to match the men.' But while her goal was votes for women it is not easy to separate her own convictions on tactical matters from her insistence on the overarching need to attract maximum support for women's suffrage. Her speeches and articles make it clear that she felt that to put her own views before the good of the movement was not only selfish but counterproductive, and suggest that she had a clearer idea of the function of leadership than John Stuart Mill.

This approach was expressed in her early and often repeated statement that the interests of men and women were not opposed,[16] and also in her stance on the contentious issue of votes for married women. The issue agitated and divided the movement to a surprising extent in view of the small number of married women who paid rates and hence would have qualified for the parliamentary franchise. Unlike Harry[17] she had no objection to the exclusion of married women, towards whose enfranchisement there was widespread hostility. Her desire was to advance a case which could secure maximum support, finding chinks in the enemy armour through which parliamentary votes for some women might be inserted. The principle once achieved, she believed that more women voters would follow. Votes for unmarried women and widows might secure parliamentary approval, because these groups would be a small minority of voters and would not be a presumed second vote awarded to husbands. Moreover, the enfranchisement of these women would lead to the gradual ending of the legal oppression of their married sisters. Hence, she declared in 1875: 'I really don't care whether married women have votes or not.'[18] Later in life when she was a short, amber-haired widow, her formula was to 'accept as an instalment a Bill which even restricted the franchise to women with dark hair, or those who were six feet high'.[19]

It was in the same spirit that in a London speech in 1878 she advised women not to neglect 'the duties of their home life' and reminded young women that 'it was not by being bad needlewomen and bad housekeepers that they would show themselves worthy of the trust they claimed. It was just the contrary.'[20] There is no reason to believe that this comment hid a deeper meaning. She was born into early Victorian England and was herself an accomplished needlewoman.[21] But she was also a political figure concerned to obtain votes and other practical benefits for women, rather than to lay down eternal principles of women's emancipation. In her view women who wanted votes would be well advised to work with the grain of their time, and good housekeepers, like attractively dressed and well-mannered women, were more likely to achieve their aims.

On the other hand it would be mistaken to suppose that, obsessed by tactical considerations, she expressed no positive convictions on the suffrage question. The argument that women's suffrage was consistent with the spirit of an increasingly democratic age was one of her deepest and most frequently expressed beliefs. Women's legislative status should correspond to their social status. Women followed university courses, were employed in the civil service, served on school boards, voted in local elections, took part in electioneering and even attended parliamentary debates, and 'nobody seems a penny the worse'.[22] It was clear that 'a very great social change has steadily been evolving itself'.[23] As she wrote succinctly on another occasion: 'The movement for the representation of women is nothing more nor less than a simple outgrowth of the democracy which has been the gradual product of this century.'[24]

However compelling the arguments for women's suffrage, the lack of parliamentary progress and the divisions within the movement must have been dispiriting even for so optimistic a campaigner as Millicent Garrett Fawcett. The development of women's education was more encouraging. Millicent continued her work for Newnham and served on the college council from 1881, soon after its establishment, until 1909.[25] She also kept an eye on developments at Girton, and her relations with the college were sufficiently cordial for her to put forward a name, though unsuccessfully, for the position of mistress in 1875. Her reasons for suggesting Eliza Cairnes, shortly to be the widow of the economist J.E. Cairnes, throw an interesting light on mid-Victorian criteria for leadership in women's education. Apart from sympathizing with the subject, she wrote, Mrs Cairnes was 'a very cultivated & refined woman: she has a very pleasing appearance & good manners, and she has a great power of influencing those about her.' A final argument in her support was that she did not need the £200 annual salary to maintain herself in comfort, a guarantee that she would not carry out her duties simply 'from the necessity of money getting'.[26]

Millicent also involved herself in the effort to improve university facilities for women in London, about which she wrote to Helen Taylor to report progress in 1875.[27] She gave a practical demonstration of her commitment by lecturing in political economy at Queen's College, London – then regarded as an institution of higher education – for at least two terms in 1879, at a fee of £10 a term.[28] She was elected president of the Women's Debating Society of London University in the same year.[29]

Her principal article on education in the period was published in *Good Words* in 1878. The growth of maturity and self-confidence since her earlier articles is striking. She argued that the great growth of human freedom in the nineteenth century should not be restricted to men. The theory that women should be 'constantly under tutelage', told what to do, think and believe, was no longer valid, for 'the supply of men runs short', many had other things to do than to instruct the women of their families, and some might lack the desire to do so. The article was an impressive attempt to demonstrate that freedom and increased opportunities for women were not only just but inevitable, a movement with 'roots deep and wide throughout the whole of society'. As with the suffrage, she attempted with considerable success to show that it was not simply a few courageous individuals but history itself which was knocking at the door.[30]

Her other main concern during this period was to attempt to secure increased opportunities for working-class women to find employment even where this involved competition with men. It appears that the Fawcetts learned together in this field and influenced each other. The first two editions of Harry's *Manual of Political Economy*, published in 1863 and 1865, did not discuss women's labour, though the author had expressed himself privately an enthusiastic supporter.[31] In July 1867, three months after his marriage, speaking in Parliament on an important factory bill which was to bring many new industries into the protective net, he gave the bill his blessing and did not mention its effect on women.[32] But in October 1868 he cautioned the Social Science Association against restrictions on employment which would be unjust to women,[33] and in the third edition of his *Manual*, published in 1869, he expresssed his support for women's right 'to follow any profession, trade, or employment to which they desire to devote their energies'. It may be significant that he warmly thanked his wife for her 'care and assiduity'; she had 'pointed out many defects and some inaccuracies'.[34]

By the early 1870s he had become a leading opponent of factory legislation. Admitting his inconsistency, he put up a strong and effective fight in 1873 against the Nine Hours Bill of A.J. Mundella, formerly a political ally, now a wounded antagonist.[35] Millicent was also involved in the controversy. She wrote a long letter to *The Times*, insisting that legally shortened hours would mean less employment for women. The spirit behind the desire for factory legislation, though hidden behind ostensible concern for women's well-being, was 'the old Trade Union spirit to drive women out of certain trades where their competition is inconvenient'. Women worked too hard for the unions' liking; if they were 'a little lazier they would not be half so objectionable'. Attempts should be made to improve unhealthy working conditions, but it was better to suffer while earning an honest living than 'be driven to the dismal alternative of starvation or prostitution'. The newspaper did not agree. In a leader on the letter it asserted that the weak should be protected: 'Professors of Political Economy are apt to fall into errors from failing to grasp all the conditions of a question.'[36]

Some months later a resolution was passed without dissent by the Trades Union Congress repudiating both Millicent's letter and Harry's parliamentary opposition to Mundella's Nine Hours Bill.[37] Why Harry changed his convictions on the extension of factory legislation is difficult to say, and Mundella's papers shed no light on the question.[38] Given the nature of his character it is also difficult to accept that Harry was decisively influenced by his wife. But her uncompromising views may have helped to persuade him that his own had been inconsistent. In any event the opposition of political friends and the loss in the general election of February 1874 of Harry's Brighton seat[39] did nothing to modify her unyielding and lifelong opposition to restricting the employment of women.

Millicent's opposition did not extend to women's trade unions. Indeed, at a time when they were identified with feminist belief in the unrestricted employment of women it would have been surprising if she had not participated in union affairs. Her support was hearty but intermittent. She was from its inception a trustee of the National Union of Working Women, a shadowy organization founded in Bristol in August 1874 and concerned with improving wages and hours, instituting sickness and other benefits and opposing new factory legislation. Despite its name the union failed to extend its activities beyond the West Country and South Wales, and its existence, which seems not to have continued beyond the end of the decade, was hampered by the apathy of potential members.[40]

The reports which chronicle the union's activities do not suggest that Millicent did more than lend her name. Nor does she seem to have been involved in the more successful Women's Protective and Provident League founded by Emma Paterson and her associates, also in 1874, until June 1881 when she presided at its seventh annual meeting and accepted a place on the league's council. Much of her speech from the chair followed the mainstream of mid-Victorian liberalism. She reminded her audience that unions could not defy the trade cycle and urged the case for the employment of women in a wider range of industries. Self-help and mutual help were complementary, not antagonistic. At the start of her speech, however, she made a striking declaration of faith in trade unionism.

She was one of those who had always been very hearty supporters of trade unions (cheers) though she knew there were some who, speaking in the name of Political Economy, would tell them that trades unions had absolutely no effect in raising the rate of wages, and that the rate was dependent upon the immutable laws of Political Economy . . . If they would turn from their books and look at facts, they would see that, in the bargaining between employer and employed to settle the rate of wages, the *employé* was not in a position to make the best bargain for himself unless he had a union to fall back upon . . . he must either accept the employers' terms or starve.[41]

The professor of political economy with whom she shared her home might not have gone so far as to reject these words, but it is difficult to imagine him using them.[42]

Sympathy with the working class is also apparent in the article on 'Communism' which Millicent wrote for the ninth edition of the *Encyclopaedia Britannica*, published in 1877. In this, her principal economics publication in the period, she demonstrated detailed knowledge of the theory and history of attempts to abolish the institution of private property, and took care to differentiate communists from the Paris Communards of 1871. The writer whom she quoted at greatest length was 'Karl Marx, a member of the International Society'. She pointed out that the earliest advocates of compulsory education, free trade, law reform and the improvement of the conditions of women were found among communists. It was salutary for wealthy people in Britain, 'the richest country in the world', to consider why so many of their fellow citizens lived in abject poverty. Communism would pose a brake on the motive of self-interest and the incentive to individual effort, but so too did the existing system under which workmen did as little work as they could for their weekly wages, and trade unions limited output and prevented the employment of women where they could. Like Harry she praised the advantages of producer co-operation, and pointed out that its origins in England were largely due to communists.[43]

Her principal objections to communism were twofold. First, under such a system there would be no motive to limit families unless an intolerable system of state control of births were introduced. Second, the advantages which communism might bring, such as co-operation, could be more effective if grafted onto existing society rather than brought about by sudden and sweeping change. 'Society', she wrote, 'is one of those things which cannot be made – it must grow.'[44] She was writing not only before the Communist revolutions of the twentieth century but before the rise of the modern British labour movement, but one can see in this article the later women's suffrage leader, unafraid to collaborate with socialists and Labour party officials.

Although the parliamentary vote was the symbol of women's aspirations in the 1870s, as it long remained, striking advances were made in the later years of the nineteenth century in securing not only votes but also the right to serve as members of the many different forms of local government which existed in the period.[45] Service in particular on school boards and boards of poor law guardians had begun, and Elizabeth Garrett secured a victory in the first London School Board election in 1870, the scale of which has probably never been repeated.[46] It would have been surprising if Millicent herself had been untouched by the growth of women's involvement in local government, but she never gave it the attention which she devoted to women's suffrage and declined all offers to stand for election. In 1875, when her name was suggested as a London School Board candidate for either Lambeth or Hackney,[47] not only Elizabeth but also Alice had served on the board.

The Fawcetts did not underestimate the importance of local government to the women's cause. Both of them were members of Elizabeth's election committee in 1870,[48] though neither was among her more prominently active supporters. At the end of 1870 Millicent joined a committee whose purpose was to promote the election of women to school boards.[49] In 1876 she wrote Helen Taylor a letter of support which demonstrated no illusions about her own sisters: 'You are the first radical woman, I think, who has stood for the school board, and your success would be a great service both to radicalism & to the women's cause.' Taylor was involved in her usual personality clashes with supporters and colleagues, and in contrast with Millicent's soapy deference Elizabeth wrote to Taylor with characteristic Garrett bluntness soon afterwards: 'The difficulty has its origin with you & that from some cause you are not able to work harmoniously with others.'[50] In the next election, in 1879, the Fawcetts supported Henrietta Muller, the Liberal candidate in Lambeth, where their position as local residents gave them considerable influence.[51] In later years Millicent became a somewhat more prominent advocate of women's role in local government, though not on behalf of individual candidates.

One field in which she was not active, surprisingly, was the movement for married women's property rights. This was one of the leading feminist campaigns of the period and her speeches often made reference to the subject. She is somewhat misleadingly associated with this campaign because of a striking and much quoted anecdote in her autobiography. This was an unfortunately romanticized and inaccurate version of an incident which she assigned to 1877, when her purse was stolen at Waterloo station and the thief was charged with stealing the property of Henry Fawcett. 'I felt', she wrote, 'as if I had been charged with theft myself.' Though almost all the details of the story were erroneous[52] the situation which it represented was real enough. In a speech made in 1880 she referred with greater accuracy to the fact that one of her books, which must have been *Political Economy for Beginners* (1870), was not her own property, so that when Harry had made his will he had had to bequeath her the copyright of her own book.[53] But the annual reports of the Married Women's Property committees contain almost no evidence of participation by either Fawcett in the organized effort to reform the law which led to the passage of acts of Parliament in 1870 and 1882.[54] Some hint of an explanation might lie in the fact that the committee's leading officials were

*Millicent Garrett Fawcett speaking in Glasgow, December 1874.*

Elizabeth Wolstenholme (subsequently Wolstenholme Elmy) with Lydia Becker and Josephine Butler in earlier years, and later Ursula Bright. Wolstenholme aroused Millicent's moral sensibilities by living unmarried with her future husband until after she was pregnant,[55] Becker and Bright were prominent among the Manchester suffragists who supported the repeal movement led by Butler. But it was not typical for Millicent to abstain from a campaign on such grounds, and her behaviour remains inexplicable.[56]

By the time that Harry was appointed a minister in the second Gladstone Government in 1880 she was a prominent and respected figure, no longer a shocking novelty as she had been a decade earlier. Some indication of her public standing is given by the invitations to preside over the Women's Debating Society of the University of London and to chair the annual meeting of the Women's Protective and Provident League. She lectured on subjects relatively remote from suffrage or education, such as the novels of Dickens, Thackeray and George Eliot.[57] She had become an acknowledged authority on almost all aspects of the 'woman question' and, in so far as a woman could be, a part of the liberal-intellectual elite. In 1873 she had served on the Mill commemoration committee. In 1877 when Charles Darwin was awarded an honorary degree at Cambridge, it was Millicent who suggested that the occasion should be marked by the presentation of a bust or portrait and she served on the organizing committee.[58] In the same year she wrote a pamphlet entitled *The Martyrs of Turkish Misrule*, championing the Bulgarian Christians, a potential 'nation of free men'[59], whose cause was led in Britain by Gladstone. As the 1880s began with a Liberal election victory and, for Harry, ministerial office, she must have looked forward to a productive and successful future.

NOTES

1. Mary Stott, *Before I Go . . .* (Virago, 1985), p. 50.
2. *Some Eminent Women of our Times* (1889). For the 'lost novel' see ch. 2, n. 27.
3. Henry Fawcett to A.J. Mundella, 12 December 1873 (Mundella Papers, University of Sheffield); *WSJ*, March 1874, p. 42; *ER*, April 1874, p. 138; Leslie Stephen, *Life of Henry Fawcett* (1885), p. 128.
4. Barbara Caine 'John Stuart Mill and the English women's movement' (ch. 4, note 1 above); Josephine Kamm, *John Stuart Mill in Love* (1977), ch. 21.
5. The leading modern books on Victorian prostitution and the repeal movement are Judith Walkowitz, *Prostitution and Victorian Society* (Cambridge: Cambridge University Press, 1980) and Paul McHugh, *Prostitution and Victorian Social Reform* (Croom Helm, 1980).
6. *MGF*, pp. 52–3.
7. Caine, p. 61.
8. *ibid.*, pp. 64, 66; Francis E. Mineka and Dwight N. Lindley (eds), *The Later Lectures of John Stuart Mill 1849–1873* (1972), vol. 4, pp. 1850, 1921.
9. *WSJ*, 1 December 1871, pp. 130–2; 1 February 1872, p. 21.
10. *ibid.*, 1 February 1872, p. 21; 1 July 1873, p. 109; Ray Strachey, *Women's*

*Suffrage and Women's Service* (London and National Society for Women's Service, 1927), p. 15.

11. Mineka and Lindley (eds), vol. 4, pp. 1921–4; Kamm, pp. 191–2. Mill's letter was dated 21 November 1872.

12. Caine, p. 66; Mineka and Lindley (eds), vol. 4, p. 1921n.

13. Mineka and Lindley (eds), vol. 4, p. 1921; *WSJ*, 1 August 1873, p. 123; *ER*, October 1873, pp. 288–9.

14. Kamm, pp. 192–3; correspondence in Mill–Taylor Collection (BLPES), vol. 12; *WSJ*, 1877–8, *passim*.

15. *WSJ*, 14 February, 1 June, 1 December 1880, pp. 33–7, 101–8, 208–16; 1 January, 1 March, 1 December 1881, pp. 10–13, 41–5, 185–9; 1 March, 1 December 1882, pp. 38–43, 182–7. See also MGF in Stanton (ch. 4, note 6 above), pp. 13–14.

16. *WSJ*, 1 January 1872.

17. *WIR*, p. 71; *MGF*, p. 96. Strachey's assertion that both Fawcetts supported votes for married women is in error; the letter dated 8 February 1884 which she cites in evidence was written by Ursula Bright to Harry only (FLALC, vol. 1a).

18. *WSJ*, 1 July 1875, p. 96.

19. *ibid.*, 1 May 1889, p. 67.

20. *ibid.*, 1 June 1878, p. 89.

21. *Review of Reviews* (ch. 1, note 11 above), p. 20. See below, pp. 72 and 81, note 7.

22. 'Never was heard such a terrible curse; But, what gave rise to no little surprise, Nobody seem'd one penny the worse!' (R.H. Barham, 'The jackdaw of Rheims', *The Ingoldsby Legends*, Bentley, 1840).

23. *WSJ*, 1 June 1881, pp. 87–8.

24. MGF, 'Women and representative government', *Nineteenth Century* (August 1883), p. 289. See also p. 138 below.

25. Newnham College *Reports*.

26. MGF to Barbara Bodichon, 8 June [1875], Girton College Archives. Marianne Frances Barnard, who was chosen mistress soon afterwards, appears to have been selected on similar criteria.

27. MGF to Helen Taylor, 18 July [1875] (Mill–Taylor Collection).

28. Queen's College Payment Book, 25 March 1879, 27 June 1879; *ER*, 15 July 1878, p. 301.

29. *ER*, 15 March 1879, p. 123.

30. MGF, 'The old and the new ideals of women's education', *Good Words* ([November] 1878), pp. 853–60.

31. See Mill to Helen Taylor, 21 February [1860]; Mineka and Lindley (eds), vol. 2, p. 683.

32. *Parl. Deb.*, 3rd ser., 189, col. 481 (30 July 1867). For the Factory Act of 1867 see B.L. Hutchins and A. Harrison, *A History of Factory Legislation* (Cass, 1966 edn), pp. 168–9.

33. *Transactions of the National Association for the Promotion of Social Science, 1868* (Longman, 1869), pp. 611–12.

34. Henry Fawcett, *Manual of Political Economy* (3rd edn, Macmillan, 1869), pp. vi, 531–2.

35. *Parl. Deb.*, 3rd ser., 217, cols 1287–303 (30 July 1873); W.H.G. Armytage, *A.J. Mundella 1825–1897* (Benn, 1951), pp. 132, 134, 144, 145.

36. *The Times*, 9 June 1873 (reprinted with additional material as *Factory Acts Amendment Bill*, 1873).

37. *Report of the Sixth Annual Trades' Union Congress, 1874* (n.d.), p. 21.

38. Harry's support for the 1867 Factory Bill makes it impossible to accept Millicent's claim that his objection was not to protective legislation as such but to

extending it to new trades (Leslie Stephen's manuscript biography of Henry Fawcett, Trinity Hall Cambridge, MGF's comment at p. 471).

39. Mundella remained sufficiently friendly to write a letter of condolence. Harry's reply blamed 'money and beer' rather than the TUC resolution (Henry Fawcett to A.J. Mundella, 10 February 1874, Mundella Papers, University of Sheffield). He was soon afterwards returned for Hackney.

40. There are two leaflets about the union's work at M50/4/10, 1 and 2, and periodic reports in the *ER* and *Women's Union Journal* until 1880. The Bristol Association of Working Women, which was represented at the TUC from 1881, may have been a successor body.

41. *Women's Union Journal*, July 1881, pp. 67–8.

42. I am grateful to Lawrence Goldman for assistance on this point.

43. Henry Fawcett was well known as an apostle of co-operation. See Stephen, pp. 164–6.

44. MGF, 'Communism', *Encyclopaedia Britannica* (9th edn, 1877), vol. 6, pp. 211–19.

45. Patricia Hollis's magnificent *Ladies Elect* (1987) has removed all reason for ignorance of this previously shrouded subject.

46. *ibid.*, pp. 72–8.

47. Eliza Orme to Helen Taylor, 1 September 1875 (Mill–Taylor Collection).

48. A list of the members of 'Miss Garrett's committee' is filed in the Emily Davies papers at Girton College.

49. *WSJ*, 2 January 1871, p. 5.

50. See Hollis, pp. 92–3; Kamm, pp. 216–17. The letters quoted, dated 21 October and 7 November 1876, are from the Mill–Taylor Collection.

51. *ER*, 15 October, 15 November 1879, pp. 444, 505.

52. *WIR*, p. 62. The theft took place in 1876 and the charge was 'feloniously stealing one purse and the sum of 14 shillings from the person of Millicent Garrett Fawcett, at Lambeth' (Surrey County Record Office, Quarter Sessions Records); *The Times*, 19 October 1876.

53. *WSJ*, 1 June 1880, p. 108; Henry Fawcett's will, Somerset House. The book was published on 25 June 1870, and the first Married Women's Property Act became law on 9 August.

54. The British, Fawcett and Manchester Public Libraries contain a variety of leaflets and annual reports of the Married Women's Property Committee, whose title was subject to periodic change. There is no record of activity by either Fawcett after the later 1860s.

55. MGF to Elizabeth Wolstenholme Elmy (copy), 10 December [1875] (FLALC, vol. 2b.) This letter entreated Mrs Elmy 'most earnestly' to withdraw as committee secretary because of 'what happened before you were married'. See also James Stuart to MGF, 16 December 1875 (*ibid.*) and Sylvia Pankhurst, *The Suffragette Movement* (1931), p. 31.

56. Lee Holcombe states in her comprehensive *Wives and Property* (Oxford: Martin Robertson, 1983, p. 134) that Millicent was an active member of the organized movement. I have been unable to confirm this statement.

57. *Pictorial World*, 2 January 1875; *The Times*, 21 May 1877.

58. MGF to Louisa Garrett, 27 November 1877 (Anderson Papers, St Brelade). See also Francis Darwin (ed.), *The Life and Letters of Charles Darwin*, vol. 3 (Murray, 1887),
p. 222.

59. MGF, *The Martyrs of Turkish Misrule* (1877), p. 6.

# CHAPTER 6

## MINISTER'S WIFE AND WIDOW 1880–4

Henry Fawcett's four-and-a-half years as Postmaster-General are part of his own biography, not his wife's. But in so close a relationship as the Fawcetts', with so many interests held in common, his ministerial career was bound to have a strong influence on her life.

It seems likely that Gladstone, irritated by a persistent parliamentary gadfly, appointed Harry to ministerial office in order to silence him. If so, he should have known better. As Millicent wrote in a biographical account a few years after Harry's death, he was anything but a reliable party man. Whether the issue was household suffrage, university religious tests, the extension of factory acts to agricultural children, compulsory universal education, the preservation of commons and open spaces or the government of India, 'his chief foes were among the leaders of his own party'. It was unlikely that such a man would stick to his stamps. His appointment to the non-Cabinet office was also based on the fact that his blindness made it difficult for him to guard Cabinet secrets. Millicent commented that he 'accepted the decision with cheerfulness' but did not regard it as final.[1] Blind at 25, professor at 30, MP at 31 and minister at 46, it is hardly surprising that he did not feel his career had reached its summit.

Whether he was more pleased to be appointed to office, at the handsome salary of £2,500 a year, or more disappointed by the office itself, he threw himself into the work of the Post Office with his usual buoyant activity.[2] He was one of the most visible and active of Postmasters-General.[3] One of his colleagues recalled in later years Harry's loud voice and 'his frank and manly ways. He treated all men alike.' His bourgeois style and disregard for convention disconcerted the Post Office's head messenger, who had served aristocratic chiefs. He was reported as saying that 'he had never expected to have to go to a house in Lambeth and to have the door opened by a Female!'[4]

There is no correspondence to suggest that Harry's Post Office reforms owed anything to his wife, and nothing in Millicent's own papers which shows any particular involvement in the affairs of the Post Office. Persuasion on her part was hardly necessary. He had made abundantly clear his sympathy with feminist aims, and the increase in the number of female clerks and the introduction of open competition in their appointment, though alarming to a conventional figure like Queen Victoria, were not surprising moves for a Liberal committed to retrenchment and equality of opportunity. The praise contained in his annual reports for the work of the female clerks and his appointment of the first woman medical officer in government employment further confirmed his support for new opportunities for women workers.[5] The officer appointed, Edith Shove, was one of the first women medical graduates of the University of London and a protégé of his sister-in-law Elizabeth.[6]

His innovative work at the Post Office was interrupted in November 1982 by a combined attack of diphtheria and typhoid which nearly killed him, grim evidence of the fact that even the most eminent Victorians walked in the shadow of disease and death[7]. His illness followed the tragically early death of Rhoda Garrett, the cousin with whom Agnes lived and worked and to whom Millicent was also close. Only 40, Rhoda Garrett was a brilliant suffrage speaker and a woman of outstanding talent.[8] Her half-brother Edmund, then a schoolboy aged 17, wrote to Lady Maude Parry, who with her husband the musician Hubert Parry were close friends: 'Rhoda was one among a thousand in her wonderful charm and influence & genius: but she was one among a million in the use she made of these.'[9] Ethel Smyth, the composer who was also an intimate, wrote of Rhoda's 'magic personality . . . cut off at the zenith of her powers'.[10] Millicent returned from the funeral late in November to find that Harry had fallen seriously ill.

Agnes Garrett, who had gone to stay with the Fawcetts soon after the funeral, wrote to Lady Maude when Harry's condition was still worsening: 'The poor thing has *four* doctors round him at three o'clock and separate ones at all other hours – enough to kill anyone . . . It was so strange to me all last night comforting poor Millie with my own heart bursting.'[11] The illness led to a remarkable outpouring of public and private concern. Gladstone's private secretary Edward Hamilton told his diary on 14 December 1882: 'There is no man probably who could have elicited so much universal sympathy and interest on the bed of sickness as he has, save Mr G. himself.'[12] Among the enquirers and well-wishers were Mrs Gladstone and Sir Charles Dilke, who was told on Christmas day that Harry was making good progress.[13] On the same day *The Times* published a letter of thanks from Millicent to a meeting of Hackney workers who had expressed their sympathy: 'I am full of hope and happiness about him. Neither he nor I will forget the universal kindness and sympathy that were shown us throughout his illness.'[14] He had by no means recovered, however, and writing the following February to the Brighton Liberal Association she made clear that she would do everything possible to prevent him from taking part in exhausting engagements for at least a year. He returned the following month to the Post Office, but suffered several subsequent minor recurrences of ill health and did not speak in public until November.[15]

The grip which the Garrett sisters were wont to keep on their emotions and which was sometimes mistaken for lack of feeling was much in evidence during this period. Hubert Parry, whose affection for Agnes and Rhoda and distress at Rhoda's death were among his strongest sentiments, noted that both Agnes and Millicent were 'wonderfully restrained' after Rhoda's death, while he had 'the greatest difficulty' to avoid breaking down in public.[16] An incident related by Ethel Smyth hints at the suffering which Millicent had endured during the previous year. 'I thought Mrs Fawcett rather cold', she commented, but late one evening in the summer after Rhoda's death when Smyth was singing an Irish melody, 'I suddenly noticed that tears were rolling down her cheeks, and presently she got up and quietly left the room.'[17]

By the time that Harry was ready to resume an active role in politics women's suffrage was about to achieve more parliamentary prominence than at any time since 1867. After the narrow defeat in July 1883 of a resolution to enfranchise qualified women Edward Hamilton wrote in his diary: 'The extension of the franchise to women on *some* basis or other is sure to come sooner or later; and more probably sooner than later.'[18] At the time, however, the women's movement was at least as concerned with the Agar-Ellis case. This affair, which had dragged on for a number of years, involved a husband who had first broken a promise to allow his daughters to be brought up as Roman Catholics and then prevented his estranged wife from seeing them. Harriet Agar-Ellis's unsuccessful attempts to secure a judicial separation from her husband and access to her children confirmed that as the law stood she was without means of redress.[19] The comments which Millicent made in a scrapbook suggest the limits of her influence over Harry and a restrained impatience at his unwillingness to become involved in the affair. It is also the only recorded conversation between the pair, valuable despite its brevity and the one-sided nature of the 'recording':

> On reading this to Harry he remarked 'What a brute.' I said 'I am told Agar-Ellis's children hate him.' He replied 'I should think so. Serve him right.' Now this sympathy is very natural but it is of no practical use to the injured woman and children because it does not lead to any alteration in the law.[20]

The Guardianship of Infants Act, passed in 1886, was an inadequate first step towards reform, and no further legislation followed until 1925.[21]

At the end of 1883 W.T. Stead, the recently appointed editor of the *Pall Mall Gazette*, wrote to Millicent to ask her to contribute an article on the work of women in the Post Office. It was the beginning of a working relationship which continued intermittently until Stead's death on the *Titanic* nearly thirty years later. She replied that she preferred to write about the suffrage question, to which she had devoted herself, and her article duly appeared in a prominent position a few days later, at the start of a momentous year.[22]

The article referred to a recent Liberal conference at Leeds, which had carried a women's suffrage resolution by a large majority. Writing in a then Liberal paper she urged Liberals to have the courage of their convictions, and insisted that the case being advanced by Liberal leaders to enfranchise rural male labourers applied equally to qualified women. One day, she predicted, it would seem 'almost incredible' that the idea of giving women the parliamentary vote had seemed 'dangerous and revolutionary'. The municipal and school board franchises had been granted to women without turning society upside down: 'We still like needlework; we prefer pretty gowns to ugly ones; we are interested in domestic management and economy, and are not altogether indifferent to our friends and relations.'[23] The article was in effect an early warning, delivered by a ministerial wife, that the proposed reform act would not omit women without a stiff fight.

The article alarmed some of the Liberal party bureaucrats. The *Pall Mall Gazette* published letters claiming that the Leeds resolution had been passed by a small and unrepresentative group of delegates after the main body had gone home.[24] Millicent, who was by this time a skilled political wirepuller herself, marshalled letters from her brother Sam and her brother-in-law Skelton Anderson, who had attended the conference, and protested to Stead about the one-sided nature of the letters which he had published.[25] She vented her wrath in a letter to Elizabeth: 'One longs to let out & tell these people what one thinks of them but we can't afford a good honest rage yet.'[26] She could not have known that before the next year had ended she would be writing to Stead as a hero.

The campaign thus started soon moved forward enthusiastically. A meeting of suffragist Members of Parliament including Henry Fawcett was held in early February and agreed that William Woodall, Liberal MP for Stoke, should move an amendment to the reform bill to give women votes on the same terms as men.[27] The next month Millicent joined other prominent Liberal women, including a sister and daughter of John Bright, champion of votes for men and opponent of votes for women, in a letter asking Gladstone to receive a deputation: 'We are, so far as the law permits us to be, your supporters, and supporters from heartfelt conviction of a great and just Liberal policy for their country.' Gladstone refused to meet the deputation, partly on grounds of ill health, partly because he claimed that the addition of women's suffrage to the bill might endanger the entire measure, but the signature of the wife of his wayward Postmaster-General was unlikely to have persuaded him to look favourably upon the request.[28] In turn, Millicent's aversion to Gladstone, already strong and later, in the form of opposition to Irish Home Rule, to become a dominating passion, was certain to have been strengthened.

In April she was a principal speaker at a great meeting held in St James's Hall, London, in support of Woodall's amendment. She referred to the large numbers of women engaged in responsible occupations and to the much greater incidence of crime and drunkenness among men than women. 'We are like starving people seated at a banquet with our hands tied behind us,' she continued. Occasionally men gave them something to eat, but they wanted the power to feed themselves. She professed to believe that the suffrage struggle was near its end. 'But even if it should not be so near as I now believe we must not lose heart or hope. What are five, ten, or fifteen years in a great historical movement like the one we are engaged in.'[29] What indeed were 34?

Woodall's amendment was introduced on 10 June 1884. A few days earlier the Liberal *Daily News* published a long article by Millicent, in which she argued for women's suffrage on the grounds that representative government was a just and Liberal cause, and that women were treated unfairly under existing inequitable laws. Married women, whose immediate enfranchisement she thought it unwise to demand, were particularly badly treated. The Agar-Ellis case was one of those summoned in support. She took the opportunity to declare herself a hearty supporter of the disestablishment of the Church of England, a commitment which is unlikely to have survived the decade, and added that women's supposed Conservatism was neither certain nor permanent. Even if that were true, she expressed her contempt for the doctrine that a political party should enfranchise only its known supporters. Women political agitators, she pointed out, were accused of being 'soured and spoiled', but this characteristic was the consequence of unjust treatment. 'Reformers and agitators', she added, 'are often more useful than agreeable people.'[30] The description was one which was generally not applicable to her, but future colleagues would learn as previous ones had done, that for Millicent, like other reformers, the cause was more important than the personalities comprising it.

The time had now come for Harry to blot his political copy book for the last time. It was no surprise that he supported women's suffrage as a minister as he had done as a backbencher. He had repeated his support in a speech at Salisbury the previous April, when he had proclaimed that household suffrage for both sexes was coming 'as surely as the sun will rise to-morrow'.[31] However, the rebellion which was now to take place was nearly the last straw for his long-suffering chief. Harry's position as a member of the Government with no share in determining its policies was an unhappy one. He was uneasy about the Government's pragmatic Irish policy and would undoubtedly have opposed Home Rule had he lived.[32] His abstention on the vote on a royal grant in 1882 aroused the severe displeasure of the Queen.[33] His greatest offence was his consistent opposition to the Government's aggressive Egyptian policy, particularly the use of Indian troops and tax revenue. Edward Hamilton speculated over the possibility of his resigning over the issue and even bringing down the Government.[34] He was a rumbling volcano, a constant threat of political eruption.

Gladstone repeatedly expressed his irritation to Hamilton, whose view of Harry was much more sympathetic. He was, the Prime Minister insisted, 'totally unable to work in concert with others – essentially "idiosyncratic" in temperament, to which possibly his physical infirmities have partly conduced'.[35] Over the reform bill his disagreement with the Government involved not only women's suffrage but also proportional representation, another Millite nostrum to which he was strongly pledged. It is not necessary to go so far as his supposed friend and fellow radical Sir Charles Dilke, who wrote later that Harry's behaviour in June 1884 was dictated by pique over the failure of the parcel post and his exclusion from the Cabinet, to conclude that trouble was inevitable.[36]

In addressing the House of Commons on Woodall's amendment Gladstone claimed to express no personal view about women's suffrage, though his opposition is undoubted.[37] He told the House that if the amendment was passed he would renounce responsibility for the reform bill and, warning of a possible veto by the House of Lords, declared: 'The cargo which the vessel carries is, in our opinion, a cargo as large as she can carry safely.'[38] It is a point worth considering, since even in 1918, with a huge House of Commons majority in favour and a wholly changed political situation, the suffragists were extremely apprehensive about the Lords. At the same time it is difficult not to sympathize with Millicent's bitter reflection that so far from being saved before men, as the nautical metaphor implied, women were thrown overboard.[39] Henry Fawcett and Leonard Courtney, also an extra-Cabinet minister as Secretary to the Treasury, abstained along with the disgruntled Dilke, a Cabinet minister (at the Local Government Board), who took care to tell Millicent that 'the vast majority in my opinion of both House & country are against the change'.[40] Whatever their motives the three men took their political lives in their hands to support women's suffrage, an act rare in the history of a struggle more often served by the lip than in the lobby. They apparently owed their survival to Gladstone's worry about the developing crisis in Egypt.[41]

Although Edward Hamilton told his diary that 'Courtney and Fawcett have both swallowed the jobation' and had expressed pleasure at not being dismissed, the letter which Harry wrote to Gladstone to acknowledge his reprimand and reprieve reads more like defiance than submission or the respectfulness of Millicent's recollection.[42] In any event when it was written he had less than six months to live. The real impact of the incident was on Millicent. In Ray Strachey's view her existing dislike and distrust of Gladstone were transformed by his behaviour over women's suffrage in 1884 into permanent enmity.[43] This may be true, though if Harry had lived or the Home Rule issue had not reared its head her hostility might have faded. Her previous dislike had not prevented her from expressing in a letter to Catherine Gladstone in 1882 'affectionate congratulations' on her husband's fifty years in politics: 'What a noble life and life's work is included in that 50 years!'[44]

Harry's death was sudden and followed a short illness. His last speech was delivered to his Hackney constituents on 13 October 1884, and it is satisfying to record that it contained a strong defence of his abstention on the Woodall amendment and of the case for women's suffrage: 'I believe the demand of women householders to be enfranchised will not rest until it is conceded. You will have to do it sooner or later, and sooner is better than later.'[45] Taken ill at the beginning of November, his condition steadily worsened. On the morning of the 6th Millicent telegraphed to Elizabeth, who had already visited Harry, to return to Cambridge bringing with her Sir Andrew Clark, the eminent physician who had tended him in 1882. That evening Elizabeth telegraphed to her husband: 'Our dear Harry is gone died suddenly at five thirty terrible shock to all.'[46]

His death occasioned much public and private expression of grief, the consequence of its unexpectedness, his relative youth and ebullient personality and the heroic conquest of his blindness. The women's press was prominent in its praise of the dead man, and a women's memorial tribute was organized without delay.[47] There was, *The Times* wrote, 'a great gathering' at the graveside in Trumpington, one of the Fawcetts' favourite spots. Many mourners had travelled by special train from London following the funeral service in Westminster Abbey. The paper's view was that Harry had achieved a measure of 'national esteem and regard' not exceeded by any other public man.[48] More valuable because privately expressed was Edward Hamilton's judgement: 'He excited the interest and sympathy of the masses; he commanded the respect of his opponents as much as of his friends; he had cut a great figure in the political world both inside and outside Parliament.'[49]

There is no reason to doubt the sincerity of such comments. But it is necessary to remember also his defects, particularly obvious before the beginning of his ministerial career: insensitivity, verbosity, and independence of mind and action carried to the point of self-indulgence. There must have been many who, like Henry Lucy the political journalist, found him unbearable as an orator or who, like Disraeli, commented with cruel wit: 'If this fellow had eyes . . . how we should damn them![50]

For Millicent Harry's death was a catastrophe as great as it had been unexpected and called on all her reserves of courage and resilience. But it enabled her to develop the independent public life begun in her dazzling youth and somewhat overshadowed subsequently by her role as academic and political wife. As her sister's biographer comments, his death was for her both an end and a beginning.[51] The £9,535 he left her together with the royalties from his books was an important factor in allowing her middle-class life style to continue.[52] His economic knowledge, his academic and political contacts and his support for feminist causes had been of the greatest assistance in her development, but they would have availed her nothing had she not been wholeheartedly involved in the same causes. There were important differences as well as similarities in the personalities of the part-ners. Millicent developed qualities of leadership which Harry, hampered by his blindness and a more competitive environment never equalled, and she inspired respect and later love while he often aroused impatience and antag-onism. But each followed the dictates of conscience regardless of con-sequences with the result that each could be a prickly and difficult colleague. Independence of thought and action was a characteristic which she was to display over and over again. Her period of mourning once ended, she was to return both to feminist and wider political activity with undiminished enthusiasm and effectiveness.

NOTES

1. MGF, 'Henry Fawcett', *Chambers's Encyclopaedia* vol. 4 (1889 edn), pp. 567–8.
2. *Whitaker's Almanack 1881*, p. 110.
3. H.S. Swift, *A History of Postal Agitation* (Manchester: Percy Brothers, 1929), esp. pp. 5–6, 113–19; Alan Clinton, *Post Office Workers* (1984), pp. 129–33. An 1882 *Punch* cartoon of him as 'The man for the post' is reproduced in Lawrence Goldman (ed.), *The Blind Victorian* (1989), p. 143.
4. Lewin Hill, 'Henry Fawcett when Postmaster General', *St Martin's Le Grand* (July 1909), pp. 247–51.
5. 27th to 30th *Reports of the Postmaster-General*, P.P. 1881–4; MGF notes on Stephen MS biography (ch. 5, note 38 above), p. 542; Hilda Martindale, *Women Servants of the State* (Allen & Unwin, 1938), p. 28. He subsequently appointed women medical officers in Liverpool and Manchester (*WSJ*, 1 December 1884, p. 257; Leslie Stephen, p. 444).
6. Louisa Garrett Anderson, *Elizabeth Garrett Anderson* (1939) pp. 222, 226, 232–3. I am grateful for the assistance of Miss C.A. Tully of the Post Office.
7. Leslie Stephen, ch. 9 and pp. 457–60.
8. *WSJ*, 1 December 1882, p. 195; *ER*, 15 December 1882, pp. 547–8.
9. Edmund Garrett to Maude Parry, 1 December 1882 (Parry Papers, Shulbrede Priory).
10. Ethel Smyth, *Impressions that Remained*, vol. 2 (1919), pp. 7–8.
11. Agnes Garrett to Maude Parry, 1 December 1882 (Parry Papers). Agnes had come 'for an hour and stayed six weeks', her grateful sister noted (Stephen MS, p. 558)
12. Dudley W.R. Bahlman (ed.), *The Diary of Sir Edward Walter Hamilton 1880–1885*, vol. 1 (1972), p. 375.
13. MGF to Catherine Gladstone, 14 December [1882], (Mary Gladstone Papers, BL Add. Mss); MGF to Dilke, 25 December [1882] (Dilke Papers, BL Add. Mss).
14. *The Times*, 25 December 1882.
15. *ibid.*, 7 February, 9 November 1883; Leslie Stephen, pp. 460–1.
16. Parry diaries, May 1876, 25 November 1882 (Parry Papers); Charles L. Graves, *Hubert Parry*, vol. 1 (Macmillan, 1926), pp. 149, 165, 225, 237. The Garrett cousins had advised the Parrys on the decoration of their home.
17. Smyth, vol. 2, pp. 12–13.
18. Bahlman (ed.), vol. 2, pp. 457–8.
19. Accounts of the Agar-Ellis affair may be found in the *ER*, 15 August, 14

September and 14 December 1878, pp. 372–3, 385–92, 537–48, and 15 August 1883, pp. 356–61.

20. MGF's cuttings book, 1884(sic)–94 (M50/2/26/2). Her comments were inspired by a comment in *The Times* on 24 July 1883.
21. See Erna Reiss, *Rights and Duties of Englishwomen* (Manchester: Sherratt & Hughes, 1934), p. 100.
22. Stead to MGF, 31 December 1883; MGF to Stead (copy), 2 January [1884] (M50/2/1/14 and 15).
23. MGF, 'Women's suffrage and the franchise bill', *Pall Mall Gazette*, 14 January 1884 (reprinted in Jane Lewis (ed.), *Before the Vote was Won* (1987), pp. 391–5).
24. *Pall Mall Gazette*, 15, 17 January 1884. A third letter (19 January) defended the Fawcett view of the vote.
25. M50/2/1/16 to 30.
26. MGF to Elizabeth Garrett Anderson, 19 January [1884] (Anderson Papers. St Brelade).
27. *The Times*, 8 February 1884. This was the meeting at which Harry manifested his support for votes for married women householders; see ch. 5, note 17 above.
28. *ER*, 15 May 1884, pp. 221–3.
29. *The Times*, 25 April 1884; *WSJ*, 1 May 1884, pp. 88–94; M50/2/4/23 (MGF, notes for speeches).
30. MGF, 'Women's suffrage and the new reform bill', *Daily News*, 3 June 1884.
31. *The Times*, 10 April 1884.
32. Leslie Stephen, pp. 411–12.
33. Bahlman (ed.), vol. 1, pp. 242–4, 247.
34. *ibid.*, vol. 1, pp. 362, 365; vol. 2, pp. 464, 581, 587.
35. *ibid.*, vol. 1, p. 341. See also vol. 2, pp. 432, 464, 546, 654, 726.
36. Dilke MS memoirs (Dilke Papers). 'How these Radicals hate one another', Sir William Harcourt told his wife in 1879, after listening to Millicent expressing the hope that Joseph Chamberlain would lose his Birmingham seat (A.G. Gardiner, *The Life of Sir William Harcourt*, vol. 1 (Constable, 1923), p. 357. Chamberlain and the Fawcetts differed on a number of issues, including women's suffrage. See John Morley, *Recollections*, vol. 1 (Macmillan, 1917), p. 157.
37. Constance Rover, *Women's Suffrage and Party Politics in Britain 1866–1914* (1967), p. 118. See also Ann P. Robson, 'A birds' eye view of Gladstone' in Bruce L. Kinzer (ed.), *The Gladstonian Turn of Mind* (Toronto: University of Toronto Press, 1985), pp. 63–96; and Bahlman (ed.), vol. 2, pp. 457–8, 613, 634.
38. *Parl. Deb.*, 3rd ser., 288, col. 1959 (10 June 1884). The amendment was duly defeated by a huge majority.
39. MGF, *Women's Suffrage* [1912], p. 28.
40. Dilke to MGF, undated but probably June 1884 (M50/2/1/46). He did have the good grace to acknowledge her letter of thanks (idem to idem, 17 June 1884; FLALC, vol. 1a).
41. Bahlman (ed.), vol. 2, p. 636. See also Stephen Gwynn and Gertrude M. Tuckwell, *The Life of the Rt. Hon. Sir Charles W. Dilke, Bart., M.P.* (1917), vol. 2, pp. 6–9, and *MGF*, pp. 97–9.
42. Bahlman (ed.), vol. 2, p. 638. Jobation and reply are quoted in *MGF*, pp. 97–9; see also *WIR*, p. 113.
43. *MGF*, p. 99.
44. MGF to Catherine Gladstone, 14 December [1882] (Mary Gladstone Papers).
45. *The Late Mr Fawcett on Women's Suffrage and the Franchise Bill* (n.d.), p. 4 (BLPES).

46. Leslie Stephen, pp. 461–3; telegrams in Anderson Papers. See also Jo Manton, *Elizabeth Garrett Anderson* (1965), pp. 271–2.
47. *ER*, 15 November 1884, pp. 503–8; *WSJ*, 1 December 1884, pp. 256–7; *Women's Union Journal*, November 1884, p. 103. For the unveiling of the memorial see *ibid.*, August 1886, pp. 75–6.
48. *The Times*, 7, 11 November 1884; Stephen MS, MGF comment at p. 564.
49. Bahlman (ed.), vol. 2, p. 725; also p. 729.
50. Henry W. Lucy, *A Diary of Two Parliaments: The Disraeli Parliament 1874–1880* (Cassell, 1885), pp. 135–8; G.E. Buckle, *The Life of Benjamin Disraeli*, vol. 5 (Murray, 1920), p. 501. The remark was made about 1876.
51. Manton, p. 272.
52. Probate Registry Calendar, 1884, Somerset House. The shares and property later left her by Newson and Louisa Garrett in 1893 and 1903 must have freed her from subsequent financial worry. Newson left a total of £57,801; Louisa, £19,432 (Wills and Probate Registries, Somerset House).

# PART II

# THE MIDDLE YEARS 1884–1905

# CHAPTER 7

## RECREATIONS OF A SUFFRAGIST

Millicent Garrett Fawcett became a widow when she was 37. There followed a long period of fruitful work in a variety of causes before the beginning of militancy in 1906 transformed women's suffrage into one of the leading controversies of the day. She never forgot the suffrage but she had many other interests, to some of which she devoted more effort over a restricted period. Had she died at Harry's age or even ten years later she would have been remembered for the variety of her contributions to the emancipation and other campaigns, rather than as the single-minded advocate of the suffrage which she is sometimes thought to have been. In the twenty years after 1884 she matured from relative youth into stable and hard-working middle age, and from a figure celebrated for her brilliant early career and her famous marriage into one of the most respected women of the day, profiled in the press and sought as a speaker and sponsor of worthy causes.

Harry's death was a crushing blow from which she did not soon recover. Nearly two years later, when she and her sister Agnes dined with the Parrys, Hubert wrote in his diary of her attempt to appear normal but that she had nearly broken down at one point. 'It is a strange nature', he added, and although he also wrote that there was 'a lot of tenderness, & sentiment hidden behind the stony [?strong] and determined front she shows to the world', the 'passionately reticent' emotional character discerned by Ray Strachey was often misunderstood and sometimes censured by outsiders.[1] Long afterwards the mention of Harry's name could cause her to lose her composure, and she devoted only two sentences in her autobiography to his illness and death, and its effect on her.[2] The sudden ending of so close an emotional and intellectual a relationship was perhaps also significant in the development of her political and social attitudes. The absence of his influence may help to explain the fact that her views and behaviour on a range of questions became increasingly dogmatic, intolerant and, for a prolonged period, Conservative.

She never remarried, and the restricted number and nature of surviving letters dealing with her personal life makes it impossible to know whether she declined the opportunity. She had a gift for friendship and many close women friends, and it was with Agnes and her unmarried daughter Philippa that she spent the remainder of her life in the Gower Street house which Agnes had earlier shared with their cousin Rhoda.

Soon after Harry's death she asked Leslie Stephen to write his biography. Though the two men had grown apart after Harry's election to Parliament,[3] it was a good choice. Stephen's book, speedily written and published, is informative and comprehensive, and as honest as possible in the circumstances. Mrs Fawcett provided the kind of assistance which biographers crave and dread, including letters and other documents and comments on the manuscript.[4] Christopher Harvie asserts that she toned down Stephen's examples of personal or political sharp practice on Harry's part, but such interventions were few and unimportant, and Stephen did not always accept her wishes.[5] Most of her comments, which mainly concerned the last phase of Harry's life, dealt with his political beliefs and policies rather than his methods of carrying them out. She also provided information about his illnesses in 1882 and 1884.[6]

Her political commitments never prevented Mrs Fawcett from enjoying life, though her ideas of enjoyment were more intellectual than frivolous. Her liking for needlework was more than suffrage propaganda. Her sister Elizabeth wrote to her husband in 1895 from Austria: 'Milly & I have done a good deal of sewing, & reading aloud.'[7] Their reading included Erasmus, a good indication of a second major interest. She was an untiring reader of history, literature and related subjects, and her speeches and writings were peppered with references to historians, poets and novelists. Although, as her friend Margaret Heitland pointed out, she did not read simply to find an apt quotation, she seemed always to have one at hand.

One notable example occurred in 1906, when she chaired a debate on women's suffrage at the Tunbridge Wells conference of the middle-class National Union of Women Workers. The anti-suffrage Countess of Dysart told the meeting that the proper sphere for a woman was not the public arena, but in the care of her family, as 'a mother in Israel'. Replying, Mrs Fawcett quoted the passage from the Book of Judges to which the countess had referred and reminded her audience that it had been spoken by Deborah, 'the warrior woman who had led her people in battle'. 'The debate collapsed in delighted laughter, Mrs Heitland recalled.[8] It would have been appropriate for her, like her contemporary Robert Blatchford, to have used the pen name 'Nunquam Dormio' ('I never sleep'), for most of her reading was of potential use in the women's struggle. In 1897, for example, she told her mother that she had read a life of Erasmus by the historian J.A. Froude. Carefully mentioning that he had been a forerunner of the Reformation, she added that the fight which he and his friends had made for 'real education . . . often reminded me of the women's fight now for the same thing'.[9]

It was appropriate that one of the three illustrations of herself published in her autobiography showed her, in 1892, with a book in her hand. (A second showed her at work with Harry.) Asked in 1914 if she enjoyed public speaking, she replied characteristically that she would prefer to spend her time with her books.[10] Some of them were of considerable value from age or association. In 1900, for example, the British Museum offered to buy from her a book of sermons published before 1500, and one of her most precious possessions was a copy of Mill's *Subjection of Women* given her by the author.[11]

In 1923 she supplied the *Woman's Leader* with a list of eight 'out-of-the-way' books recommended for holiday reading. They included Elizabeth Blackwell's *Pioneer Work in Opening the Medical Profession to Women*, to the 1914 edition of which she had written an introduction, and two anthologies of poetry. The other five books, by Disraeli, Robert Curzon, A.W. Kinglake, George Borrow and W.H. Hudson, combined travel with autobiography or fiction.[12] The list was compiled with the preoccupations of the holiday season in mind and reflected the interest which she had developed in old age in the Middle East, but it serves as a useful reminder that one of her favourite preoccupations was travel, despite the fact that she was an inveterate sufferer from seasickness. Writing from Bayreuth to their mother in 1891 Elizabeth commented that the Rotterdam boat had been 'fairly comfortable' and that she not been ill, 'tho' Milly was'.[13] Six years later the sufferer herself reported after a twelve-hour crossing to Corfu: 'After a good night we are none the worse though I did say when I set foot on shore that I should spend the rest of my life in Corfu!'[14]

She travelled with Harry, and both before and after his death with various friends and relations.[15] She kept her eyes and ears open, asking an English-speaking German how the people of the small town of Rothenburg lived,[16] and regretting having missed bread riots in Siena. With the dispassion of the social scientist she added: 'It seems rather brutal to wish to have seen the row; but if they were bound to have it, I am rather sorry just to have missed it.'[17]

In the same letter she wrote: 'Nothing can be more lovely than Italy in the Spring.' The comment represented one of her strongest sentiments at this period of her life. In 1884 she wrote two informative chapters, almost exclusively on Italy, for W.J. Loftie's *Orient Line Guide* (1885). Despite her frequent visits to Italy she might seem an unexpected choice as a guidebook writer but for the fact that Skelton Anderson's firm had founded the line in 1878.[18] Engagingly disclaiming any pretence of expertise, she feelingly described the debt of Western civilization to Italian history. She took the opportunity to point out that the Italian Renaissance had not been confined to men, that there had been 'four lady professors' at Bologna, and that modern Italy had been a leader in the education of women. She stressed the fact that Italian sculpture and architecture would be better appreciated in their native setting than in South Kensington, in the museum later named for Victoria and Albert. With a display of emotion more characteristic of nineteenth-century romantics and guidebook writers than of her own suffrage speeches she wrote:

> The traveller, who for the first time sees Giotto's tower at Florence, and at a stone's throw distant on the one side the Baptistery with its marvellous storied gates, and on the other the matchless dome of Brunelleschi, feels that the fairy tale has come true and that he is in the land of the giants.

To visit Italy one was truly to spend the rest of one's life longing to return. She was a specialist in none of Italy's specialities, she added, but 'I can honestly say that if I was told at this moment that I was dying, not my first, nor my second, but certainly my third thought would be that I should never see Italy again.'[19]

She was sufficiently experienced as a tourist to counsel her readers against exhaustion. Visitors who never took more than an hour's daily exercise at home, she pointed out, rushed round Italian churches, galleries, museums and theatres, then wondered why they felt unwell. They decided not to return to Italy because it was 'so unhealthy', ignoring the fact that it was the activity rather than the climate which had exhausted them. Her advice was to visit the sights in the morning, 'when one [was] at one's freshest', followed by 'a plain substantial meat luncheon', an hour's rest and a driving excursion. After dinner 'the wise and prudent will read their guide-books for an hour, and go to bed at half-past nine.'[20] Here indeed was the familiar voice of moderation associated with the author.

She took advantage of a visit to Egypt early in 1897 to write an account for a subsequent edition of the *Guide*. She characteristically prepared for the trip by a short course of reading, supported by visits to the Egyptian galleries of the British Museum. She found Egypt poised between what, like other travellers, she termed 'barbarism and civilisation', in no respect more than in the relative position of young men and women of the upper classes. She visited two wealthy and refined young ladies, granddaughters of the Khedive Ismail, whose cultural and educational level contrasted sharply with the restrictions on their movements and the arranged marriages to which they were subject. The main problem in improving the education of Egyptian girls, she commented elsewhere, was 'the complete absence of desire for improvement on the part of the natives, and the apathy of those in authority'.[21] She then went to Greece, where she found the inhabitants 'manly, vigorous and straightforward', in contrast to the Egyptians, whom she described as inveterate liars.[22] As this comment illustrates, the breadth of vision and freedom from stereotype which she applied to Englishwomen were often strikingly absent from her descriptions of foreigners, including within the term the Celtic inhabitants of the British Isles.

Her passion for travel was so great as to take precedence on occasion over her suffrage activities. The trip to Egypt and Greece, which also included a visit to Italy, took place over a fifteen-week period in 1896–7 and meant that she missed the debate in the House of Commons in February 1897 when for the first time women's suffrage secured more than 200 votes, and the bill comfortably passed its second reading.[23] Later she missed an opportunity to join an unprecedented women's suffrage deputation to Sir Henry Campbell-Bannerman, the recently installed Liberal Prime Minister, on the eve of the outbreak of the militant suffrage movement. She wrote to one of the organizing secretaries from Palermo in April 1906 to say that she had been 'pondering deeply' whether to return for the deputation a month later but had finally decided not to do so: 'We are travelling to & from Naples by Sea by the Orient Line, and their steamers are exactly wrong for being home on the 19th.'[24] Her decision reflected not only her love of Italy but also the sporadic level of suffrage activity and the fact that she had not yet become the symbol and figurehead of the constitutional movement, her absence unthinkable from all major occasions.

She was an enthusiastic traveller not only abroad but at home. Apart from her native Suffolk, with which she continued to have close family links, she was specially fond of Harry's home county of Wiltshire and neighbouring Hampshire, as well as Yorkshire and Scotland, all of which she visited repeatedly. Parts of *Janet Doncaster* (1875) were set in the New Forest, and in 1884 she wrote two articles on the forest which showed an intimate knowledge of its topography and history, pointing out that to see it properly it was necessary to travel on foot or horseback. She also expressed strong opposition to attempts to exploit the forest commercially and restrict the rights of the commoners, which would greatly reduce its attraction to the public. This was true Millite radicalism, for the land question and the preservation of commons was a prominent radical cause, in which Henry Fawcett had been frequently and successfully involved.[25] She referred to the felling of 300 ancient yews in 1851 by a government department as 'wanton acts of vandalism' and added that the saving of the forest by parliamentary action ranked as a victory 'worth a good deal more to England than many of her victories of gunpowder and glory'.[26] She wrote another article on Burnham Beeches, displaying less detailed knowledge but similar attention to its preservation for the public and warm appreciation of its literary associations.[27]

As she grew older she travelled further afield, to South Africa (originally at the behest of the Government), the Middle East and finally Ceylon in the year of her death. She resisted, however, all the attempts of American suffragist leaders over a prolonged period to persuade her to visit the United States, including Julia Ward Howe's decorous assurance that a visit would be 'greatly appreciated' and 'helpful to the Cause', Susan B. Anthony's peremptory 'do you not ever intend coming to this country?' Anna Shaw's hint of a plan to 'lure you to America' or Carrie Chapman Catt's touching 'Please, dear Mrs Fawcett, come.'[28] Her vulnerability to seasickness undoubtedly helps to explain her reluctance to cross the Atlantic, and Frances Willard, the American temperance leader and suffragist may have been

correct in a tart remark to her compatriot May Wright Sewall: 'Mrs Fawcett
. . . I think considers America to be on some other planet, but she evidently
looks upon the Republic across the water through the wrong end of her
telescope – if indeed she ever look (*sic*) at all.'[29] Whatever the explanation
she was to remain on her own side of the Atlantic.

Travelling allowed her to indulge two of her other favourite recreations,
physical exercise and music. She enjoyed riding and mountaineering,
though both pastimes had caused Harry some alarm,[30] as well as skating and
gardening. Her visits to the Cambridge gymnasium with the Newnham
students may have contributed to her admirably succinct reply to a ques-
tioner who asked if she accepted the claim that higher education for women
benefited the mind at the expense of the body: 'No, I think it's all rub-
bish.'[31] (Soon afterwards sport, especially hockey, was to take the women's
colleges by storm; her daughter Philippa was a member of the Newnham
hockey side.[32] Like the rest of the population Mrs Fawcett took up cycling
in the mid-1890s.[33] She wrote to her mother in March 1896 that she had
begun to learn, but that after three lessons was 'rather stupid at it'. She must
have persevered, for some months later she wrote again to ask if she could
visit with her friend Jane Walker: 'if fine we could have a bicycle ride'.[34]

The recreation which proved most durable, however, was walking, a
holiday pastime which left its traces in London, where she briskly outpaced
her companions even in old age.[35] Evelyn Sharp, the author and militant
suffragist, visited the holiday home which Elizabeth Garrett Anderson had
bought at Newtonmore in the Scottish Highlands, in the company of her
friend Louisa, Elizabeth's daughter. She left a vivid picture of an undated
visit or visits which probably belonged to the period around 1910 when
Millicent was 63, Agnes 65 and Elizabeth 74:

> There was a strong family likeness in all the Garretts . . . Miss Agnes Garrett
> used to accompany Mrs Fawcett everywhere, and when they joined us at
> Newtonmore, the conversation became noticeably more racy, enlivened as it
> was with many excellent anecdotes gathered in their wanderings about the
> world. Nothing seemed to daunt these doughty women, and . . . I felt
> nothing but an artificial inhabitant of cities when I saw them tuck up their
> skirts – there was plenty to tuck up in those days – and don indescribable
> boots, before starting out to brave inclement weather and face really difficult
> rambles in the mountains above Speyside.[36]

The portrait was one which might have surprised those who only knew Mrs
Fawcett on the public platform, but it was in keeping with a personality
long known to her intimates to enjoy life to the full, possess a keen sense of
humour and marked skill as a raconteur.[37]

Harry's biographer implied that he never cared greatly for music, and it is
difficult to think that so restless a nature could have attended a concert or
opera with much pleasure.[38] With Millicent it was quite otherwise. From
childhood to old age music was one of her greatest loves.[39] Hubert Parry,
who stayed with the Fawcetts in Cambridge in 1883 when his music for *The*

*Birds* of Aristophanes was first produced, recorded his appreciation of their hospitality.[40] She was also friendly in her Cambridge years with the composer Charles Stanford, whose subsequent opposition to women's suffrage was at least as strong as Parry's support, and more publicly expressed.[41]

The high point of her musical life was undoubtedly her repeated visits to Bayreuth to the Wagner festivals which began in 1882. She described for the Orient Line travellers the staging and surroundings of the performances in exalted tones and *Parsifal* in terms of a religious experience, 'like nothing else that has ever been put upon the stage'. She did not lose the opportunity to snipe at a pet aversion, the London concert wrecker: 'The painted, over-dressed women whose object it apparently is to attract as much attention to themselves as possible, and who frequently talk, even at concerts, all through the performance, are conspicuous by their absence at Bayreuth.'[42] She must have had in mind in writing this sentence an incident which had taken place in 1885, when her enjoyment of a series of concerts was so blighted by a group of chatterers that she wrote them a reprimanding letter. It was perhaps appropriate that one of her tormentors was Mary Gladstone, the daughter of the Prime Minister whose Irish policy was soon to incur her unyielding hostility, and that a second was Margot Tennant, later the wife of the Prime Minister and arch-opponent of women's suffrage, H.H. Asquith.[43]

Travel, physical exercise and music were all sources of deep satisfaction to her, and she also enjoyed attending art galleries and the theatre. As ever she made use of her periods of leisure to recruit allies for the women's cause. As early as 1891 she acknowledged Ibsen as one of 'the foremost thinkers' of the day on the rights of women and pointed out that he had taken a lead in asserting that women had a duty to themselves as well as their families.[44] She wrote appreciatively of the plays of Barrie and Shaw and even referred humorously to the *Medea* of Euripides as 'such a good suffrage play'.[45]

It was books, however, which were her inseparable companion and probably the source of her greatest satisfaction. She could not adapt Disraeli by saying that if she wanted to read a book she wrote one, but her output was remarkable for a busy woman with many different spheres of public work, a wide circle of friends and many other leisure interests. After her early rash of publications her output declined until after Harry's death, but in the next twenty years articles, pamphlets and books poured from her pen. Many of her articles dealt with her suffrage and other campaigning activities and will be considered in their place, but in addition she wrote four books between 1889 and 1905 which demonstrated her ability to advance her causes in a wider context.

In order of publication these were *Some Eminent Women of our Times* (1889), *Life of Her Majesty Queen Victoria* (1895), *Life of the Right Hon. Sir William Molesworth* (1901) and *Five Famous French Women* (1905). She would probably have been the first to admit that the three books on women were written to serve a limited contemporary purpose and possessed little historical merit, while her life of Molesworth, a serious and well-researched study, has suffered because her subject has long been forgotten by all but specialists. All but one of the twenty-three accounts of eminent women had originally appeared in the pages of the *Mother's Companion* in 1887–8. Intended 'chiefly for working women and young people', they were published at a time when, a few years after Harry's death and some time before her father's, she may have had a financial motive for writing.[46] The chapters were short sketches of women, mostly British, who had lived in the century prior to publication. Her aim was to show that women were capable of the highest achievements without losing the 'womanly' qualities of care for others, purity of moral character and self-sacrifice. Both aspects, she insisted, had developed together.

A century later this is not an inspiring message, and it may seem to any modern readers that the book was a contribution to the subjection of women rather than their emancipation. Such an assumption would be to ignore the historical context in which the sketches were written and a good deal of their content. They demonstrated that talented women had had to struggle against the opposition of their families and their male-dominated world, that high achievement was compatible with support for women's rights and that a powerful mind was not an attribute exclusive to men. Moreover, this 'simple record of noble women', written with 'characteristic clearness and simplicity and . . . refinement and dignity of literary style'[47] reminded a readership generally ignorant of the women's movement of what had been achieved in the past and, by implication, what might be achieved in a more enlightened world than that confronted by the subjects of the book. In later years a number of chapters were kept in print by the National Union of Women's Suffrage Societies to instruct and inspire its members.

One of the subjects was Queen Victoria, to whom Mrs Fawcett devoted her next book. It is no more appealing to the modern reader than its predecessor; even the loyal Ray Strachey suggested that it was 'perhaps a little over-enthusiastic about the Queen' and historically 'a little too simplified to be quite convincing'.[48] Patriotism was one of her strongest emotions and it was natural for her to identify it with the female monarch. In praising the Queen, she believed, she could simultaneously advance the cause of other British women. Certainly the book contained a number of what Strachey termed 'feminist touches'.[49] Her feminist aim was to show that Victoria was a woman successfully involved in demanding political work, who was none the less a loving wife, a prolific mother and a good housekeeper, the epitome of the domestic virtues. 'She has ever been the true woman, and because a true woman therefore a great Queen.' She also pointed out that Prince Albert had successfully carried out the function of being his 'wife's husband', a subordinate role familiar to women but rarely experienced by men.

The book is notable for two other revelations of the author's character, one political, the other movingly personal. In referring to the revolutions which broke out on the continent in 1848 she observed smugly that 'revolution' in Britain tended to take no more violent a form than the presentation of a petition. 'The utter inability of the revolutionary germ to thrive in the soil of constitutional liberty was the lesson of 1848.' The personal revelation arose from the death of Albert. Presumably thinking of her own renewed public activity after Harry's death she referred to women compelled by economic necessity after their husbands' deaths to seek employment: 'If the inner history of such lives can be told', she wrote,

> would it not often be found that the curse was transformed into a blessing, that the necessity to seek active work, the friends found in seeking it and in doing it, gave relief to the heartache, and that the rod of chastisement had been converted into the staff of strength?

Victoria's grief, she added, was the consequence of a happy marriage. 'Death itself could not rob her of this enormous happiness.'[50]

Her final venture into biography was a study of five famous Frenchwomen of the late Middle Ages and the Renaissance. Had she not confined herself to this restricted period she could have included a more obviously relevant figure like the Polish-born Marie Curie, whom Mrs Fawcett herself later called 'the originator of the greatest scientific discovery of modern times'.[51] But her theme was political leadership, and this could best be demonstrated by studies of Joan of Arc and four royal or aristocratic women.

All of them contrasted sharply with their weak or ignoble male contemporaries, and several showed their independence of mind by Protestant convictions or sympathies obviously congenial to the author. The point she was most concerned to stress was that though women and men had different qualities, both had important contributions to make in the political as in other spheres. This was particularly apparent in her treatment not only of Joan of Arc but also of Jeanne d'Albret, Queen of Navarre and mother of Henry IV: 'Jeanne was a thorough woman, and was not the less so for her intelligence, capacity, and courage, and the power of inspiring courage in others.'[52] The book was accused, not unreasonably, of 'scrappiness' by *The Athenaeum*,[53] but Mrs Fawcett had not written it for professionals. The appreciation of suffragists[54] and the propaganda value offered to the suffrage cause by the publication must have compensated for any lack of critical enthusiasm.

Her biography of Sir William Molesworth (1810–55) was a study of the mid-century radicalism which had inspired the young Henry Fawcett in the years before Millicent had became politically conscious.[55] It was her only book after the early period not concerned with the rights of women and her last book published by Macmillan, originally Harry's publisher, to whom she had been faithful for thirty years. Her negotiations with the firm are well documented and show her to have been a competent businesswoman. In February 1901 she wrote to Maurice Macmillan, father of the future Prime Minister, to tell him that she had been working on the book for 'the last few months', at a time when the women's movement had suspended its activities because of the contemporary war in South Africa. She had obtained 'volumes of most interesting unpublished letters' from Molesworth's surviving sister. His identification in the last twenty years of his life, she added, 'with what we now know as an Imperial Colonial policy' would make the book particularly topical.

Macmillan agreed to publish the book, but offered her half its profit rather than a royalty. Her demur was of no avail, but she assured him a little stiffly that she had 'no wish to offer my life of Sir William Molesworth to any other publisher'. She sent him the manuscript on 19 June and received the proofs a month later. The book was published before the end of the year and she asked for twelve gratis copies to be sent to friends and relations.[56] She wrote again in February 1902 expressing justified pleasure at the general tone of the reviews, especially the *Spectator*'s, which had called the book 'a literary masterpiece'. She added that as the report on the women's commission on South African concentration camps which she had led had just been published and was thought likely to create a stir, 'it would be a favourable moment for advertising Molesworth'.[57]

The book was particularly concerned with Molesworth's views on colonial policy. He advocated close relations with self-governing colonies rather than the neglect favoured by most of his fellow radicals and a wide swathe of public opinion. 'He foresaw, as very few did in his time, that the root of Colonial loyalty could flourish only in Colonial freedom.' His policy had been justified by the transformation of the colonies from 'burden' to 'jewel' in the half century since his death, and the strong links between them and Britain, had grown even closer in time of war. A second theme was the justification of Molesworth's religious independence, which he expressed in 'sincere, outspoken and manly' fashion. Like him she regarded the religious orthodoxy of his day as both evil and obscurantist. She added a dash of feminism in her condemnation of a society in which a woman who loved him was unable to marry him because her family opposed her marriage to a radical and infidel. It was a mistaken policy, she added with a jab at the orthodoxy of her own day, for the churches to prefer ignorance to 'the reverent searching for truth in the physical universe'.[58]

Ray Strachey rightly pointed out that the book gave her the opportunity to express her views on topics with which her writing did not normally deal.[59] But the careful reader should, even so, have been able to guess the name of the author without reference to the title page. Her condemnation of the 'iniquitous sentence' served on the trade unionist Tolpuddle Martyrs of 1834 was strikingly expressed and recalled the radicalism of her youth. Her sympathy with Molesworth's opposition to the Chartist movement, however, which had mounted a much more sweeping attack on established society, illustrated the limits of her commitment to reform. Patriotism was a final theme, her emotions roused by a war to which she was deeply committed. She deserted Molesworth, who had opposed Palmerston's swashbuckling foreign policy in the Don Pacifico incident of 1850, to express a deeply held conviction with a rush of sentiment:

> Who is there that does not feel that it is worth something to be a British subject? That if he is wronged anywhere in the ends of the earth, Great Britain will see him righted? When Great Britain acts up to this character, every Briton repays the debt he owes his country with love and gratitude, and with his life if need be.[60]

Mrs Fawcett's *Molesworth* was without a successor, though letters which she wrote in 1902 indicated that she would have worked on the life of Lord Durham (1792–1840), a colonial reformer of a slightly earlier period, had she not been anticipated by Stuart Reid, whose two-volumed *Life and Letters* appeared in 1906.[61] But her only venture into general history and biography was evidence of a formidable intellect, while the open expression of her prejudices in a scholarly work conformed to the common practice of the period. If she had not written normally for political and propagandist purposes there seems little doubt that she could have established herself in a successful career as a serious writer.

It would be misleading to accept at face value Mrs Fawcett's own claim that she would have been happier among her books than carrying out speaking engagements,[62] however weary or dispirited she may sometimes have been. She was primarily a political figure, dedicated to the cause of women's emancipation. But it is clear that she was a woman of unusually wide interests, with the means and determination to follow them. Had she been confined to her recreational and intellectual pursuits she would have found no difficulty in leading a rich, varied and productive life.

NOTES

1. Parry diaries, 1 October 1886 (Parry Papers, Shulbrede Priory); *MGF*, pp. 102–3.
2. *MGF*, pp. 102–3; *WIR*, p. 134.
3. Leslie Stephen, *Life of Henry Fawcett* (1885) Preface; *idem, Mausoleum Book* (1977), p. 87; Collini in Lawrence Goldman (ed.) *The Blind Victorian* (1989), pp. 43–4.
4. Stephen, preface.
5. Harvie, *The Lights of Liberalism* (1976) pp. 178 and 309 n. 24; also in Goldman (ed.), p. 181. She made no comment on the passage which Harvie thinks best illustrates Harry's 'political acumen'.
6. The manuscript, as indicated in ch. 5, note 38 above, is in the archives of Trinity Hall, the Cambridge college of both men. I am indebted to Sandra Raban for facilitating my access to it.
7. Elizabeth Garrett Anderson to Skelton Anderson, 15 August 1895 (Anderson Papers, St Brelade). Soon afterwards a profile of Mrs Fawcett in a women's magazine commented typically that she was 'a very expert needlewoman' and that her daughter Philippa could 'make everything she wears except her boots' (Tooley; ch. 1, note 31 above).

8. National Union of Women Workers, *Women Workers* (P.S. King, 1906), pp. 96–8; M[argaret] H[eitland], *The Times*, 13 August 1929.
9. MGF to Louisa Garrett, 11 October 1897 (Anderson Papers).
10. Brian Harrison, *Prudent Revolutionaries* (1987), p. 24.
11. R.E. Graves to Richard Garnett, 13 March 1900 (Richard Garnett Collection, University of Texas). The book was *Sermones Quadrigesimales* by Robertus Carracciolus de Litio. The British Museum bought ten editions of this book after 1899, but none from Mrs Fawcett (John Goldfinch, British Library, to author, 10 March 1989). See also *WIR*, p. 87.
12. *WL*, 17 August 1923, p. 229.
13. Elizabeth Garrett Anderson to Louisa Garrett. 26 July 1891 (Anderson Papers).
14. MGF to Louisa Garrett, 7 March 1897 (*ibid.*).
15. *WIR*, p. 103.
16. Elizabeth Garrett Anderson to Louisa Garrett, 26 July 1891. 'They practice economie' [*sic*] was the disconcerting reply (Anderson Papers).
17. MGF to Louisa Garrett, 10 May 1898 (*ibid.*).
18. Jo Manton, *Elizabeth Garrett Anderson* (1965) p. 270. Loftie had supported Elizabeth Garrett's campaign for the London School Board in 1870 (Anderson, *Elizabeth Garrett Anderson* (1939), p. 147).
19. MGF, 'Italy' in W.J. Loftie (ed.), *Orient Line Guide* (2nd edn, 1885), pp. 140–53. Quotations are from pp. 141 and 153.
20. *ibid.*, pp. 154–5.
21. *ibid.*, 6th edn [1901], pp. 92–6; *London Pupil Teachers' Association Record*, 20 May 1897, p. 19.
22. MGF to Louisa Garrett, 7 March 1897 (Anderson Papers).
23. *idem* to *idem*, 22 March 1897 (*ibid.*); Brian Harrison, *Separate Spheres* (1978), pp. 28–9.
24. MGF to Frances Sterling, 17 April 1906 (FLALC, vol. 1bii).
25. Stephen, ch. 7. For Fawcett's efforts for the New Forest see *ibid.*, pp. 322–6.
26. MGF, 'The New Forest', *Magazine of Art*, October and November 1884, pp. 1–8, 45–52. The quotations are from pp. 50 and 51.
27. MGF, 'Burnham Beeches', *ibid.*, September 1885, pp. 485–92.
28. Letters to MGF from Julia Ward Howe, 26 December 1890 (M50/2/1/102), Susan B. Anthony, 18 May 1903 (FLA, box 89 vol. 1), Anna Shaw, 13 April 1907 (*ibid.*), Carrie Chapman Catt, 23 November 1915 (M50/2/22/74). Other invitations came from a party of American suffragists offering to pay all expenses (17 July 1890, M50/2/1/96) and from Mrs Catt on an earlier occasion: 'You know I have spoken to you often of coming to the United States . . . Do come!!!' (19 October 1909, Catt Papers, Library of Congress).
29. Frances Willard to May Wright Sewall, 27 January 1893 (Sewall Papers, Indianapolis Public Library).
30. See above, page 45; *WIR*, pp. 103–04.
31. See above, page 27; 'Mrs Millicent Garrett Fawcett', *Women's Penny Paper*, 3 November 1888, pp. 4–5.
32. Kathleen E. McCrone, *Playing the Game* (1988) pp. 35–8. Ann Phillips (ed.), *A Newnham Anthology* (Cambridge: Cambridge University Press, 1979), reprints a photograph of the side, including Philippa, in 1891 (opp. p. 50).
33. See David Rubinstein, 'Cycling in the 1890s', *Victorian Studies* (vol. 21, 1977), pp. 47–71.
34. MGF to Louisa Garrett, 7 March and 19 October 1896 (Anderson Papers).
35. See below, page 240.
36. Evelyn Sharp, *Unfinished Adventure* (1933), p. 125.
37. *Review of Reviews*, July 1890, p. 23.

38. Stephen, p. 55. But see *WIR*, pp. 80–1, for a description of the Fawcetts' musical life in Cambridge, including chamber music in their own home.
39. *WIR*, pp. 27–8; *MGF*, pp. 359–60 and *passim*.
40. Parry diaries, 26 November–1 December 1883 (Parry Papers); Charles L. Graves, *Hubert Parry* (1926), vol. 2, p. 92.
41. *WIR*, pp. 80–1; *The Times*, 16, 19, 21, 23 July 1910.
42. Loftie (ed.) (3rd edn, 1888), pp. 117–18.
43. *MGF*, pp. 136–8.
44. *ibid.*, pp. 139–40; MGF, introduction to Mary Wollstonecraft, *A Vindication of the Rights of Woman* (T. Fisher Unwin, 1891 edn), pp. 28–9.
45. MGF, 'Great expectations', *WL*, 27 July 1923, p. 205; Helena Swanwick, 'Millicent Garrett Fawcett; an appreciation', *Time and Tide*, 16 August 1929, p. 979.
46. This speculation draws some support from the fact that she taught economics at Queen's and King's Colleges soon afterwards. There is, however, no direct evidence that she was financially embarrassed then or later.
47. *ER*, 15 July 1890, pp. 313–14; *Women's Penny Paper*, 7 December 1889, p. 82.
48. *MGF*, p. 180.
49. *ibid.*
50. MGF, *Life of Her Majesty Queen Victoria* (1895). Quotations are from pp. 153, 203–04, 212, 253. See also *MGF*, pp. 103–5.
51. MGF, 'The international aspects of women's suffrage', *The Englishwoman*, April 1909, p. 276.
52. MGF, *Five Famous French Women* (1905). The quotation is from p. 232.
53. *The Athenaeum*, 30 December 1905, p. 892.
54. Mary A. Ewart to MGF, 16 January 1906 (M50/2/1/226).
55. Stephen, pp. 190–1; *MGF*, p. 187.
56. She also presented a copy to King Edward VII, taking much care to choose a suitable binding (MGF to J. and J. Leighton, 25 October 1902; Holborn Public Library).
57. MGF to Maurice Macmillan, 25 February, 12, 13, 19 June, 21 July, 17 December 1901, 21 February (190[2]; 1901 written in error) (Macmillan Archive, University of Reading); *The Spectator*, 8 February 1902, p. 215.
58. MGF, *Life of the Right Hon. Sir William Molesworth* (1901). Quotations are from pp. 4 and 257.
59. *MGF*, p. 188.
60. MGF, *Molesworth*, pp. 85, 222, 296 (quotation).
61. MGF to Richard Garnett, 28 February, 12 March 1902 (Richard Garnett Collection, University of Texas).
62. Above, page 73.

# CHAPTER 8

—————— · ——————

# MORALITY

Morality was at the heart of what Mrs Fawcett understood by women's emancipation. As Barbara Caine has pointed out, the exploitation of girls and young women brought out the emotions usually hidden in her work for women's suffrage, education and employment.[1] Morality meant to her in large part the relations of the sexes. She believed in female 'purity' and the family and was unhesitatingly hostile to advocacy of 'free love'. Similarly, she condemned individuals whose private behaviour she felt was harmful to morality and hence particularly to women, and she justified the censorship of books now regarded as literature. Hers is no longer a point of view acceptable to feminists.[2]

A biographer's concern is not to justify or condemn but to explain. It seemed obvious to Mrs Fawcett and many other late Victorian feminists that it was women who paid the price of sexual irregularity, in the form of poverty, social obloquy or even death. As she pointed out, the admiration expressed for Shelley's attitude to free love by the heroine of Grant Allen's egregious novel *The Woman Who Did* (1895) was admiration for a man who deserted his pregnant wife.[3] The strength of her feeling and her public prominence meant that she was noticed, not that hers was a marginal point of view.

The economic and political power of men meant that most women were, ultimately, at their mercy with consequences which could mean abuse, desertion and prostitution. At the end of her life Mrs Fawcett recalled two cases of young 'gentlewomen' being solicited in the London streets in 1870. Similar cases were daily occurrences, she wrote, in the lives of 'poverty-stricken working girls'.[4] It was a situation in which conventional morality seemed to her not to imprison women but to offer them a form of protection. She was in some respects less bound by convention than is sometimes thought, but her attitude is not surprising in a period before contraception became socially acceptable and widely available. The fact that she clothed her views in moral conviction illustrates little more than that morality is largely socially determined.

Her decision not to combine her work for women's suffrage in the years following her marriage with support for Josephine Butler's campaign to repeal the Contagious Diseases Acts was a tactical one.[5] Soon after Harry's death in 1884 she was to work vigorously and simultaneously for the suffrage and against the sexual exploitation of girls and women. Janet Doncaster's determination in 1875 not to stay with her drunken husband, and Mrs Fawcett's letter in the same year to Elizabeth Wolstenholme Elmy, insisting that her earlier defiance of sexual convention 'has been and is a great injury to the cause of women',[6] were early examples of a moral stance which in these 'middle years' was a dominant feature of her life.

Her concern with public morality, which never ceased, took a variety of forms. In this period she was closely involved in the work of the National Vigilance Association and in combating 'white slavery', the organized attempt to force girls and young women into prostitution. The nature of her work indicates the range of dangers faced by poor and inexperienced women in late Victorian London and helps to explain behaviour which in a later age would be regarded as censorious assaults on personal freedom. Three striking incidents illustrate her view of the sexual exploitation of women and the lengths to which she was prepared to go to oppose it.

The first was W.T. Stead's famous exposé of the nature and extent of white slavery in London, which appeared in July 1885 in the pages of the *Pall Mall Gazette* under the sensational heading 'The maiden tribute of modern Babylon'.[7] The articles and their aftermath were to have a profound effect on her thought and behaviour. Her grievance against Stead in the previous year now forgotten, she demonstrated her support by letters to the press, including one which Stead gratefully published in a leading position in the *Pall Mall* after *The Spectator* had refused letters on the subject. In it she defended the morality and value of his articles; they had influenced parliamentary and public opinion about crimes against children as nothing else had done. They had also called forth 'a deep yearning for purity' which would be of permanent value in saving young men and women 'from condemning themselves to wallow in the quagmire of vice'.[8] Her position both as a feminist leader and as the widow of a popular political figure whose death was still fresh in the public memory must have given her a standing in the controversy of special value.

She was asked by Stead to interrupt a holiday to speak at a conference at the St James's Hall on the protection of girls, at which the National Vigilance Association was established. He was 'most anxious', he wrote, 'that you should present the women's suffrage side of the movement.'[9] Although she did not speak on this occasion, probably her first speech after Harry's death was in his constituency at a meeting convened by the NVA. She took the opportunity to defend Stead and insist that the cause which he championed was far more important than whether or not he had 'unwittingly overstepped the limits of legality'. If women had the parliamentary vote, she stressed, the purity campaign would be greatly strengthened.[10] Mrs Fawcett was, according to a later account, the author of a letter of thanks to Stead signed by 436 women and published in August 1885.[11] Soon afterwards he was prosecuted for abduction, convicted on technical grounds and sent to prison. She associated herself with his defence, raised money and condemned the prosecution vehemently:

> The government reserves itself and all the resources given to it by its control of the public purse to prosecute those men who descended into the pit of infamy in order to be able to compel the attention of all decent men and women to the hideous crimes that were going on around them.[12]

Once Stead was in prison she exerted herself to increase his comfort[13] and wrote him a remarkable series of letters. In one she told him that he had set on foot a movement 'as great as Wycliffe's or Luther's'; in a second, after writing in similar terms she added: 'Everything I have written sounds so cold compared to what I feel.'[14] Writing to Mrs Stead she said that his 'true character' was that of 'the hero saint who in every age of the world's history has been picked out for special persecution & misrepresentation'.[15] Another letter, of which only a fragment remains, contains neither a date nor the name of the recipient, but it is probable that it was written to Stead at about the same time. It contained a revealing confession. She had not previously spoken in public about sexual abuses, she wrote, because she had thought that the law on the subject would not be reformed until women had gained the parliamentary vote. Moreover, she could not speak about 'all those horrible facts about children . . . without crying and I had a morbid horror of breaking down in public.' She now felt ashamed of this attitude and understood that if she could do good it did not matter if she broke down.[16]

Despite this letter, however, she was to remain in public a model of dispassionate clarity. Over a decade later, Josephine Butler, to whom she became closely attached during this period, commented to friends that though Mrs Fawcett was an invaluable colleague, she 'lacks warmth rather'. Long after her death the verdict of another colleague, Philippa Strachey, was that 'any display of her private feelings wd seem to her indecent'.[17]

In an article written that autumn in the wake of Stead's revelations she stressed unanswerably that the situation which he had exposed resulted from the economic and political subjection of women, including wages at such a level that prostitution became almost inevitable. 'The evil state of the law', only rectified after the *Pall Mall's* sensational articles, resulted from 'the notion that women are possessions or chattels' with whom men should be able to deal as they pleased.[18] A year later a case arose which illustrated her point. A servant girl aged 17 was accosted in the West End of London by a fashionably dressed man of about 60, who asked her to accompany him to Greenwich or to his home. She refused, but having obtained her address he wrote to her and offered to take her to the zoo or into the country. The case was brought to Mrs Fawcett's attention by the employers, who happened to be her close friends, and with the assistance of the NVA a trap was laid for the man, an army doctor named Muschamp. When the servant met him outside the British Museum a reception committee was with her. Quickly assembling a sizeable crowd they badgered and berated the offender, according to one account throwing flour in his eyes and down his back. He denied having intended to harm the girl 'but', as an NVA report commented, 'Mrs Henry Fawcett . . . who had been present the whole of the time, remarked, "Dr Muschamp, we have your letter." This seemed to convince the fellow that silence was the best policy.'[19]

The incident was unremarkable in contemporary London apart from the exposure of Muschamp, who as Mrs Fawcett pointed out to a friend, had done nothing illegal.[20] What is significant is the light which it throws on her character. A profile of her in the *Review of Reviews*, edited by Stead, retold the story a few years later, pointing out that when faced by 'cruel wrong . . . she has not the quality of Moses. She is not meek. She is vengeful and remorseless . . . Mrs Fawcett had no pity; she would have cashiered him if she could.' The article also referred more candidly than sympathetically to her 'orderly and well-balanced life' and to 'what seems like hardness' in her character. It concluded by saying in effect that though her stern rectitude could be uncomfortable, the nation would be better with more women like her.[21]

Nearly a decade later she was a great deal too vengeful and remorseless for Harry Cust. Her intervention in this affair, whose details are known only in part, showed her in a light which many contemporaries who knew the story found unacceptable. Modern readers are likely to find it not only unacceptable but inexplicable.

In 1893 Cust was Conservative MP for Stamford and editor of the *Pall Mall Gazette*, which had lost the radicalism of its years under Stead. He was attractive to women and is supposed to have been the father of a number of unacknowledged children.[22] He had seduced Nina Welby-Gregory, his cousin and 'a young girl of good Lincolnshire family',[23] who apparently became pregnant and subsequently miscarried.[24] Cust, much against his will, was forced to marry her, and as might be expected the marriage was for many years an unhappy one.[25] It was at that time that Mrs Fawcett became involved.

She learned Cust's story late in 1893, and found to her horror the following February that, having fallen foul of the Lincolnshire Conservatives, he had been adopted for the Liberal seat of Manchester North. She wrote in strong terms to her friends and contacts in Manchester to attempt to enlist their opposition to Cust. Among them was the secretary of the Manchester branch of the Women's Liberal Unionist Association, a body of which she was at the time one of the national leaders. She did this, she explained to the Conservative leader A.J. Balfour, 'because I considered that Cust's conduct struck at the root of everything that makes home and marriage sacred'. She also wished to save the Conservative party from adopting such a candidate, who if elected would have promoted religious education and laid the foundation stones of churches and church schools. Neither the local nor the national WLUA was willing to act, members of the latter body asserting that men did not like women to interfere in this type of affair. The Liberal Unionist agent, and her WLUA and suffragist colleague Lady Frances Balfour, A.J. Balfour's sister-in-law, also refused to assist. In consequence she had acted independently, un-deterred by Cust's blandishments and threats.[26]

Balfour's reply, in his own hand, occupied twelve pages. He was evidently in a state of cold fury, but he attempted to put the case of the man of the world calmly to the emotional woman. He pointed out that 'from the purest sense of duty' Mrs Fawcett had 'made public, through the length and breadth of Manchester, the unhappy story of a most unhappy woman. Her shame has become the common topic of political gossip.' Had she really been wicked enough to deserve such treatment? He insisted that it was in the interests of public morality that a man's private life should not be dragged before the public.[27]

Such a reply from such a source might have daunted many crusaders. It did not shake Mrs Fawcett. Cust, she replied, was not a fit person to be a parliamentary candidate. Having failed with the politicians she had ap-proached two friends involved in social and religious work in Manchester. She denied that doing so was to make the affair public. In any case the story was widely known to the political world in London and it was Cust himself who had brought it before a new political public in Manchester. Public men could not expect their private lives to remain above scrutiny, particularly at a time when the women's movement was bringing about greater equality between the sexes, when the practice of visiting 'the whole of the social punishment . . . on the woman' was beginning to change.[28]

Eventually Cust's candidacy was withdrawn and he did not find a parliamentary seat until 1900, when apparently without further opposition from Mrs Fawcett he was elected for Bermondsey. But the Manchester story had in March 1894 still another year to unfold. It is dificult to piece together all the details, particularly as only about a tenth of the surviving letters postdate June 1894. It is fairly clear, however, that Mrs Fawcett was not satisfied when Cust formally withdrew in September but attempted to drive him out of public life. The most interesting letters in the file are from Lady Frances Balfour, who was recruited by the Conservative party chiefs to attempt to persuade Mrs Fawcett to desist.[29] Lady Frances did what she could. She warned Mrs Fawcett that she had become 'the best abused woman in London' and was harming the suffrage cause. She pointed out that the attempts under the Puritans in the seventeenth century to reform public morals had ended in failure. She appealed to her to consider the views of her colleagues as well as the morals of Harry Cust. Finally she threatened to leave the suffrage movement and explain her reasons if Mrs Fawcett re-peated her behaviour over Cust. This letter bears a note: 'To this I sent no answer at all. M.G.F.'[30]

If the political world had really been ruffled by the affair it was quickly pacified. Cust, as seen above, eventually found another seat. A.J. Balfour, who according to Ray Strachey's discreet account of the case never entirely forgave Mrs Fawcett,[31] continued to give the suffrage cause limited moral and virtually no practical support. Within two years women's suffrage had secured a significant victory in the House of Commons, though Mrs Fawcett was not there to witness it.[32] Six weeks after the breach between the two women Lady Frances was writing to Mrs Fawcett about the tactics of the suffrage cause and a year later as a respected leader.[33] The affair is of importance in the largely wasted life of Harry Cust. It is more important in demonstrating Mrs Fawcett's attitude to sexual morality, which was representative of a good deal of feminist opinion,[34] and the fact that when convinced of the rectitude of a certain course of action she was not to be stopped by arguments of political expediency from even the highest source. The contrast with her cautious, pragmatic behaviour over women's suffrage and other issues is an important illustration of the depth of her emotional commitment to moral questions.

It would be easy to go through her career during this period finding examples of moral censoriousness. A note in her cuttings book about Tolstoi's *Anna Karenina*, probably dating from the late 1880s, swept aside a reviewer's comment that love had raised and purified Vronsky, the hero, with the comment that it had had the opposite effect on Anna.[35] In 1889 she associated herself with a successful attempt to prevent her former friend Sir Charles Dilke, whose fall from political prominence had been due to sexual scandal, being selected for the post of alderman on the new London County Council.[36] In 1891 the NVA executive was told that she had persuaded Macmillan to alter or delete an objectionable sentence in a biography of Admiral Rodney which the firm was about to publish.[37] In 1891 and 1895 she moved two almost identical resolutions at the annual meetings of the NVA, expressing satisfaction with 'the success which has attended the efforts to suppress objectionable pictures, books and pamphlets'.[38] The success included the prosecution and imprisonment of Henry Vizetelly, the British publisher of the works of Zola.[39]

Moral censoriousness is also apparent in her attitude to Mary Wollstonecraft, to whose *Vindication of the Rights of Woman* (1792) she wrote a long introduction for a new edition in 1891. Modern writers have drawn attention to passages in which she expressed disapproval of 'the errors of Mary Wollstonecraft's own life' and specifically her 'irregular relations'.[40] It is irritating to read that Wollstonecraft was an 'essentially womanly woman' who exalted the 'truly feminine' including 'women's domestic duties'.[41] But her intention was to make Wollstonecraft acceptable to the later Victorian reading public and, indeed, to herself.[42] Giving the sanction of her prominent and widely respected name she introduced Wollstonecraft to a new audience as a pioneer feminist who urged the case for political representation and economic independence of women, and insisted that their first duty was to themselves. The women's rights movement owed her as much as political economy owed to Adam Smith, her contemporary.[43]

When the introduction was reprinted in 1907 Elizabeth Wolstenholme Elmy, a more 'advanced' feminist who had long before felt the lash of Mrs Fawcett's moral disapproval, called it 'deeply interesting' and said that Mrs Fawcett had written 'wisely and justly of Mary Wollstonecraft'.[44] It was, in short, a valuable service to show that the women's movement could claim links with a tradition dating from the enlightenment of the eighteenth century and a powerful and original feminist mind.[45] The price was a somewhat distorted and sanitized Mary Wollstonecraft.

The provisional council of the National Vigilance Association met for the first time at the end of 1885. Twenty-five years later Mrs Fawcett recalled the atmosphere of the early days: 'We were looked on with some suspicion, and I think we were regarded as about half crazy and wholly undesirable.' She was elected to its preventive (later preventive and rescue) sub-committtee and chosen as its president.[46] She was also a member of the association's executive, though her attendance was irregular, and her offer to resign was declined in 1889.[47] She was elected an NVA vice-president in 1891, and continued to serve on the executive and the preventive sub-committee until about 1893. Even after severing her formal links with the association's leadership she could be counted on to appear at annual meetings and speak in support of its work.[48]

There is no doubt that Mrs Fawcett was wholly committed to the work of the NVA and that she worked assiduously for its objectives. Nor is there a doubt that she enlisted it to work for hers, above all the attempt to put an end to the employment of young children on the stage.[49] Her sub-committee was especially concerned with preventing girls and women from becoming prostitutes and with rescuing those who had done so. Among the measures adopted were the establishment of a medical home for women administered by women; the promotion of rescue work and assistance with individual cases; advocacy of compulsory detention of feeble-minded women and girls to prevent them from becoming prostitutes and mothers of illegitimate children; and the end of the practice whereby women were turned out of courts of law when criminal offences against their sex were considered.[50] Mrs Fawcett stressed the importance of 'raising the tone of public amusements in theatres and elsewhere' and urged the licenser of plays to do so. She also took the opportunity to point out that improvements in the law could be achieved more easily and efficiently if women had the right to vote.[51] 'It was simply perfect', the veteran suffrage worker Priscilla Bright McLaren wrote to her after reading a newspaper report of an NVA annual meeting; 'your allusion to woman's suffrage was so well timed – everything so calmly & clearly spoken.'[52]

Having delivered the valedictory address in 1891 to the third meeting of the middle-class Central Conference (soon to become National Union) of Women Workers,[53] Mrs Fawcett returned the next year to speak at a meeting of rescue workers to appeal for amendments to the Criminal Law Amendment Act of 1885, the law passed in the wake of what she called the 'moral earthquake' inspired by W.T. Stead's revelations. Using material supplied her by the NVA office, she cited in detail cases of sexual abuse of young girls by older men, in some cases their fathers.[54] Her main point was that legislation setting 16 as the age at which girls could legally consent to sexual intercourse was riddled with loopholes and subject to constant abuse. She also pointed out that incest was not an offence punishable in law. The legal problems and delays were the result of political expediency:

> The House of Commons is too fully occupied with redressing the grievances of people who have votes, and can therefore decide the fate of members and ministries, to have time to attend to the wrongs and injuries of those who have no votes.

Women's suffrage was to her in this as in other cases not only an abstract right but the most practical means of fighting abuses: 'But we must work with what weapons we have, and not fold our hands and do nothing because the most effective and most constitutional weapon is denied to us.'[55]

Closely related to her NVA work was the assistance which Mrs Fawcett gave to the Travellers' Aid Society. This was an offshoot of the YWCA, founded in 1885 with Lady Frances Balfour as its president.[56] The society's purpose was to give help to young girls who arrived at ports and railway stations in London and other large cities seeking employment or pleasure. Mrs Fawcett wrote an article in the *Pall Mall Gazette* in 1887 describing its work and appealing for money. 'There is', she wrote, 'a class of fiends in human form who haunt railway stations specially for the purpose of entrapping ignorant and foolish girls, often little more than children, to their ruin.' TAS representatives worked with railway officials to protect the girls, and in consequence fewer of them thought it safe to go off with a stranger 'because she is well dressed and apparently respectable'. The article raised £85 in donations and was reprinted as a leaflet, and Mrs Fawcett accepted membership of the TAS general committee.[57] She made a further appeal in *The Times* the following year, in which she referred to the many ruses adopted by the 'harpies' who sought to trap the girls. One who had dressed as a nurse 'is at present, I am glad to say, in temporary retirement in one of Her Majesty's prisons; but many others are at large.'[58]

She was capable of appealing to the emotions on behalf of girls who had been abducted into prostitution, but she was unsentimental about those who had voluntarily adopted it as a livelihood.[59] Her real anger, however, was reserved for the 'harpies' and for men who were the cause of punishing prostitutes without risk of punishment to themselves. One example was the

Spinning House case of 1891, in which moral outrage got the better of what her friends thought was good judgement.

Charles Russell of Jesus College Cambridge accosted the 17-year-old Daisy Hopkins and asked to accompany her to her lodgings. Apprehended by the university authorities, who had jurisdiction in the matter, Russell admitted that he had initiated the encounter, but on his evidence Hopkins was sentenced to a fortnight's imprisonment in the Spinning House. 'This married man', Mrs Fawcett angrily told a meeting, 'her senior in age, her superior in education and social position', suffered no penalty apart from the publicity which the case had aroused.[60] A week later her close friend Emma Miller, who lived in Cambridge, wrote to her that Daisy Hopkins was 'a noted prostitute' and a member of a family of prostitutes. Russell had lost his college position and an Indian appointment and his wife had left him. Moreover, when prostitutes were sent to the Spinning House attempts were made by ladies to reclaim them.[61] For Mrs Fawcett, however, the nub of the matter was that a woman had been punished, while a man who was the guiltier of the two had not been. Her reply appears not to have survived, but it is unlikely that she spent much time regretting the fate of Charles Russell.

Her most important speech on the white slave trade was delivered to an international congress held in London in June 1899. She said that there had been no concerted attempt to stop the trade. Girls could be 'shipped from country to country like so many head of cattle' and were virtually powerless to escape. It was necessary to institute 'a higher moral standard in the community at large, and especially a higher moral standard among men'. At present, 'low debauchery, and cowardly villainy' were looked on as manly or at least as inevitable, and in such conditions rescue and prevention work among women could not hope to succeed. She found hope in the growing movement for equality among men and women; men were being asked to practise what they preached.[62]

The Contagious Diseases Acts, the target of the struggle led by Josephine Butler, had been repealed in 1886. Their threatened application to India in 1896–7 led to an unequivocal speech by Mrs Fawcett to the National Union of Women Workers. Moving a long resolution which, among other things, encouraged the provision of 'further occupation and recreation for soldiers on foreign service, or suitably modifying their food, and of giving increased facilities for marriage', she again argued that men should adopt a higher moral standard. She opposed the view that prostitution was a necessary evil and that it was 'impossible for the British soldier to be anything but a brute'. She insisted that in France, where legal regulation had long applied the birth rate was low, the death rate high and art 'too often degrading rather than elevating in its general influence'.[63] Interestingly, this brief campaign pro-duced a rare adverse comment about her equanimity under fire. Working with Josephine Butler and others she suggested amendments to a draft manifesto which Mrs Butler regarded as defeatist. 'Mrs Fawcett could *never* be a *leader*, dear woman', she wrote to friends, 'for a leader should always be *most* full of hope & courage in the darkest hour.'[64] It was this very quality for which she was later to be renowned.

This chapter has attempted to explore the range and nature of Mrs Fawcett's activities in moral questions. Much of the distaste which modern readers may feel towards her behaviour will stem from her assumption that girls and women, especially of the working class, needed to be protected against men; her firm belief in a pattern of female chastity which has largely disappeared; and her readiness to invade individual liberty in the name of morality. But her age is not ours. The society in which she lived was built in large part on the savage and largely uncontrolled exploitation of women. If her solutions now seem often to have been grotesquely intolerant, there is a case for the view that they were appropriate in the conditions and circumstances of late Victorian England.

## NOTES

1. I am indebted to Barbara Caine for her then unpublished paper 'Millicent Garrett Fawcett: a Victorian Liberal feminist?', and for several conversations which have done much to clarify my thinking on this subject.
2. Constance Rover, *Love, Morals and the Feminists* (1970), pp. 52–5; Lucy Bland, 'The married woman, the "new woman" and the feminist: sexual politics of the 1890s' in Jane Rendall (ed.), *Equal or Different* (Oxford: Blackwell, 1987), pp. 160–1.
3. MGF, 'The woman who did', *Contemporary Review*, May 1895, pp. 625–31.
4. MGF and E.M Turner, *Josephine Butler* (1927), pp. 54–5.
5. See above, page 46.
6. See above, pages 55/57 note 55.
7. Stead's campaign and Mrs Fawcett's role in it are well summarized in *MGF*, pp. 107–16.
8. *Pall Mall Gazette*, 14 August 1885.
9. W.T. Stead to MGF, 14 August 1885 (FLALC, vol. 11). There is no indication that she took part in the conference (fully reported in a special edition of the *Pall Mall Gazette*, 22 August 1885).
10. *Pall Mall Gazette*, 24 October 1885.
11. *ibid.*, 5 August 1885; *CC*, 16 May 1912, p. 86.
12. *ER*, 15 October 1885, p. 455.
13. *MGF*, pp. 113–16; Frederic Whyte, *The Life of W.T. Stead*, vol. 1 (1925), p. 206.
14. Quoted in Whyte, pp. 159, 207.
15. MGF to Emma Stead, 11 November 1885 (Stead Papers, University of Cambridge).
16. FLALC, vol. 8b.
17. Josephine Butler to Anna Maria and Mary Priestman, 15 October [1896] (Butler Letter Collection, Fawcett Library; quoted in Caine, note 1 above). Both Mrs Fawcett and Ray Strachey wrote that she did not meet Mrs Butler until the Stead agitation (Fawcett and Turner, p. 10n.; *MGF*, p. 108), but as early as April 1871 she had moved a resolution at a women's suffrage conference

'on behalf of her friend Mrs Josephine Butler' (*WSJ*, 1 June 1871, p. 69). Philippa Strachey's comment was made in a letter to Betty Vernon, 20 May 1957 (Fawcett Library, unclassified).

18. MGF, 'Speech or Silence', *Contemporary Review*, September 1885, p. 330.
19. NVA, *Report and Balance Sheet Presented to Annual Meeting*, 8 November 1887, pp. vi–vii (Fawcett Library); *Review of Reviews*, July 1890, p. 22; *MGF*, pp. 117–18.
20. *MGF*, p. 118.
21. *Review of Reviews* (note 19 above), pp. 22–3. There are nine entries in the index of the Strachey biography under MGF, ' "unforgivingness" to public enemies'.
22. Jane Abdy and Charlotte Gere, *The Souls* (Sidgwick & Jackson, 1984), p. 70.
23. MGF to A.J. Balfour (copy), 19 March 1894 (FLA, box 90a file 14).
24. This is another part of the story about which knowledge is incomplete.
25. MGF memoranda in *ibid.*; Abdy and Gere, p. 70; Angela Lambert, *Unquiet Souls* (Macmillan, 1984), pp. 79–80.
26. MGF to Balfour (note 23 above).
27. Balfour to MGF, 22 March 1894 (*ibid.*).
28. MGF to Balfour (copy), 26 March 1894 (*ibid.*). The Fawcett–Balfour correspondence has been summarized and analyzed by Susan Kingsley Kent, *Sex and Suffrage in Britain, 1860–1914* (1987), pp. 153–5.
29. Her account is in *The Times*, 7 August 1929.
30. Frances Balfour to MGF, 15 March 1894, 19 March 1895 [March 1895], 25 March 1895 (FLA, box 90a files 12 and 13).
31. *MGF*, pp. 118–20. Mrs Fawcett's is the only name mentioned in this account.
32. See above, pages 74–5.
33. Frances Balfour to MGF, 9 May 1895, 25 June 1896 (FLALC, vol. 1bi).
34. See Kent (note 28 above) esp. ch. 5, and Sheila Jeffreys, *The Spinster and her Enemies* (Pandora, 1985), esp. ch. 4.
35. MGF's cuttings book, 1884–94 (M50/2/26/2). The comment was undated, but *Anna Karenina* was published in English in 1886.
36. A petition against Dilke's selection was signed within 'an incredibly short time' by 1,604 women, including four of the Garrett sisters (*Women's Penny Paper*, 2 February 1889, p. 3).
37. NVA, executive committee minutes, 24 November 1891 (FLA, box 194).
38. *Vigilance Record*, November 1891, p. 103; August 1895, p. 18.
39. *ibid.*, June 1889, pp. 54–7.
40. Rover, *Love*, pp. 52–5; Bland, p. 161; Brian Harrison, *Prudent Revolutionaries* (1987), p. 21; Ann Oakley, 'Millicent Garrett Fawcett' in Dale Spender (ed.), *Feminist Theorists* (Women's Press, 1983), p. 193.
41. MGF, introduction to *A Vindication of the Rights of Woman*, pp. 3–4, 22–3.
42. Dale Spender, *There's Always Been a Women's Movement This Century* (Pandora, 1983), pp. 178–9.
43. MGF, introduction (note 41 above), pp. 24, 29–30.
44. Elizabeth Wolstenholme Elmy, 'The enfranchisement of women', *Westminster Review*, September 1907, p. 279. The reprint was in Brougham Villiers (ed.), *The Case for Women's Suffrage* (T. Fisher Unwin, 1907).
45. Spender (note 42 above), p. 179.
46. W.A. Coote (ed.), *A Romance of Philanthropy* (1916), pp. 16, 126, 220.
47. NVA, EC minutes (note 37 above), 15 January 1889.
48. NVA, *Annual Reports*. She continued to serve as a vice-president until 1926 (*ibid.*). See *Vigilance Record*, February 1893, p. 4; August 1895, p. 18; July 1897, p. 92; July 1904, pp. 1–3.
49. See ch. 9 below.

50. NVA, EC minutes, 29 July 1890, 29 December 1891; *Annual Reports*, 1890–2; *Vigilance Record*, March 1888, p. 20; June 1890, p. 50; February 1893, p. 4.

51. *Vigilance Record*, December 1889, pp. 124, 127; November 1891, pp. 103–4; NVA, EC minutes, 29 October 1889.

52. Priscilla Bright McLaren to MGF, 6 November 1891 (FLA, box 89 vol. 1). She had seen the report in *The Times* on the same day.

53. There is a copy of her speech at M50/6/6/2, and a summary in the *ER*, 15 January 1892, pp. 36–7.

54. NVA, *Annual Report*, 1892, p. 21.

55. Appendix to *Report of the Central Conference of Women Workers* (?1892), pp. 3–12. Quotations are from pp. 6 and 11.

56. *YWCA Monthly Journal*, June 1887, pp. 114–16; September 1887, pp. 199–200; M50/5/12/1–9.

57. *Pall Mall Gazette*, 12 February 1887; Travellers' Aid Society, EC minutes, 15 March 1887 (FLA, box 201); general committee minutes, 13 May 1887 (FLA, box 202).

58. *The Times*, 24 July 1888.

59. *Vigilance Record*, November 1891, pp. 103–4; *Review of Reviews*, July 1890, pp. 21–2.

60. *The Times*, 5 December 1891. The paper's report of the case had been carried the previous day.

61. Emma Miller to MGF, 13 December 1891 (M50/2/26/20). Other relevant letters are at M50/2/26/19, 21 and 22.

62. MGF, *International Congress. The White Slave Trade: Its causes, and the best means of preventing it* (1899) (M50/5/13/1). Quotations are from pp. 2, 3, 5. She observed that Shakespeare's Laertes had had ample time to lecture Ophelia about morality until, challenged about his own, he hastily replied: 'Oh, fear me not. I stay too long' (*ibid.*, p 8).

63. MGF, *Speech . . . on the New Rules for Dealing with the Sanitary Condition of the British Army in India* [?1897] (M50/6/9). Quotations are from pp. 3, 22, 23. See also Fawcett and Turner, ch. 11.

64. Josephine Butler to Anna Maria and Mary Priestman, 4 November [1896], (Butler Letter Collection).

# CHAPTER 9

<h1 style="text-align:center">CHILDREN AND OTHERS</h1>

Between 1887 and 1889 Mrs Fawcett was a leading figure in a campaign to abolish or control the employment of children on the London stage. The campaign had its origin in her work for the National Vigilance Association, and the issue was for her one which raised moral questions of the most fundamental kind. But it also had a life of its own and involved wider questions than many of those with which the NVA was normally interested.

Late Victorian London, and to some extent other British cities, had a marked and increasing appetite for watching young children on the stage.[1] Pantomimes could last for up to four months after Christmas, and ballets and melodramas also employed children. It was difficult to estimate with any accuracy the number involved; Mrs Fawcett herself was told that it was as high as 1,000 in London, and Cardinal Manning referred to an estimate of 3,000. There were in any case enough children for private schools and 'academies' of theatrical dancing to be opened for children of school age.[2]

The rapid and uncontrolled growth of urban society had important consequences for child neglect and prostitution. The exciting and monied atmosphere of the theatre made it a source of potential abuse. It was also possible for parents who wished to do so to live off their children to an extent not otherwise possible, though there can be no doubt that Mrs Fawcett exaggerated their numbers. But it was certainly true that the education of theatrical children was in danger of neglect, at a time when the process of universal elementary education was being established against heavy odds.[3] On the other hand employment in the theatre gave children a focus of excitement and commitment which school could not hope to rival, and for every father who battened off his child's earnings there must have been many families who were able to pay the rent or improve their diet thanks to their children's theatrical employment.

The NVA's first annual report noted that its preventive sub-committee had held a conference in June 1886, chaired by Mrs Fawcett, in which the employment of children in theatres and pantomimes had been discussed.[4] In February 1887 the NVA executive agreed to support Sir John Lubbock's parliamentary bill which sought to regulate the employment of children, and to ask to give evidence to the Royal Commission on Education, which was then holding its sessions.[5] Mrs Fawcett's first substantial publication on the subject appeared the following May, when her article in the *Contemporary Review* brought it before a wider public and made her a target for the attacks of London theatre managers and their supporters.

She was at pains to point out that contrary to 'unfair misrepresentation [by] a vested interest', the desire to extend the factory acts to the theatre was not motivated by prejudice against acting. 'To object to the employment of young children upon the stage', she wrote, 'no more involves the condemnation of the theatre, than to advocate the Factory Acts involved a condemnation of calico.' Audiences liked watching children on the stage, children preferred acting to school, parents and theatre managers liked the money. None of this justified the practice. Children should not become wage-earners at the age of 4 or 5. Teachers complained that they were exhausted and learned nothing, while a minority of parents were concerned only to live 'in dissolute idleness' on their children's earnings.[6]

The article was amplified by the evidence which she gave the next month to the Royal Commission on Education, supported by her NVA colleague Charles Mitchell. She objected to the strains on the children's health, their low level of general educational attainment, theatrical apprenticeships of seven to nine years contracted at a very early age, and the fact that in some cases the children's wages ended in the public house. Pressed hard on the alleged moral danger to young girls she refused to agree that it was unreal. She advocated that the principle of the factory acts should be invoked to forbid the employment of children in theatres before they reached the age of 10. Between 10 and 13 they should be allowed to appear at afternoon performances.[7]

In view of the opprobrium which she incurred in the course of this campaign, less prolonged but no less strongly expressed than the opposition to her work for women's suffrage, it is interesting to note that the Royal Commission accepted the accuracy of her evidence and somewhat timidly endorsed her solution. They agreed that the state should step between the children and their employers, and acknowledged that 'one remedy' would be to include theatres under the factory acts.[8]

Inspired by Mrs Fawcett the NVA proceeded on two fronts, urging the London School Board to undertake prosecutions when children did not attend school and advocating the changes in the law which she and Mitchell had put before the Royal Commission. Sensing a changed public mood the board fell into line, declaring its opposition to the employment of children under 10 'for purposes of gain', sending a deputation to the Government and successfully prosecuting a number of theatrical employers.[9] Meetings were held and Mrs Fawcett wrote further articles, notably a series in *The Echo* in December 1888.[10] Like her earlier article in the *Contemporary Review* they were reprinted by the NVA as a pamphlet.

She insisted that she did not regard theatres as 'haunts of vice' or 'dens of iniquity'; she pointed out that she frequently visited them, often in the company of children and young people.[11] She stressed the danger to which young girls on the stage were subject at a time when juvenile prostitution was already a serious social problem. A 'home for fallen children' in London admitted only girls aged 12 and under. She also stressed the adverse effects on the children's health and educational attainment and, relying on information which teachers had passed on to her from school board officers, implied that one or both parents of most theatrical children drank to excess:

> Hence all the sentiment which good people so often utter, that we are so hard-hearted as to wish to take the bread out of the mouths of starving children, should be translated into the rather different statement that we wish to take the gin from the mouths of the drunken parents.[12]

Those who depended on theatres or theatrical advertising for their living, or disliked the work and expense of the school board, or who, like some of the royal commissioners, thought of the issue as one primarily involving individual liberty, were quick to take issue with Mrs Fawcett and the NVA.[13] The fact that both she and her husband had been widely known as apostles of individualism made her an easy target for accusations of cant, which many papers were not slow to deploy.[14]

One of her early opponents, though he did not criticize her by name, was Lewis Carroll, who in July 1887 defended a Brighton production of *Alice in Wonderland* in which three girls aged 7, 10 and 15 had been appearing since Christmas. All three were in 'blooming health and buoyant spirits', he wrote, adding that 'a taste for *acting* is one of the strongest passions of human nature'.[15] The articles in *The Echo* brought a reply from Mary Jeune, a prominent figure in social and political circles, and, less prominently, a supporter of women's suffrage.[16] She accused Mrs Fawcett of ignorance of theatre management and of exaggerating the moral risks to the children: 'A woman need no more be immoral because she is an actress than because she is a housemaid. Every profession has its temptations.'[17]

Augustus Harris, the famous Drury Lane impresario, had established a private elementary school for theatrical children of a type which Mrs Fawcett frequently attacked as lax and inefficient, notably in the course of a long letter to *The Times* in February 1889. Harris angrily accused her of 'wild, unfounded, and libellous' statements and referred to 'the powerful imagination of this misguided lady'.[18] *The Times* itself supported the employment of children in theatres without mentioning Mrs Fawcett, but another paper called her a 'noisy virago'.[19] Harry Furniss, the *Punch* cartoonist, drew a picture of an idyllic 'Palace of Happiness', surrounded by dancing children, menaced by a grasping ogre labelled 'school board' and a bonneted, umbrella-waving moral protestor.[20] Mrs Fawcett wrote to Furniss, acknowledging ironically his 'lifelike portrait of myself' and insisting

*Pantomime children, a partisan view, 1889.*

that she had no prejudice against the theatre, 'but I have the very strongest feeling against children being sent to work and to earn wages for the family during their early infancy'.[21]

As so often in her life persistence paid, though as so often final victory was delayed and its achievement more formal than real. The 1880s was marked by increased public concern about cruelty to children,[22] and in 1889 the Prevention of Cruelty to Children Act was passed. Its passage followed a further hard-fought correspondence in *The Times* and a theatre managers' deputation to Lord Dunraven, a sympathetic peer, which gave Augustus Harris new opportunities to denounce Mrs Fawcett's allegations as 'fabrications' and the product of her imagination.[23] Section 3 of the act prohibited the employment of children in places of amusement under the age of 7 and required individual licences from a magistrate for children of 7 to 9. Commenting on its passage the *Vigilance Record* expressed the view that without Mrs Fawcett the clause would not have passed: 'It is in great part due to her able advocacy, her untiring correspondence, and her personal interviews, that success was ensured.'[24] The Act as passed, however, abandoned a clause inserted by the House of Commons which would have forbidden employment under the age of 10. This was not achieved until the Employment of Children Act 1903. In the interval the lax attitude of magistrates to the stage employment of children aged 7 to 9 drew trenchant protests from Bernard Shaw, then a music and drama critic not known as a prude or a supporter of the NVA.[25]

It will be clear that the sympathy which Mrs Fawcett felt for wage-earning children did not extend to their parents, especially their fathers. In 1889 the first of three surveys carried out for the London School Board showed that nearly 44,000 undernourished children attended their schools, providing statistical reinforcement of claims widely publicized during the board election of 1888.[26] As with the free school issue nearly twenty years earlier Mrs Fawcett did not hesitate, and as in 1870 her chosen weapon was a letter to *The Times*. Drawing heavily on a single case she claimed that the provision of free meals by charity would discourage work and thrift, encourage a neglectful father to spend his wages at the Welsh Harp and conclude: 'There is no harm done if you do spend your wages in your own indulgences instead of buying food for your children, because kind ladies and gentlemen will feed them if you don't.'[27] In the social conditions of late Victorian London hers was a rigid and simplistic attitude which by that time had been widely abandoned by social reformers.

Mrs Fawcett's philosophy held that adult men and women, no matter how low their income, must learn to look after themselves and their families, for to assist them was to sap their greatest asset, their independence. Her concern for children was primarily to protect them where necessary from exploitation by their parents. This point of view predisposed her to sympathize with the plight of Indian girls, the victims of compulsory early marriage. Her original interest in India was probably due to Harry, who had participated in Indian issues since before his marriage and whose concern gave him the informal title of 'Member for India'.[28] Mrs Fawcett continually encouraged the education and career opportunities of Indian women, and when Philippa came of age in 1889 she and her mother gave £400, which had originally been raised in India to meet Harry's election expenses, to found two Henry Fawcett prizes for Indian female medical students.[29]

The campaign against Indian child marriage seems to have been another offshoot of her work with the NVA. It began in 1889,[30] and the following year she wrote several articles in her usual forthright fashion, asserting that child marriage was little more than slavery. Girls in some parts of India were married at the age of about 8 and transferred to their husbands' families where they were subjected to physical mistreatment which could extend to murder or result in suicide. But no political party stood to make capital out of the sufferings of little Indian girls, and in consequence the outrage which had been expressed about atrocities in Turkey, Crete or Armenia was conspicuously absent. It was said, she wrote, that it would be politically dangerous to interfere with Indian social and religious customs. This was probably true. But British rule had abolished female infanticide, suttee, slavery and immolation of human victims in religious rites. If Britain now lacked the courage to deal with child marriage 'we have lost the qualities of a governing race' and deserved to lose India to 'some other nation, with more backbone in it'.[31]

Feminism, humanity and imperialism were a remarkable but effective combination. Her campaign was successful in its immediate aim, and the age of consent was formally raised to 12 in India in 1891. Once raised, however, the law remained a dead letter.[32]

Advocates of further restrictions on women's work remained active and influential in these years, and as previously Mrs Fawcett remained one of their most vigorous opponents. In her view women had the same right to employment as men, and it was better for them to work at low wages and for long hours than to face the alternatives of prostitution or starvation. When attempts were made to add new categories of employment to those from which women were prohibited or add new restrictions to their working hours, she was a valuable asset to the opposition.[33] Angela John notes that Mrs Fawcett was among those who fought to prevent the exclusion of women from the pit-brow in Lancashire, and refers to a speech in which she declared that women pit-brow workers were cleaner than men who did similar work. She compared them with the chimney sweep who never failed to wash on Sunday whether his face was dirty or not, and added: 'She was told by those who had watched these girls at work, that it was quite picturesque to see their rosy faces shining through the coal-dust, and the labour was said to be far more healthy than that in factories.'[34]

Another group of women whose employment was controversial in the period were the women chain-makers of the Black Country, whose working conditions shocked some sections of parliamentary and public opinion and led to a colourful and long-remembered defiance of the House of Commons by the radical-socialist R.B. Cunninghame Graham.[35] She was fond of quoting a comment made to her by a chain-maker after a deputation to the Home Secretary, Henry Matthews, which she had accompanied: 'It's very hard for him, poor gentleman, to have to make the laws, and not know nothing about it.'[36] She also lobbied influential individuals in the same cause. Lord Derby, for example, wrote to her in April 1891, probably soon after the deputation: 'I always listen with respect and interest to opinions of yours', but declined to support her stand on the issue.[37] She was more successful some weeks later with the Earl of Wemyss, who agreed to oppose, though unavailingly, a clause of a factory bill which prohibited the employment of mothers for four weeks after childbirth. She and her sister Elizabeth were among the influential women whom Wemyss cited in addressing the House of Lords.[38]

Her links with the women's trade union movement weakened during this period, especially after the Women's Protective and Provident League became the Women's Trades Union League at the start of the 1890s and abandoned its opposition to protective legislation.[39] She again took the chair at annual meetings in 1884 and 1887, however, and again strongly supported the role of the unions in defending otherwise defenceless workers against their employers. She also attacked 'any kind of political or social disturbance which lessened the security of investments' because of their adverse effect on trade and hence wages, but addressing a meeting not long after Annie Besant had championed the cause of the match girls in 1888 she commented:

> It has not often been my fortune to find myself in agreement with Mrs Besant, so I the more gladly take this opportunity of saying how much working women owe to her for the courage with which she conducted the Match Strike to a successful termination.[40]

In 1886 she intervened in an industrial dispute at the Army Clothing Factory in Pimlico, where there had been bitter complaints by the women workers of wage cutting. She acted at the behest of the Government in the person of William Woodall, champion of women's suffrage and Surveyor-General of Ordnance in the brief third Gladstone ministry. Woodall told the House of Commons that she had carried out her mission both confidentially and successfully, and that her report had 'smoothed away a great many of the differences which existed'. She apparently succeeded in pleasing the women trade unionists as well, for some of the former wages were restored and the union quoted Woodall's praise in its own annual report.[41] Mrs Fawcett later recalled that she had 'acted as a sort of peace-maker'. She examined all the wages books and asked every woman worker if she was supporting any other person with her wages: 'Nearly all of them had some relatives dependent upon them.'[42]

Support for women's right to employment did not necessarily imply support for the principle of equal pay for equal work. The principle had been endorsed by the Trades Union Congress in 1888, but it was a double-edged concept, as likely to keep women out of work as to benefit them.[43] Two articles by Mrs Fawcett in the early 1890s made her position clear. The first followed Sidney Webb, who had written in the *Economic Journal* in 1891

that women and men seldom did the same work and hence seldom com-
peted against each other. Her two main points were that too few occupations were open to women, and that the law of supply and demand should
be left to determine the level of their wages. Women needed training, and
more skilled and professional occupations should be open to them. Women
domestic servants were paid more in Lancashire than in Dorset, because in
the former county they had to be tempted away from mill work. To insist
on equal pay in existing conditions was a mistake both of principle and of
tactics.[44]

The second article appeared two years later in the *Leeds Mercury*, one of a
series on 'A living wage'. She insisted that a rigid rule of equal pay would
mean that many women would find no work. She accused the factory acts
of having kept down women's wages, and strongly opposed both the proposed suppression of domestic workshops and the prohibition of married
women's employment. Again she urged the case for training and accused the
unions of wanting to keep women out of work to reduce competition.
Women needed unions of their own and also joint unions with men. But
above all they had to rely upon themselves: 'One of the worst results of the
perpetual interference by Parliament with women's work is that it under-
mines the principle of self-help, which is, in the long run, the only true
safeguard for the interests of the worker.'[45] In short, her view was that the
weakness of women's industrial position owed more to parliamentary and
union interference than to their inability to combat oppressive employers
without outside assistance.

Mrs Fawcett's most prominent intervention in women's employment
questions in the period came in 1898, when the smouldering question of
necrosis of the jaw among the women match workers of Bryant and May was
brought before the public by the radical press, especially *The Star*. In May it
carried a dramatic headline: 'They profit by phossy jaw! An Appeal to Bryant
and May shareholders'. Among the shareholders listed were noble and ecclesiastical names, and also her own.[46] The sequel was an affair in which once
again she showed herself to be an informed and merciless opponent.

Some weeks after *The Star* article Bryant and May were fined for not
notifying a case of necrosis as required by the Factory Acts. Evidence from a
factory inspector revealed that since 1893 the firm had failed to report
seventeen other cases, including six deaths.[47] At the time Mrs Fawcett was a
small shareholder of about a year's standing, disinclined, as she wrote in an
account of the affair, 'to pocket dividend warrants reeking of phosphorus'.[48]
She wrote to Gilbert Bartholomew, managing director of the firm, to
express her concern and to ask for further information. Bartholomew
invited her to visit the factory in Bow, East London, and she accepted,
prepared if necessary to make herself 'disagreeable' at the shareholders'
meeting.[49] She was favourably impressed by what she saw and by
Bartholomew's frankness in answering her questions, as she explained in a

long letter to *The Standard*. Bartholomew told her that the firm had made consistent efforts to combat necrosis, spending large sums to prevent the disease, providing medical treatment and financial compensation to sick employees. 'One great difficulty was the indifference or ignorance of the workers themselves.' She acknowledged that only an expert could say whether the firm's precautions were adequate, but she added that the factory was 'splendidly ventilated' and that the girls and women employed looked healthy, happy and robust.

She then visited a girls' club to talk to some of the Bryant and May workers, whom she found unanimous in their praise of their working conditions. Necrosis, they told her, was the consequence of not washing before eating: ' "If yer wants to 'ave it, yer can 'ave it; it's yer own fault." ' They hated having their teeth seen to and thought it a joke to deceive the doctor into thinking that they had sound teeth. Mrs Fawcett described them as 'high-spirited, healthy, boisterous girls', not shy, depressed or downtrodden, who sang as they worked.

> I told them some people wanted to forbid girls and women working at all where phosphorus was used. They expressed great indignation . . . 'Where are we to go,' they said, 'to earn the same money?' ' 'Oo's going to keep my widder mother and two little 'uns too small to work?' and so on.[50]

Her usual discernment was wholly missing from this account, marked as it was by eagerness to accept what she was told by Bartholomew and his employees, whom she was ready enough to term indifferent and ignorant in a slightly different context. What was even more distasteful was the manner in which she rounded on Canon Basil Wilberforce and the group of titled and other notables whom he recruited to publicize Bryant and May's wrongdoings and work towards the prohibition of matches containing phosphorus.[51] Mrs Fawcett had been invited to take part in a meeting which Wilberforce had intended to hold in his drawing-room until the pressure of numbers dictated otherwise. Unable to be present she sent a letter defending the firm and asked for it to be read to the meeting. Wilberforce did not do so or permit Bartholomew to be present, and from these and other episodes she concluded that he was dishonest and not to be trusted, a conclusion partly justified by his own evasive behaviour.[52] She agreed with Bartholomew's view that Wilberforce was 'unChristian, mean & contemptible', and replied that 'commercial morality' had shown itself in a favourable light when compared to 'ecclesiastical morality'. She added that the possibility of libel action should be considered by the firm.[53] No respecter of persons, she also tilted at the Duchess of Sutherland, who had taken part in Wilberforce's meeting but admitted in a private letter that she had never visited a match factory.[54]

The conclusion of Mrs Fawcett's letter to *The Standard* was a vicious attack on the 'professional philanthropist':

> The managers of the business must not be believed; it is their obvious interest to deceive. The workers must not be believed; they are too ignorant to know

what is good for them. The Shareholders must not be believed, because they care for nothing but their dividend. If you want the real truth about match girls and phosphorus poisoning you must go to fashionable drawing-rooms, in which all expressions approaching criticism have been carefully silenced, and then listen to what people have to tell you who have never been into a match factory in their lives, or whose knowledge of the subject has been largely reinforced by the imagination.[55]

The passage was not without a measure of justification. But if gullibility had been displayed it had not been limited to the Wilberforce side, who had attacked neither Mrs Fawcett nor Bryant and May with such venom. Bryant and May was a prosperous firm, its employees suffered from necrosis, and the firm had concealed the fact not once but repeatedly. It is hardly surprising that Mrs Fawcett's role in the affair has been treated with little sympathy by historians.[56]

In a further letter she asked readers to suspend judgement until the report of experts appointed by the Home Secretary in consequence of the furore raised by the case had been published.[57] It was advice which she would have done well to follow. The report appeared the following March and was severely critical of the match companies, of which Bryant and May was the largest and best known.[58] So too was an article published a few years later by one of the experts, who pointed out that use of the dangerous yellow phosphorus had slowly declined: 'English methods of manufacture, like national customs, die hard.'[59] So too did Mrs Fawcett's convictions; she was blinded by faith in self-help and belief in the importance of women's employment to the possibility that even 'professional philanthropists' were sometimes right, and that publicity often led to reform.

Her continuing efforts to improve the education of girls and women required less aggressive qualities. Much of her work in this field, like much of her later suffrage activity, was as a standard bearer in a cause in which others carried out the burdensome daily toil. It was a role which evidently pleased her as well as those who sought her assistance. In 1888, for example, she addressed the pupils at Clapham High School, where her daughter Philippa had studied, and gave the prizes to both boys and girls at an educational ceremony in Salisbury, Harry's birthplace.[60] She addressed the supporters of the blind and spoke at Toynbee Hall, the East London settlement.[61] She was a faithful friend and governor of Bedford College, London, which Philippa also attended, and on several occasions addressed student or other meetings with a wealth of historical and literary references.[62] She was a patron of the London Pupil Teachers' Association, serving as president and later vice-president of the girls' association. She was a generous friend, giving money and books, taking part in social activities and contributing articles to its journal.[63]

She was also a member of the advisory council of the women's branch of Swanley Horticultural College. She told a meeting in 1895 that she intended to become a student once women's suffrage was carried, 'in order to secure for herself a happy old age'.[64] In 1905 when a quarrel broke out at the college involving the principal, Fanny Wilkinson, Lady Frances Balfour and others, Mrs Fawcett acted as a conciliator, earning the thanks of another participant, the social worker Emma Cons: 'It is very good of you (who are always so busy) to take this matter up.'[65] She spoke in 1898 at the first conference of the Alexandra College Guild, a social and charitable organization attached to a college of higher education for women in Dublin. She was elected a vice-president and crossed the Irish Sea to speak or take part in guild activities.[66]

She also participated in education as a teacher. She returned to Queen's College to give a series of lectures on political economy in 1889.[67] From 1888 till 1891 she lectured also at the King's College Department for Ladies, and she declined an invitation to give lectures elsewhere in October 1890 because of the demands of her existing courses.[68] Among her students was Margaret Ethel Gladstone, later a prominent champion of working women, who married Ramsay MacDonald in 1896. She was to become a socialist and a strong supporter of factory legislation, and even at this stage she was not satisfied with the limitations of traditional political economy. She wrote in her journal that she found Mrs Fawcett's lectures 'very interesting; but I often want to go further to the root of the matter than she does, & to be more unorthodox.'[69] Mrs Fawcett also lectured for the university extension movement, which was founded by her old friend James Stuart, the Cambridge professor and Henry Fawcett's successor as Liberal MP for Hackney, and took part in at least one of its summer schools.[70] In addition she was a friend of adult education colleges in London. She had been a supporter of the College for Working Women since the 1870s, and by the 1890s was associated with the mixed-sex Working Men's College, where she lectured occasionally and was a sponsor of the building appeal.[71]

It was Stuart who was responsible a few years later for awarding her an honorary doctorate of laws at the University of St Andrews, to which he was appointed rector in 1898. He wrote to her at the end of the year, saying that he hoped she would accept the award since he was particularly anxious to nominate a woman.[72] The award, one of the first to a woman, was made specifically for her services to education and was greeted jubilantly by the leaders of the women's movement.[73] Her close friend Dr Jane Walker made the long journey to St Andrews with Agnes Garrett, and wrote gleefully to Philippa that *The Times* had reported only the speech honouring Mrs Fawcett and ignored the other recipients. The award was a moving occasion:

> When Millie's turn came the students all got up and cheered tremendously and waved their caps in the air, and the rest of the audience got up and cheered. Both Agnes and I had big lumps in our throats, we felt so proud and happy.[74]

For the next quarter of a century, until she was made a Dame, she was to be known as 'Mrs Henry Fawcett, LL. D.'

One intimate who did not make the journey was her sister Elizabeth. James Stuart had been a leading participant in the struggle against the Contagious Diseases Acts and the fight for an equal moral standard with which Mrs Fawcett was belatedly but closely associated.[75] Elizabeth had not been a supporter of the movement, and a letter to her mother showed no weakening of the Garrett grasp of moral principle:

> The particular work which Mr Stuart and Milly shared is not one wh. we think useful, so that there would be a kind of insincerity in our being there. We must be content to differ on a good many points, and it is no good trying to pretend that there are no differences when there are in fact important ones.[76]

Mrs Fawcett's strongest educational loyalty, however, still lay with Cambridge. Despite her Newnham affiliations she had no objection on principle to working with Girton supporters, and her name was suggested as mistress of Girton soon after the death of Henry Fawcett in 1884.[77] According to Emily Davies it was a reference in one of her speeches, probably to the Bedford College students in October 1886, which inspired the abortive attempt in 1887 to secure degrees for women at Cambridge. The two women worked together in lobbying activities, apparently without friction.[78]

The attempt was bolstered by the fact that in the 1887 examinations Agnata Ramsay was the only candidate to win a first class in the classics tripos. Three years later an even greater triumph was recorded when Philippa Fawcett finished 'above the senior wrangler' in the mathematics tripos. This famous examination result occasioned the greatest celebration which the women's movement had ever known. The success was particularly prized because the movement was small and intellectually biased, because success in mathematics was regarded as specially important and because the candidate was Philippa Fawcett. Soon after the result was announced Mrs Fawcett herself was publicly congratulated and loudly cheered when she attended one meeting, and enthusiastically embraced at another.[79] The moving chapter in her autobiography[80] may be supplemented by the abundant press reports and by unpublished letters of congratulation. Clara, Lady Rayleigh, wrote: 'It quite makes one feel that things are opening out to our sex & it reflects glory on us all!'[81] Elizabeth's daughter Louisa wrote to her mother from her school in Scotland: 'Oh! It is too lovely about Philippa! Too utterly lovely.' The sentiment was shared throughout the school.[82] An incomplete letter from Mrs Fawcett to her father described a visit which Agnes had paid to an elderly man who may have been George Frederick Watts the painter. He had 'talked of nothing else for days when he first heard about it. He said to Agnes "And I hear she is so good too, & *makes her own frocks!*" '[83]

The cheers of the Cambridge undergraduates for Philippa, however sincere, had no positive consequences and may, as Rita McWilliams-Tullberg suggests, have led to a new male hostility to women students.[84] In any event, when a new and stronger movement for degrees for women at Cambridge came to a head in 1897 the cheers of 1890 had long since died away. The new movement began late in 1895 and Mrs Fawcett again played an important part. After a resolution by the Associates of Newnham College, an elected body of former students and tutors, to campaign for degrees and membership of the university for women, a meeting of the college council was held on 16 November. Mrs Fawcett's successful resolution 'received with pleasure' the Associates' resolution and accepted its views. She then moved, originally as an amendment, the decisive resolution to confer with members of the Girton council and the university senate, with the aim of choosing a suitable time to apply to admit women to university membership and degrees.[85]

The campaign which followed was arduous, complicated and unsuccessful, culminating in a crushing defeat, by 1,713 votes to 662, in May 1897.[86] It was not the result of her inactivity, for she lobbied hard, sometimes with amusing or revealing results. A don, W.G. Adams, recalled a colleague who had told him many years previously of his opposition to examining women candidates, before announcing: ' "My best man is Ogle"!!', unaware that the 'man' in question was a Newnham woman. Lord Farrer, another supporter, told her that at a recent dinner at Trinity College his host had argued against degrees for women 'on the loftiest philosophical grounds', only to be betrayed by his colleagues, who admitted that 'if they gave women degrees they must give them fellowships of which there were not enough for the men'.[87] But there remained, as she pointed out shortly before the decisive vote, the problem of 'a deep-rooted belief . . . in the intellectual inferiority of women'.[88]

The defeat, paralleling an earlier though less bitter battle at Oxford in which Mrs Fawcett had also taken part, was a severe blow and she did not attempt to disguise it.[89] But it was possible to ward off even greater disaster. Some of the women's opponents proposed to drive them out of Oxford and Cambridge altogether and establish a women's university, perhaps based on Royal Holloway College, Egham, and such other colleges as might wish to join it. At a conference held in December 1897 she declared herself 'uncompromisingly hostile' to the proposal. It would be 'the height of folly', she asserted, for women to surrender their position at Oxford and Cambridge, where they possessed 'important privileges . . . in favour of some fancy scheme the merits of which yet remain to be proved'. Her speech was received with 'loud applause' and expressed the general view of women in education and their male allies.[90] Satisfied with their resounding victory at Cambridge the opponents did not press the point and little more was heard of the women's university.

It is hardly possible to deal with the full range of Mrs Fawcett's activities in this period, which included a trenchant, knowledgeable attack on compulsory vaccination, gratefully reprinted and long remembered by the anti-vaccinationists. Better England pockmarked than devoid of personal independence, she wrote.[91] An aspect of medicine in which she was more closely involved was an ambitious venture in which she collaborated with her friend Jane Walker. This was an open-air sanatorium administered by women for tubercular patients of both sexes at East Nayland, Suffolk. The record of the East Anglian Sanatorium Company, later the Jane Walker Hospital, show that Mrs Fawcett played an active role in establishing the sanatorium in 1899 and was an early shareholder.[92] She became the leaseholder of the site and was chairman of its three separate hospital institutions until nearly the end of her life. The first building was opened in 1901, and when a department for the poor was established in 1904 she appealed to the public for financial support. She told the writer Sidney Lee: 'The sanatorium is very much needed. The poor patients flowed in even before we could get the workmen out of the place.'[93] In the years before 1914 the demands of the suffrage campaign reduced the commitment of time which she could give to the hospital, but she remained chairman and her interest in its activities was unbroken.[94]

She also retained a continuing, though less than wholehearted interest in local government. The passage of the bill in 1888 to create powerful elected county and county borough councils and the doubt about women's eligibility to serve on them led to the formation of the body which in 1893 took the title Women's Local Government Society.[95] In November 1888 the National Vigilance Association's preventive committee resolved to ask Mrs Fawcett to stand for election to the new London County Council, and 'failing her some other suitable ladies'. She was also asked to stand by a group of women concerned with local government.[96] She refused, as she had already declined a new opportunity to contest a school board seat, and as she rejected offers to contest elections outside the women's movement throughout her life.[97] In 1894 she and Agnes also refused to join the WLGS committee, and it was not until the unsuccessful struggle to secure a place for women as councillors on the new London metropolitan boroughs in 1899 that she came into closer contact with the society.[98]

After chairing a conference for the WLGS on women's role in London local government she agreed in January 1900 to become the society's treasurer. She made clear that she lacked the time to be an active officer, but she offered her name and her attendance at annual meetings and was accepted on this basis.[99] Three years later, however, she resigned over the society's opposition to the Education Act of 1902. The act aimed to establish an efficient system of administration in which elementary and secondary education were strictly separated, putting an end to attempts to develop an informal system of quasi-secondary education. It gave rate aid to church schools and, against Liberal, trade union and some feminist opposition abolished the school boards in England and Wales, thus depriving women of an important position in local government. Mrs Fawcett was at this time a Liberal Unionist and a government supporter, and like Lady Frances Balfour, also a Liberal Unionist, she endorsed this major piece of Unionist legislation.[100] It was a rare case in which she put party considerations before the interests of women.[101]

She did not resign her membership of the society, however, and was a speaker at a dinner which it held in December 1903.[102] Two years later she chaired a more ambitious WLGS dinner attended by 350 people, and delivered a speech full of fire and wit. She encouraged the civic patriotism of both sexes and praised the work which women had carried out on school boards and as poor law guardians. Victor Hugo had said that the great discovery of the nineteenth century had been woman, but the discovery had been withheld from many local councils. Quoting Hamlet's 'What a piece of work is a man!' she remarked that he was too often prone to forget the existence of woman: 'He is all the better for keeping an eye on him. If he is left quite alone, he fancies he is alone.'[103]

Mrs Fawcett was primarily concerned to make women's demands seen and heard in public. She did not, however, ignore individual cases in which she could intervene privately, such as that of her neighbour Louisa Wilkinson. She was a bookbinder, excluded because of her alleged amateur status from classes at the Central School of Arts and Crafts, although as a woman she had little opportunity to secure any other status. Mrs Fawcett's intervention was unsuccessful, though it forced the London County Council's Technical Education Board to undertake an elaborate exercise in self-justification.[104] The case, small in itself, illustrated the problems faced by women seeking places in male-dominated occupations and the reforms which, if elected to positions in local government, they might have been able to bring about on behalf of their sex. It also demonstrated the range of Mrs Fawcett's activities. The enemy was a hydra-headed monster, to be fought wherever it was found.

### NOTES

1. See Tracy C. Davis, 'The employment of children in the Victorian theatre', *New Theatre Quarterly* (vol. 2, 1986), pp. 116–35. I owe this reference to Don Roy.
2. *Third Report* of the Royal Commission on Education (P.P. 1887, vol. XXX, C. 5158), pp. 305–15 (MGF's evidence). Davis suggests a nationwide total of nearly 5,000 child actors in the 1880s (p. 117).
3. David Rubinstein, *School Attendance in London* (1969), esp. p. 63.
4. NVA, *Annual Report*, 1887, p. 15.
5. NVA, EC minutes, 22 February 1887 (FLA, box 194).

6. MGF, 'Holes in the education net', *Contemporary Review*, May 1887, pp. 639–53. The quotations are from pp. 647–8. Both Percy Bunting, the journal's editor, and his wife Mary were leading figures in the NVA.

7. C. 5158 (note 2 above), especially qs 50,431–2, 50,435, 50,441, 50,451, 50,454, 50,479–86, 50,529–31.

8. *Final Report* of the Royal Commission on Education; P.P. 1888, vol. XXXV, C. 5485, p. 110.

9. *Vigilance Record*, February 1889, pp. 6–7; *The Times*, 6 February 1889; School Board for London, *Minutes*, 17 January, 7 February, 21 March, 11 April 1889; School Board for London, *Annual Report*, 1888–9, pp. 32–3.

10. *The Echo*, 10, 12, 15, 18 December 1888.

11. *ibid.*, 10 December 1888. She allowed herself in her 15 December article, however, to refer to 'the low tone of stage morals'.

12. *Vigilance Record*, November 1888, p. 110; *The Echo*, 12 December 1888 (from which the quotation is drawn).

13. Rubinstein, ch. 5; C. 5158 (note 2 above), q. 50,693 and MGF's evidence, *passim*.

14. C. 5158, q. 50,518.

15. *St James's Gazette*, 19 July 1887.

16. Lady St Helier, *Memories of Fifty Years* (1909), pp. 343–5; MGF to Mary (later Lady) Jeune (subsequently Lady St Helier), 18 July 1889 (Yale University Archives).

17. Mary Jeune, 'Children in theatres', *English Illustrated*, October 1889, pp. 6–14. The quotation is from p. 13. Mrs Fawcett replied to this article: 'The employment of children in theatres', *Contemporary Review*, December 1889, pp. 822–9; and 'Theatre children', *Sunday Magazine*, February 1890, pp. 124–8.

18. *The Times*, 5, 7 February 1889.

19. *ibid.*, 4 February 1889; unidentified paper quoted in *Review of Reviews*, July 1890, p. 20.

20. *Punch*, 16 February 1889, p. 83. See illustration no. 4.

21. MGF to Harry Furniss, 22 February 1889; quoted by Furniss in *Some Victorian Women* (John Lane the Bodley Head, 1923), p. 117. Pointing out that he and Mrs Fawcett disagreed about 'politics and other things', he wrote of her as 'a very brilliant conversationalist and extremely witty' (p. 116).

22. Ivy Pinchbeck and Margaret Hewitt, *Children in English Society*, vol. 2 (Routledge & Keegan Paul, 1973), pp. 621–9.

23. *The Times*, 18 and 19 July (MGF), 18 July (deputation), 20 July (Harris), 30 July (Benjamin Waugh of the NSPCC), 5 August 1889 (Mary Jeune), etc.

24. *Vigilance Record*, September 1889, p. 85.

25. *The Works of Bernard Shaw* (Constable, 1931), vols 25, pp. 297–8, 395–7; 26, pp. 58–60, 132. See also Davis, pp. 131–4.

26. Rubinstein, pp. 81–3; *idem*, 'Annie Besant and Stewart Headlam: the London School Board election of 1888', *East London Papers* (vol. 13, 1970), pp. 3–24.

27. *The Times*, 21 December 1889. See also *ibid.*, 11 October 1890.

28. Leslie Stephen, *Life of Henry Fawcett* (1885), p. 341 and ch. 8; *MGF*, p. 356.

29. *MGF*, pp. 86, 163, 336; *The Times*, 8 June 1889; *Cabinet Portrait Gallery* (?May 1890), p. 68; Cornelia Sorabji to MGF, 6 July 1899, 6 August 1904 (FLA, box 90 vol. 4).

30. *Vigilance Record*, December 1889, pp. 124–5, 128.

31. MGF, 'Infant marriage in India', *ibid.*, January 1890, pp. 138–9; 'Infant marriage in India', *Contemporary Review*, November 1890, pp. 712–20; 'Indian child marriage', *New Review*, November 1890, pp. 450–4 (quotations, p. 452).

32. Katherine Mayo, *Volume Two* (New York: Harcourt Brace, 1931), esp. chs 1, 6, 7; Eleanor Rathbone, *Child Marriage: The Indian minotaur* (Allen & Unwin, 1934), pp. 17–20.

33. For the background see Rosemary Feurer 'The meaning of "sisterhood"' (ch. 3, note 29 above); David Rubinstein, *Before the Suffragettes* (1986), ch. 8.

34. Angela John, *By the Sweat of Their Brow* (Routledge & Kegan Paul, 1984 edn), pp. 148, 150; *WSJ*, 1 May 1886, p. 63.

35. *Parl. Deb.*, 3rd ser., 331, cols 732–4 (1 December 1888). 'I never withdraw', he declared.

36. Quoted in Rubinstein, *Before The Suffragettes*, pp. 113, 130 n. 11.

37. Derby to MGF, 24 April 1891 (FLALC, vol. 2b).

38. Carol Dyhouse, *Feminism and the Family in England 1880–1939* (1989), pp. 81–2.

39. See James Schmiechen, *Sweated Industries and Sweated Labor* (Urbana: University of Illinois Press, 1984), pp. 150–1.

40. *Women's Union Journal*, July 1884, pp. 59–60; 15 December 1887, pp. 91–2; *Women's Penny Paper*, 2 February 1889, p. 6.

41. *Parl. Deb.*, 3rd ser., 302, col. 1222 (25 February 1886); 308, cols 1449–50 (6 September 1886); Women's Protective and Provident League, *Twelfth Annual Report*, 16 November 1886, pp. 2–3.

42. *Women's Penny Paper*, 2 February 1889, p. 6.

43. *Report of the Twenty-First Annual Trades Union Congress* (?1889), p. 43; Rubinstein, *Before the Suffragettes*, pp. 103–5. The TUC resolution had been moved by Clementina Black on behalf of a group of women's trade unions.

44. MGF, 'Mr Sidney Webb's article on women's wages', *Economic Journal*, March 1892, pp. 173–6.

45. *Leeds Mercury*, 8 May 1894. See also her review of Ramsay MacDonald (ed.), *Women in the Printing Trades, Economic Journal*, June 1904, pp. 295–9.

46. *The Star*, 5 May 1898. Most of the material relating to the Bryant and May controversy is contained in the file M50/4/22/1–51. See also Lowell Satre's excellent article, 'After the match girls' strike: Bryant and May in the 1890s', *Victorian Studies* (vol. 26, 1982), pp. 7–31.

47. Satre, p. 24; *The Times*, 2 June 1898.

48. *The Times*, 27 July 1898; 'A shareholder in pursuit of the truth, a chapter of autobiography', incomplete narrative (M50/4/22/51).

49. M50/4/22/51.

50. *The Standard*, 23 July 1898.

51. *Daily Chronicle*, 12 July 1898.

52. M50/4/22/16, 18, 26, 38, 39, etc.

53. Bartholomew to MGF, 23 July 1898; MGF to Bartholomew (draft), 27 July 1898 (M50/4/22/46, 50).

54. Millicent, Duchess of Sutherland, to MGF, 16 July 1898, M50/4/22/30.

55. *The Standard*, 23 July 1898.

56. Marian Ramelson, *The Petticoat Rebellion* (1967), pp. 106–7; Sheila Lewenhak, *Women and Trade Unions* (Benn, 1977), p. 74.

57. *The Times*, 27 July 1898.

58. *Reports . . . on the use of Phosphorus in the Manufacture of Lucifer Matches*, P.P. 1899, vol. XII, C. 9188, esp. pp. 15–16, 96; *The Times*, 17, 29 March 1898; Satre (note 46 above), pp. 11, 27–8.

59. Thomas Oliver, 'Phosphorus and lucifer matches', in *idem* (ed.), *Dangerous Trades* (Murray, 1902), pp. 417–33. The quotation is from p. 432.

60. MGF, 'Altissima Peto', *Time*, May 1888, pp. 528–32; *Salisbury and Winchester Journal*, 9 June 1888.

61. *Pall Mall Gazette*, 29 March 1886; *The Times*, 11 October 1886, 14 March, 26 November 1888, 27 March 1889.
62. *The Times*, 14 October 1886, 8 October 1897, 24 June 1899. The first address was published in the *Contemporary Review*, November 1886, pp. 719–27.
63. M50/4/8/1–4; *London Pupil Teachers' Association Record*, 1896–1907 *passim*.
64. *ER*, 15 July 1895, p. 176.
65. Emma Cons to MGF, 26 February 1905 (FLALC, vol. 4b). Adjacent letters in the same file are also relevant.
66. *Alexandra College Magazine*, June 1898, pp. 255–7, 275–7; June 1904, pp. 3–9 and *passim*; *ER*, 15 July 1904, pp. 191–2; *CC*, 29 May 1914, p. 163.
67. Queen's College *Prospectus*, July 1889, p. 5.
68. King's College Department for Ladies, EC minutes, 1 and 8 June 1888; King's College *Calendar*, 1888–9, pp. 341–3 (kindly supplied by Jane Platt of King's College London); *ER*, 15 July 1891, pp. 159–60; MGF to 'Dear Sir', 31 October [1890] (Holborn Public Library).
69. Margaret Gladstone journal, 4 March 1891 (MacDonald Papers, PRO); J. Ramsay MacDonald, *Margaret Ethel MacDonald* (Hodder & Stoughton, 1912), p. 80.
70. *The Times*, 11 October 1890, 3 August 1893; *WIR*, pp. 74–6.
71. *Journal, Annual Reports*, and correspondence of the Working Men's College, 1894–7 (I am grateful for the assistance of staff of the college); June Purvis, *Hard Lessons* (Cambridge: Polity Press, 1989), pp. 174, 213.
72. James Stuart to MGF, 17 December 1898 (FLALC, vol. 8c).
73. Helen Blackburn to MGF, 3 January 1899 (*ibid.*); Elizabeth Blackwell to MGF, 21 January 1899 (*ibid.*).
74. *MGF*, pp. 182–3; *The Times*, 24 January 1899.
75. Her obituary tribute to Stuart was published in the *CC*, 28 November 1913, p. 612.
76. Elizabeth Garrett Anderson to Louisa Garrett, 7 January 1899 (Anderson Papers, St Brelade).
77. *MGF*, pp. 106–7. The Girton archives contain no record of the proposal.
78. M50/3/1–4; Barbara Stephen, *Emily Davies and Girton College* (1927), p. 328; Rita McWilliams-Tullberg, *Women at Cambridge* (1975), pp. 91–2.
79. *The Times*, 12 June 1890; Frances Balfour, *Ne Obliviscaris*, vol. 2 [1930], p. 120.
80. *WIR*, ch. 15.
81. Clara E.L. Rayleigh to MGF, 17 June 189[0] (1896 written in error); M50/3/1/28.
82. Louisa Garrett Anderson to Elizabeth Garrett Anderson, 8 [June] (May written in error) 1890 (Anderson Papers).
83. MGF to Newson Garrett [1890] (*ibid.*).
84. McWilliams-Tullberg, p. 102.
85. Minutes of Newnham College Council, 16 November 1895; McWilliams-Tullberg, pp. 109–10. Mrs Fawcett's own account of this incident is at M50/3/1/7.
86. McWilliams-Tullberg, ch. 8.
87. Adams to MGF, 7 February 1896; Farrer to MGF, 11 February 1896 (M50/3/1/20, 21). Amy Ogle secured a first in Natural Sciences in 1876.
88. *Westminster Gazette*, 17 May 1897.
89. *MGF*, p. 167; A.V. Dicey to MGF, 11 February 1896 (M50/3/1/22); MGF, 'Degrees for women at Oxford', *Contemporary Review*, March 1896, pp. 347–56. She had publicly supported the case for women taking examinations at Oxford as early as 1884 (*Daily News*, 26 April 1884).
90. *University Degrees for Women* (M50/3/3/23), pp. 31–3; *The Times*, 6 December 1897.

91. MGF, 'The Vaccination Act of 1898', *Contemporary Review*, March 1899, pp. 328–42; obituary notice in *Vaccination Inquirer*, 2 September 1929 (copy in Fawcett Library).

92. Records of the Jane Walker Hospital, Suffolk Record Office, Bury St Edmunds. Her family and friends were also induced to buy shares.

93. *The Times*, 29 June 1904; MGF to Sidney Lee, 29 October [?1904] (Lee Correspondence, Bodleian Library).

94. *MGF*, pp. 171, 224; Maltings Farm Sanatorium *Report*, 1 October 1910–31 December 1912, p. 3 (Jane Walker Hospital Records).

95. Patricia Hollis, *Ladies Elect* (1987), pp. 306–7.

96. NVA, EC minutes, 6 November 1888; *ER*, 15 November 1888, p. 508.

97. *The Times*, 13, 14 October 1885.

98. WLGS, EC minutes, 18 January, 15 February 1894; 12 June 1899 (GLRO).

99. *ibid.*, 23 June 1899 and inserted conference report 19 July 1899; 23 March 1900; sub-committee minutes, 23 January 1900.

100. *ibid.*, 12 February 1901, 10 April 1902, 7 April 1903; EC minutes, 17 February 1903.

101. See Hollis, p. 328.

102. WLGS, *Report to Eleventh Annual Meeting*, 1904, p. 22.

103. WLGS, *Report to Thirteenth Annual Meeting*, 1906, pp. 19–20; WLGS leaflet, *Speech by Mrs Henry Fawcett*, 29 November 1905 (GLRO).

104. *Minutes* of London County Council Technical Education Board, 6 February 1899 (*ibid.*). The case is discussed in Anthea Callen, *Angel in the Studio* (Astragal Books, 1979), pp. 189–91. A further letter from Mrs Fawcett to Frank, Lord Russell, dated 6 January 1899, is in the Bertrand Russell Papers, McMaster University. I am grateful to Godfrey Rubens for assistance with this case.

# CHAPTER 10

——————— · ———————

## PROTECTING THE EMPIRE

Her love of country was one of Mrs Fawcett's strongest and most enduring passions, equalled only by the emotions aroused by the struggle against sexual exploitation of women. Her fervent patriotism stood in sharp contrast to her shifting party political allegiance. Isolating her political beliefs is difficult, and it is not surprising that historians have been unable to fit her into a neat category. Schooled in Liberalism, she retained a strong but critical attachment to the Liberal party for twenty years. For nearly as long she was a Liberal Unionist, her beliefs barely distinguishable from Conservatism. Thereafter non-party, she worked closely with the Labour party in the period before the outbreak of war in 1914, when new conditions called forth new alliances.

There was no such variation in her patriotism. It was in a sense curious that so committed a feminist should have been so passionate a patriot. Britain was a country in which poverty often reached the level of destitution, in which working women were more vulnerable than any other group. Sexual exploitation of girls and women was common and horrifying, as Mrs Fawcett herself did much to show. Politicians protested their support for women's aspirations while destroying suffrage bills by shady tricks of parliamentary procedure. British institutions and policies were man-made, claiming, one might suppose, only a qualified allegiance from feminists.

Convictions are complex, patriotism more than most. Whatever it may have owed to her Suffolk upbringing or her pride in recent English achievements,[1] her belief in a personified England was uncomplicated and unquestioned. It had its first opportunity to express itself publicly in the new political situation created by the general election of 1885. Though the Liberals had a large lead they did not have an outright majority, and the Irish nationalists were greatly strengthened by the votes of the male agricultural labourers enfranchised in 1884. It was in these circumstances that Gladstone made known his conversion to Irish Home Rule. This development was widely assumed to owe more to expediency than conviction, and Mrs Fawcett was from the first a bitter and effective opponent.

115

In our own day the apparently insoluble question of Ulster with its attendant tragedies may well lead to the wish that Gladstone had been able to 'solve the Irish problem' a century ago. It is now so generally accepted that the independence of at least the bulk of Ireland from British rule was inevitable, just and belated that it is an effort to think ourselves into a period when it was widely regarded as repugnant, even immoral, by wide sections of educated opinion.[2] So far as Mrs Fawcett was concerned there were four reasons to oppose Home Rule. The first was the strong links which had been built up over the centuries between the two islands, a process which she looked on as England's civilizing mission and a sensible imperialism of mutual benefit to England and Ireland alike.

The second was that a measure of devolved government would have been to reward the violence which had marked Irish history, particularly since the formation of the Land League in 1879 and the rise of Charles Stewart Parnell, the most dynamic and effective leader whom Ireland had produced for many years. She was convinced that it was better to rule Ireland by force than to surrender to force. In this view she was typical of much middle-class opinion, as also in believing that Catholic Ireland was in general idle, priest-ridden and shiftless. Ancient hostility, prejudice and stereotyped thinking had not lost their force. Finally, her distrust of Gladstone, one of her strongest political sentiments, reinforced her opposition to a policy which in any case she thought wholly misguided.

In November 1885 she voted for the Liberal candidates for her division of the London School Board, probably the first votes she had cast.[3] It was one of her last acts as a loyal Liberal. The following June, when the fate of the first Irish Home Rule bill was about to be decided by the House of Commons, she wrote to *The Times*, quoting from Henry Fawcett's speeches in an effort to show that if he had been alive he would have strongly opposed Home Rule. He had tried to 'approach the Irish question and other political questions', she wrote, 'in a broad and national spirit, unprejudiced by party'.[4] Though one may accept this statement at less than face value, there is no doubt that Harry opposed Home Rule until his death.[5] It is highly probable that he would have continued to do so even in the changed conditions of 1885–6, but it is doubtful whether a man of such strong radical convictions would, like his wife, have allowed himself to sever irrevocably his ties with the Liberal party.

The earlier years of the 1880s were marked by the establishment in a number of towns of women's Liberal associations, leading to the formation of the Women's Liberal Federation at a meeting held early in 1887.[6] Mrs Fawcett refused to let her name go forward for election to the WLF executive, citing her dislike of party politics.[7] Her break with Liberalism, however, did not follow immediately. She addressed gatherings of women Liberals in Wolverhampton and Peckham in March 1887, urging the Wolverhampton women to support Liberal principles rather than the party itself 'through thick and thin'. Such behaviour would be 'creditable to their good sense of patriotism'.[8] Soon afterwards, however, she declined an invitation to attend a meeting of women in Hackney called to protest an Irish 'coercion' (or Crimes) bill, telling the organizers (and the readers of *The Times*): 'I am one of those who think that those who kill or shoot their neighbours, maim cattle, cut off the hair of girls and pour tar over their heads ought to be punished whether they live in Ireland or in England.'[9] In an article published the following August she was still calling for the Irish problem to be resolved outside party lines by a national body which should have for its aim 'the Unity of the Empire'.[10]

A non-party solution to the leading political controversy of the day was not possible, and in May 1888 the first meeting of Liberal Unionist women was held at the home of Kate Courtney, sister of Beatrice Potter (later Webb). Her husband Leonard had been a close friend and ally of Henry Fawcett, and was in a sense his political heir.[11] Some husbands had forbidden their wives to attend the meeting, but a committee was successfully formed. Mrs Fawcett was from the start one of its most reliable members.[12] In July she spoke at the first general meeting of sympathizers held in the West End drawing room of Lady Stanley of Alderley; Kate Courtney thought that her speech was one of the best.[13] Home Rule, she said, was a moral question and as such a women's question. Enduring political institutions could not be built on crime. If women believed that Home Rule would bring peace, goodwill and prosperity to Ireland, she commented in a revealing passage, many of them would be willing to grant it, 'notwithstanding that we might also believe that it would be a blow to the greatness and prosperity of England'. But Home Rule would be a disaster to Ireland itself.[14]

Kate Courtney became the Women's Liberal Unionist Association's hard-pressed secretary. In that office she had to deal with a variety of political and personal problems, and relied heavily on Mrs Fawcett's experience, ability to calm passions and willingness to assume the burden of the secretaryship at moments of crisis.[15] She spent several days helping Leonard's election campaign in Bodmin in 1886 and 1892, and a week in 1895. Kate recorded of the 1895 election that she was 'liked & asked for everywhere – a real good friend!'[16] The following year Leonard's failing eyesight became apparent, and Mrs Fawcett wrote Kate a kindly and tactful letter, offering comfort based on Harry's experience. She also sent Leonard a book on the Oxford reformers which Kate read to him, and went out of her way to befriend the Courtneys when they were in Germany at the same time: 'Mrs F. taking up her abode in lodgings close to,' Kate recorded, 'ready to read & do anything else kind & helpful.'[17] When in 1899 Kate's opposition to the war in South Africa led to her resignation from the WLUA committee, Mrs Fawcett did her best to minimize the breach and soothe her feelings.[18] It is clear that though, as her colleague Frances Balfour wrote, Mrs Fawcett was in favour of the WLUA pursuing 'a bold policy',[19] her humour and competence were major factors in holding the organization together until the crisis in 1903 over free trade which led to her resignation.

As in other spheres, however, her most valuable role as a Unionist was as a standard bearer for women opposed to Home Rule. After her death T.P. O'Connor, one of the most colourful of Irish nationalists, recalled her as 'more bitter and more tenacious against Home Rule than even the original Tory . . . She was virulent in her attacks on my unfortunate party and policy.'[20] It was typical but unhelpful to the women's suffrage cause that her speeches and published letters failed to look forward to a time when the large Irish parliamentary group might be the difference between victory and defeat on the issue.

Her speeches were as intemperate as any she ever made except on other occasions when her outraged sense of patriotism was involved. In September 1888 she was the only woman speaker at a Liberal Unionist meeting in Nottingham. The Irish question, she insisted, was one of character, on which rested the greatness of a nation. The Irish had 'many attractive and charming qualities', but they made heroes and patriots of men who bore false witness against their neighbours and did not pay their debts. The concessions won by Irish tenants were not based on skill or honesty but on political agitation. These concessions had tended to 'weaken in the Irish character that which was already weak – I mean the honesty, the industry, the self-reliance, upon which alone any permanent economic well-being must be founded'.[21]

The speeches continued relentlessly. She told a WLUA meeting in London in 1889:

> The question before them was one of life and death both for England and Ireland, for it would be a disgrace to England if a surrender were made to those anarchical people who would favour the severing of the two countries. If that should ever come to pass England would never be the same, either in power or influence.[22]

Two years later, again in Nottingham, she said that there was little comfort to be found in either of the two parties into which Irish nationalism had by that time divided. One 'embodied the red spectre of revolution', while the other represented 'the black spectre of priestly domination'. Hatred of England was the dominant sentiment of both.[23] The speeches were highly effective; the Earl of Derby said in what was taken as a reference to Mrs Fawcett that one of the best speeches he had ever heard on the Irish question had been delivered by a woman.[24] Philippa followed where her mother led, taking office as Home Secretary in 1888 in a Liberal Unionist 'government' at Newnham, and in 1893 making an attack on Home Rule the occasion of her first public speech.[25]

Mrs Fawcett's selective perception of morality was not restricted to the public platform. In February 1890 a special commission appointed by the

Government and composed of Unionists vindicated Parnell of the charges of support for nationalist murders alleged in forged letters purchased by *The Times*. This was widely regarded as a striking victory and an enormous moral boost for the Home Rule cause.[26] Mrs Fawcett, however, seized on the commission's denunciation of the incitements to intimidation of which they found the nationalist party guilty. The report proved, she told her mother, 'Parnellism to have been a criminal conspiracy, based on hatred of England, financed by the advocates of dynamite & assassination in the U.S.A. and aiming ultimately at complete separation from England'.[27] It is easy to discern in this letter and elsewhere the sentiment that 'hatred of England' was, if not the greatest crime, at least the root of the evil.

By the beginning of the 1890s she was in considerable demand as a speaker on Unionist platforms. She made clear, however, that she was not prepared to speak for candidates who did not support women's suffrage.[28] W.R. Bousfield, the Conservative candidate in a by-election in 1892, assured her of his support and asked her to address his meetings in Hackney: 'Personally I shall consider your assistance as a privilege & an honour.' Mrs Fawcett spoke twice for him and received a letter of thanks couched in similarly obsequious terms.[29] Invited to address a WLUA meeting in Birmingham in 1892 she was asked not to raise the suffrage question since it was a divisive issue among Unionists. She replied, refusing to give an undertaking: 'If others take the opportunity of speaking against it, I shall show my dissent from their views.'[30] She took the same line in a letter to the *Liberal Unionist*, which she accused of making use of women's political work while denying them the right to a political voice.[31] Enough candidates satisfied her criteria at the general election of 1892, however, for her to support Unionists in Cambridge, where an earlier meeting of hers had been broken up by angry Liberals, as well as London, Sheffield, Suffolk and her Cornish expedition to assist Leonard Courtney.[32]

Her Unionist activities, which included repeated visits to Ireland, drove Mrs Fawcett, like most other Liberal Unionists, sharply to the political right. She was a repeated and scathing critic of Gladstone, whose political morality, she alleged, was based on arithmetic, the search for enough votes to put him into office.[33] In 1890 she manifested her support for the financial and foreign policies of the Unionist Government, and when in 1891 the WLUA met to consider the moderate version of socialism expressed in *Fabian Essays* it was Mrs Fawcett who was reported as specially concerned with the question of private property.[34]

A few months later she attacked the 'socialist microbe' which had manifested itself in Ireland as Home Rule, in England as the new trade unionism. 'As lovers of their country' Liberal Unionists must support 'a firm and righteous government' as well as working to remove just grounds of complaint.[35] Her arguments for women's suffrage in the decade after 1886, to be considered in the next chapter, were often couched in terms of women's support for policies of order and stability. Home Rule declined as a crucial issue with the fall of the Liberals in 1895 and Gladstone's retirement, but it is fair to say that in this period she was as closely and influentially identified with Conservative policies as she had ever been with Liberal ones.

The place of Home Rule in political life was taken by the equally dramatic issue of South Africa, an issue with which Mrs Fawcett was again to be heavily involved. Queen Victoria's diamond jubilee in 1897 came in good time to keep patriotic fervour at a high pitch, and Agnes, Millicent and Philippa were enthusiastic participants. Their cousin Edmund Garrett wrote from Cape Town on the day after the celebrations, correctly assuming that 'no people wd take keener delight in the tributes to our Queen, & our national sense of pride & unity, than my own dear people in Gower Street'.[36] Millicent wrote a detailed letter to her mother about the celebrations, for which she had a ringside seat. The Queen, she wrote, 'looked very well and happy; not so red as she sometimes does. The pageant was most beautiful; the colonial and Indian troops called forth the most enthusiasm.'[37]

Edmund Garrett, who was born in 1865, was the younger half-brother of Rhoda. Like her he was of delicate health, dying of tuberculosis when little over 40. Also like her he possessed great charm and was much loved by his cousins, especially Agnes, who was almost his foster mother. He had entered journalism in 1887 on W.T. Stead's *Pall Mall Gazette*, with the recommendation and support of his cousin Millicent.[38] He visited South Africa in 1889–90 in the hope of recovering his health; in 1895 he went again, this time to edit the *Cape Times*, and became actively involved in political life.[39] At the start of 1896 he wrote to Agnes in partial defence of the Jameson Raid, the quixotic freebooting attempt to invade the Transvaal and abet an English settler rising against its Boer Government. 'Tell Millie I look to her to put the right head on this in England, & the Liberal press especially.'[40] When war broke out between Britain and the Boers in October 1899 Edmund had left Cape Town and soon entered a German sanatorium. (Later he was to be a patient at the East Anglian sanatorium at East Nayland.) Her affection for him undoubtedly increased Millicent's concern about developments in South Africa, but there is little doubt that she would in any case have given a highly controversial war her wholehearted support.

For Mrs Fawcett and those who thought like her the war was a struggle for freedom, a campaign on behalf of the English and other 'Uitlanders' in the Transvaal who were denied the rights of citizenship in the Boer republic. The connection between the plight of her compatriots abroad and voteless women at home was obvious, though the immediate impact of the war was not to stimulate but to stifle suffrage propaganda: 'Two fires cannot burn together', she wrote later.[41] From an early stage she played a part in supporting the war at home and presenting it in a favourable light abroad.

The fact that it was widely seen as an imperialist struggle fought by a major power on behalf of a knot of wealthy capitalists against an heroic small nation made it easy for Boer propaganda to find a ready reception.[42] Mrs Fawcett conceived a plan to counter this propaganda by distributing literature abroad explaining the British case, and she was heavily involved in its execution through the agency of the Women's Liberal Unionist Association. Pamphlets were published in English, French, German and Italian, and by March 1901 the WLUA committee had distributed a total of 75,000 publications, as well as sending explanatory letters to consuls and other leading British figures on the Continent and in the United States. Special effort was paid, as a letter written by Mrs Fawcett and two other WLUA leaders claimed, to countering 'the stream of calumny and falsehood' which the Boers'

> European supporters have directed against everything British, and specially against British soldiers in the field . . . It is lamentable to reflect . . . that in some cases Englishmen have taken part in the dissemination of villainous charges against their countrymen, charges which they at least ought to have known to be both false and ridiculous.[43]

Such an aggressive statement must have been of the utmost assistance to the Government, coming as it did from a respectable group with no direct responsibility for waging the war. In private, however, she may have been less confident of the rectitude of British soldiers than her public stance suggested. Josephine Butler, with whom she was in close contact during the war years, wrote to a friend in February 1901 about particularly agonizing charges of rape and brutality against groups of soldiers: 'My heavy grief is *lest it should be true* . . . Mrs Fawcett is greatly distressed & has asked me to take it up.'[44]

Her activity in connection with the South African war now entered its most important phase. As Kitchener's armies progressed after their initial reverses they constructed concentration camps in the Transvaal, the Orange River Colony and Natal for the dependants of the Boer soldiers. They were designed to prevent the camp inhabitants from helping the soldiers and to provide food and shelter in a countryside which had been systematically deprived of means of support.[45] It was at this point that Emily Hobhouse rose to prominence. A member of the Liberal family which included the philosopher L.T. Hobhouse, she visited South Africa early in 1901 and wrote a devastating indictment of the conditions which she saw in the concentration camps. They were overcrowded and insanitary, with inadequate supplies of such basic amenities as water, food, fuel, beds, clothing and soap. Her report, made to a leading anti-war body which the parlance of the day termed 'pro-Boer' and published in June 1901, achieved wide publicity.[46]

Perhaps obeying her cousin Edmund's injunction in an earlier crisis to 'put the right head on this in . . . the Liberal press', Mrs Fawcett wrote an article on the Hobhouse report, soon after its publication, in the Liberal *Westminster Gazette*. Her mode of defence was twofold. First she picked out the places in the report which praised the work being done by camp staff against enormous odds to improve conditions and quoted these effectively (though the *Gazette* observed in an editorial note that she said nothing about the high death rate in some of the camps). Second she pointed out that the Boer farms had naturally been used as rallying points for the enemy and sources of misinformation for British soldiers. No one could blame the Boer women for this. 'But no one can take part in war without sharing in its risks, and the formation of the concentration camps is part of the fortune of war.'[47]

Eleven days after the appearance of this article the War Office was asked in the House of Lords to appoint a commission of inquiry, to include some women, to visit the concentration camps and report on their conditions. The reply was that such a commission was in process of being appointed and that it would consist exclusively of women.[48] This, it should be remembered, was at a time when the appointment of women to any government committee was still a novelty. The name of one member was already known to the initiated, for on the same day Lady Frances Balfour, with whose view of patriotism Mrs Fawcett was closely in accord, wrote to her: 'I *am* pleased, you are exactly the right person – I hoped it wd come, when I heard the WO was going to send them out.'[49] It would seem a particularly blatant example of reward for services rendered were it not for the fact that several months of grinding toil lay ahead of the commission, to say nothing of the seasickness which always plagued Mrs Fawcett. A second Liberal paper, the *Daily News*, praised her personally when the news was announced a week later, but pointed out that she was 'a strong politician' and her *Westminster Gazette* article heavily biased. If she was to be a member of the committee, the paper asked, 'why was Miss Hobhouse not placed on it also?'[50]

In fact Emily Hobhouse was not only rejected but refused permission to return to the camps. St John Brodrick, the Secretary of State for War, declined her offer of service with the strikingly disingenuous comment: 'We are sending out no one specially identified with any form of opinion.' There is, however, no reason to doubt his further observation: 'We hope that the result of their visit will be satisfactory to us from every point of view.'[51] It proved impossible for the three commissioners based in England to meet Hobhouse and her friends before setting sail for South Africa, a failure for which each side blamed the other,[52] but it is improbable that they regarded an interview with a notorious 'pro-Boer' committee as a very high priority in the few days before they left Southampton on the Orient Line's *Orotava* on 22 July.

The remainder of the commission was as unlikely to be accused of impartiality as its best-known member. Only Lucy Deane, one of the first women factory inspectors, was not publicly known to support the war, and later in life showed herself to be a woman of independent spirit. But she was the daughter of a soldier and a junior government employee, and was presumably judged to be a safe appointment. Alice, Lady Knox, was the wife of a

British general serving in South Africa. The remainder of the commissioners were already there, and consisted of two doctors and a nurse. The most prominent of the three was Dr Jane Waterston, Edmund Garrett's former doctor, who on 24 July wrote to the *Cape Times* denouncing the agitation against the concentration camps:

> Judging by some of the hysterical whining going on in England at the present time, it would seem as if we might neglect or half starve our faithful soldiers, and keep our civilian population eating their hearts out here as long as we fed and pampered people who have not even the grace to say thank you for the care bestowed on them.[53]

This letter caused great offence in anti-war circles in England and South Africa, as Mrs Fawcett discovered when she visited a 'pro-Boer' relief committee in Cape Town. The committee asked to have one of their number co-opted onto the commission, a request subsequently rejected.[54] The fact that Waterston had written it when she had initially declined to serve on the commission could have done little to reassure anti-war opinion about the good faith of a woman known to be a strong patriot.[55]

Mrs Fawcett kept a diary during part of her visit to South Africa. It was fullest and most interesting for the period before the visits to the camps began on 20 August, for much of the remaining material was incorporated into the report itself. It began with her visit to Brodrick at the War Office. Perhaps not knowing his woman he sought to stiffen her resolve by pointing to the unprecedented humanitarian role of the concentration camps. She neatly outbid him by pointing out that infant mortality rates were high in England and elsewhere, and that the high proportion of young children and the very old in the camps would naturally lead to heavy mortality: 'He seemed struck by this point and had not thought of it before', she noted.[56]

Each of the women travelling from England had provided herself with a companion. In Mrs Fawcett's case it was the faithful Philippa, who had remained at Newnham as research student and lecturer since her examination triumphs in 1890–1. An obituary notice commented that she was pleased to leave, and there is certainly no evidence that her mother compelled her to do so.[57] The voyage was not without incident. Soon after departure Mrs Fawcett was woken by a rat which jumped down from the upper berth, but Philippa was not disturbed by her 'great yelp'. Later she was told by the ship's captain, a friend of the Andersons, that 800 rats had been killed while the vessel lay in Southampton.[58]

Other incidents were less alarming. Mrs Fawcett worked on the index of her biography of Molesworth, and all three commissioners worked on the papers supplied them by the War Office. There was, however, ample time to observe a whale, flying fish and the Southern Cross: 'A more second class constellation I have never seen', she recorded tartly. They experienced the death of one of their few women fellow passengers, who was going with her baby to join her husband in South Africa. All of the commissioners and

*Newnham College staff, 1896; Philippa Fawcett seated, fourth from left.*

companions declined an invitation to attend a boxing match, 'I am glad to say', but they could not avoid an evening in the chief engineer's tiny cabin, listening to his gramophone and 'packed in like herrings'. They had been promised sacred music, but instead the evening's highlights were music-hall songs such as ' "Mary was a housemaid" & such like ditties . . . Fortunately I was not next Philippa or I think we shd both have given way.' Philippa distinguished herself at hopscotch and Mrs Fawcett to her surprise survived a round of the ladies' egg-and-spoon race. They also survived the attentions of a fusilier, 'a well known bad lot' found wandering near their cabin, and she noted patriotically the approach of Trafalgar. Just before landing at Cape Town on 10 August she enjoyed the magnificent view of Table Mountain: 'It looks like a country worth fighting for', she wrote. Upon disembarking they received a telegram from the War Office appointing her president of the commission.[59]

After a few days of acclimatization and consultation the party set out by special train for the camps on 15 August, reaching the first, Mafeking, on the 20th. The journey gave the women the opportunity to establish good working and personal relationships and their collective outlook.[60] Mrs Fawcett recorded a number of revealing episodes. Ella Scarlett, the second of the South African-based doctors, had brought with her a man servant named Collins. He aroused the dislike of the other women: 'He looked like a half caste – he spoke Dutch and none of us fancied him at all . . . We felt he would very likely be a spy upon us and report what we were doing to the enemy.' It fell to Mrs Fawcett as president to tell the distressed Scarlett that Collins must remain behind. Two days later Jane Waterston asked that grace should be said before meals and the Church of England evening service introduced. 'To both these wishes I of course assented', Mrs Fawcett wrote. The next day Waterston dined with friends, returning with stories of 'the dissatisfaction of the loyalists about the amount done for the Boer con. camps and little or nothing for the loyalists'.[61]

Their report, signed on 12 December 1901, was published the following February, just over three months before the end of the war. It is unlikely that it did much to change fixed opinions and it is probably as important an event in the history of women's emancipation as of the South African war. It is, however, a remarkable document.[62] The dominant commissioners were the president and Jane Waterston, both of whom had previously publicized their unalloyed support for the British Government and their conviction that the camps were at worst an unfortunate necessity. Their perspective was supplemented by that of Lady Knox, the general's wife, who had previously lived for two years in South Africa: 'In her opinion the Boers of today are in social circumstances very much where the Scottish people were 200 years ago.'[63] But while its patriotic perspective was the report's first feature, its second was the many criticisms of detail and recommendations for reform which it contained. The third was the painstaking care which the commissioners took over their work, evidence for those prepared to accept it that a group of women could be as competent as men. When it was published Mrs Fawcett's friend Kathleen Lyttelton wrote to her: 'Your Report has apparently done the impossible & pleased everyone. It is a great triumph for it shows you have been just & fair.'[64] This of course was an oversimplification, but the report was certainly more than the coat of whitewash which Brodrick probably anticipated, and it provided ample ammunition for the 'pro-Boer' faction.

The published document consisted of 208 foolscap pages, the first 24 of which were a general report. This was followed by detailed accounts of all but one of the thirty-four camps, half of them in the Transvaal, most of the remainder in the Orange River Colony. The general report contained a number of passages in which the civilian Boer inmates were largely blamed for their own plight: 'Every superintendent', they wrote, 'has to wage war against the insanitary habits of the people.' Tents were 'stinking' and many of the deaths of Boer children were the result of the 'noxious compounds' given them by their mothers.[65] ('One hoped that Englishwomen would have been above such accusations', Emily Hobhouse wrote, adding that superstition and folk remedies were also characteristic of English villages.[66]) The high death rate, they concluded, was caused 'in a very large degree' by the conditions of war. Even if the Boer children had stayed on their farms many of them would have died. The commissioners also pointed out that large sums had been spent to provide amenities for the inhabitants. One old man had exclaimed, they were told, that the British must be God's chosen people, 'for he had never heard of any other nation paying for the education of the children of their enemies'.[67]

The general report's defence of the British administration was balanced by criticisms of individual camps couched in terms almost savage for an official publication. As Emily Hobhouse pointed out, the commissioners recommended 'sweeping reforms . . . They do not shrink from condemning ill-chosen sites, dismissing incompetent superintendents, reforming entire hospitals, urging various improvements in food, fuel, and water, recommending beds and ameliorating sanitation.'[68] Even the relatively lenient general report urged that much more attention be given to water supply and sanitary conditions and the provision of adequate supplies of both fresh food and medical staff.[69]

Those who read the report found in it what they looked for. Not only Emily Hobhouse and her friends but the Liberal press and parliamentary critics found ample ammunition for their attacks on the Government.[70] On the other hand the pro-government *Times* wrote complacently that nobody who read the report without prejudice 'can fail, we believe, to be satisfied that everything which could be done by forethought, sympathy, and a lavish expenditure of money has been done'.[71] To this extent Kathleen Lyttelton's praise had been justified. The commissioners must

also have drawn satisfaction from the drop in the death rate which followed their report.[72]

In March 1903 Mrs Fawcett returned to South Africa to visit Philippa,
who had taken up a position as education organizer in the Transvaal. She
found that 'the order of the day was rebuilding, restoring, repairing'. Emi-
grating Englishwomen could do their share by taking up gardening and
related land work. It was as yet too soon for reconciliation between the
British and the Boers, but small beginnings had been made, out of which
would emerge in time 'a great united nation'. Her main criticisms were of
the government-operated railways and the shortage of labour, with attendant adverse results on the country's economy. Marmalade from Dundee,
for example, cost less than to make it from local oranges in South Africa.[73]
In a letter to her cousin Amy Badley, Edmund Garrett's sister, she wrote
that Philippa's black domestic servant, who was paid the large sum of £36 a
year, had left her when she refused to pay more, claiming that he could earn
£6 a month elsewhere. 'To our great satisfaction this turns out to be
invention', and he was left without employment.[74]

Her defence of the British Government was as strong after her return as
before her departure and must have contributed to the public snubs which
she received from some erstwhile friends.[75] Probably a more important
reason was her continued onslaughts on the opponents of the war. 'Boers
are generally far more reasonable than pro-Boers', she wrote. In four
months visiting the camps she had never heard a syllable critical of the
British soldier, and she quoted a Boer woman who had declared: 'I will
speak up for the British until I lie in my grave.'[76] It was Emily Hobhouse,
another indefatigable combatant, who pointed out that she had gone to
South Africa 'as an official, not as a friend', and would have been an unlikely
confidante of Boer women.[77]

The problems presented by the Boers were to Mrs Fawcett similar to the
Irish struggle in which she had been so heavily involved. Both Boers and
Irish opposed the British and must be treated firmly. In addition, both were
in her eyes people who preferred to mount protest movements and appeal
to the gullible in England rather than help themselves. She reflected on one
similarity after visiting a Boer farm on the veldt. The occupants, she wrote,
were 'well to do people, but the farm & house are the most awful pig hole I
have ever seen except an Irish cabin'.[78] Boer habits were in sharp contrast to
those of English families, even in concentration camps.[79]

She never changed her views about the behaviour of the British forces in
South Africa. Shortly before her death she wrote to the *Times Literary
Supplement* after a sympathetic review of a biography of Emily Hobhouse by
Ruth Fry. She referred to 'the aspersions cast by the late Miss Hobhouse' on
the administration of the camps, blamed much of their squalor on the Boer
women and praised the British soldier as 'the best of peacemakers'.[80] Her
letter was followed by dignified replies from Ruth Fry and L.T. Hobhouse,

Emily's brother, who praised the work of the women's commission but regretted Mrs Fawcett's inability 'to understand that one may do a far greater service to one's country by withstanding its errors than by accepting all its doings without criticism'.[81] It was a telling point, for her version of patriotism was narrow to the point of vindictiveness, as Home Rulers and 'pro-Boers' had discovered. It was once again to be given full play during the wider tragedy of the Great War.

NOTES

1. *MGF*, pp. 1, 139–40.
2. See, for example, Christopher Harvie, *The Lights of Liberalism* (1976), pp. 218–32; D.A. Hamer, *Liberal Politics in the Age of Gladstone and Rosebery* (Oxford: Clarendon Press, 1972), pp. 116–21.
3. *Pall Mall Gazette*, 1 March 1886.
4. *The Times*, 4 June 1886.
5. Leslie Stephen, *Life of Henry Fawcett* (1885), p. 412; Justin McCarthy, *Reminiscences*, vol. 1 (Chatto & Windus, 1899), p. 288.
6. Linda Walker, 'Party political women' in Jane Rendall (ed.), *Equal or Different* (Oxford: Blackwell, 1987), pp. 167–8.
7. *MGF*, p. 122.
8. *The Times*, 9 March 1887; *WSJ*, 2 May 1887, p. 54.
9. *The Times*, 5 May 1887.
10. *Liberal Unionist*, 3 August 1887, p. 2.
11. G.P. Gooch, *Life of Lord Courtney* (Macmillan, 1920), pp. 111, 200, 205, 206, 209–12, 234.
12. Kate Courtney's diary, 11 May 1888 (quoted in Patricia Hollis, *Ladies Elect* (1987), p. 62n. and Pat Jalland, *Women, Marriage and Politics 1860–1914* (1986), p. 218).
13. Kate Courtney's diary, 5 July 1888 (Courtney Papers, BLPES).
14. *Speeches on the Formation of the Women's Liberal Unionist Association*, pp. 8–14 (quotation p. 12) (Fawcett Library).
15. Kate Courtney's diary, esp. 5 July 1896, Jubilee Week, 1897; Barbara Caine, *Destined to be Wives* (Oxford: Clarendon Press, 1986), p. 165.
16. Kate Courtney's diary, 20 June 1886, 18 June 1892, 6 July 1895; *Liberal Unionist*, 1 August 1892, p. 19.
17. MGF to Kate Courtney, 3 August 1896 (quoted in Gooch, pp. 339–40); Leonard Courtney to MGF (typescript copy), 8 October 1896; Kate Courtney's diary, 1 September 1896 (Courtney Papers).
18. Kate Courtney's diary, 7 and 24 October 1899.
19. Frances Balfour, *Ne Obliviscaris* vol. 2 [1930], p. 119.
20. *The Sunday Times*, 11 August 1929.
21. *The Times*, 29 September 1888.
22. *ibid*, 11 February 1889.
23. *ibid.*, 8 April 1891.
24. *Parl. Deb.*, 3rd ser., 345, col. 279 (9 June 1890). *Review of Reviews*, July 1890, p. 17. The occasion was probably the first annual meeting of the WLUA, at which Derby was the principal speaker and Mrs Fawcett followed him (*The Times*, 28 June 1889).

25. Philippa Fawcett to MGF, 21 October 1888 (Rossetti Collection, State Historical Society of Iowa); *ER*, 15 July 1893, pp. 183–4.
26. J.L. Hammond, *Gladstone and the Irish Nation* (Longman, 1938), ch. 29; R.C.K. Ensor, *England 1870–1914* (Oxford: Clarendon Press, 1936), pp. 181–3.
27. MGF to Louisa Garrett, 1 March [1890] (Anderson Papers, St Brelade).
28. Lord Feilding to Mrs Shaw, 26 August 1890 (M50/2/1/101); *The Times*, 1 March 1890.
29. W.R. Bousfield to MGF, 5 and 13 May 1892 (M50/2/1/165, 173); *The Times*, 10 May 1892.
30. MGF to Margaret C. Farrow (draft), 13 January 1892 (M50/2/1/153). The meeting was cancelled for unspecified reasons (M50/2/1/155).
31. *Liberal Unionist*, 1 January 1892, p. 109; see also *MGF*, p. 129.
32. *MGF*, pp. 150–1; *Liberal Unionist*, 1 March 1892, p. 159; 1 August 1892, pp. 18–19; *ER*, 15 July 1892, pp. 171–5.
33. *The Times*, 21 January 1887, 27 April 1889, 1 July 1892.
34. *Liberal Unionist*, 1 June 1890, p. 217; 1 March 1891, p. 159.
35. *ibid.*, 1 July 1891, p. 229.
36. Edmund Garrett to Agnes Garrett, 23 June 1897 (Edmund Garrett Papers, BL Add. Mss).
37. MGF to Louisa Garrett, 22 June [1897] (Anderson Papers).
38. MGF to Stead, 1 June 1887 (Stead Papers, Cambridge); Stead to MGF, 30 December 1887 and 11 October 1895 (FLALC, vol. 11).
39. E.T. Cook, *Edmund Garrett, a Memoir* (Edward Arnold, 1909), esp. pp. 5–8; Alfred Milner, biography of Edmund Garrett in *Dictionary of National Biography 1901–1911*, vol. 2 (Oxford: Oxford University Press, 1920 edn), pp. 83–4; *MGF*, pp. 171, 183–4.
40. Edmund Garrett to Agnes Garrett [8 January 1896] (Edmund Garrett Papers). I have been unable to find evidence that she did so.
41. MGF, *Women's Suffrage* [1912], pp. 58–60.
42. Thomas Pakenham, *The Boer War* (Weidenfeld & Nicolson, 1979), pp. 249–50.
43. *The Times*, 24 May 1900, 30 March 1901 (quotations); *MGF*, pp. 184–6. For Mrs Fawcett's activities in the war *MGF* ch. 9 and *WIR* ch. 17 are indispensable reading.
44. Josephine Butler to Fanny Forsaith [12 February 1901] (Butler Letter Collection, Fawcett Library).
45. Pakenham, pp. 493–5.
46. Emily Hobhouse, *Report of a Visit to the Camps of Women and Children in the Cape and Orange River Colonies* [Friars Printing Association, 1901]; Pakenham, pp. 501–8; Jill Liddington, *The Long Road to Greenham* (Virago, 1989), pp. 45–8.
47. *Westminster Gazette*, 4 July 1901.
48. *Parl. Deb.*, 4th ser., 97, cols 373–4 (15 July 1901).
49. Frances Balfour to MGF, 15 July 1901 (FLALC, vol. 2c).
50. *Daily News*, 23 July 1901.
51. St John Brodrick to Emily Hobhouse (draft), 19 July 1901 (War Office Papers, PRO). This letter may not have been despatched. For a subsequent, similar letter see Emily Hobhouse, *The Brunt of the War* (1902), p. 135.
52. Hobhouse, *The Brunt of the War*, p. 136n.; *The Times*, 25–8 March 1902 (Hobhouse–MGF correspondence).
53. *Cape Times*, 24 July 1901 (cutting in FLA, box 90b, MGF diary of her South African trip, henceforth 'MGF diary').
54. *ibid.*, 12 August [1901]; *The Times*, 26 March 1902. Brodrick had given permission for the commission to co-opt additional members (MGF diary, 20 July).

55. *WIR*, pp. 154–5; MGF diary, 12 August.
56. MGF diary, 20 July.
57. Newnham College Roll *Letter*, January 1949, p. 48.
58. MGF diary, 23–4 July.
59. *ibid.*, 24 July–10 August.
60. *WIR*, pp. 157–8.
61. MGF diary, 15–19 August.
62. It was published as P.P. 1902, vol. LXVII, Cd. 893 (henceforth Cd. 893).
63. MGF diary, 22 July.
64. Kathleen Lyttelton to MGF, 28 February 1902 (FLALC, vol. 2c).
65. Cd. 893, pp. 1–2, 15–17.
66. Hobhouse, *The Brunt of the War*, p. 290.
67. Cd. 893, pp. 5, 15.
68. Hobhouse, *The Brunt of the War*, pp. 291–2. Examples may be found in Cd. 893, pp. 56, 103, 151, 178 and elsewhere.
69. Cd. 893, p. 18.
70. *Daily News, Manchester Guardian*, 22 February 1902; *Parl. Deb.*, 4th ser., 104, cols 407, 409, 415–17 (4 March 1902).
71. *The Times*, 22 February 1902.
72. Hobhouse, *The Brunt of the War*, pp. 327–46.
73. MGF, 'Impressions of South Africa, 1901 and 1903', *Contemporary Review*, November 1903, pp. 635–55 (quotations pp. 636, 655); 'Openings for women in South Africa. I. Gardening', *Imperial Colonist*, March 1904, pp. 28–30.
74. MGF to Amy Badley, 4 July [1903] (FLALC, vol. 14).
75. *MGF*, p. 203.
76. *The Times*, 22 March 1902, 9 January 1903.
77. *ibid.*, 13 January 1903.
78. MGF diary, 3 September [1901].
79. *ibid.*, 4 September; Cd. 893, p. 56.
80. *Times Literary Supplement*, 30 May 1929, p. 436.
81. *ibid.*, 6 June 1929, p. 454.

# CHAPTER 11

—————— · ——————

## WOMEN'S SUFFRAGE

Asked in 1910 to provide some notes about her mother for publicity purposes and to emphasize her non-suffrage interests, Philippa Fawcett replied: 'There is really very little else, as the main part of my mother's life (for 42 years) has been devoted to suffrage work.'[1] Such a reply from such a source may seem scarcely comprehensible in the light of previous chapters, but the kernel of truth is that while Mrs Fawcett was absorbed for relatively short periods in morality campaigns and imperial issues, the 'main part' of her life was indeed devoted to women's suffrage.

The reply may also hint at the nature of the relationship between mother and daughter, who shared both their interests and their home. There was a deep bond between them; as their friend Philippa Strachey wrote much later, Philippa was 'the apple of her [mother's] eye & the joy of her heart'. But the closeness of the relationship may have inhibited her own personality and her independence, for some among her contemporaries found her timid and colourless.[2] Mrs Fawcett made constant plans for Philippa's future, attempting through her to introduce women into previously barred occupations, and she was instrumental in 1905 in Philippa's application for a high-ranking position in the education service of the London County Council. There Philippa worked successfully for thirty years, developing schools and colleges and doing much to improve the conditions of female staff.[3]

In the mid-1880s the outlook for women's suffrage was bleak. It became even dimmer as the years passed, partly because of quarrels within the ranks of suffragists, but chiefly as the nature and extent of male opposition became clearer. If there had ever been a chance of slipping women's votes past an unwary Parliament it was now definitively lost. Nevertheless the suffrage movement between 1884 and the first years of the new century was full of incident, and deserves a better press than it has received at the hands of those primarily interested in an earlier or later period.[4]

The significance of the defeat of the women's suffrage amendment to the reform bill of 1884 was that henceforth women were on their own. No one expected that another act would be passed to enfranchise the large but powerless groups of men who still lacked the vote, and it was not until the social convulsions of the Great War that universal male suffrage was generally acceptable to political opinion. It would not have been surprising if the women's movement had given up the struggle for a period, but this did not happen. There were few parliamentary votes on women's suffrage in the twenty years after 1884,[5] partly because of intrigue in the House of Commons. As a result there were few high points in the campaign, but meetings, petitions and publications continued vigorously.

During the first year of her widowhood Mrs Fawcett took no part in public affairs, but from 1886 she was again a frequent speaker on women's suffrage, addressing meetings in many different parts of country.[6] On the occasion of Queen Victoria's jubilee in 1887 she was the first of four signatories of an address presented by the Central Committee of the National Society for Women's Suffrage.[7] In the same year she became president of the Guild of the Unrepresented, a body based in Southport which received a good deal of publicity among feminists.[8] In 1888 she was at the centre of the developments which resulted in the break-up of the NSWS, a division which lasted for nearly a decade.

The principal issue which led to the schism was whether to admit to the NSWS women's social and political organizations. These, it was universally anticipated, would be branches of the Women's Liberal Federation, for the Primrose League, to which Conservative women devoted their energies, took no stand on such a contentious political question, and the Women's Liberal Unionist Association was not a wholeheartedly suffragist body. It is difficult to feel that had the NSWS accepted the women Liberals without a struggle women's suffrage would have gained greatly.[9] Liberal men were more inclined to support women's suffrage than Conservatives, but as Mrs Fawcett wrote many years later, Liberal suffragists were 'an army without generals'.[10] Some of the best-known Liberals were wily and determined opponents of the cause, while few members of the 'army' could be relied on under fire. In addition a link with the Women's Liberal Federation would have led to the loss of many prominent suffragists, for some were Conservatives and the Home Rule split had reinforced the Unionist camp and brought an unprecedented element of bitterness into political life.[11] But women Liberals were mostly sympathetic to the suffrage, and by the late 1880s their numbers were growing rapidly.[12]

When the question came to a head within the NSWS in December 1888 Mrs Fawcett led the opposition to rule changes which would have admitted party organizations. There is no doubt of her sincerity, but her convictions could only have been strengthened by the hostility to the Liberal Party which now dominated her life. Speaking to Manchester suffragists the previous month she was quoted as saying: 'Although she had a great respect for individual members, yet for parties in themselves she had no respect whatsoever, for she thought they would get all they could out of women and give them as little as possible in return.'[13] She repeated this view at the crucial debate of the Central Committee of the NSWS on 12 December, pointing out that if politicians had kept their word women's suffrage would have succeeded long before. To accept the new rules would be 'a most fatal and suicidal act', taken when the movement might be close to success. The vote seems to have been on party lines, ninety-four supporting the proposed rules revision and sixty-three opposing.[14] In essence the NSWS had fallen victim to the violent political passions of the age.

The majority formed a new suffrage body under the title Central National Society for Women's Suffrage, while the minority retained the original name. Mrs Fawcett became honorary secretary of the NSWS, a position which she held almost without a break until the two societies reunited in 1900. She was also for two years its treasurer, a responsibility not wholly free from anxiety. Reporting to the annual meeting in July 1890 she confessed that she was 'a treasurer with nothing to treasure' and that the society, known to be a moderate body, had allowed its moderation to extend to the subscription list.[15]

It was equally serious that the split in the suffrage forces, though initially attracting much publicity and nominal support for one society or the other,[16] provided an excuse for parliamentary inaction or opposition. In 1891, for example, a flagrant piece of political chicanery involving figures from both main parties and including Gladstone, prevented William Wood-all's women's suffrage bill from being discussed in the House of Commons.[17] Mrs Fawcett had lobbied for this bill to the point of exhaustion.[18] Both the Liberal Woodall and the Conservative Edward Cotton Jodrell told her that there was not a majority for women's suffrage in the House of Commons. Jodrell wrote: 'As was expected the unfortunate "split" a year or so ago has greatly injured us for the present.'[19] The loss of the bill caused severe anguish and anger among suffragist women. Mrs Fawcett's Cambridge friend Emma Miller wrote unequivocally: 'The longer I live and the more I have to do with men, the stronger I realise, in every way, their inferiority to women.'[20]

Given that the split had taken place suffragists increasingly succeeded in working together with a good will which women were sometimes accused of lacking. Mrs Fawcett remarked at the critical meeting with a lightness of touch typical of her suffrage activities: 'They need not emulate the two grammarians, one of whom hoped the other would go to an unpleasant place because of his theory of irregular verbs.'[21] This sentiment was widely shared. The Liberal-dominated CNSWS selected a number of its vice-presidents from the ranks of Conservatives, and one Conservative MP congratulated the society on having recruited as supporters men and women from all political parties.[22] In 1892 Mrs Fawcett was asked to second a resolution at the CNSWS annual meeting. She made an appealing and witty speech, in which she succeeded in making a complimentary reference to Gladstone, and observed: 'I am anxious to show that women can work together for a great political object, and I am only too delighted to have this opportunity of addressing a meeting which has been called together by a Society to which I have not the honour to belong.' This statement was greeted with cheers.[23] In turn she invited Eva McLaren, a Liberal whose husband was a strong parliamentary supporter of women's suffrage, to speak to the annual meeting of the Unionist NSWS. The invitation was accepted, Mrs McLaren writing that she would 'feel it a pleasure and a privilege to show that I can work with those who differ with me on some subjects if united by the bond of sympathy in the cause of women'.[24]

In the late 1880s the women's suffrage movement was too divided and decentralized to be led by a single figure, though Lydia Becker, editor of the *Women's Suffrage Journal*, who died in 1890, was probably its most prominent personality. It is clear, however, that its intellectual leader was Millicent Garrett Fawcett. It was she who in 1888–9 was the most effective opponent of Goldwin Smith, a prominent writer with a reputation as a formidable controversialist, who had emigrated to Canada where he had become a self-appointed expert on the dangers of women's suffrage as illustrated by limited American experience. She attacked him in several articles and letters, not neglecting to remind her readers that Smith claimed to be an expert on the threat posed by women's suffrage to the country he had abandoned. She exposed some of his allegations as errors and remarked: 'It may be truly said of him that on this subject of women's suffrage he relies on his memory for his eloquence and on his imagination for his facts.'[25]

Goldwin was not the only member of 'that numerous and influential family' of Smith[26] to feel her lash. Samuel Smith was a well-known Liberal MP who in 1891 published his objections to women's suffrage as a pamphlet. Mrs Fawcett replied with another pamphlet, in which she called attention to the 'curious mixture' in his mind of 'sentimental homage and practical contempt' for women. He had claimed that Parliament had legislated away most of the women's grievances; this comment, she wrote, was evidence of the fact that those without complaint were prepared to accept suffering which did not directly touch them.[27] It could hardly have been expected that either Smith would be moved to a public recantation, but the shallowness of their arguments had been impressively exposed.

A more serious test of Mrs Fawcett's intellectual stature came in June 1889, when the famous 'appeal' against women's suffrage appeared in the pages of the *Nineteenth Century*. Within two months the original 104 signatories were supported by another 1,796 women. Most of the 104 were the wives of prominent men rather than well known in their own right, but the novelist Mary Augusta Ward was one of the organizers. She was flanked by such conspicuous women as the writer, Eliza Lynn Linton, famous for her opposition to the 'advanced' woman, the educationists Alice Ottley and Lucy Soulsby, and Beatrice Potter, who as Beatrice Webb was many years later to repudiate her anti–suffrage views.[28]

The supporters of women's suffrage recognized the appeal as a challenge not to be ignored and Mrs Fawcett was at the centre of the effort made to counteract it. She wrote a reply published in the *Nineteenth Century* in July and was one of the organizers of a counter-appeal which collected the names of over 2,000 suffragists; a representative sample was published in the *Fortnightly Review* the same month. Many of them were women who had distinguished themselves in education, philanthropy, medicine, local government and other spheres. The list was preceded by an article in support of the suffrage, and although it did not bear a signature its author was unmistakable.[29] Both articles were impressively written. Her friend Lilias Ashworth Hallett told her:

> I doubt whether anything better has ever appeared. The two articles convey the impression of real joy in the writing . . . We owe you a great debt for these articles – but it was too bad that you should have had to write both. I cannot imagine *how* you could do them in the time & produce the variety.[30]

After the effort involved in the riposte to the anti-suffrage appeal her brush with Frederic Harrison in 1891 must have seemed like light relief. Unlike the Smiths he was a man of considerable intellectual stature. He was also a proven friend of the working class, but a notorious opponent of women's suffrage. Women, in his view, should remain in the home as wives and mothers, thus fulfilling their 'true function'. This view savoured to Mrs Fawcett of the 'social quack'. She wrote a reply which even *The Times*, excelled by none in its sententious dismissal of women's aspirations, found 'healthier and more advantageously flexible' than Harrison's point of view.[31]

When women's suffrage finally reappeared in the Commons in April 1892 she acted as inspirer before the vote and professional optimist afterwards. She must have enjoyed the opportunity to attack Gladstone, the leader who had 'denounced almost every political change that he had finally led to success', and Henry Labouchere, wit, radical, and unscrupulous opponent of votes for women.[32] Despite the weight and influence of the parliamentary opposition the bill was defeated by only twenty-three votes, a result which, she said, delighted its friends and dismayed its opponents.[33]

The following year the Central Committee of the NSWS took the lead in launching a national appeal for women's suffrage. A special committee was established in June 1893 representative of most shades of suffrage opinion. Mrs Fawcett was elected its president. The petition was not presented to Parliament until 1896, but most of the meetings took place in the first year, when almost all the 258,000 signatures were obtained. Mrs Fawcett took her presidency seriously, speaking in many different parts of England.[34] She told one meeting in 1894 that she had never been 'so actively engaged in the work' and that the women's movement 'was becoming a real, permanent, political force in the country'.[35] Making due allowance for her propagandist role it seems reasonable to see the suffrage movement as a force whose strength was at least maintained until it was eclipsed by the outbreak of the South African war in 1899.

Her election to the presidency of the appeal committee was the first public indication that she was not only the intellectual leader of the suffrage movement but, in the post-Becker period, its pre-eminent figure. It was true that she was, in the contemporary phrase, 'a strong politician', whose views on the Irish question were probably unacceptable to most women who supported the suffrage. But despite her Unionist loyalties she generally put the suffrage first. After the general election of 1892 she sent out a private leaflet urging suffragists not to work against supporters of women's suffrage or on behalf of candidates who opposed it.[36] She was also attractive to the wider public in a sense which dowdy figures like Lydia Becker or Helen Blackburn were not.[37] Lady Frances Balfour, seeking to persuade her to moderate her stance in the final stages of the Cust affair, told her that she was 'the representative, most before the eyes of the world, of suffrage'.[38] Georgiana Hill, a well-known writer on women's history and related topics, commented in 1896 that her name had 'become a household word' and her speeches more influential than those of any other suffrage leader, and a few years later Helen Blackburn referred to her as 'the most prominent upholder of the movement in England'.[39]

The closer relations fostered by the united suffrage appeal and the desire to avoid parliamentary confusion and duplication of effort – acutely highlighted by the damaging freelance activities of Mary Cozens[40] – led to a conference of the two London-based societies in June 1895 at which Mrs Fawcett presided. The meeting in turn resulted in parliamentary and electoral co-operation in 1895, and on Mrs Fawcett's initiative was extended into 1896.[41] The culmination of these moves was a private meeting held in Birmingham on 16 October 1896 of delegates from about twenty societies representing suffragists as far afield as Edinburgh, Dublin and Belfast. Significantly it was 'by common consent' that she was chosen to preside.[42] The need for the meeting was underlined not only by the divisions within the movement but also by the fact that while the suffrage societies could collect 260,000 signatures, far more women and many areas of the country remained untouched by the movement.[43] Mrs Fawcett told her mother that it had 'passed off very harmoniously and pleasantly'; Philippa had attended as the Cambridge delegate. She hoped that 'a vigorous winter campaign' would follow,[44] but the ramifications of the meeting, as she must have anticipated, were considerably greater.

At the annual meeting of the Central Committee of the NSWS in July 1897 it was Mrs Fawcett who moved a resolution approving of the proposed National Union of Women's Suffrage Societies and called for 'closer union and co-operation between the various societies'.[45] The reference to the national union was an early mention of an organization in which she was to be the dominant figure for over twenty years. At combined committee meetings in June and October 1897 it was agreed that the national union should be created, with about seventeen member organizations.[46] It is important not to mistake this body for the democratic and centralized organization which the NUWSS was to become in the twentieth century. At its start it had little power and few funds and was hardly more, as Leslie Parker Hume remarks, than a liaison committee.[47] Nor was Mrs Fawcett its president from its inception, though both she and Ray Strachey later believed that she was,[48] and a number of historians have repeated the error. She was for a period one of its treasurers, but it was not until 1907 that the NUWSS was reconstituted as a body with a president and an elected executive.[49]

At the end of the nineteenth century Mrs Fawcett had not yet become the indispensable leader of a decentralized and relatively leisurely movement. As seen above she was abroad when women's suffrage won a considerable moral victory with the passage of the second victory of Faithfull Begg's suffrage bill in 1897, and she was content to suspend her suffrage work while Britain was engaged for nearly three years in a controversial colonial war.[50] She was apparently absent from the first 'national convention' of the NUWSS held in October 1903. She attended the second convention, held in November 1904, and chaired a public meeting, though not the private working meetings, and was again absent the following year when a further convention was held in Hull.[51] As late as May 1906 she was missing from the first women's suffrage deputation to the Prime Minister,[52] an absence unthinkable in later years. When, however, the International Congress of Women was held in London in June 1899 it was Mrs Fawcett who, as the voice of the British movement, chaired an international women's suffrage meeting at the Queen's Hall.[53]

The years between 1884 and 1905 formed a period when suffragists kept their flag flying in difficult conditions. The movement remained active, its supporters (though not its income)[54] buoyant and its structure flexible. Its gradual reunification and the second reading triumph of the Begg bill showed that it remained a force to be reckoned with, though not one to which ambitious politicians devoted much attention. It had, however, reached the limit of what could be achieved by meetings, petitions and private members' bills. New forms of activity were required and were to be introduced by both the new militant suffragists and the moderates.

It is now necessary to consider the arguments which Mrs Fawcett deployed in support of women's suffrage during these middle years of her life. Even more than previously her speeches and writing were characterized by arguments which she thought would be acceptable to particular audiences. This was a political stance rather than an heroic one, but she was a political leader rather than a revolutionary theorist, and there is no reason to suppose that her words belied her convictions.

Three of her principal arguments for women's suffrage may be termed sociological, conservative and feminine. Constance Rover has quoted one of her articles, published in 1886, in which she argued that women's suffrage would be the result of changed social conditions rather than 'an isolated phenomenon'.[55] Mrs Fawcett stressed the same point in her Mary Wollstonecraft introduction in 1891, insisting that the emancipation of women was not the work of individuals but of a broad democratic movement: 'The hour had to come as well as the man.'[56] The case was perhaps most interestingly expressed in an article which she wrote in the same year for the *Fortnightly Review*. The women's movement, she asserted in a passage which ran parallel to Marxist thought, had followed paid employment. 'Economic independence' had transformed women's position: 'That the movement for women's emancipation has an economic foundation, based on the changes in methods of production utilising the labour of women, affords strong grounds for believing in its durability.' It was for this reason that the movement had advanced furthest in England and the United States, where economic conditions were most favourable.[57] Though there were fewer institutional barriers to women's progress elsewhere, she added privately, citing degrees at the University of Paris and various reforms in Australia, these concessions had been 'in machinery & from without'. Improvement in access to higher education for women in England, on the other hand, had been their own achievement, 'the outcome of a social movement on the part of women themselves'.[58]

The insistence on the economic and social basis of the movement was an argument which she was to develop subsequently. The 'peaceful revolution' which women had experienced, she commented, was the result not only of economic but of educational change. Among its 'social instruments' were the sewing machine and the bicycle.[59] With the development of a larger women's movement she thought in more sweeping terms. Writing in the socialist *New Statesman* in 1913 she claimed that 'The awakening of women' was 'one of the biggest events which has ever taken place in the history of the world' and part of something still larger, the rise of democracy.[60] In 1923, with the battle for women's suffrage largely won, she compared the spiritual and mental revolution of the women's movement with the spread of Christianity, the Renaissance and the Reformation.[61] But the twenty years before the rise of the militant movement was a period of Conservative domination and Mrs Fawcett was during most of the period the close ally of the Government. Liberals had shown themselves untrustworthy, 'false to the very essence of liberalism' and afraid that the enfranchisement of women householders would strengthen the Conservatives.[62] If women's suffrage was not attractive to Liberal leaders and much of the rank and file, perhaps Conservatives could be persuaded to adopt it.

The arguments which she developed in this context would have surprised her when she was a young radical, republican and disestablishmentarian. They were boldly enunciated in a speech which she gave to a gathering of Midland Conservative women in 1890. She acknowledged that she was not a Conservative but pointed out that there was little difference between Conservatives and Liberal Unionists. Many voters were grossly ignorant and the Liberal party was putting forward the case for 'one man one vote'. To emancipate educated, propertied women would benefit the country:

> Looked at from the broadest point of view, and not merely from the narrow party point of view, she regarded the women of the country as an immense and very valuable Conservative force in the country . . . There were many things which tended to make women a force for the preservation of order – many things which convinced women of the value of order, and which brought home to them the fact that order was essential to liberty.[63]

A fortnight earlier she had written privately to the editor of *The Scotsman*, an influential Unionist paper, urging in similar terms that the Government should emancipate women householders: 'To face the next general election without women's suffrage is very like going into battle with half your forces unarmed.' Long before suffragists are supposed to have understood the disadvantages of a non-party stand she pointed out that a private member's bill would not pass through Parliament without the support of the Government.[64]

In November of the next year she attended the conference of the National Union of Conservative Associations where she addressed a women's meeting and the conference itself. To both audiences the message was the same, but she expressed herself to the women's meeting in very different terms from her usual dispassion:

> What new forces were they prepared to bring against the anarchy, socialism and revolution which were arrayed against them? The granting of women's suffrage would be against the disintegrating power of the other side, as women were everywhere anti-revolutionary forces.

She was well received by the conference and a somewhat guarded resolution in support of women's suffrage was passed by a large majority, accompanied by loud cheers.[65]

With the decline of Home Rule from its former position of political pre-eminence, the failure of the Conservative leaders to do more than express passive sympathy for women's suffrage, and the drawing together of the various suffrage organizations in the mid-1890s this type of appeal for a Conservative solution to the suffrage question was heard less frequently.[66] Her central message was now more commonly a speech delivered in a variety of versions on the theme 'men are men and women are women'.[67] The speech like others was directed at a particular audience. Anti-suffragists based much of their case on the alleged fact that the two sexes had different qualities and that for women to take part in politics would 'unsex' them, a word whose menace was aggravated by its vagueness.[68] Mrs Fawcett there-fore took her stand on the ground that men and women differed in nature, occupation and training, but that both would benefit from the passage of women's suffrage. 'If men and women were exactly alike', she argued in a speech published as a pamphlet in 1894, 'the representation of men would represent us, but not being alike, that wherein we differ is unrepresented under the present system.'[69]

The home, she claimed, was 'the most important institution in the country'. It should be of greater importance in political life, and granting the parliamentary vote to women would be a means of improving its status. True womanliness, however, should not be confused with false manifestations. 'Is there anything truly feminine in fainting fits, or in screaming at a mouse or at a black beetle?'[70] Women would do much for the community by voting, but they would also have much to gain. The horizons of most women were narrow. To care only for their families and domestic comfort and not the wider community was 'merely selfishness writ large'. The vote would bring 'the ennobling influence of national responsibility' into the lives of women.[71]

If women were not men, neither were they of a single type. Human beings were infinitely variable and each woman should discover her own gifts and learn to develop them like men. Women were not goddesses, objects to be 'set in a shrine and worshipped'. The theory that they should be received a shock 'when brought into contact with the realities of life'.[72] Women, she commented with some bitterness in 1886, were the only sizeable group who were taxed but not represented. 'Women did not blow up gaols, or break windows, or loot shops, and therefore Governments did not pay much attention to them', she observed.[73] But if women did not do these things they took a full part in public life and particularly in elections, providing another argument for the right to vote.

The 1880s was the decade in which women's political organizations were formed, including the Women's Liberal Federation and the Women's Liberal Unionist Association, and senior to both, the Primrose League, whose mass membership and extensive social activities did not hide an efficient and often female-dominated political machine.[74] All contested elections, Mrs Fawcett wrote in 1889, required women's assistance. It was anomalous that women were encouraged by party leaders to make speeches and canvass electors without being able to vote, a function which any 'quiet, retiring woman' could safely undertake. Women were elected to school boards and as poor law guardians, and carried out strenuous duties without ill efffect. It was difficult to see how their physical constitution could inhibit them from putting a piece of paper in a ballot box.[75] She attributed the surprisingly narrow defeat of the women's suffrage bill in 1892 to the fact that MPs required the assistance of women in elections. In consequence 'the most rabid parliamentary opponent of women's freedom hesitates to declare that politics are unwomanly, or that women who care for politics are unsexed harridans.'[76]

She made the same point in an article on women's political activities which she prepared for an American journal in 1892 with her usual thoroughness.[77] The women who were most eagerly sought by political agents, she insisted, were those whose 'looks, dress, and manners' were most womanly. Political participation did not unsex women; if it did it would not be right to take part, and she counselled any woman seduced by the lure of the committee room to abandon political activity at once. She was herself a reluctant participant in the political process, hating to be away from home and counting the minutes 'like a child at school' till she could return.[78] This was a sentiment doubtless shared by many other political figures, though most men would have been unlikely to acknowledge it.

Her arguments for women's suffrage as thus far summarized were designed to reassure particular groups of opinion rather than to challenge the basis of male political power. Women's suffrage was part of the great democratic movement of the day. Women were conservative and would support political stability. They differed from men in character and action and the difference should be recognized in political life. They were already active in political work; to grant them the vote was logical and involved no new point of principle.

In any event the women householders who stood to be enfranchised under existing electoral law would number only about a million as compared to about six million men,[79] since most women were married to householders and would not themselves be enfranchised. Wives would gain enormously from the enfranchisement of single women, however, she wrote in 1886, for the interests of the two groups were similar. She added a poignant comment: 'Unmarried women are every day becoming wives, and, wives, alas! are every day becoming widows.'[80] Her attitude to this question illustrates the fact that while she ridiculed the frequently used concept of 'the thin edge of the wedge' she deployed it herself with considerable skill.[81] She also insisted that advocates of women's suffrage did not wish to turn society upside down or women into men. 'We are seeking to give women the power which would enable them the better to fulfil their duties as women.'[82]

There is no doubt, however, that her primary aim was to redress the existing state of the law in the interests of women. There was scarcely a case of conflict between 'the supposed interests of men and women', she declared, 'in which the state of the law is not flagrantly unjust to women'.[83] Factory acts discriminated against them. Trade unions sought to ban their employment in many trades. The laws of intestacy and probate were grossly unfair to widows. Women and girls had little protection against those who sought to exploit them sexually, especially by driving them into prostitution. Access to divorce was unequal and a woman divorced by her husband had no legal right of access to her children. On the other hand in most cases a woman was solely responsible for her illegitimate child.[84] She suggested ironically that the word 'man' in an act of Parliament included 'woman' only if a tax or penalty were involved. 'Where it is a question of privilege, the word man is apt to bear the more restricted meaning of male person.'[85] She frequently quoted a letter from Charles Pearson, a leading Australian politician and historian, who wrote to her late in 1891 that he hoped to return to live in England. He intended to keep his Victorian domicile, he wrote, for the sake of his daughters. He hoped that if they married they would have good husbands, but if one did not, 'I should not like her to be under the tender mercies of the English law.'[86]

Women's suffrage could not eradicate legal injustice overnight, but it was reasonable to think that it would be women's most effective weapon in their attempts to change the law. The strength of male opposition and the tortured arguments used to justify it lend credence to this belief. Mrs Fawcett pointed out that legal reforms in the position of women in the late nineteenth century had often been inspired by suffragists, and she was to maintain in the last decade of her life with a considerable degree of evidence that the enactment of women's suffrage in 1918 was followed by important and numerous reforms.[87] The problem was not the likely effect of the suffrage but how to achieve it. By 1905 the organized movement had existed for nearly forty years. She had been one of its most active participants during the entire period and was now its most prominent and influential figure. Yet support was too frequently passive and academic, advocates hampered by the very arguments and methods which they intended to maximize their support.[88] It was this stultifying atmosphere of relatively leisured debate, in which few serious politicians devoted more than fleeting attention to the issue, that the militant movement was to shatter and transform. In the process Mrs Fawcett's life, like that of other suffragists, was also to be transformed.

## NOTES

1. Philippa Fawcett to Miss Varty Smith, 15 September 1910 (D/Mar/3/10).
2. Philippa Strachey to Betty Vernon, 20 May 1957 (Fawcett Library, unclassified); Alan Bishop (ed.), Vera Brittain, *Chronicle of Friendship* (Gollancz, 1986), p. 53; Fawcett Library biographical cuttings file.
3. Fawcett Library biographical cuttings file; *MGF*, pp. 204–5.
4. Andrew Rosen, *Rise Up, Women!* (1974), p. 12; Brian Harrison, 'Women's suffrage at Westminster 1866–1928' in Michael Bentley and John Stevenson (eds), *High and Low Politics in Modern Britain* (Oxford: Clarendon Press, 1983), pp. 87, 91. I have considered the fortunes of the suffrage movement in the 1890s in *Before the Suffragettes* (1986), ch. 9.
5. Brian Harrison, *Separate Spheres* (1978), pp. 28–9.
6. *WSJ*, 1 April, 1 May, 1 December 1886, pp. 44, 59, 159–60, 162–3; 1 January, 1 March, 1 April, 1 December 1887, pp. 6, 28, 32–3, 39, 136–7; 1 February, 1 March 1888, pp. 17, 27 (Bedford, Colchester, Manchester, Leicester, Edinburgh, Cambridge, Reading, Nottingham, Bristol, Southport, Brighton, Gloucester, Hastings, Portsmouth).
7. *ibid.*, 1 July 1887, pp. 77–8.

8. For example, *Women's Penny Paper*, 15 December 1888, p. 7.
9. Here I take issue with Brian Harrison. See his 'Women's suffrage at Westminster', esp. p. 96.
10. Quoted in Rosen, *Rise Up*, p. 12.
11. Prominent suffragist Unionists included Lydia Becker, Helen Blackburn, Emily Davies, Millicent Garrett Fawcett, Lilias Ashworth Hallett and Isabella Tod.
12. Membership figures are given by Linda Walker, 'Party political women' (1987), p. 169.
13. *WSJ*, 1 December 1888, p. 113.
14. *ibid.*, 1 January 1889, pp. 7–14; *Women's Penny Paper*, 15 December 1888, pp. 4–5; *ER*, 15 December 1888, pp. 557–60. The best modern account of the split is Marian Ramelson, *The Petticoat Rebellion* (1967), ch. 8.
15. Central Committee of the NSWS, *Report of Executive Committee*, 15 July 1890 (M50/2/11/2).
16. *WSJ*, 1 February 1889, p. 22.
17. Lord Wolmer to MGF, 30 April 1891 (M50/2/1/133); *The Times*, 1 May 1891; *MGF*, pp. 156–7.
18. Lilias Ashworth Hallett to MGF [May 1891] (M50/2/1/142).
19. Jodrell to MGF, 1 May 1891; Woodall to MGF, 2 May 1891 (M50/2/1/136, 138).
20. E[mma] M[iller] to MGF, 1 May 1891 (M50/2/1/135).
21. *WSJ*, 1 January 1889, p. 10.
22. *Women's Penny Paper*, 12 January 1889, p. 4; *WSJ*, 1 May 1890, p. 54.
23. *Woman's Herald*, 5 March 1892, pp. 6–7.
24. Eva McLaren to MGF, 6 May 1892 (M50/2/1/167).
25. MGF, 'Women's suffrage: a reply', *National Review*, March 1888, pp. 44–61; *St James's Gazette*, 7 January 1889; *The Times*, 4 January, 25 February 1889; 'The women's suffrage bill. I. The enfranchisement of women', *Fortnightly Review*, April 1889, pp. 555–67 (quotation, p. 566).
26. MGF in *Woman's Herald*, 5 March 1892, p. 6.
27. MGF, *A Reply to the Letter of Mr Samuel Smith, M.P. on Women's Suffrage* (1892), pp. 4, 6. See also Constance Rover, *Women's Suffrage* (1967), pp. 179–80. The pamphlet has been reprinted in Jane Lewis (ed.), *Before the Vote was Won* (1987), pp. 434–42.
28. 'An appeal against female suffrage', *Nineteenth Century*, June 1889, pp. 780–8. For Beatrice Webb's change of heart see below, page 152.
29. [MGF], 'The appeal against female suffrage, a reply', *ibid.*, July 1889, pp. 86–96; 'Women's suffrage: a reply', *Fortnightly Review*, July 1889, pp. 123–39; Mary St Helier, *Memories of Fifty Years* (1909), pp. 343–5; MGF to Mary Jeune (ch. 9, note 16 above).
30. Lilias Ashworth Hallett to MGF [July 1889] (FLALC, vol. 1a).
31. *The Times*, 7 (Harrison), 12 (MGF), 14 (leader) September 1891. See also MGF, 'The emancipation of women', *Fortnightly Review*, November 1891, pp. 673–85.
32. Central Committee of the NSWS occasional paper, *Conversazione* (1892), p. 73.
33. MGF, 'The women's suffrage question', *Contemporary Review*, June 1892, p. 763.
34. *ER*, 15 July, 16 October 1893, pp. 157–60, 240; 17 January, 16 April, 16 July 1894, pp. 22–4, 104–5, 170; 15 July 1896, p. 169.
35. *The Times*, 7 July 1894.
36. Leaflet in Fawcett Library, marked 'Private and confidential'. This leaflet is cited by Rosamund Billington, 'Women, politics and local liberalism', *Journal of Regional and Local Studies* (vol. 5, 1985), p. 7, which I have followed gratefully through the suffrage morass of the 1890s.

37. Lilias Ashworth Hallett wrote to Mrs Fawcett: 'Both Lady Frances & Miss Curry spoke to me about Miss Bl. being made more presentable. If I were in London I would insist on this' [June 1892] (FLALC, vol. 1a). See also *MGF*, p. 161. For Becker see Rover, *Women's Suffrage*, p. 57.
38. Frances Balfour to MGF [March 1895] (FLA, box 90a file 12).
39. Georgiana Hill, *Women in English Life*, vol. 2 (Bentley, 1896), p. 340; Helen Blackburn, *Women's Suffrage* (1902), p. 225.
40. For whom see Billington, 'Women, politics and local liberalism', p. 8; Rubinstein, *Before the Suffragettes*, pp. 145–6.
41. CNSWS, EC minutes, May–December 1895, *passim* (FLA, box 136); Leslie Parker Hume, *The National Union of Women's Suffrage Societies* (1982), p. 4 & n.
42. *Speeches to Resolution I* (n.d., bound with Fawcett Library women's suffrage pamphlets, 1898), pp. 3–5. Estimates of attendant societies varied from nineteen to twenty-three.
43. *ibid.*, pp. 6–7.
44. MGF to Louisa Garrett, 19 October 1896 (Anderson Papers, St Brelade).
45. Central Committee of NSWS, *Annual Report* 1896, pp. 16–17.
46. The names and number of societies invited to join varied slightly in different accounts.
47. Hume, pp. 4–7. For diagrams of the evolution of suffrage organizations in these years see Rover, *Women's Suffrage*, pp. 54–5, and Brian Harrison, *Prudent Revolutionaries* (1987), pp. 4–5.
48. MGF to Mary Sheepshanks, 9 February 1918 (JRL, IWSA Papers, box 1); *MGF*, p. 178.
49. See below, pages 153–4.
50. See above, pages 74–5, 120.
51. *Women's Suffrage Record*, December 1903, pp. 8–14; 31 December 1904, pp. 7, 10–11; 31 October 1905, p. 12; *ER*, 16 January 1905, pp. 15–19.
52. See above, page 75.
53. *Speeches at a Great Meeting held in Support of the Political Enfranchisement of Women* [1899] (BLPES).
54. Harrison, 'Women's suffrage', pp. 87–8.
55. Rover, *Women's Suffrage*, p. 2. Ann Oakley also discusses this point in 'Millicent Garrett Fawcett' (1983) (pp. 184–5).
56. MGF, introduction to *A Vindication*, pp. 1–3.
57. MGF, *Fortnightly Review* (note 31 above), 681.
58. MGF to Charles H. Pearson, 3 February [1892] and 5 September 1890 (Pearson Papers, Bodleian Library).
59. MGF, *Women's Suffrage* (speech at Owens College, Manchester, 1899), p. 13.
60. MGF, 'The remedy of political emancipation', *New Statesman*, 1 November 1913 (supplement), p. viii.
61. MGF, 'Historical survey' in G. Evelyn Gates (ed.), *The Woman's Year Book 1923–1924* (Women Publishers Ltd [1923]), p. 15. See also *MGF*, pp. 240–1.
62. MGF, 'Women in English politics', *Forum*, December 1892, p. 454.
63. *ER*, 15 October 1890, pp. 372–5.
64. MGF to Charles A. Cooper, 28 July 1890 (M50/2/1/97); Harrison, 'Women's suffrage', pp. 92–4.
65. *The Times*, 25 November 1891.
66. A later example was her address to the Junior Constitutional Club entitled *Women's Suffrage* (1897).
67. This was the title of an article which she wrote for *The Englishwoman* in February 1909, subsequently reprinted by the NUWSS. See below, page 202.
68. See Harrison, *Separate Spheres*, esp. ch. 4.

69. MGF, *Home and Politics* [1894], p. 3; reprinted in Lewis (ed.), pp. 418–24. Sandra Stanley Holton, *Feminism and Democracy* (1986), quotes a similar comment made in 1889.
70. MGF, *Home and Politics*, pp. 4, 7.
71. MGF, *Fortnightly Review* (note 25 above), p. 560; Owens College speech (note 59 above), p. 5.
72. *The Times*, 12 September 1891; *Fortnightly Review* (note 31 above), p. 685.
73. *The Times*, 21 October 1886.
74. Walker, pp. 165–91; Rubinstein, *Before the Suffragettes*, pp. 150–8; Martin Pugh, *The Tories and the People* (Oxford: Blackwell, 1985), esp. ch. 3.
75. *Fortnightly Review* (note 29 above), pp. 124, 128–9.
76. *Contemporary Review* (note 33 above), p. 763.
77. Replies from the Women's Liberal Federation and the Primrose League to her requests for information are filed at M50/2/26/29 and 30. For the article see note 62 above.
78. MGF, 'Women in English politics', p. 459.
79. For this estimate see her *Women's Suffrage* (note 66 above), p. 4.
80. MGF, 'Women's suffrage: a reply', *Nineteenth Century*, May 1886, p. 747.
81. *Women's Suffrage* (note 66 above), p. 12; Owens College speech (note 59 above), p. 11; *Speeches at a Great Meeting* (note 53 above), p. 6.
82. *Speeches to Resolution I* (note 42 above), p. 4.
83. *Reply to Samuel Smith* (note 27 above), p. 6.
84. *ibid.*, pp. 6–7; *Fortnightly Review* (note 29 above), pp. 126–8.
85. Owens College speech (note 59 above), p. 8.
86. Pearson to MGF, 25 December 1891 (M50/2/26/2).
87. *Fortnightly Review* (note 29 above), p. 128. See below, page 258, 264.
88. This claim was persuasively advanced by Teresa Billington-Greig, 'Feminism and politics', *Contemporary Review*, November 1911, p. 697.

# PART III

## THE SUFFRAGE AT LAST 1906–18

# CHAPTER 12

·

# THE ADVENT OF MILITANCY 1906–9

In June 1905 Mrs Fawcett celebrated her fifty-eighth birthday. It would have been natural for her to have assumed that she was moving towards the end of her career in the women's suffrage movement rather than standing on the threshold of its most active phase. Despite triumphs in a few American states, Australia and New Zealand, and the development of the National Union of Women's Suffrage Societies, the movement seemed no closer to success than it had ever been. Unionist and Liberal politicians alike continued to offer only honeyed words. Moreover, she had resigned from the Women's Liberal Unionist Association in 1904 after the Unionist leaders' conversion to a protectionist policy and thus lost her privileged access to party circles. Her old loyalty to free trade was too strong to accept tariff reform, and she told the WLUA council that she and other free-traders 'were not prepared to spend a shilling of their money, nor one hour of their time' to assist protectionist candidates.[1]

The Women's Social and Political Union was founded in 1903 and launched its militant activity in October 1905,[2] but the symbol of a new age was the sweeping victory of the Liberal party in the general election of January 1906. It was followed by a period of intense political controversy unparalleled since Chartist days sixty years earlier. Discussion was exciting and hope was great. Suddenly everything seemed possible and women's suffrage moved closer to the centre of the political stage than it had ever been. The election of thirty Labour MPs, members of another disadvantaged group, provided evidence that a more democratic age was dawning and gave suffragists an unprecedentedly faithful nucleus of parliamentary supporters.[3] By this time there was a number of suffragists with a labour movement background, including Isabella Ford, Charlotte Despard and Emmeline Pankhurst. They were followed by a generation of younger women who were unafraid of organizational association with the labour movement. With their support the NUWSS was to form a working relationship with the Labour party which, though not free from problems, was of a wholly different character from any previous alliance with politicians.

149

The year 1906 witnessed dramatic developments in the suffrage campaign, pallid as they were to seem in contrast with subsequent events. But its principal significance lay in the fact that the triumphant Liberal Government proved to be no more amenable than its predecessors. In the new conditions of political life the consequence was to be the development of militancy. By the end of the year it was an established fact of political life, though Mrs Fawcett was not alone in refusing to recognize an unbridgeable division between militant and constitutional methods.

Sir Henry Campbell-Bannerman, the new Prime Minister, professed to sympathize with women's suffrage, though he did so with little enthusiasm.[4] He consented after some pressure to receive a deputation of MPs, suffragists and other women's leaders, a concession never previously granted by a prime minister. At the meeting, in May 1906, he acknowledged that the suffragists had established an 'irrefutable' case for their cause. His own sympathy was not shared by all his colleagues, and like all ambitious or successful male politicians he put the perceived needs of his party firmly before justice to women. He advised the deputation to 'go on converting the country as you have been doing during the last half-dozen years', advice widely reported as 'go on pestering'. It is not surprising that dissent was expressed at the meeting itself nor that he should be regarded by militants as 'that false smiling C.B.'[5]

Although in early 1906 the WSPU was 'still a tiny provincial movement', it had succeeded in making its presence known by heckling and interruptions at Liberal election meetings.[6] Even these early moves caused considerable alarm to some suffragists,[7] and it was to allay their fears that Mrs Fawcett wrote a letter to the *Westminster Gazette* which was widely read and discussed in suffrage ranks. The WSPU had originally been an organization of labour movement women, and Mrs Pankhurst introduced herself to Campbell-Bannerman in May as a working women's representative.[8] It was therefore natural that in her letter published the previous January Mrs Fawcett should have characterized militant methods as the actions of working-class women newly recruited to the suffrage struggle.

Women, she observed, were universally welcomed as canvassers, but when they asked for the right to vote the response was outrage and ridicule. 'The societies which have worked for Women's Suffrage consist mainly of middle-class women. We have conducted ourselves with perfect propriety in our middle-class way, and have got nothing for our pains.' Working-class women conducted themselves in their own fashion. 'Their way is not our way', but it might prove to be more effective, for politicians were often more responsive to those who proved themselves troublesome. Supporters of women's suffrage should not denounce those whose methods differed from their own.[9] The development of militancy in subsequent years caused her to disregard her own advice, but her fundamental belief never altered; suffragists should confront the common enemy rather than attack each other.

Not all the surviving correspondence stimulated by this letter or its re-publication in other journals[10] was sympathetic. One suffragist reduced her contribution to the cause in consequence and Margaret Ashton, soon to be an NUWSS leader, denied that those responsible were working women. 'It has been most deplorable from all points of view', she wrote.[11] On the other side her friend Isabella Ford expressed her delight: 'I feel so grateful to you for your name carries such tremendous weight of course.' W.T. Stead, now editor of the *Review of Reviews* and a valued suffragist ally, also wrote to express his wholehearted agreement with her defence of 'our fighting For-wards'.[12] It is likely that at this stage most constitutional suffragists would have agreed with Mrs Pollard of the Women's Institute, a women's club and centre, who wrote to a member who had resigned in protest at an invitation to the militant Annie Kenney to address members: 'I do not like Miss Kenney's methods and have no wish to join them; but I am perfectly prepared to benefit by the suffrage if she and her party succeed where we have failed.' She associated herself with the Fawcett view that quiet, respect-able methods had failed and must be supplemented by other forms of protest.[13]

Mrs Fawcett remained sympathetic towards militancy throughout 1906 and beyond. In June, Annie Kenney, Teresa Billington and other militants besieged the London home of H.H. Asquith, the Chancellor of the Exche-quer who was known to be a powerful enemy of women's suffrage. Several were arrested and imprisoned,[14] and in July Mrs Fawcett wrote a long letter to the *Women's Tribune* in their support. Again her concern was to prevent a breach between working-class suffragists and educated, refined women alarmed by militant methods. Every movement, she wrote, attracted 'excit-able temperaments'. In addition it was a matter of historical fact that exten-sions of the franchise had in almost every case been accompanied by militant methods. Prison sentences often carried more weight than pamphlets or speeches:

> The verdict of history has not hitherto placed the responsibility on the excit-able people who land themselves in prison, but on the stupid people who will not listen to any claim to justice until the claimants show that they are able to make themselves in some way unbearable nuisances.[15]

On 23 October 1906 the impact of militancy was further sharpened when a WSPU demonstration took place in the lobby of the House of Commons. Ten women were arrested, most of whom were already known as promi-nent figures in the militant movement. They included Mary Gawthorpe, Emmeline Pethick-Lawrence, Annie Kenney and Annie Cobden Sander-son, a friend of Mrs Fawcett and, embarrassingly for the Government, a daughter of Richard Cobden. Tried and found guilty, they refused to be bound over and were sentenced to two months in prison.[16]

The next day, in Tunbridge Wells, Mrs Fawcett took the chair at a discussion of women's suffrage. The occasion was the annual conference of the National Union of Women Workers, of which she had been a vice-president since 1895. She told the meeting, which manifested overwhelming support for women's suffrage, that to attempt to secure legal reforms without votes was 'like pulling a bell rope with no bell at the other end'. She praised the assistance which the Labour party had given to the suffrage cause, a bold declaration before a middle-class audience, and ended her contribution by appealing for unity among suffragists: 'We have plenty of enemies outside, let us hold together.'[17] It was a generous statement, as Elizabeth Robins, the American-born actress and writer who had made a striking intervention at the NUWW meeting, recognized in a letter of thanks. Mrs Fawcett's attitude, she wrote, had been 'an invaluable help' to suffrage newcomers like herself.[18] Another participant at the Tunbridge Wells meeting was Evelyn Sharp, who had been sent to report it for the *Manchester Guardian*. She recalled that Mrs Fawcett's speech 'rose to the drama of the occasion' and that the meeting altered the course of her own life; soon afterwards she joined the militant movement.[19] Another significant development was the recantations of Louise Creighton and Beatrice Webb, formerly prominent opponents of women's suffrage.[20] It must have seemed likely that the long log jam of indifference and hostility was about to break up.

Mrs Fawcett followed her statement at Tunbridge Wells with a letter to *The Times* which was reprinted and widely quoted. Nearly half a century's work for women's suffrage had achieved nothing, she pointed out, and 'more sensational' methods were the consequence. The militant women had been insulted and abused, particularly in the 'reptile' press. 'But', she declared:

> I hope the more old-fashioned suffragists will stand by them; and I take this opportunity of saying that in my opinion, far from having injured the movement, they have done more during the last 12 months to bring it within the region of practical politics than we have been able to accomplish in the same number of years.[21]

It is acknowledged even by critics of the militant movement that in its early phase it awakened interest in women's suffrage as never before.[22] It was, however, a courageous admission for Mrs Fawcett to make in 1906. She not only acknowledged the failure of the movement to which she had devoted her life but risked the loss of suffragists who were unwilling to be associated with militancy. The pragmatism of her approach on this question and her ability to work in harmony with the strong personalities of the NUWSS helps to explain her success as a suffrage leader. It stands in stark contrast to her uncompromising behaviour towards Harry Cust, Irish nationalists and the 'pro-Boer' opponents of the South African war.

Letters to Mrs Fawcett from the Liberal suffragist and parliamentarian Walter McLaren reveal that after the imprisonment of the ten militants in October 1906 she wished to stage a protest demonstration, a desire supported by McLaren. His belief that the imprisonment of the ten had done more to make women's suffrage 'a real live question . . . than all the work of years [had] been able to do', however, was not shared by other colleagues and the plan was abandoned.[23]

Instead, she and other leading suffragists staged a banquet at the Savoy Hotel on 11 December to welcome the ten upon their release from prison. Speaking from the chair she praised the courage and self-sacrifice of the militants and the inspiration which they had given to other suffragists. She warned MPs that the patience of women was at last exhausted. It was, as *Women and Progress* wrote, 'one of those splendid addresses for which she is famous'.[24] Two slightly awed accounts, one in an American journal, described her appearance and manner shortly before her sixtieth birthday. One wrote that she had 'a most motherly face, with the fine rosy complexion of a hunting squire's wife, crowned with the high expansive forehead of a great statesman'. It also mentioned the logic, enthusiasm and humour of her speech. The other described her as 'a dignified, oldtime lady with lilies-of-the-valley in her dress and diamonds on her neck'. Support for the alliance between conservative and militant suffragists, it wrote, 'was sanctioned with her unrivalled authority'.[25]

It might be appropriate to term 1906 an age of innocence, before the unbridgeable gulf between opposing suffrage factions became first obvious and then inescapable. After the prisoners had begun their sentences in Holloway, Mrs Fawcett wrote a comprehensive and thoughtful article defending law-breaking as a political tactic. The article was a restrained and moving declaration of faith in the prisoners and the potential of women. She acknowledged the achievements of the older suffragists: 'But John Bull still will not move without something in the nature, I will not say of a kick, but of an electric shock. We older workers were plodding but not magnetic; we could not give the requisite electric shock.' To do so was the achievement of the younger generation: 'The prisoners have roused the country, and Women's Suffrage has become practical politics.'[26]

Until the start of 1907 Mrs Fawcett could speak largely for herself, for the NUWSS was still a loose federation without a strong central leadership. In January 1907, however, a new constitution was adopted which provided for elected oficers, an executive committee and a quarterly policy-making council. Although she had achieved a unique position in suffrage circles, the question of the presidency had not been decided before the annual council meeting convened in Newcastle on 31 January with Bertha Mason, subsequently the NUWSS treasurer, in the chair. Several societies had nominated Lady Frances Balfour, president of the Central (soon afterwards London) Society for Women's Suffrage.[27] Lady Frances had agreed at Mrs Fawcett's suggestion to stand for the presidency of what was still the Central Committee of the National Society for Women's Suffrage in 1896, while protesting that Mrs Fawcett herself would have been the better choice.[28] By 1907, however, she appeared to have conquered her inhibitions and an election was arranged, though its details were confidential.[29] In any event Mrs Fawcett emerged from the Newcastle council as president of the NUWSS. With its new structure and the new prominence which militancy had given to the suffrage cause, the union was clearly going to exert a much greater impact on the political scene than in its first decade.

A week later the rejuvenated NUWSS took part in the first large-scale public demonstration of the new suffrage era. This was the so-called 'mud march', held in bleak London rain on 9 February. Organized by the Central Society (which Mrs Fawcett had chaired since the separatist London societies had merged in 1900) it was an unprecedented event supported by women of all social classes and political convictions, and unofficially by a number of militants, in a remarkable display of unity in the common cause. The NUWSS leaders claimed that the march was a mile long and the biggest demonstration held in London in their generation. Mrs Fawcett was one of the leaders, and though she did not preside over the subsequent rally at Exeter Hall as she was to do in later years, she was, with Keir Hardie and the novelist Israel Zangwill, among the principal speakers. The event secured wide publicity and was regarded as a success. It was not an easy matter, however, for all the marchers to decide to take part. It required considerable courage to ignore one's upbringing, the surprise or disapprobation of acquaintances and the jeers of bystanders.[30] Lady Frances Balfour, for one, was a reluctant participant in this type of event. But, she recalled, 'Mrs Fawcett thoroughly enjoyed [marching], and pirouetted through her part as leader with the step of a girl of seventeen.'[31]

Now that the attention of the public had been caught it was necessary to hold it by evidence of the continued growth of the movement, publicity-attracting events and the hint of the mailed fist. It was a relatively easy matter for the WSPU leadership to intensify militancy, though both con-temporaries and historians have insisted that the policy was self-defeating. For the constitutionalists, however, more imagination was required as well as meticulous organization and administration. It was fortunate that women with the necessary skills were willing to put them to the service of the movement.

Later in February 1907 five women, including Mrs Fawcett, requested Parliament to be allowed to plead at the bar of the House of Commons in support of a petition to remove the political disabilities of women. The novel gesture failed, but it enabled the petitioners to claim that they acted on behalf of women of all social classes and political parties. Mrs Fawcett herself wrote as a Unionist as she did in a further statement the following month,[32] but it was a designation which she shortly abandoned, a sensible move in face of a Liberal Government with an overwhelming majority. By the time that Irish Home Rule again became a major political controversy after the elections of 1910 she was too strenuously engaged in negotiations over women's suffrage bills to allow herself to damage the cause by taking part in extraneous battles. Her behaviour was a revealing indication not only of her changed priorities but of the growth of support for women's suffrage since the 1890s.

Skelton Anderson's death prevented her from presiding as advertised at a mass meeting at the Queen's Hall in March 1907 at which Bernard Shaw was the principal speaker.[33] She was, however, heavily involved in the same period in establishing the NUWSS by-election policy. In distinction to the WSPU, which had already determined on a policy of opposition to Liberal candidates, the national union decided to support friends of women's suffrage regardless of their party affiliation.[34] There followed the famous by-election at Wimbledon at which Bertrand Russell, already a leading mathematician and philosopher, a strong Liberal and NUWSS executive committee member, courageously stood as a women's suffrage candidate and unofficial Liberal in a hopeless seat. Mrs Fawcett warmly supported him, gave what a local paper described as 'a most eloquent speech' at an election meeting and £20 to his election fund. Large numbers of suffragists worked strenuously on Russell's behalf, and despite his heavy defeat the campaign produced useful publicity and much enthusiasm. It involved, however, an unacceptable expenditure of money and effort, and though the union was active in later by-elections, it was careful not to shoulder the entire burden as it had done with Russell.[35]

Mrs Fawcett, now the acknowledged leader of the largest suffragist organization, was already beginning to be treated with the veneration which was to be so marked a feature of her later years. Her reserved and unemotional manner, however, meant that she disappointed those who sought impassioned leadership. The militant sympathizer Maud Arncliffe-Sennett, whose archives provide an essential record of the later years of the suffrage struggle wrote in a moment of irritation that she was 'all brains but utterly without *heart*'.[36] A picture more acceptable to NUWSS members was drawn a few months earlier by her colleague Edith Palliser in a published profile. She was, Palliser wrote, 'not demonstrative; her feelings do not lie near the surface; nevertheless the strong motive power is there, the fire, the force and the passionate belief in the justice and expediency of women's claims'.[37] This was also the privately expressed view of Lady Frances Balfour, who had seen her in many different situations: 'She is the most extraordinary mixture of emotion, with a steel control.'[38]

As a speaker she excelled not with the bludgeon but with the rapier. A by-election speech in Hull in November 1907 provides an illustration. Opponents of votes for women, she pointed out, constantly reiterated that women's place was the home: 'To that I would say that man doesn't live by bread alone, but very largely upon catchwords.'[39] Her wit, respectability and lucidity made her the natural choice as the first woman to address the

*Millicent Garrett Fawcett speaking at the Oxford Union, November 1908.*

Oxford Union a year later. Inevitably the occasion was a debate on women's suffrage, in which she supported the case put forward by the 20-year-old 'Ronnie' Knox, who already enjoyed a reputation for brilliance and was later a celebrated Roman Catholic priest, wit and author.[40] She claimed that votes for women would be likely to result in higher wages for sweated workers, a benefit to the entire community. Women had proved themselves in local government, she pointed out, paying a scarcely veiled tribute to her sister Elizabeth who had, a few days earlier, again established a precedent for women by her election as mayor of Aldeburgh. It was said that women were too ignorant to vote: 'At election times it was wonderful how desirous the candidates were to get the help of these peculiarly ignorant people, who were asked to persuade others to vote, but were not considered good enough to have the vote.' The defeat of the motion to remove the electoral liabilities of women by 329 to 360 in an all-male assembly as inclined to contemptuous frivolity on the subject as the late Victorian House of Commons was a considerable achievement.[41]

One of the principal problems confronting Mrs Fawcett in this period came from within her own ranks. This was the demand for adult suffrage, which the Labour Representation Committee had adopted in place of women's suffrage at its conference in 1905.[42] There was much to be said on both sides. The aim of both constitutional and militant suffragists was to add women with the same property qualifications as men to the existing electoral register. Votes for women ratepayers, whose numbers were relatively small, would satisfy a crucial principle without offering a serious challenge to male control of political power. Whatever Mrs Fawcett had said in her speeches it was a classic case of the thin end of the wedge. But a Liberal Government was in office, conscious of its increasing need to appeal to a working-class electorate. The various attempts to prove that women voters would be mostly 'working women'[43] appeared contrary to the dictates of common sense. In any case the Liberal leaders did not believe them, and regarded the women's suffrage leaders with understandable scepticism.

For Mrs Fawcett and those who thought like her the issue was simple. Their goal was women's suffrage. At a time when the level of male enfranchisement was less than 60 per cent, adult suffrage would have been a reform so sweeping as to attract only those committed to full-scale political democracy. These included the Women's Co-operative Guild and its remarkable secretary Margaret Llewelyn Davies, leading women socialists and trade unionists, and within the ranks of the NUWSS Marion Phillips, for a period its secretary, and Bertrand Russell.[44]

Mrs Fawcett was in no doubt as to what was at stake: 'To ask for adult suffrage now', she wrote in 1906, 'is in reality to oppose Women's Suffrage.' In a country in which women outnumbered men, adult suffrage would mean a female majority in every constituency and 'the demand for this would put off Women's Suffrage to the Greek Kalends.'[45] There seems little point in arguing which side was fighting the correct battle, but it should be stressed that women's suffrage was a cause which was already widely popular and was to become a mass movement. Adult suffrage was not and never became so.[46] Even Russell admitted in a letter to Llewelyn Davies in November 1907: 'It seems to me 90% of working men don't wish their wives to have votes.'[47]

Although the adult suffrage strand within the national union was never more than a vocal minority, it was one which Mrs Fawcett took seriously. It was coupled with what seemed to her a wholly misguided faith in the good intentions of the Liberal party and particularly H.H. Asquith, its strongest figure. Her feeling was reinforced when she led an NUWSS deputation to Asquith at the Treasury in January 1908. She remembered with scorn his apparent fear of assault by members of the deputation and with bitterness the contempt with which he subsequently treated them.[48]

Asquith became Prime Minister in April 1908. In retrospect it almost seems that suffragists should have taken up some other issue until he left office, for it seems inconceivable that any women's suffrage bill would have been passed during his tenure whatever the behaviour of its advocates.[49] They took such comfort as they could from the fact that he led a party some of whose members were apparently firmly committed to women's suffrage, while others felt it was a cause which they should or dared no longer oppose. On 20 May he promised a deputation of suffragist MPs that his intended electoral reform bill would be framed so that women could be included by amendment,[50] an offer which then seemed more attractive than in later years when it was devalued by repetition and disappointment.

Bertrand Russell enthusiastically supported Asquith's statement and Mrs Fawcett warned him that in her view Asquith had done no more than to lift the issue

> another rung or two up the political ladder. We must remember that he has always been and remains an enemy of the movement and it looks to me now very much as if he were heading us off (or trying to do so) with the Adult Suffrage trap . . . I have as a suffragist suffered too much from the political tricks of official liberalism for the last 30 years, not to be on my guard against them now.[51]

It is difficult not to sympathize with her scepticism, but her long memory, her years of hostility to the Liberal party and her animosity towards Asquith could not have been helpful in the years of negotiations with 'official liberalism' which lay ahead.

Russell, who replied 'I fear you must think me a person very easily taken in',[52] told readers of the *Women's Franchise*: 'Success is now at last in sight.' He was publicly rebuked by Mrs Fawcett, who pointed out that he did not write on behalf of the NUWSS executive, and by his brother Frank, Lord Russell, but told Margaret Llewelyn Davies that he was 'unrepentant'.[53] Writing to him at about the same time, as a member of the younger, democratic wing of the constitutionalist movement, Llewelyn Davies assessed the position of the NUWSS leader: 'I should think Mrs Fawcett and her "trap" view, might be disregarded. She is useful as a re-assuring element to the backward – & by mere advocacy of the suffrage does more good than harm to us whatever she advocates.'[54]

Russell believed early in 1909 that he was making progress in converting the executive to support for a wider franchise, and correspondence in his papers suggests that he may have been right.[55] Certainly Mrs Fawcett was the leading figure among those who insisted that votes should be demanded for women householders only. She estimated their numbers in March 1909 at two million or less.[56] She wrote to Russell a few days earlier, defending herself against the charge of having exceeded agreed policy and expressing regret at his threatened resignation from the executive, 'especially if it is I who have driven you off it'.[57] The following autumn he led an attack on her for allegedly again ignoring executive decisions. He had denounced her at the NUWSS quarterly council meeting and had himself been denounced for doing so, he told an American friend.[58] The simmering quarrel continued until he resigned from the executive at the end of 1909 and Marion Phillips left her position as secretary the following spring.

In resigning, Russell told Phillips that his primary concern was not women's suffrage but the bitter struggle between the Liberals and the House of Lords.[59] This was a logical position for a democratic Liberal but untenable for one to whom women's suffrage came before all else. Mrs Fawcett was pre-eminently a suffragist, and she had now succeeded in shaking off the challenge of Russell and his sympathizers. He may have been right in suggesting that 'long advocacy of a reform almost always destroys judgment'[60], but it seems more accurate to point out that she was a political leader while Russell was not. He admitted to one of his correspondents as he was about to resign from the union's executive that 'the Liberals . . . can't carry Adult Suffrage till the country is willing to have it'.[61] Women's suffrage, however remote it might still be, seemed a more practicable aim than the political never-never land of a trebled electorate.

It is improbable that Mrs Fawcett was an enthusiast for adult suffrage before the sweeping electoral change of 1918. But it is a mistake to group her, as Margaret Llewelyn Davies did in 1907, with her aunt Emily Davies, a lifelong Conservative.[62] A political leader could not lag behind events. As time passed and enfranchisement on democratic lines seemed increasingly possible she repeatedly made clear her support for such a solution. Two years after Russell left the executive, when the Government was preparing its own franchise bill, the union issued a statement, signed by Mrs Fawcett, which affirmed: 'We want as much suffrage for women as we can get.'[63] In the same month C.P. Scott, editor of the *Manchester Guardian*, noted in his diary that he had been told that Mrs Fawcett's principle was ' "The more suffrage for women the better.' "[64] In one of her last speeches before the outbreak of war in 1914 she declared her support for a law 'framed on a broad and democratic basis'.[65] Her constant concern was to break through the blanket ban on women voters by whatever means seemed most likely to find political acceptance. The arithmetic of enfranchisement was of secondary importance.

The adult suffrage–women's suffrage controversy was one of Mrs Fawcett's principal problems in the early militant years, but it was overtaken by the growing crisis in relations between the NUWSS and the WSPU. Militancy was changing its form and becoming increasingly violent; neither the union nor its leader could be shielded from the consequences. One consequence was that not only politicians' meetings but their own were increasingly likely to be disrupted. The age was still turbulent. As Brian Harrison comments: 'Physical force . . . was the occupational hazard of the reformer in Britain before 1914.'[66] Young men willing to create a disturbance were always at hand, and likely to make their presence known given any excuse for intervention. As early as November 1906 a meeting which Mrs Fawcett chaired in Brighton was disrupted. It was a meeting held to persuade men of the reasons for women's suffrage and about a thousand attended, but after her opening remarks neither Charlotte Despard, Ethel Snowden nor Mrs Fawcett herself could gain a hearing.[67]

Eighteen months later she made a short tour of South Wales with Mrs Despard, a militant leader in her mid-sixties who had broken with the Pankhursts in the autumn of 1907, and with other dissidents established the Women's Freedom League. A meeting in Cardiff was broken up and an hour spent in the streets 'dodging crowds of hooting young hooligans', Mrs Despard wrote, though it proved possible to stage another meeting in a different hall. 'Mrs Fawcett['s] . . . dignity and coolness never once deserted her.' At Pontypridd the meeting was also broken up and a meeting held for sympathizers only in a darkened hall with lowered curtains and without applause.[68] In an interview with the *Pontypridd Observer* Mrs Fawcett said that she had always advocated women's suffrage by constitutional means and would continue to do so. 'It was indeed a pleasure to listen to her', the reporter wrote. 'Her pleasing countenance, combined with her vivacity and wit, charmed one . . . Mrs Despard enthused, while Mrs Fawcett convinced.'[69]

In July 1909 a public meeting held in Nottingham before an NUWSS council meeting was equally rowdy and Mrs Fawcett's colleagues feared for her safety. She managed to obtain a hearing before her platform was rushed and wrote to her colleague Frances Sterling that she had never been in danger. The next day she appeared 'serene and self-possessed as ever' at the council meeting.[70] Although she made light of the incident it could not have been pleasant for a mid-Victorian lady approaching old age.

More important than being shouted down at meetings or even 'hooted & chased through the streets of Cardiff by howling students & miners',[71] was the impact of the militant suffragists on the prospects for women's suffrage. It gradually became clear that militancy not only antagonized many suffragists, but after its initial propaganda successes roused strong opposition in politically powerful quarters. Few of the opponents would have been likely to support women's suffrage whatever the circumstances, but a moderate movement facing moderate opposition was in danger of being eclipsed by the rise of a militant movement, whose political challenge could be ignored and its use of violence dismissed as posing no more than a problem of law and order.[72]

In March 1907 Mrs Fawcett replied to a letter from the importunate Maud Arncliffe-Sennett, stating friendly but firm opposition to a suggestion that the NUWSS and WSPU should amalgamate: 'We can and I hope we shall help each other most, by promoting our common cause each in our own way.'[73] She wrote to the press the following November, stressing the union's commitment to constitutional methods but pointing out the disadvantages of such a policy in terms of publicity. 'The Press . . . loves sensation' and constitutional demonstrations were often ignored.[74]

Enormous publicity, however, attended the separate peaceful demonstrations staged by the two unions in June 1908.[75] Writing to *The Times* a month earlier Mrs Fawcett and three of her colleagues called attention to the fact that in staging its march and rally the national union was emphasizing its constitutional status, although 'most of us recognise the help our cause has received from the courage and self-sacrifice of the members of the "militant" societies'. There was 'no rivalry or hostility' between the two events, she added later.[76] The union organized a march from the Embankment to the Albert Hall, a distance of two miles, led by Mrs Fawcett in her doctor's robes, Lady Frances Balfour, Emily Davies who at 78 was a veteran of the women's suffrage petition of 1867, and Sophie Bryant, a prominent London headmistress and doctor of science who also wore academic dress. The march was a blaze of flags, banners and colour, which almost defeated the descriptive powers of the press. James Douglas, a leading journalist, wrote in the *Daily Leader*: 'It was more stately and more splendid and more beautiful than any procession I ever saw.'[77] At the Albert Hall the presentation of thirty bouquets of flowers to Mrs Fawcett by representatives of the 10–15,000 marchers reduced her to tears. When she had recovered she told her audience that their cause was as great as any the world had ever seen and urged them to dedicate their lives to its success.[78]

The WSPU rally in Hyde Park the following week was a very much larger affair, attracting between 250,000 and 500,000 participants and spectators. Not unfairly Henry Nevinson, a famous journalist with militant sympathies, contrasted the 'cultured procession' with the 'vast democratic assembly' and pointed out that without the WSPU the national union's procession 'would never have been held or thought of'.[79] Whatever the outside stimulus, however, the NUWSS had demonstrated both its ability to mount an imaginative and impressive spectacle and the wide range of its support.

*Women's suffrage procession, June 1908.*

The divisions between the two unions displayed in June 1908 began to move towards an open breach at the end of the same month, when WSPU supporters first added stones to their offensive armoury.[80] Once begun the resort to violence soon became increasingly marked, and Mrs Fawcett was particularly distressed by a call from Christabel Pankhurst to 'the lowest classes of London roughs and the dangerous hordes of unemployed' to 'rush the House of Commons' when it reassembled on 13 October.[81] Like most people of her age she believed that women should behave in a more dignified and restrained manner than men, and that law and order were particularly precious to them.[82] But even after this incident she was unenthusiastic about demands to attack the WSPU, fearing that 'the enemy' wanted to divert suffragists from their proper target.[83]

November was the critical month for relations between the two organizations. Mrs Fawcett wrote to Lady Frances on the 7th:

We are all tarred with the same brush in the eye of the general public. We must just go on: and take every opportunity of emphasising that our set do care for law and order and are citizens even before we are women's suffragists.

The national union must be identified with constitutional methods and those who could not accept them should resign: 'I think we could dwell on this without *attacking* the militants. I still feel that they have "roused the country" more than we were ever able to do. More shame for the country.'[84]

A few days later, in a letter from its officers to members of the House of Commons, the national union recorded its 'strong objection' to the resort to violence. Mrs Fawcett recalled in a covering statement her defence of the militants in 1906 and pointed out that in the interval violence had become more frequent and more extreme. Societies which stood for the use of lawful methods should say so. She again acknowledged the courage and self-sacrifice of the militants, 'but when they adopt methods which we believe to be wrong in themselves, we are compelled to dissociate ourselves from them.'[85] Criticized for initially defending women whose actions she now sought to disown she replied without embarrassment: 'I do not sit in judgment on those who believe that injustice can best be met by violence. They have a good deal of history on their side.' But those who thought their new methods 'wrong in themselves' must say so.[86]

The national union moved carefully, for some of its local societies were not convinced that a breach with the WSPU would help either the suffrage cause or their own effectiveness.[87] The London Society for Women's Suffrage was deeply divided by the issue in 1908–9 and Mrs Fawcett was so concerned that she cancelled speaking engagements in Yorkshire in November 1908 to attend the society's annual meeting.[88] She and her friends issued a slate of preferred candidates for its committee and a three-line whip in favour of a resolution limiting membership to adherents of 'lawful and constitutional methods'[89] The successful battle was the more piquant because one of her defeated opponents was her niece Louisa Garrett

Anderson, who had vainly attempted to convince 'Dearest Aunt Millie' of the desirability of supporting the WSPU.[90]

As violence intensified in 1909 the breach between the two organizations became irrevocable. It was illustrated by the increasingly peremptory manner in which Mrs Fawcett rejected three times in little more than three months appeals from Maud Arncliffe-Sennett for amalgamation or cooperation between them.[91] Early in October the NUWSS held its quarterly council meeting in Cardiff. Shortly before it took place she wrote to the suffragist Helena Auerbach: 'I feel the present crisis to be most serious & that strong steps ought to be taken in the most authoritative manner to dissociate the NU [from WSPU violence].'[92] At the council meeting she traced the evolution of her own position from admirer to opponent of the WSPU. After a long discussion the council passed by a large majority a resolution which 'strongly condemns the use of violence in political propaganda' while also strongly protesting against the Government's response to the suffrage agitation.[93]

At the end of 1909 the impasse was total. With a divided movement and a hostile government, women's suffrage, which had so recently seemed within reach, was apparently as tantalizingly far away as ever. The mixture of hope and frustration which had thus become established was to remain a familiar characteristic of subsequent years.

NOTES

1. *The Times*, 15 March 1904; WLUA notes (FLA, box 90a file 5).
2. E. Sylvia Pankhurst, *The Suffragette Movement* (1931), pp. 168, 189.
3. Brian Harrison, *Separate Spheres* (1978), p. 42.
4. John Wilson, *CB: A life of Sir Henry Campbell-Bannerman* (Constable, 1973), p. 510.
5. *ibid.*; *Women's Suffrage Deputation* [1906], pp. 13–14, 16 (BLPES); *The Times*, 21 May 1906; Jill Liddington, *The Life and Times of a Respectable Rebel* (1984), p. 169; Dora B. Montefiore to Selina Cooper, 31 May [1906] (Cooper Papers, Lancashire County Record Office).
6. Andrew Rosen, *Rise Up, Women!* (1974), pp. 54–7.
7. For example, Caroline Skinner to MGF, 10 and 14 January 1906 (M50/2/1/214, 215).
8. Rosen, *Rise Up*, pp. 30–5; *Women's Suffrage Deputation*, p. 9.
9. *Westminster Gazette*, 12 January 1906.
10. These included the *Manchester Guardian* and, in abridged form, the *Daily News*, 13 January 1906.
11. G.M. Fullerton to Edith Palliser, 19 January 1906 (FLALC, vol. 1bi); Margaret Ashton to MGF, 16 January 1906 (M50/2/1/225). See Jill Liddington and Jill Norris, *One Hand Tied Behind Us* (1978), pp. 194–5.
12. Isabella O. Ford to MGF, 14 January 1906; W.T. Stead to MGF, 13 January 1906 (M50/2/1/222, 219); see Sandra Stanley Holton, *Feminism and Democracy* (1986), pp. 35–7.
13. Mrs Pollard to Miss Somerville, 6 June 1906 (FLALC, vol. 1bii); quoted in Billington thesis, p. 614n.

14. Pankhurst, pp. 212–13; Rosen, *Rise Up*, pp. 67–8.
15. *Women's Tribune*, 13 July 1906, pp. 197–8; Billington thesis, pp. 615–16.
16. Pankhurst, pp. 228–9; Rosen, *Rise Up*, p. 74.
17. *The Times*, 26 October 1906; NUWW, *Women Workers* (1906), pp. 82–3.
18. Elizabeth Robins to MGF, 27 October 1906 (M50/2/1/232); Leslie Parker Hume, *The National Union of Women's Suffrage Societies* (1982), p. 31.
19. Evelyn Sharp, *Unfinished Adventure* (1933), pp. 129–30.
20. *The Times*, 1 and 5 November 1906.
21. *ibid.*, 27 October 1906.
22. See Martin Pugh, *Women's Suffrage in Britain* (1980), p. 23; Brian Harrison, 'Women's suffrage at Westminster' (1983), pp. 112–13; *idem, Peaceable Kingdom* (Oxford: Clarendon Press, 1982), p. 62.
23. Walter McLaren to MGF, 25 October 1906 (M50/2/1/231); *idem* to *idem*, 18 November 1906 (FLALC, vol. 1bii); Billington thesis, p. 618.
24. *The Times*, 12 December 1906; *Women and Progress*, 14, 21 December 1906, pp. 103, 117–18.
25. Extracts from the *Weekly Dispatch* and the *New York Tribune* were published in the *Woman's Journal* (Boston, Massachusetts), 5 January 1907; cutting in Fawcett Library scrapbook *In Memory of Millicent Garrett Fawcett*.
26. MGF, 'The prisoners of hope in Holloway gaol', *Contemporary Review*, December 1906, pp. 820–6 (quotations, pp. 821–2).
27. Hume, pp. 32–3; Edith Dimock to Frances Sterling, 3 January 1907 (FLALC, vol. 1biii).
28. Frances Balfour to MGF, 25 June 1896 (FLALC, vol. 1bi); *ER*, 15 July 1896, pp. 168–9.
29. NUWSS annual council, 31 January 1907, *Report of Proceedings* (FLA, box 301); *The Tribune*, 1 February 1907.
30. *Women and Progress*, 15 February 1907, pp. 248–50; *The Times*, 11, 13 February 1907. There is a fine illustrated account of the march in Lisa Tickner, *The Spectacle of Women* (1987), pp. 74–8.
31. Frances Balfour, *Ne Obliviscaris*, vol. 2 [1930], p. 169.
32. *The Times*, 23 February, 8 March 1907; *ER*, 15 April 1907, pp. 87–9.
33. *The Tribune*, 25 March 1907; *The Times*, 27 March 1907.
34. Hume, pp. 35–8; *The Times*, 25 March, 9 May 1907.
35. *The Times*, 2 May 1907; *Wimbledon Boro' News*, 11 May 1907; Hume, pp. 39–40; Thomas Kennedy, 'The woman's man for Wimbledon, 1907' in *Russell* (vol. 14, 1974), pp. 19–26.
36. Quoted in Brian Harrison, *Prudent Revolutionaries* (1987), p. 28. This comment, made on the reverse of a letter from Mrs Fawcett (25 September [1909]), was undoubtedly influenced by her curt rejection of a plea by Arncliffe-Sennett for joint action by all suffragists.
37. *CC*, 22 April 1909, pp. 23–4.
38. Frances Balfour to Betty Balfour (copy), 27 November [?1907] (Balfour Papers, Scottish Record Office).
39. *Hull Daily Mail*, 21 November 1907.
40. R.A. Knox to MGF, 22 December 1908 (FLALC, vol. 1c); unidentified cutting in Fawcett Library scrapbook (note 25 above) [21 November 1908].
41. *Women's Franchise*, 3 December 1908, pp. 273–4.
42. Liddington, pp. 164–6. The Labour Representation Committee was soon renamed the Labour party.
43. *ibid.*, pp. 144–5, 162–3; Constance Rover, *Women's Suffrage* (1967), pp. 182–4; F.M. Leventhal, *The Last Dissenter: H.N. Brailsford and his world* (1985), p. 82 & n.; Rosen, *Rise Up*, pp. 34–5.

44. Holton, pp. 53–64.
45. *Contemporary Review* (note 26 above), p. 826.
46. For an opposing perspective see Harrison, 'Women's suffrage at Westminster', pp. 101–3.
47. Russell to Llewelyn Davies, 16 November 1907 (Russell Papers, McMaster University).
48. MGF, *The Women's Victory – and After* (1920), pp. 16–19; *MGF*, pp. 250–1. An account of the deputation is contained in *Women's Franchise*, 6 February 1908, pp. 364–5.
49. The biographies by J.A. Spender and Cyril Asquith (two volumes, 1932), R.B. McCallum (1936), Roy Jenkins (1964) and Stephen Koss (1976) outline his attitude. The hope that a measure might be passed to enfranchise women against his opposition was more optimistic than realistic. See below, pages 186–7.
50. *The Times*, 21 May 1908.
51. MGF to Bertrand Russell, 25 May 1908 (Russell Papers).
52. Russell to MGF, 26 May 1908 (FLALC, vol. lc).
53. *Women's Franchise*, 28 May, 4 June 1908, pp. 565, 579, 587; Richard A. Rempel, Andrew Brink, Margaret Moran (eds), *The Collected Papers of Bertrand Russell*, vol. l2 (1985), pp. 274–5.
54. Llewelyn Davies to Russell [?29 May 1908] (Russell Papers).
55. Rempel *et al.* (eds), pp. 285–90; Bertha Mason, Frances Sterling, Helena Swanwick to Russell, 18 February, 13 March, 23 and 27 November 1909 (Russell Papers).
56. *The Times*, 15 March 1909.
57. MGF to Russell, 12 March 1909 (Russell Papers). He did not resign on this occasion (Russell to MGF, 15 March 1909, M50/2/1/278).
58. Russell to Lucy Donnelly, 18 October 1909 (Russell Papers).
59. Russell to Phillips, 25 November 1909 (*ibid.*); *CC*, 9 December 1909, pp. 463–4. For Phillips's own departure from her post see Holton, p. 64.
60. Russell to Llewelyn Davies, 27 May 1908 (Russell Papers).
61. Russell to Donnelly, 17 November 1909 (*ibid.*). See also Rempel *et al.* (eds), p. 242.
62. Llewelyn Davies to Russell, Easter Sunday [1907] (Russell Papers).
63. *The Times*, 10 November 1911.
64. C.P. Scott diary, 16 November 1911 (Scott Papers, BL Add. Mss); Holton, p. 71.
65. *MG*, 29 June 1914. See also *CC*, 16 May 1912, p. 90; MGF, 'Our balance sheet', *The Englishwoman*, August 1914, p. 126.
66. Harrison, *Separate Spheres*, p. 187.
67. *The Times*, 26 November 1906.
68. Charlotte Despard, 'Ungallant little Wales', *Women's Franchise*, 28 May 1908, p. 569.
69. *Pontypridd Observer*, 16 May 1908.
70. *Evening Standard*, 6 July 1909 (MAS, vol. 7); *CC*, 15, 22 July 1909, pp. 173, 181, 196; *MGF*, pp. 231–2.
71. MGF to Mrs Atkinson and Evelyn Atkinson, 8 October 1927 (FLALC, vol. 1m).
72. Martin Pugh, *Electoral Reform in War and Peace* (1978), p. 18.
73. MGF to Maud Arncliffe-Sennett, 27 March 1907 (MAS, vol. 1).
74. *The Times*, 23 November 1907.
75. Lisa Tickner's splendid account (pp. 80–98), on which I have drawn, is essential reading for both events.

76. *The Times*, 8 May, 13 June 1908.
77. *Daily Leader*, 15 June 1908 (MAS, vol. 3).
78. *The Times, Morning Post*, 15 June 1908 (MAS, vol. 3).
79. *Daily Chronicle*, 23 June 1908 (MAS, vol. 4).
80. For this incident: Pankhurst, p. 286; Rosen, *Rise Up*, pp. 107–8. For accounts of deteriorating relations between the NUWSS and WSPU see Hume, pp. 50–5; Holton, pp. 46–50.
81. MGF to Alice Stone Blackwell (copy), 22 February 1909 (M50/2/1/270); Hume, pp. 50–1; Holton, p. 47.
82. See Hume, p. 52; Holton, p. 47.
83. MGF to Philippa Strachey, 16 October 1908 (FLA, box 298).
84. MGF to Frances Balfour, 7 November 1908 (FLALC, vol. 1c).
85. *The Times*, 12 November 1908; *Women's Franchise*, 19 November 1908, p. 237.
86. *The Times*, 19, 20 November 1908.
87. Holton, pp. 48–9.
88. MGF to Philippa Strachey, 28 October 1908 (FLA, box 298).
89. The dispute in the LSWS is well documented. The preferred slate of 1908 is among Fawcett Library pamphlets; the three-line whip of 1909 in FLA, box 89 vol. 1. A contemporary account is contained in *ER*, 15 January 1910, pp. 34–5. See also Hume, pp. 53, 55; Holton, pp. 48–9.
90. Louisa Garrett Anderson to MGF, 22, 25 June 1908 (M50/2/1/246, 248).
91. MAS, vols 7–8. Mrs Fawcett wrote on 16 June [1909], 21 July 1909 and 25 September [1909]. Her assessment of 'the immediate outlook for our cause' as 'gloomy in the extreme' (16 June) is quoted by Rosen, *Rise Up*, p. 17, Hume, p. 49.
92. MGF to Helena Auerbach, 1 October 1909 (Fawcett Collection, IIAV).
93. *The Times*, 8 October 1909; *CC*, 14 October 1909, pp. 339, 341, 343.

# CHAPTER 13

## TURBULENT YEARS 1909–14: MODERATES AND MILITANTS

The period between 1909 and the outbreak of the Great War was the most intense and dramatic in the history of the women's suffrage movement. As president of the largest suffrage organization Mrs Fawcett was at the centre of events, her prestige as a veteran of the movement whose experience dated almost from its start unique and unchallenged. Her main responsibility in difficult but exciting conditions was to keep up the spirits of her growing army and to interpret the National Union of Women's Suffrage Societies and its cause to the outside world. From the time of her election in January 1907 her work for the national union gradually overtook in importance her work in the London Society for Women's Suffrage, of which she remained chairman until 1909. She continued to serve on its executive until 1913, however, spoke frequently at its meetings all over London and remained in close touch with its activities. Her affection for its secretary, Philippa Strachey, and her popularity with the members ensured that her attempts to sever her formal links with the LSWS committee were unsuccessful.[1] In London and throughout the country she was the personification of the constitutional suffragist movement both to suffragists themselves and to the interested public. Her main problems were the increasingly violent and uncontrolled actions of supporters of the Women's Social and Political Union, and negotiations with politicians whose commitment to women's suffrage could not be relied upon however blandly sympathetic their words.

Between the adoption of its new constitution in 1907, when it was still a small organization looking back to its Victorian roots, and 1914 the NUWSS built itself up into a formidable fighting machine. In April 1909 it gained in the *Common Cause* an impressive and indispensable weekly journal which, while nominally independent, became the authoritative voice of the NUWSS. It was edited by Helena Swanwick, a leading suffragist and an experienced journalist.[2] In the summer of 1912 its circulation stood at 10,000.[3] By 1912 it employed 32 full-time organizers, by the end of 1913 it had 52,336 members and almost as many affiliated supporters, and by 1914 it claimed 602 affiliated branches and societies.[4] These local bodies, like the

*Helena Swanwick, about 1910.*

national office and executive committee, became much stronger and more effective over the years, and it needed tactful leadership and a winning personality to persuade the collection of talented and determined women committed to the suffrage cause to work with reasonable harmony through the problems and pitfalls of the period. It is difficult to imagine that any other leader could have carried out this task so successfully.

It was Mrs Fawcett's natural role. She had acted as a reconciler of differing opinions since she was little more than a girl,[5] except when roused to uncompromising passion by the kind of moral or patriotic issue examined in earlier chapters. She was not drawn to administration and was not good at it. An obituary notice which may have been the work of Helena Swanwick pointed out that she was 'always more a teacher or a heartener of her party than a tactician or organiser'.[6] Committee work was not her strong point, Mrs Swanwick observed in a contemporary profile, and 'it must be confessed that procedure and points of order are, and will probably to the end of time be, to her a very evil and never completely mastered necessity.'[7] Indeed, she engagingly admitted as much in a letter to Helena Auerbach in 1910.[8] Her wit and good fellowship, however, compensated for the missing points of order: 'Her humour irradiates the dullest committee, and peeps out in witty repartee or in graphic reports of interviews and statements which might be dull from the lips of another.'[9] Swanwick commented in another obituary, often quoted: 'She was a great encourager.' In the darkest times she would remind her colleagues of reasons for optimism. 'She was the sundial that recorded only the sunny hours. Who knows how much fortitude went to keep to herself the dark ones?'[10]

She travelled constantly to rally her forces and to put the case for women's suffrage. In the last three months of 1909, for example, she was scheduled to speak in Cardiff, Manchester, London, Shrewsbury, Chester, again in Manchester, Sussex, Kent, Glasgow, Edinburgh, again in Kent and a number of intermediate places. She followed this with a week in North Wales in February 1910 and then returned to Surrey.[11] She wrote to Mrs Auerbach from Dundee on 10 September 1910 that she had twenty-one meetings arranged before the end of the following month.[12] Unlike some other NUWSS speakers she did not request fees and imposed no conditions as to geographical area or type of audience.[13] It is worth reflecting on the discomforts involved in an age of relatively arduous transport facilities, the loneliness of hotels and the tensions which could arise from the hospitality of well-meaning strangers. There must have been many incidents parallel to an undated one in which a tipsy commercial traveller on a long rail journey tried to force drink on her. She refused, but when the train hit a goods waggon and both she and the man were thrown on the floor, she agreed that it was a suitable moment for brandy.[14]

Typical of her activities was a tour of Cumberland and Westmorland in October 1908. The consequence was a good deal of local publicity, increased interest in women's suffrage and the formation of new branches of the NUWSS. She returned to this part of the country early in 1910, and although it cost four guineas to hire County Hall, Carlisle, the meeting made a profit. The guinea spent on her bouquet was largely raised by local suffrage workers themselves.[15] Her speaking tours, despite her continuing claim to dislike them, were among her greatest services to the suffrage cause, attracting large audiences and providing reassurance to workers that the movement was continuing to progress.[16] Her acceptance of an invitation to

Glasgow in 1914 produced a reply which may have lightened the burden of constant travelling: 'It would have amused you if you had heard the hearty cheer which went up when I informed the office here. We are *very* glad indeed.'[17] The tours also afforded an unrivalled opportunity for local suffragists to publicize the cause; 2,500 handbills advertised another meeting in Glasgow in November 1909, and 2,000 copies of her speech were printed.[18]

By 1910 she had become almost a legend. At a London meeting in that year a new member asked which Mrs Fawcett was addressing the audience. She was told that there was only one Mrs Fawcett. ' "Oh, but it cannot be" ', came the reply, ' "she is much too young!" '[19] This was a common reaction, though it may seldom have been expressed so ingenuously.[20] At the end of the same year she visited Winchester, where the correspondent of the *Common Cause* had been converted to women's suffrage after hearing her speak twenty years earlier:

> It seemed to her that those twenty strenuous years had passed over Mrs Fawcett's head leaving her untouched by their burden. The same calm, noble face; the same clear, emphatic voice; the same sane, reasonable, logical speech, only more fluent with practice; the same flashes of wit and humour.[21]

In an age in which formality and publicly displayed emotion co-existed happily, there were many public demonstrations of the affection of her followers. One such was the occasion in 1908 when she was presented with bouquets of flowers in the Albert Hall. Another was the annual meeting of the London Society in 1911 at a time of exceptional parliamentary tension. When she rose to speak the audience greeted her with an obviously heartfelt standing ovation. It was, the *Common Cause* reported, an 'electric' moment.[22]

An even more emotional occasion took place early in 1913. After the Speaker of the House of Commons had thwarted the long-anticipated vote on the suffrage issue, ruining the prospect of success for the foreseeable future, Mrs Fawcett wrote a short message in the *Common Cause* appealing to the membership to display 'courage and steadfastness'. The response was a reception held a few weeks later at which she was given four volumes of beautifully lettered and bound messages of loyalty from hundreds of local societies. She was also presented with a brooch composed of pearls, fire opals and green enamel, the colours of the national union. On the reverse were inscribed the words 'steadfastness and courage'.[23] She would have been less than human had she not been encouraged by such a demonstration and constant reiteration in the *Common Cause* of the love and reverence felt for her by members to think that in time of crisis she had the moral authority to speak for the union as a whole. The assumption was to be put to a disastrous test in 1915.

It is difficult to follow her work as a conciliator in any detail from the existing records, not least because though she was the national union's president she did not take the chair at meetings of its executive. As Ray Strachey later wrote, with the benefit of her own years of committee service, the union contained 'hosts of intelligent and eager women' whose dedication to the suffrage movement was equalled by the articulate manner in which they argued their case.[24] Even if there were no issue of principle at stake, passions could be aroused in the conduct of ordinary business, as pressure groups have always discovered. A letter to Catherine Marshall, the union's parliamentary secretary, from her assistant Mollie Mackenzie in November 1913, conveys the flavour of some meetings: 'I have to report to you most serious misconduct on the part of the Executive Committee today. There was a long agenda, & they would all talk at once, & keep hurling suggestions at the head of the unfortunate Chairman.' Only 'a solemn lecture' from the chair restored comparative order.[25]

Mrs Fawcett's influence in persuading such ardent personalities to work together was based not on an authoritarian temperament but partly on ignoring the details of many of the quarrels, partly on distracting the participants by anecdotes or other irrelevancies, and partly by the personal loyalty she inspired.[26] This, not the charisma of Mrs Pankhurst, was her great gift. 'Never', Mary Stocks recalled, 'were two women who served the same cause so wholly unlike one another.'[27] Yet ignoring quarrels did not mean apparent support for everyone. Lady Frances Balfour, who acknowledged in a letter written in 1913 that she was 'a head and shoulders above us all', had written some years earlier: 'Not a really sympathetic nature, & if I don't see eye to eye with her I never feel she understands my view.'[28]

The essence of the union's internal strains and fundamental unity was captured at a tense moment at the start of 1913 by Philippa Strachey, who as secretary of the LSWS was a privileged observer of the fray. Writing to 'Dearest Mrs Fawcett' she commented:

> Internecine feuds are more hateful than can be said & it is a great addition to their horror to think that you are being worried about them. I do not think though, that you need ever be afraid of any really grave scandals because we are all of us too deeply attached to the N.U. in the abstract & to the President in the concrete.[29]

There was a kernel of truth in this otherwise over–emollient passage. However inclined to bicker in the committee room the members of the executive were all dedicated workers in the common cause.[30] It was this fundamental unity of aim as well as her determination to present an encouraging front to the world which enabled Mrs Fawcett to write to a friend in 1912 that she and her colleagues were 'like Nelson's "band of brothers". That is one of the joys of our work.'[31]

Quarrels, though often deflected by her personality, were neither infrequent nor insignificant, either on the executive or the council, which she did chair. They often concerned matters of substance, and it was probably helpful both to herself and to the union that she rarely staked her moral authority on particular points of principle. Early in 1911 a dispute about election policy and the appropriate allocation of power between the national executive, local societies and regional federations led to the replacement of an honorary officer and the resignation of two other members of the executive. According to the resigning members Mrs Fawcett would have joined them had the issue not been compromised.[32] At the same time she defused the potentially explosive issue of tax resistance by expressing her sympathy in principle but doubting that it had sufficient adherents to be effectively pursued. This view was accepted by the union council.[33]

She attempted the following year to persuade Helena Swanwick to remain editor of the *Common Cause* when her executive committee colleagues repudiated Swanwick's bitter attacks on the militant suffragists. Her expressions of support and assurance that she had contemplated resignation on the same issue did not succeed in averting Swanwick's own resignation, but she wrote to her friend C.P. Scott of the *Manchester Guardian*: 'Mrs Fawcett . . . is always so reasonable & so considerate.'[34] Maude Royden, her antagonist on this occasion, expressed the same view.[35]

A characteristic of a good leader is the ability to attract and retain supporters of high calibre. This was certainly true of Mrs Fawcett. Although such women as Margaret Ashton, Kathleen Courtney, Catherine Marshall, Maude Royden, Helena Swanwick[36] and others came into the movement as suffragists rather than Fawcett loyalists they were her devoted colleagues until after the outbreak of war in 1914. Royden wrote truly in a letter to Marshall in 1912 of women 'who toil all day & every day & often half the night, without pay & at the cost of their health very often, exactly as if it were a highly-paid profession in which they would earn fortune & fame!'[37] The union depended heavily on their imagination, hard work and fresh approach to women's suffrage, unhindered by bitter memories of past betrayals by politicians.

Mrs Fawcett's most important function outside the union was to present an intellectually impressive and personally attractive case for women's suffrage. She must have grown weary both of the ritual tributes interspersed with personal attacks paid her by opponents of the cause, and the repetition of her name by suffragists as a kind of talisman.[38] It may be true that while the militants antagonized the wider public by violence, a leader grown old in the movement, universally respected and widely known in the worlds of politics and journalism, was taken for granted and hence sometimes ignored.[39] This was the accusation of militant sympathizers who despaired at the lack of passion which marked her speeches. The Unitarian minister and militant sympathizer Alexander Webster, writing to the *Aberdeen Free Press* in October 1913, claimed that her meeting in the city had been 'pithless pulp', her speech inaudible and devoid of inspiration. 'The subject of Women's Suffrage sank into clammy torpor.' A second letter, borrowing a term from the music-hall comedian Harry Lauder, called her 'a frost' on the movement and alleged that, 'Micawber-like', she was merely ' "waiting for something to turn up" '.[40]

Like any militant she valued the vote not for itself but for what it could achieve, but she did not glory in fighting for its own sake. Others did, both militants and non-militants. There was no joy in a victory won by compromise, Margaret Llewelyn Davies told Bertrand Russell in 1914.[41] For Christabel Pankhurst too the very purpose of the movement was the struggle itself: 'Realising what has been gained by militancy', she wrote to Lady Constance Lytton in 1914, 'we are positively *sorry* for the women in other countries who have got the vote without fighting for it. We want, when the vote comes, to be able to say that we got it ourselves.'[42]

It is hardly possible to state with confidence whether Mrs Fawcett's respectability, privileged contacts and lack of charisma were a 'frost' on the movement. The growth of the national union's numerical and financial support, however, does not suggest that she was a leader out of touch with her time. Certainly those with whom she was most closely associated thought that she had a uniquely favourable impact on the public. One of the most lively brief accounts of the adulation of her colleagues and the admiration of the public was published in an article by Maude Royden. The occasion was a procession of militant and constitutional societies in 1911, during a period of truce in the WSPU campaign of violence:

> We left a little space between Mrs Fawcett and the rest of us, so that the crowd could see her. And we heard 'That's Mrs Fawcett – that's Mrs Henry Fawcett – Bravo, Madam!' and hats were taken off as she went along, with her unassuming air of being just like all the rest – which she isn't![43]

Although relations between the two main suffrage organizations had sunk to a low ebb by 1909, the subsequent years were not a period of unrelieved hostility between them. Within the ranks of the NUWSS, the larger and less regimented body, the WSPU retained both admiration and support. According to Mrs Fawcett the London Society of Women's Suffrage lost 133 members at the end of 1909 when it adopted its new rules, though the recruitment of 293 new members suggests a wide measure of agreement with the policy of excluding the militants.[44] Among the resigning members were Hertha Ayrton, the pioneer woman engineer, and her step-daughter Edith, whose husband, the writer Israel Zangwill, was a prominent supporter of the suffrage movement.[45] Ayrton and Mary Murdoch, the well-known Hull doctor and suffragist leader, both wrote to the *Common Cause* in March 1912 to protest against attacks on the militants. Ayrton renounced her subscription to the paper and Murdoch resigned from the union with the succinct explanation: 'The public condemnation of one body of women by another working for the same cause is to me unthinkable.'[46]

It is difficult to know for how many women she spoke, but there were certainly some who were unwilling to admit a final breach between the camps, at least until the last stages of militancy began early in 1913. Lady Betty Balfour, a well-known constitutional suffragist, was the sister of Lady Constance Lytton, a famous militant. The Blathwayt family of Somerset entertained militants and moderates almost indiscriminately, sometimes simultaneously.[47] Within the Garrett family both Elizabeth Garrett Anderson and, as seen above, her daughter Louisa were for a considerable period supporters of the WSPU, and Millicent's cousin Amy Badley, the sister of Edmund Garrett, had a foot in both camps.[48] Mrs Fawcett too continued to have divided emotions throughout the period, but the evidence that the increasing violence of the militants alienated the public and allowed politicians to betray their promises drove her to condemn both suffragist violence and politicians' untrustworthiness.

She wrote to Lady Frances Balfour in June 1909 after a battle between the WSPU and the police: 'The physical courage of it all is intensely moving. It stirs people as nothing else can.'[49] A year later she concluded a speech with a quasi-militant flourish, surprising and perhaps shocking some suffragists, especially those who read the necessarily abbreviated report in the *Morning Post*. Even the fuller version published in the *Common Cause* was striking enough:

> This movement will not be put down by persecution and by punishment . . .
> The more the Women Suffragists are persecuted, either by prison, or by other forms of suffering . . . the more determined they are to go on until they have succeeded in their work. It is hardship and persecution that rouse heroism in the heart of man – yes, and of woman too . . . But if the opportunity [of obtaining women's suffrage by agreement] is denied us, then we will seek rougher and harsher methods. Because things happen to us that are unpleasant, we will not be deterred from the path that we have mapped out, and we will not cease until we get that for which we have been fighting, and which has been denied us for so many years.[50]

There is no evidence that the speech led to mass revulsion among suffragists, and some thought that a critical letter by Marion Phillips should not have been published in the *Common Cause*.[51] It provided useful ammunition for anti-suffragists, however, whose attacks on Mrs Fawcett were unremitting. One of the most savage was a detailed letter to the press by a prominent anti-suffragist named Audrey Mary Cameron, who in 1914 accused her of 'double-dealing'; she had, the letter claimed, 'ruined her own cause, and proved herself unfitted for political power'.[52] Mrs Fawcett claimed fairly enough that she had supported the militants when they were the victims of violence and ceased to support them when they began to inflict it, but this was a distinction which her opponents were happy to ignore.[53] Her denunciation of forcible feeding as 'a form of torture which ought to be absolutely forbidden' and her private admiration of Emily Wilding Davison's martyr's death after the 1913 Derby, an action deplored by many suffragists, were further evidence of her continued deep respect for the women who risked their lives to obtain votes.[54]

It was impossible to draw a clear line between suffering and violent militants from 1908, as the NUWSS had realized in statements dissociating itself from violence in November 1908 and October 1909,[55] but the

WSPU's announcement of a truce in January 1910 temporarily ended the controversy. Mrs Fawcett, while publicly deploring the 'futile silliness' of violence, counselled against a formal protest when the truce was briefly broken in November 1910, asserting that 'perpetual protesting' was 'a sign of weakness'. Following the resumption of militancy in November 1911, however, she moved a resolution at a special union council, opposing 'the resort to methods of violence', which after considerable discussion was carried by a large majority.[56] Further violence led to the union executive issuing another statement in March 1912, expressing its 'deep indignation' at the WSPU's behaviour.[57] Mrs Fawcett had opposed issuing the further statement as unnecessary and even 'rather ridiculous', she told Frances Balfour,[58] but on this occasion her view was not accepted. Speaking two days earlier she had made clear her own strong disapproval of violence, but she asked her audience 'not to speak too harshly of those other suffragists who, they thought, were damaging their cause'. She believed that large numbers of them were sincere though misled: 'And they must not let the breach between them be made any wider than necessary.'[59]

Attempts to secure collaboration between the two unions were only once successful, when the WSPU-organized 'Women's Coronation Procession' attracted huge numbers of marchers in June 1911. Despite the truce the NUWSS executive had an anxious discussion on whether to take part, and there was considerable opposition to its eventually favourable decision.[60] Mrs Fawcett wrote to the *Common Cause* assuring readers of her own continued belief that 'force is no argument', reminding them of previous expressions of NUWSS disapproval of WSPU methods but asserting that 'this seems to me no reason for refusing to co-operate with them when they are acting on lines which we heartily approve. We are all asking for the same thing.'[61] She missed the Stockholm congress of the International Woman Suffrage Alliance, of which she was first vice-president, to lead the NUWSS contingent on the procession, despite anguished letters from IWSA leaders.[62] The procession was another notable success, and the press did not fail to note that the NUWSS had attracted more of the 40,000 marchers than any of the other suffrage societies.[63] A jubilant Mrs Fawcett wrote in an unusually friendly tone: 'My dear Mrs Sennett . . . I was delighted with the procession and I never was surer of anything in my life than that it was the right policy for the Cause, for the Nat. Union to co-operate in it.'[64]

The 1911 joint procession was especially gratifying because failure to stage a joint event in July 1910 had resulted in bitter recriminations. The occasion was a demonstration in support of the Conciliation Bill, whose moving spirit was the radical journalist H.N. Brailsford. His sympathies were with the WSPU of which his wife Jane was an adherent, but the bill which he planned early in 1910 and which was limited to women occupiers, was designed to attract maximum support from Liberals and Conservatives, militant and constitutional suffragists. It was a doomed attempt to square the circle, but at first he seemed to make surprising progress in securing approval and even co-operation from his team of incompatibles.[65] Mrs Fawcett followed her usual line, which closely paralleled Brailsford's: 'My own view is that I would accept any W.S. bill which had a reasonable chance of passing.'[66]

The failure to mount a joint demonstration in July stemmed chiefly from the WSPU's refusal to promise to abstain from militancy until it was over. They also alienated Mrs Fawcett by refusing to agree on an acceptable resolution to put from the suffrage platforms and insisting on a timescale which the national union could not meet.[67] In consequence the union held a rally in the Queen's Hall on 28 June and a demonstration in Trafalgar Square on 9 July, while the WSPU held its own events on 18 June and 23 July.[68] Despite the breach the militants managed to secure the participation of a number of other suffrage societies,[69] and on 23 July Mrs Fawcett was in attendance, apparently in her individual capacity. Among the souvenirs which she kept until her death was a spray of ivy, with a note in her hand: 'WSPU demonstration – July 23 1910 a man stepped out of the crowd close to the Apsley House and gave me a bunch of these ivy leaves "from Lancashire".'[70] The events of the summer highlighted the incompatibilities between the style and constitution of the two organizations to which Leslie Parker Hume has drawn attention,[71] but also Mrs Fawcett's concern to work with the WSPU if possible.

The 1911 march was thus the exception to the otherwise consistent failure of the two suffrage bodies to collaborate. After the WSPU truce came to an end in November 1911 the national union, as seen above, expressed its opposition to militant tactics in a resolution moved by Mrs Fawcett. When the Conciliation Bill was defeated by 14 votes in March 1912 she did not hesitate to blame the militants: 'I am personally of the opinion that the militant suffragists have destroyed for the time being much of the sympathetic support that the women's movement has hitherto enjoyed from the general public.'[72] An NUWSS statement on the same day referred to 'the disastrous effect of militancy on public opinion'.[73] After attempted assaults by militants on leading Cabinet opponents of women's suffrage in July Mrs Fawcett vainly signed a public appeal to the WSPU on behalf of the NUWSS executive: 'Our best friends . . . are convinced that militancy is doing the greatest possible harm to the suffrage cause.' Violence led to greater violence; a fire once started could not easily be extinguished.[74]

July 1912 marked a turning point in her attitude to the WSPU. She had now abandoned hope of reconciliation and of attempts to avoid widening the breach. She had opposed sending the appeal: ' "It sticks in my gorge to sign it" ', Helena Swanwick reported her as saying.[75] National union statements, joint declarations and personal expressions of opposition to violence were frequent in the two years before the outbreak of war in 1914. The militants were 'the most powerful allies the anti-Suffragists have', she wrote in July 1912, 'the chief obstacles' to the success of the movement in August.

Hope of a forthcoming parliamentary victory would 'almost certainly be destroyed' if militancy was continued.[76] Her opposition to the WSPU was also expressed privately. She wired the NUWSS office in August, following sensational acts of militant violence in Dublin, strongly opposing taking part in a joint deputation to the Canadian Prime Minister. 'My view is that we cannot co-operate with the Society which was guilty of the Dublin outrages & does its best to encourage similar crimes', she told Helena Auerbach.[77] The national union again protested against violence in July 1913,[78] and on 13 June 1914 *The Times* published 'A manifesto of protest against militancy'. It was issued jointly by the NUWSS and the Conservative and Unionist Women's Franchise Association; Millicent Garrett Fawcett was the first signatory. The protests of the Women's Liberal Federation had appeared two days earlier.

The breach was now wide though occasional overtures continued to be made.[79] Mrs Fawcett did not, however, lay the whole of the blame for violence at the door of the militants. Their methods were tragically mistaken, but the responsibility was that of the Government. This was her publicly expressed attitude until the end of the pre-war suffrage campaign, but her most important statements were an open letter to Lloyd George in December 1911 and an article in the *Daily News* in March 1912. She began her letter to 'My dear Mr Lloyd George'[80] by pointing out that she regretted and deplored violence – 'condemn[ed] also, if the word must be used' – but asserting that the role of the statesman was to remove grievances rather than exacerbate them. The English, she wrote, were not naturally revolutionary and preferred constitutional means if they were available. As force was no argument for suffragists so it was no remedy for governments.[81] In 'Broken windows – and after', reprinted both in the *Common Cause* and as an NUWSS leaflet, she told her Liberal readers that the responsibility of the statesman was to heal the disorders of the body politic. In India far worse crimes than those of the militant suffragists had been committed by nationalists, and the Government's response had been to maintain a policy of political reform. This was the path of wisdom or, 'at any rate, the manly and courageous course'.[82]

She expressed a similar view privately to politicians who showed more inclination to blame the militants than to demand women's suffrage. The issue had been 'played with' in the House of Commons, she told Ramsay MacDonald. If any question affecting men had been treated in similar fashion 'there would have been rioting of a very different & much more serious kind than any women have been guilty of'.[83]

The argument that it was the function of Liberal statesmen to preserve or restore social consensus was a powerful one, which might have been expected to be convincing in other circumstances. It did not persuade the Asquith Government, partly because it was led by an irreconcilable anti-suffragist whose supporters at least acquiesced in his stand, and partly because the militants were powerful enough to irritate, even infuriate, but not compel.[84] Politicians were not to be intimidated by the degree of violence which the militant women could muster, nor by the mass meetings and growing numbers of the moderates. Gradually the NUWSS leaders became convinced that a subtler weapon must be found, some means of persuading politicians that they faced the likelihood of losing power and place. The union embarked on this course, at first cautiously, then systematically, involving it in new challenges and strains, and its president in a role which she could hardly have anticipated.

NOTES

1. FLA box 298 contains two large files of correspondence, mostly relating to speaking engagements and other business details, between Mrs Fawcett and the LSWS, principally Philippa Strachey.
2. Helena Swanwick, *I Have Been Young* (1935), p. 207; Sandra Stanley Holton, *Feminism and Democracy* (1986), p. 43.
3. MGF to Helena Auerbach, 13 August 1912 (Fawcett Collection, IIAV).
4. NUWSS, *Annual Reports*; 1912, p. 43; 1913, p. 18; *CC*, 14 August 1914, p. 385. In the first seven months of 1912 alone 103 new societies affiliated to the union (MGF to Helena Auerbach, 13 August 1912, IIAV). See also Leslie Parker Hume, *The National Union of Women's Suffrage Societies* (1982), pp. 229–31, and Brian Harrison, 'Women's suffrage at Westminster' (1983), p. 88.
5. *MGF*, pp. 43–4. See above, page 36.
6. *MG*, 5 August 1929.
7. Helena Swanwick, 'An appreciation of Mrs Henry Fawcett', *Everyman*, 7 February 1913, p. 524 (MAS, vol. 20). A letter from Mrs Fawcett to C. Sarolea about this interview (21 January 1913) is contained in the Sarolea Collection, Edinburgh University.
8. MGF to Helena Auerbach, 10 September 1910 (IIAV).
9. *Everyman* (note 7 above), p. 524. Mary Stocks, a later colleague, recalled the same quality (*My Commonplace Book* (1970), p. 72).
10. *Time and Tide*, 16 August 1929, pp. 979–80. The obituary was first and most fully quoted in Swanwick, *I Have Been Young*, pp. 185–6.
11. *CC*, 23 September 1909, p. 302.
12. IIAV Collection.
13. NUWSS, *List of Speakers*, June 1911, October 1913 (D/Mar/3/12, 23).
14. *Evening News*, 5 August 1929.
15. D/Mar/3/1 and 2.
16. NUWSS, Eastern Counties Federation, *Annual Report* 1912, p. 12; West Riding Federation, *Annual Report* 1914, p. 9 (D/Mar/3/14,26); *CC*, 3 November 1910, p. 492.
17. Glasgow and West of Scotland Association for Women's Suffrage, letter book; Katherine Lindsay to MGF, 6 June 1914.
18. Glasgow and West of Scotland Association for Women's Suffrage, minutes, 3 November and 22 December 1909.
19. *CC*, 10 March 1910, p. 678.
20. See, for similar: B.M. Willmott Dobbie, *A Nest of Suffragettes in Somerset* (1979), p. 15.

21. *CC*, 3 November 1910, p. 487. Over seventy-five years later Fenner Brockway recalled her 'decisive convincing sentences, spoken with authority and very effective' (to author, 30 August 1986).
22. *CC*, 23 November 1911, p. 571.
23. *ibid.*, 31 January, 7 March 1913, pp. 735, 818–19; *Standard, MG*, 28 February 1913. The volumes are now filed at M50/2/5/1–4.
24. *MGF*, pp. 227–8.
25. Mollie Mackenzie to Catherine Marshall, 20 November 1913 (D/Mar/3/24). Mrs Fawcett did not attend this meeting.
26. *MGF*, pp. 227–8. This combination of qualities may have been in Philippa Strachey's mind when she wrote to Ray Strachey about 'the quasi impossibility of giving a vision of Foss as a leader' (Feb. [?1927], FLA, Ind/PHS).
27. Stocks, p. 71.
28. Frances Balfour to Betty Balfour (copies), 28 January 1913, 27 November [?1907] (Balfour Papers, Scottish Record Office).
29. Philippa Strachey to MGF, 1 January 1913 (FLALC, vol. 1k). For a delightful cameo of 'Pippa' Strachey see Harrison, *Prudent Revolutionaries* (1987), pp. 150–4.
30. 'That was why the pre-war Executive of the NU was so fine' (Maude Royden to Kathleen Courtney, 16 January 1918; FLA, box 456).
31. MGF to Mrs Atkinson, 1 February 1912 (FLALC, vol. 1jii).
32. NUWSS EC minutes, 8 February 1911 (FLA, box 84/2); duplicated letter from Ethel Bentham to 'Dear Madam', 21 February 1911 (D/Mar/3/12); Edith Palliser to Philippa Strachey, 6 January 1911 (FLALC, vol. 1ji); Holton, pp. 40–1.
33. M50/2/1/319–22, 324–34; *CC*, 15 December 1910, p. 598; 9 February 1911, p. 714; 13 July 1911, p. 248. The controversy rumbled on and in February 1913 she issued a statement reiterating that her opposition to tax resistance was not a matter of principle but of tactics (copy in IIAV).
34. Swanwick, *I Have Been Young*, pp. 23–4; Swanwick to C.P. Scott, 23 July 1912 (C.P. Scott Papers, University of Manchester); *CC*, 3 October 1912, p. 441.
35. Maude Royden, 'A great experience' (typescript, FLA box 224).
36. These are the women picked out by Jo Vellacott, Catherine Marshall's impending biographer, in 'Feminist consciousness and the First World War', *History Workshop Journal* (23, 1987), p. 82.
37. Maude Royden to Catherine Marshall, 8 April 1912 (D/Mar/3/14).
38. *Woman at Home*, December 1898, p. 214; *The Times*, 13 June 1908; *Eastbourne Chronicle*, 9 April 1910 (MAS, vol. 9); *The Scotsman*, 8 January 1914.
39. See Hume, pp. 13–14. A letter from Kathleen Courtney to Lady de la Warr (29 November 1912), outlining Mrs Fawcett's journalistic contacts, is filed at D/Mar/3/33.
40. Alexander Webster and 'A working girl' in *Aberdeen Free Press*, 1 and 2 October 1913.
41. Llewelyn Davies to Russell, 17 May [1914] (Russell Papers, MacMaster University).
42. Christabel Pankhurst to Lady Constance Lytton, 1 May 1914 (Pethick-Lawrence Papers, Trinity College, Cambridge).
43. *CC*, 22 June 1911, p. 190.
44. Holton, p. 49.
45. Hertha Ayrton to Miss McKee, 7 July 1909 (FLALC, vol. 1e); Edith Zangwill to NUWSS secretary, 7 November 1909 (FLALC, vol. 1g).
46. *CC*, 14, 28 March 1912, pp. 840, 871.
47. Willmott Dobbie and diaries of Emily and Mary Blathwayt (Blathwayt Diaries, Dyrham Park), *passim*. Mary recorded an amicable meeting between Mrs Fawcett and the militant Annie Kenney when both were among the Blathwayts' guests on 3 July 1910.

48. Billington thesis, p. 695 & n.
49. MGF to Frances Balfour, 30 June 1909 (FLALC, vol. 1e); *MGF*, p. 223.
50. *CC*, 23 June 1910, p. 162; *Morning Post*, 10 June 1910.
51. *CC*, 16, 23 June 1910, pp. 155, 162. Marion Phillips, who had recently lost her post with NUWSS (above, page 159) may be supposed to have had her own axe to grind.
52. *Standard*, 29 June 1914 (JRL, women's suffrage cuttings collection, vol. 28); 20 June 1914 and also *Anti-Suffrage Review*, July 1914, p. 103.
53. *The Times*, 8, 9, 11–13 March 1912; 9, 10 June 1914.
54. *MG*, 16 April, 9 June 1913; *CC*, 13 June 1913, p. 152. Mrs Fawcett was abroad at the time of the event and appears not to have commented publicly. Her remarkable tribute to Emily Wilding Davison was published several years later in *The Women's Victory* (1920), pp. 66–7.
55. Above, pages 163–4.
56. *CC*, 1, 15 December 1910, pp. 552, 589; 14 December 1911, p. 633.
57. *ibid.*, 14 March 1912, p. 836.
58. MGF to Frances Balfour, 5 March [1912] (FLALC, vol. 1hi; *MGF*, p. 232) (both sources misdate this letter as 1910); *Standard*, 6 March 1912 (MAS, vol. 16).
59. *Standard*, 6 March 1912. This remark was greeted with applause.
60. NUWSS, EC minutes, 27 April 1911 (FLA, box 84/2); Lisa Tickner, *The Spectacle of Women* (1987), p. 123.
61. *CC*, 4 May 1911, p. 60.
62. Carrie Chapman Catt and Signe Bergman to MGF, 15 and 16 May 1911 (M50/2/22/12, 13). Bergman wrote: 'We need you, the Convention needs you. Sweden needs you.'
63. *The Times*, *The Star*, 19 June 1911; Tickner, pp. 122–31.
64. 26 June 1911 (MAS, vol. 14).
65. F.M. Leventhal, *The Last Dissenter* (1985), pp. 68–7; Hume, pp. 65–80; Tickner, pp. 111–19.
66. MGF to H.N. Brailsford (draft), 21 March 1910 (M50/2/1/301).
67. Two circular letters from Mrs Fawcett for internal NUWSS consumption, dated 29 June and 16 July 1910, are filed in FLA, box 89 vol. 1.
68. Hume, pp. 75, 81; Andrew Rosen, *Rise Up, Women!* (1974), p. 137.
69. Rosen, p. 137.
70. Fawcett Library scrapbook (ch. 12, note 25). Philippa Fawcett had been among the participants on 18 June.
71. Hume, pp. 79–80.
72. *The Standard*, 30 March 1912 (MAS, vol. 17). See also Hume, p. 138.
73. *The Times*, 30 March 1912.
74. *CC*, 25 July 1912, p. 267.
75. NUWSS, EC minutes, 18 July 1912 (FLA, box 83); Helena Swanwick to C.P. Scott, 23 July 1912 (note 34 above).
76. *CC*, 25 July 1912, p. 265; *MG*, 22, 27 August 1912.
77. MGF to Auerbach, 25 August [1912] (IIAV).
78. A copy of the union's *Protest Against Violence* is in the BLPES.
79. *Standard*, 6 November 1912; Holton, p. 95.
80. ' "*Her dear* Mr Lloyd George, indeed!" exclaimed Mrs Pankhurst with scorn and indignation' (Ethel Smyth, *Female Pipings in Eden* (Peter Davies, 1933), p. 208). See also Hume, p. 125.
81. *CC*, 7 December 1911, pp. 612–13.
82. *Daily News*, 9 March 1912.
83. MGF to Ramsay MacDonald, 2 February 1912 (MacDonald Papers, PRO).
84. Rosen, *Rise Up*, p. 243.

# CHAPTER 14

## TURBULENT YEARS 1909–14:
## POLITICS AND POLITICIANS

An important reason for Mrs Fawcett's success as leader of the women's suffrage movement was her flexibility. After forty years in the suffrage movement she unexpectedly found herself president of an organization with a dense network of branches, tens of thousands of members and its own weekly journal. New forms of activity were devised, including marches extensively covered by the press and large outdoor rallies, at which violence inspired by her political opponents was often a threat. It was this flexibility which enabled her to accept such new departures with her habitual calmness and to work harmoniously with women half her age.

One of her principal problems was the complications of party politics and the political perspectives of her own membership. The Liberal party as a whole was not unsympathetic to women's suffrage, but it had an important component of anti-suffragist members which from 1908 included the Prime Minister, a strong suspicion that the women for whom the vote was demanded were mainly Conservatives, and a deep unwillingness to divide the party over what seemed to most politicians a fringe issue. The Conservatives or Unionists contained a minority of suffragists whose support in the evenly balanced House of Commons after 1910 was vital for parliamentary success, but they were unwilling to enfranchise the mass of working-class women favoured as voters by suffragist Liberals, for both narrow party and broader political reasons. Irish nationalist MPs were not motivated to vote for women's suffrage by strong popular demand in Ireland and feared that it would distract from the battle for Home Rule, for which they had struggled for so many years. As for Labour, its parliamentary numbers were small and its nominal support complicated by the allegiance of many of its members to adult suffrage.[1]

Mrs Fawcett has been regarded by some modern writers as at heart sympathetic to Liberalism and mistakenly inclined to accept the unreliable promises of Liberal politicians.[2] But her major political handicap in this period of Liberal domination was in fact her record of hostility to the Liberal party. She was free from party ties, she told an interviewer in 1912: 'I am not a Protectionist and therefore cannot be a Conservative. I am not a

Home Ruler and cannot be a Liberal. And I cannot join the Labour Party because I am not a Socialist.'[3] She did not revise this formulation,[4] but her primary loyalty had been to Unionism for many years. She retained her belief not only in free trade but also in rational debate and democratic decision-making, often supposed to be the hallmarks of a Liberal cast of mind. But her uncompromising assaults on Home Rule and its advocates and her consistent support for controversial Conservative policies were not forgotten, either by Liberals or by Irish nationalists. Nor had they ended with her resignation from the Women's Liberal Unionist Association in 1904. During the general election campaign at the end of 1905 she un-equivocally defended the controversial import of indentured Chinese labour in South Africa, in 1907 she still called herself a Unionist and as late as 1910 she allowed herself to engage in a blatant attack on major Liberal policies.[5]

She was in these years the Unionist-leaning leader of an organization whose leading figures tended to be Liberals or radicals, though they worked loyally within the accepted non-party framework.[6] In 1908 she had to defend the National Union of Women's Suffrage Societies and the London society from charges of Liberal bias by an aggrieved member, who complained that the union offices had been used by the Women's Liberal Federation for a meeting in support of the Government's proposed licensing bill. Mrs Fawcett replied that this had been done in error and commented: 'I may add unofficially that I think the Licensing Bill is a most dishonest measure and that I hope the Lords will throw it out.'[7] Five years later Lord Robert Cecil, the most prominent of Conservative suffragists, wrote to Catherine Marshall alleging that there was 'too much Liberal prejudice in the National Union'. His objection, he added, was not to 'party prejudice' but to attitudes of mind,[8] and it was to the credit of the national union that it was able in a period of intense party feeling to attract many more members than it lost and to recruit support from so many quarters.

A legitimate criticism of the union and its president was that it was unable to devise and follow a consistent policy towards the Government, and particularly the Prime Minister. It would have needed the patience of a team of saints and the political perspicacity of a Machiavelli to cope with the wiles of H.H. Asquith, but it was he who held power and had to be placated or overcome. There were two obvious methods of dealing with him. The first was to assault his motives and honesty, the second to pretend to believe his dubious promises and to coax or shame his party into making them law. In fact both courses were followed erratically and unsuccessfully, compounded by Mrs Fawcett's dislike and mistrust for Asquith and his contempt for 'foolish Suffragette' demands.[9]

Although he had promised suffragist MPs in May 1908 that women could be added to a government reform bill without facing the united opposition of the Government, his previously expressed views and his almost imme-diate dismissal of the importance of the concession indicate that his intention was to avoid internal party strife without giving suffragists a fair chance of parliamentary success.[10] None the less, instead of labelling Asquith 'more Tory than the Tories', declaring bluntly 'I have no faith in him' and calling on suffragists to vote against him in the University of Aberdeen rectoral election, Mrs Fawcett could have welcomed his undertaking as 'a great advance' on Gladstone's position in 1884, as she did belatedly in her little book on *Women's Suffrage* in 1912. In the book she acknowledged that the press had unanimously hailed Asquith's promise as raising prospects for women's suffrage to an unprecedentedly high level, and she might have gained more from joining them than from attacking him.[11] Bertrand Russell was undoubtedly mistaken in his optimistic view of Asquith's intentions, but he made a valid point in commenting to Margaret Llewelyn Davies: 'I think that the Suffragists, by minimising Asquith's concession, may succeed in persuading him into taking their view of his meaning.'[12]

When in 1910 the first Conciliation Bill was debated in the House of Commons Mrs Fawcett displayed greater political acumen and less willingness to yield to her own feelings, perhaps because by this time she had defeated the adult suffrage challenge within the national union. Writing to Frances Balfour on the eve of an NUWSS rally in support of the bill she urged that nothing be said to give the Liberals the opportunity to desert their commitments: 'Place an implicit and childlike faith in their vague promises.' Above all, she cautioned, it was important not to 'chaff Asquith for being squeezable'. That would be the best way to defeat their purpose.[13] She had led a deputation to Asquith the previous week and put as good a gloss on it as she could to the press. She told the rally that he was 'a man of his word; he [had] left the door ajar' and women must attempt to open it.[14]

Subsequent developments were to show that Asquith's opinion of women's suffrage were not to be altered by applying soft soap, and it may be doubted whether Mrs Fawcett's attacks had been resented or even noticed. Lloyd George, however, was another matter. More democratic, volatile and magnetic than the Prime Minister, he was a declared supporter of women's suffrage and as the leading figure in domestic politics could have been an important ally, whatever his moral or personal deficiencies.[15] Like Winston Churchill he opposed the Conciliation Bill in 1910 on the grounds that only a limited number of women would have been enfranchised, and though its second reading was carried by a large majority it made no further progress.[16] Writing to *The Times* shortly afterwards Mrs Fawcett gave vent to her anger and to prejudice which recalled her earlier attacks on Irish nationalism: 'The political genius of the Celt is for destruction. He can destroy, but he can seldom create.' Lloyd George was unable to accept, she asserted, what he was convinced would be 'a preservative and constructive force' in the electorate.[17]

Lloyd George, the acknowledged master of political invective, denounced her bigoted generalizations before an audience of Welsh women

Liberals as an 'ill-natured, ill-conditioned, and fatuous observation'.[18] She hardly improved matters in a further letter: 'The patient constructive states-manship which builds up and creates is the invaluable political contribution of the non-Celtic element in the English poeple.' Lloyd George, she pointed out, wished to destroy the existing constitutional rights of the House of Lords, the established Church in Wales and the union between Britain and Ireland: 'He does not want the creation of an extension of political liberty to women, which might possibly tend to preserve those things which he wishes to destroy.'[19] Her words suggest no lingering attach-ment to the Liberalism of her youth and an uncharacteristic lack of concern about the non-party status of the NUWSS.

This passage of arms is unlikely to have endeared the two leaders to each other, but Lloyd George continued to declare himself a supporter of women's suffrage, and both he and Mrs Fawcett had more to gain from co-operation than from continued hostility. Before the end of 1911 she was writing to 'my dear Mr Lloyd George', and a few months later she intro-duced him at an NUWSS meeting in the Albert Hall, calling him the 'strongest and most forceful personality in the present Government'. Not to be outdone he referred to her as 'a leader worthy of [the] dignity and greatness' of the women's movement.[20] Yet at a crucial moment at the end of 1912 he suggested that support for women's suffrage had declined, a malicious claim which he repeated more emphatically in 1913, adding that if it became Liberal party policy Asquith would probably resign and the party be 'hopelessly wrecked for the moment'. The House of Commons would not pass a suffrage bill while militancy continued.[21] He could not have been ignorant of the impact of his words, and it is not surprising that he was widely distrusted within the movement.[22]

It was Asquith, however, who remained the great and acknowledged enemy. Towards the end of 1911 the gloom momentarily lifted when he met a joint deputation from the suffrage societies and made explicit promises to questions from Mrs Fawcett. The Government intended to introduce and pass a reform bill enfranchising almost all the remaining voteless men in 1912. It would be drafted so that women could be included by amendment, an amendment which the Government would not oppose and would, if carried, treat as 'an integral part of the bill'. In addition, Mrs Fawcett recalled, he was 'far more conciliatory than [he] had ever been before'.[23] For a short period it seemed that suffragists had a greater hope of obtaining their objective than ever before.

The hope was brief. It is unnecessary to examine Asquith's behaviour, some of it in any case not fully documented, in the period after meeting the suffrage deputation. What is clear, however, is that suffragists believed that he worked as concentratedly as his rather indolent nature and disdain for the subject permitted to prevent his promises from being realized. Even in making them he had effectively cost the suffragists their parliamentary majority, for the votes of Conservative suffragists who opposed enfranchisement on 'democratic lines' was essential to the women's success.[24] Suffragists also believed that it was widely and intentionally rumoured that if women's suffrage were carried Asquith and other ministers would resign and in consequence Irish Home Rule be jeopardized. The rumour of resignations was rebutted by Lloyd George only at the last minute before the expected crucial vote in the House of Commons.[25] What Mrs Fawcett characteristically termed 'the ratting of the Irish', the heavy concentration of votes by Home Rulers against the 1912 version of the Conciliation Bill and its defeat, was the consequence.[26] Within a month of making his promises to the suffrage deputation Asquith told a group of anti-suffragists that women's suffrage would be 'a political mistake of a very disastrous kind'. After the defeat of the Conciliation Bill in 1912 he ignored its previous successes and his promises about an amendment to his own reform bill which could enfranchise large numbers of women, coolly telling the House of Commons that he believed it 'altogether improbable' that it would 'stultify itself' by voting for the broader measure.[27]

It is hardly surprising that in February 1912 Mrs Fawcett should write to Frances Balfour expressing the fear that 'we shall probably be tricked again'.[28] She hinted at the same fear in an article in the *Common Cause*, pouring scorn on plans circulating among anti-suffragists for an electoral referendum on the issue which, they hoped, would kill women's suffrage while allowing politicians to disclaim responsibility. 'I *hope* this may come to nothing', she wrote to Mrs Auerbach three weeks earlier, 'but I cannot help feeling anxious.' Her article also directed attention to a report in *The Times* which suggested that the proposed women's suffrage amendment to the government reform bill would be ruled out of order as not relevant. 'So desperate seems the plight of the Anti-Suffragists', she observed, 'that they catch at the most delusive of straws in their struggle to reach dry land.'[29] A year later, however, the Speaker was to destroy the women's suffrage amendment by just such a ruling.

In October 1912, when hope was still theoretically alive, Mrs Fawcett told a Manchester rally that 'pledge or no pledge, Mr Asquith will leave no stone unturned to defeat the women's suffrage amendments'. He and other anti-suffrage ministers, she charged, wanted to provoke an outburst of militancy as a means of rousing parliamentary antagonism to the women's cause.[30] By this time it was probably too late for a personal attack to influence the outcome, had the House of Commons been allowed to vote on the issue. A few weeks after the parliamentary fiasco she expressed her 'absolute want of faith in the honour and faith of Mr Asquith'.[31] At a suffragist deputation to him in August 1913 she could only suggest that he should stand aside while his Government introduced a women's suffrage bill. Although he did not reject outright the possibility of such a bill being introduced by a future Liberal Government, it is difficult to believe that she expected much from her suggestion.[32] She had spoken in more realistic mood to a London audience the previous April: 'We feel that no woman suffrage is possible while Mr Asquith is Premier.'[33]

Being forced by 1912 to eliminate the Liberals as impossible, the NUWSS was left, however improbably, with the Labour party, the only political party which had given consistent support to women's suffrage. The history of the union's collaboration with Labour has been told in detail by Leslie Parker Hume and Sandra Stanley Holton, and from the Labour point of view by Martin Pugh.[34] Here it is necessary to examine Mrs Fawcett's role in the collaboration.

It was certainly anomalous that she should have presided over such an arrangement, which was secured only by the initiative and persuasion of the national union. She and Harry had been known as supporters of the working class, but her adamant opposition to the factory acts and other social reforms, and her denunciation of trade union attempts to limit the employment of women might have made her almost as suspect in the eyes of a trade union-dominated party as her stance on Home Rule made her to Irish nationalists. Late in 1906 she expressed her hostility to the Government's Trade Disputes Bill, which by liberalizing the law of picketing would, she claimed, strengthen the powers of the unions to intimidate women workers and exclude them from the skilled trades. 'The Labour vote must at any cost be conciliated', she wrote bitterly. Women had gone almost unmentioned at the committee stage in the House of Commons: 'It was no one's business to take care of them.'[35]

Yet even at this stage she was by no means unremittingly hostile to Labour. 'I can never forget that the Labour party was the first to put women's suffrage on their electoral programme', she commented at about the same time.[36] This virtue more than compensated for the party's deficiencies. Moreover, it claimed to speak for the class to which the bulk of women belonged. Working women were a section of the female community of which the NUWSS was at least intermittently conscious, as its predecessor bodies had been. Mrs Fawcett wrote in 1884 about ward and district meetings held for working women in preparation for the huge meetings held in 1880–2 by suffragists in the principal cities.[37] She entertained a deputation of factory women from Lancashire when they came to London in 1901 to present a suffrage petition, and when several years later the national union appointed a team of paid organizers, working-class women like Selina Cooper and, later, Ada Nield Chew were among their number.[38] Despite the heavy handicap of the contemporary class system, the belief that women as an entity were a class in themselves was a significant strand of thought within the contemporary feminist movement.[39]

In June 1911 the London Society for Women's Suffrage held a meeting for working women in the Queen's Hall. It was presided over by Lady Frances Balfour, whose origins and social contacts could hardly have been more different from those of her audience. It was a highly unusual occasion in the South of England, in contrast to the North-West, where working women were much more involved in political life.[40] Ida O'Malley, active in both the London society and the national union, wrote ecstatically to Catherine Marshall about the 'very thrilling meeting . . . entirely composed of really poor working women, such as . . . one is not used to seeing at Queen's Hall. They *were* so poor & so loaded with babies & so gloriously enthusiastic . . . It really was thrilling!'[41] Mrs Fawcett seconded a resolution moved by George Lansbury, a Labour MP of whom suffragists were soon to hear much more. She told the audience that her friends among women were those of all classes who worked for justice to women, and proclaimed the existence of 'a grand freemasonry between different classes of women'.[42]

Within months of this meeting the NUWSS and the Labour party began to draw closer together. Although committed to adult suffrage Labour's short voting record in the House of Commons had been solidly in favour of women's suffrage, in marked contrast to the other parties.[43] In Keir Hardie, Philip Snowden and Arthur Henderson, to all of whom she was to pay lavish public and private tribute, the movement possessed friends who held influential positions within the party.[44] In January 1912 on Henderson's motion the party supplemented its allegiance to adult suffrage with the declaration that no suffrage bill would be acceptable which did not include women.[45] On its second reading two months later the Conciliation Bill was narrowly defeated, the first defeat of a suffrage bill on the floor of the House of Commons for twenty years. The spectacle of so many supposed friends deserting women's suffrage at the overt or concealed bidding of Liberal party leaders 'gave a fatal shock to what had hitherto been our election policy', Mrs Fawcett wrote later, namely the support for the candidate in each constituency who was judged to be 'the best friend of women's suffrage'.[46]

By deciding to abandon its previous policy the leaders of the national union can again be criticized for inconsistency. There had long been a case for opposing the Liberals, as the Women's Social and Political Union had decided in 1906,[47] and a case for maintaining 'an implicit and childlike faith' until the Government reform bill had finally been disposed of. To declare opposition to the Liberals, especially in collaboration with the small and only semi-independent Labour party, while simultaneously attempting to persuade them to honour such commitments as they had been compelled or cajoled to make, can be regarded as unsure judgement. It was even more hazardous in view of the Liberal allegiance of so many suffragists and the consequent likelihood of vocal internal opposition to a Labour alliance. On the other hand, if the electoral result of an NUWSS–Labour pact was successful, wavering Liberals might be persuaded of the folly of opposing women's suffrage. Moreover, given the blanket hostility of Asquith and some of his ministerial colleagues, the unreliability of many other Liberals and the opportunities to 'rat' offered by the continued militant campaign of violence, the NUWSS had probably little to lose in attempting to work from two corners of the British party triangle, while not abandoning its links with Conservative suffragists. These last, indeed, might be reassured by evidence of the union's hostility to the Liberal party.

Early in April 1912 the idea of a Labour alliance, previously mooted among the NUWSS officers, began to be considered seriously.[48] Mrs Fawcett pointed out in an article in the *Common Cause* that every Labour member present in the House of Commons had supported the Conciliation Bill, in marked contrast to other members. General support for Labour candidates at contested elections, she suggested, was a policy which might have to be considered by the union.[49] A month later she expressed herself more fully. She called attention to the resolution passed by the party in January 1912 and the subsequent statement by Ramsay MacDonald, the party leader, that it would be prepared to vote against the Government over the issue. It was essential, she pointed out, not to infringe the non-party character of the union, but the fact that Labour was the only party committed to women's suffrage made the pledges of its candidates more reliable than those of members of other parties.[50]

In the meantime negotiations had begun with an exploratory letter from Kathleen Courtney, the union's honorary secretary, to Arthur Henderson.[51] Mrs Fawcett was to be heavily involved in the thorny task of convincing the Labour leaders that the union should establish and maintain an Election Fighting Fund to support Labour by-election candidates. Arthur Henderson and, in particular, Ramsay MacDonald were wary of a formal commitment to the union. MacDonald, though a nominal supporter of women's suffrage, was scarcely more trustworthy than Lloyd George. He was concerned about the potential divisiveness of the suffrage question, about forming financial links with a non-Labour source and, perhaps paradoxically, about jeopardizing links with the Liberals on whom most Labour seats depended. His hostility to the militants was also deeper than that of other Labour leaders, and, despite his own bourgeois marriage, he repeatedly professed mistrust of the middle-class nature of the suffrage movement.[52] It required considerable pressure, including an angry letter from H.N. Brailsford, the originator of the scheme, and a pained one from the NUWSS, to persuade the party to give the plan for an EFF its hesitant support.[53]

The problem within the national union was no less thorny and, unlike relations with the Labour party, grew no easier with time. Its special council held in mid-May 1912 agreed by a large majority that the attitude of parties should be taken into account as well as that of individual candidates. Labour candidates should be supported by suffragists, particularly against Liberal anti-suffragists. The opposition, however, was weighty, its political complexion ranging, in the form of Emily Davies, Eleanor Rathbone and Margery Corbett Ashby, from Conservative through independent to

Liberal.[54] Even the loyal Frances Balfour wrote sceptically to her sister-in-law some months later: 'Mrs Fawcett believing the Labour party will stick to us – I don't agree but I never contradict a word she says, any more than I should contradict Deborah under the Palm Tree.'[55]

Mrs Fawcett's task within the union was now twofold. The first was to reassure members that the non-party policy had not been abandoned, the second to persuade them that they should support the Labour party, probably the party with least support among suffragists. It is reasonable to accuse the new policy and Mrs Fawcett herself of trying to achieve the best of both worlds,[56] but a shattered union, the certain result of an open party affiliation, would have done little to help either Labour or women's suffrage.

She had lost none of her wit and power of persuasion. Addressing a meeting in October 1912 she 'delighted the audience', the *Common Cause* wrote appreciatively, by explaining that her own attitude to political parties was that of the young French lady to her fiancé: 'I do not lôv him – I do not hate him – he is to me as that footstool!'[57] Three weeks later she told a crowded meeting at the Albert Hall, attended by large numbers of working women from the poorest parts of London that the national union had adopted the new course

> not because we support Labour politics (some of our members support and some, probably the majority, oppose Labour politics), but . . . because [Labour] is the only one among the various parties which has definitely and of its own initiative, long before anyone dreamed of any support from us, boldly declared itself as a party in favour of women's enfranchisement (Cheers).[58]

The only change in previous union policy, she maintained shamelessly, lay in its application to parties rather than to individuals.[59]

The following February the union increased the pressure. It now decided that it would support no Liberal by-election candidate, though abstaining from opposing 'tried friends' unless an approved Labour candidate was already in the field. The effort to replace Liberals with Labour members was to be intensified, and supplemented by campaigning against those Government ministers who opposed women's suffrage. Moreover, faith in private members' bills was officially abandoned, as, in Mrs Fawcett's words, 'looking in a dark room for a black cat which is not there'. Only a Government suffrage bill would now be acceptable. The background to these decisions was the Speaker's ruling which had doomed the women's suffrage amendments to the Government reform bill, followed almost immediately by a new and stronger resolution of the Labour party conference to call on its parliamentary party to oppose any franchise bill which excluded women.[60]

She explained some of her thinking in a letter to Annie Leigh Browne of the Women's Local Government Society shortly after the Speaker's ruling. She had spoken, she wrote, to Lloyd George, a 'conversation which left . . . a *very unfavourable* impression on my mind, and deepened my conviction

# ARE WOMEN CITIZENS?

The National Union of Women's Suffrage Societies says—**"YES."** But

## "MEN ONLY ADMITTED!"

This is what meets the women's eyes, when the gates of citizenship, at which they have knocked for forty years, are to be opened at last. Is this Justice?

Who says it?—THE LIBERAL GOVERNMENT, by introducing a Bill to extend the Franchise of men, whilst leaving the women out.

The Liberal Party professes to believe that Government should be by consent—BUT NEVER ASKS THE LEAVE OF WOMEN before passing laws which women have to obey.

It talks of Government by the People—BUT LEAVES HALF THE PEOPLE OUT.

It says that Taxation and Representation should go together—AND TAXES WOMEN WHO HAVE NO VOTE.

Will this be tolerated? **NO!** THE LABOUR PARTY WILL NOT ALLOW IT.

The best men in the Labour Party maintain that men cannot honourably accept more for themselves UNLESS WOMEN SHARE IT, and Labour, alone among the parties in Parliament, is UNITEDLY determined to fight the women's battle through.

What, then, should women do? They must do all in their power to help a party which is prepared to risk something for the Women's Cause.

That is what the National Union of Women's Suffrage Societies is doing. It is raising a Fighting Fund, which already exceeds £4,000, for use in three-cornered contests.

At Holmfirth, Crewe, and Midlothian, it worked for the Labour Candidate, roused immense enthusiasm and undoubtedly influenced votes.

Are you a Suffragist? Then join the National Union of Women's Suffrage Societies. Contribute to the Fighting Fund, and help us to prove to this Liberal Government that it will **lose seats as well as honour** by a refusal to enfranchise women.

This is the surest and quickest way to get

**VOTES for WOMEN.**

Labour Party : "They are not reckoning with the Working Men if they think they can keep you out."

*Suffragists and the Labour party, about 1913.*

that it is impossible to get a free vote on the merits of Women's Suffrage as long as there is a divided Cabinet.' Many Liberal suffragists, she explained, would oppose suffrage bills so as not to embarrass the Government.[61] A subsequent meeting with Sir Edward Grey, another ostensible supporter of women's suffrage, was equally discouraging.[62] At the same time the patent unfairness of the Speaker's decision had, she felt, 'caused a great wave of sympathy with us', on which she was determined to capitalize.[63]

In the eighteen months which followed she steadily supported the link with Labour while attempting to placate those of her members who continued to reject it. Despite the influential opposition the policy continued to receive the backing of the NUWSS council, and large sums of money, separately raised and administered from the union's ordinary income, were spent on the EFF.[64] As previous writers have pointed out, the operation of the fund combined with the recruitment of a younger generation of radically minded women tended to drive the union to the political left.[65] In December 1913, for example, the poster issued to the South Lanark electors by Clementina Gordon the NUWSS organizer, heavily implied that women's suffrage and social justice were related aspects of the same cause: 'The interests of men and women cannot be divided . . . The Labour candidate stands for justice and fair play.'[66] Catherine Marshall told Lloyd George that 'the new spirit of comradeship' established between suffragists and the labour movement would transform the political scene.[67]

The most notable Labour by-election of the period involved neither the party itself nor the EFF, and the NUWSS decision to participate placed a strain on its relations with party leaders.[68] This was the Bow and Bromley by-election of November 1912, in which George Lansbury, later a leader of the party but then a backbencher with a tendency to unreliability and rebellion, resigned his seat and fought the resulting by-election on the suffrage issue. Both the WSPU and the NUWSS were active on his behalf.[69] Mrs Fawcett issued an appeal to electors, calling attention to the fact that she was the widow of Henry Fawcett, another former East London MP, and spoke on Lansbury's behalf at an eve-of-poll meeting.[70] After his defeat she wrote him a graceful letter of regret, assuring him that his efforts for justice to women had not been wasted and that his life's work of 'helping to lift up your fellow citizens to a higher material & moral level' would continue.[71]

The bonds between the NUWSS and the Labour party were reinforced so far as the union was concerned by its final pre-war effort to secure national publicity and public support for women's suffrage. This was the Pilgrimage, a walk to London in June and July 1913 by eight columns of marchers from all over England. Mrs Fawcett, who had initially been hostile to marching for votes, reflected after it had ended: 'She did not exactly understand how people's minds worked, but if walking could bring them any nearer the Suffrage, then by all means let them walk.'[72] She took an

*NUWSS deputation to Asquith, August 1913.*

active part after her return from the international suffrage congress in Budapest, justifying the *Common Cause*'s description of her as 'a famous walker'.[73] She was not immune from the violence which intermittently marred the walk, but it was less severe in the North of England where EFF organizers had been at work among trade unionists, and working-class women were often prominent suffragists.[74]

After the Pilgrimage had ended Mrs Fawcett led a deputation to Asquith and also held private meetings with suffragist ministers and with Bonar Law, the Unionist leader.[75] The meeting with the Prime Minister was as success-ful as they could have expected, but they wrote to Lloyd George and his colleagues that they had been 'deeply disappointed' by their reception at the hands of supposed friends. To the ministerial claim that women's suffrage was unpopular and required 'rehabilitation' they replied that their experi-ence dictated otherwise. If it was to be made popular in the sense sought by ministers they should champion it rather than apologizing for it.[76] Shortly before this meeting Mrs Fawcett and other NUWSS leaders saw Ramsay MacDonald who, though refusing to accord women's suffrage the primacy which the NUWSS sought, assured them that Labour was 'absolutely solid in your favour'.[77] The EFF must never have seemed so justified and so necessary.

In January 1914, however, it ran into serious trouble when the Liberals nominated Aneurin Williams to contest the North-West Durham by-election. Williams was a suffragist and a friend of Mrs Fawcett, and pressure was put on her by Mrs Williams and by leading local suffragists not to oppose him. Mrs Fawcett was in no doubt that the future of the EFF was at stake in such a difficult case. It was necessary to support not only the individual candidate but the party pledged to women's suffrage. Moreover, the Labour candidate had been in the field for several weeks with NUWSS support before the Liberals decided to adopt a suffragist. Mrs Williams was naturally dissatisfied and expressed her opposition to the EFF, which she pointed out was used to assist a party with which few suffragists were in general sympathy and whose power was 'negligible'.[78]

Among the critics of the decision to confirm support for Labour in North-West Durham was Eleanor Rathbone, a member of the NUWSS executive with whose Liverpool shipowning, business and philanthropic family Mrs Fawcett had long been friendly.[79] For the rest of her life she was to be closely involved with Eleanor's feminist activities, whether in alliance or in opposition. Mrs Williams's point that the connection with the Labour party was of little practical use to the union was shared by Rathbone, a political independent. It was also shared by other members whose Liberal convictions made them resist a policy which seemed to make a Conservative Government more likely and women's suffrage less so.[80] Rathbone moved a Liverpool resolution at the NUWSS council in February 1914 which sought to restrict the operation of the EFF in the next general election to constituencies in which it had already been committed. The resolution was defeated by only five votes. A few days earlier she had sent out a circular seeking support from suffrage societies which opposed the EFF policy.[81] Thus began a row which lasted until she, Margery Corbett Ashby and two other members of the executive resigned in May.[82]

Mrs Fawcett continued to believe strongly in continued collaboration with Labour, but her real anger was reserved for the members of the executive and their outside supporters who had organized themselves into a pressure group. Writing to Rathbone in March she commented:

> If various groups of the Executive take action of this kind it seems to me to mean the necessary break up of the Union. I regard the whole matter as most serious. Where should we be if three or four different groups of the Executive Committee took independent action and acted separately in antagonism to one another?[83]

In similar vein a letter which she and the other union officers sent to the half-yearly council, held in April to resolve the controversy, pointed out that the executive committee was not a royal commission which was free to issue majority and minority reports, but a body concerned 'to carry out the work of the Union'.[84]

A number of resolutions and amendments at this council expressed unease about the EFF policy or, in the words of a resolution moved by Cardiff, supported 'the right of free discussion'. They were all defeated or withdrawn and an executive resolution was carried which declared that its members were not free outside its meetings to advocate courses which prejudice 'the effectiveness of the existing policy'.[85] The rebellion had been put down, but in Eleanor Rathbone's view 'discontent with the Labour policy' was widespread, the executive's victory no more than 'one long series of votes of confidence in Mrs Fawcett'.[86]

Had 'the existing policy', which still related only to by-elections, been continued into the general election due to take place by December 1915, the cost to the unity of the NUWSS might have been heavy. It was by no means clear what would have happened. In February 1913 Mrs Fawcett herself supported concentrating on 'a group of seats now held by anti-Suff Liberal ministers, for the general election', and pro-Labour sentiment was strong among influential members of the executive, officers and organizers.[87] But it is possible that in any case the Labour party, anxious about its own ties with the Liberals and by no means unanimous about the importance of women's suffrage, would not have accepted the support of the NUWSS in the general election.[88] In any event a possible split was averted by the postponement of the election, at the price of an actual split on a wholly different issue. The quarrel in early 1914 throws an interesting light not only on Mrs Fawcett's attitude to publicly voiced disagreement among her colleagues, but also on the contemporary functioning of pressure groups. It is also worth noting that her supporters on this issue included

Catherine Marshall, secretary of the EFF committee, Kathleen Courtney, Isabella Ford, Maude Royden, Margaret Ashton and Helena Swanwick.[89] All were to dissent from her attitude to the war and to resign from the executive a year later.

It is difficult to estimate the success of the EFF policy between 1912 and 1914 or, conversely, the effect of government obduracy on women Liberals. Martin Pugh and Sandra Holton have uncovered interesting evidence of their disillusion and defection, but the fact that membership of the Women's Liberal Federation rose by over 50 per cent between 1906 and 1912 before losing about a third of the increase by 1914 suggests a rather more ambiguous conclusion.[90] Pugh, Holton and Brian Harrison suggest that Asquith might have yielded on the suffrage issue, but the more sceptical view of Andrew Rosen and Leslie Parker Hume appears to fit the available evidence more closely.[91] The Liberals lost several seats to Conservatives when Labour candidates intervened in by-elections,[92] but it is difficult to discern the part played by the NUWSS in these results and what benefit was gained by the suffrage cause in consequence. It is safer to conclude only that the union continued to advocate the cause until the outbreak of war and that its president remained at the heart of its activities. Whether the future would have yielded Liberal concessions, suffragist divisions, or more working-class support for the suffrage cause is a point on which, however tantalizing, speculation can yield no firm conclusion.

## NOTES

1. There is a useful account of party attitudes to women's suffrage in Constance Rover, *Women's Suffrage* (1967), ch. 8.
2. For example, by Leslie Parker Hume, *The National Union of Women's Suffrage Societies* (1982), p. 11.
3. *Christian Commonwealth*, 26 June 1912, p. 625.
4. A 1924 repetition is quoted by Brian Harrison, *Prudent Revolutionaries* (1987), p. 22.
5. *The Times*, 28 December 1905. See above, page 154; pages 184–5.
6. See Les Garner, *Stepping Stones to Women's Liberty* (1984), pp. 16–19; Hume, p. 153; Sandra Stanley Holton, *Feminism and Democracy* (1986), pp. 68–9, 81.
7. M50/2/1/254–6; Holton, pp. 49–50. The Lords did throw out the bill.
8. Lord Robert Cecil to Catherine Marshall, 25 September 1913 (D/Mar/3/23).
9. Michael and Eleanor Brock (eds), *H.H. Asquith Letters to Venetia Stanley* (Oxford: Oxford University Press, 1985 edn), p. 378. Asquith was writing on 14 January 1915 about Eleanor Acland, the wife of one of his ministers and a constitutional suffragist.
10. David Morgan, *Suffragists and Liberals* (1975), pp. 49–51. See above, page 158.
11. *Women's Franchise*, 23 July, 29 October 1908, pp. 41, 197; MGF, *Women's Suffrage*, p. 70.
12. Russell to Llewelyn Davies, 5 June 1908; quoted in Rempel *et al.* (eds), *The Collected Papers of Bertrand Russell* (1985), p. 275.

13. MGF to Frances Balfour, 27 June 1910 (FLALC, vol. 1hii). This letter is quoted more fully in Hume, p. 76.

14. *Daily Mirror*, 22 June 1910 (MAS, vol. 10); *The Times*, 29 June 1910; *CC*, 30 June 1910, p. 186.

15. For Helena Swanwick's scathing view of him see her *I Have Been Young* (1935), pp. 214–16; Hume, p. 116n.

16. Hume, pp. 81–5; Brian Harrison, *Separate Spheres* (1978), p. 165.

17. *The Times*, 23 July 1910.

18. *ibid.*, 12 August 1910.

19. *ibid.*, 16 August 1910. After Lloyd George introduced the national insurance bill in 1911 she withdrew her allegation about 'the Celt' with an apology (MGF, 'Women's suffrage', *The Englishwoman*, June 1911, p. 247).

20. *CC*, 29 February 1912, pp. 799–800.

21. *The Times*, 4 December 1912, 24 October, 8, 24 November 1913; David Lloyd George, 'Votes for women and organised lunacy', *Nash's Magazine*, July 1913, pp. 412–17; Morgan, pp. 127–8.

22. Constance Rover (*Women's Suffrage*, p. 134) quotes Sylvia Pankhurst's gibe that Lloyd George 'appeared to be making an unsuccessful attempt to gather the sweets of two worlds' (*The Suffragette Movement* (1931), p. 360).

23. *The Times*, 18 November 1911; MGF, *The Women's Victory* (1920), pp. 8–10.

24. Eleanor Cecil to MGF, 24 December 1911 (M50/2/1/346); Morgan, p. 86.

25. *The Times*, 24 January 1913.

26. MGF to Helena Auerbach, 29 March 1912 (Fawcett Collection, IIAV).

27. *The Times*, 15 December 1911; Morgan, p. 104. A bitter account by Mrs Fawcett of these events appeared in the *Common Cause*, 14 November 1913, pp. 574–5. See also her *The Women's Victory* (1920), pp. 11–13, 20–3, 27–9.

28. Quoted by Hume, pp. 131–2; Morgan, p. 92.

29. *CC*, 8 February 1912, p. 749; *The Times*, 29, 30 January 1912; MGF to Auerbach, 17 January 1912 (IIAV). *The Times* engaged in further procedural trouble-making on 26 November and 9 December 1912.

30. *MG*, 11 October 1912.

31. *CC*, 14 March 1913, p. 833.

32. *Deputation to the Prime Minister* (Hull University Library), 8 August 1913 (n.d.), pp. 18–19, 26–8. See Morgan, p. 128.

33. *The Standard*, 24 April 1913 (JRL cuttings, vol. 15).

34. Hume, esp. ch. 5; Holton, chs 4–5; Martin Pugh, 'Labour and women's suffrage' in Kenneth D. Brown, *The First Labour Party 1906–1914* (1985), pp. 233–53.

35. MGF, 'Why we women want votes', *Daily Mail*, 20 November 1906; MGF marginal note on A.V. Dicey, 'A protest against privilege', *National Review*, October 1906, p. 221 (M50/4/26/6).

36. *Women Workers* (1906), p. 83; see above, page 152.

37. MGF in Stanton (ed.) (1884), pp. 13–14. See above, page 48.

38. *ER*, 15 April 1901, pp. 109–11; Jill Liddington and Jill Norris, *One Hand Tied Behind Us* (1978), pp. 148–9; Liddington, *The Life and Times of a Respectable Rebel* (1984), esp. pp. 106–7, 181; Doris Nield Chew, *The Life and Writings of Ada Nield Chew* (Virago, 1982), pp. 42–54; NUWSS, *Annual Report*, 1908, p. 10; Holton, p. 68.

39. Holton, pp. 21–2.

40. See Liddington and Norris, esp. ch. 12.

41. Ida O'Malley to Catherine Marshall [3 June 1911] (D/Mar/3/12).

42. *CC*, 8 June 1911, pp. 151–2.

43. Brian Harrison, *Separate Spheres* (1978), pp. 28–9, 42.

44. Hardie: 'No more sincere, true-hearted, and strenuous advocate of the principles of liberty and justice, as applied to women, ever breathed' (*CC*, 1 October 1915, p. 313). Snowden: 'I shall never forget his services to us' (MGF to Ray Strachey, 15 March 1928; Strachey Papers, Oxford). Henderson: *WIR*, p. 216.
45. Marian Ramelson, *The Petticoat Rebellion* (1967), pp. 158–9 gives a useful summary of the debate.
46. MGF, *The Women's Victory*, pp. 28–9.
47. Andrew Rosen, *Rise Up, Women!* (1974), p. 70.
48. Kathleen Courtney to MGF, 8 April 1912 (M50/2/1/357).
49. *CC*, 4 April 1912, p. 880.
50. *ibid.*, 2 May 1912, pp. 51–2.
51. Courtney to Henderson, 19 April 1912 (Labour Party Archives, National Museum of Labour History, Manchester).
52. Hume, pp. 141–52; Holton, pp. 76–8, 85; Martin Pugh, 'Labour and women's suffrage' (1985), pp. 247–8.
53. Hume, pp. 148–9, 155–6; Holton, p. 78.
54. Hume, pp. 152–5; Holton, pp. 79–80; *CC*, 23 May 1912, pp. 103–4.
55. Frances Balfour to Betty Balfour (copy), 16 October 1912 (Balfour Papers, Scottish Record Office). 'And Deborah, a prophetess . . . dwelt under the palm tree . . . and the children of Israel came up to her for judgment' (Book of Judges, 4: 4–5). See above, page 72.
56. Hume, p. 152.
57. *CC*, 31 October 1912, p. 515. See also Hume, pp. 153–4n.
58. *MG*, 6 November 1912.
59. *CC*, 8 November 1912, p. 531.
60. *ibid.*, 7 March 1913, p. 817; NUWSS, *Annual Report*, 1912, pp. 8–11; *The Standard*, 28 February 1913 (JRL cuttings, vol. 13); Holton, p. 97.
61. Annie Leigh Browne to MGF, 29 January 1913; MGF to Annie Leigh Browne (copy), 30 January 1913 (D/Mar/3/33).
62. NUWSS, EC minutes, 6 February 1913 (FLA box 83).
63. MGF to Helena Auerbach, 11 February 1913 (Fawcett Collection, IIAV).
64. NUWSS, *Annual Reports*, 1912, p. 45; 1913, p. 70; 1914, p. 56; Holton, pp. 80–1, 88, 97, 100, 113–14.
65. Garner, pp. 16–20; Hume, esp. pp. 154, 163–4.
66. D/Mar/3/24. For Gordon's pro-Labour sympathies see Holton, p. 110.
67. Marshall to Lloyd George, 28 July [1913] (Lloyd George Papers, House of Lords Record Office).
68. Hume, p. 166.
69. The WSPU has dominated the attention of historians: e.g, Pugh, 'Labour and women's suffrage', pp. 245–6.
70. *The Standard*, 23, 26 November 1912 (JRL cuttings, vol. 9, which contains excellent coverage of the election).
71. MGF to George Lansbury, 27 November 1912 (Lansbury Collection, BLPES).
72. MGF to Maud Arncliffe-Sennett, 25 September 1912 (MAS, vol. 19); *CC*, 14 November 1913, p. 573.
73. *CC*, 11, 25 July 1913, pp. 227, 237, 265, 273; *MG*, 25 July 1913.
74. *CC*, 11, 18, 25 July, 8 August 1913, pp. 237, 253–4, 265, 309; Hume, pp. 195–8; Lisa Tickner, *The Spectacle of Women* (1987), pp. 141–7, esp. p. 145.
75. A verbatim report was published of the deputation to Asquith (note 32 above); a typescript verbatim report of the meeting with suffragist ministers is contained in the Lloyd George Papers.
76. MGF and eleven others to suffragist ministers, 11 August 1913 (FLA, box 89 vol. 2); Tickner, p. 148.

77. *Daily Citizen*, 11 August 1913 (JRL cuttings, vol. 19).
78. FLA, box 90a file 8; M50/2/7/5; M50/2/9/7; Holton, p. 111.
79. Her first letter to Eleanor's mother in the Liverpool University Rathbone Collection is dated 2 December [1880].
80. George Armstrong to MGF, 23 April 1914 (FLA, box 89 vol. 2).
81. NUWSS, EC minutes, 5 and 19 March 1914 (FLA, box 83).
82. *ibid.*, 7 May 1914; Holton, pp. 111–13.
83. MGF to Eleanor Rathbone (copy), 8 March 1914 (FLA, box 89 vol. 2).
84. MGF, Helena Auerbach, Kathleen Courtney, Catherine Marshall, confidential undated letter to delegates to April council (M50/1/1).
85. *Final Agenda* (annotated) for April council (filed at *ibid.*).
86. Eleanor Rathbone to Helen Fraser, 7 May 1914 (Fraser Papers, Museum of London).
87. MGF to Helena Auerbach, 11 February 1913. (IIAV). For dissent within the union see also Holton, pp. 114–5; Liddington and Norris, p. 250.
88. Hume, pp. 208–9.
89. NUWSS, EC minutes, 5 and 19 March 1914.
90. Pugh, *Women's Suffrage* (1980), p. 21; *idem, The Making of Modern British Politics* (Oxford: Blackwell, 1982), p. 156; Holton, pp. 119–20, 178 n. 15; Linda Walker, 'Party political women' (1987), p. 169.
91. Pugh, *Women's Suffrage*, pp. 21, 29; Holton, pp. 124–5; Harrison, *Separate Spheres*, pp. 50, 204; Rosen, *Rise Up*, p. 237; Hume, pp. 220–1 and n. 114.
92. Hume, pp. 161, 206; *WIR*, p. 208.

# CHAPTER 15

---· ---

## TURBULENT YEARS 1909–14:
## OTHER INTERESTS

Despite the enormous amount of time involved in speaking, organizing and negotiating for the National Union of Women's Suffrage Societies, Mrs Fawcett did not lose sight of her other interests in the period. Their changed status or the need not to antagonize potential votes in the House of Commons, however, were instrumental in reducing her commitment to such causes as women's higher education and employment opportunities, and Irish unionism. Even the campaign for an equal moral standard had passed beyond its initial heroic phase and she did not resume her earlier activity, though her speeches were frequently punctuated by references to the need to secure the vote to protect women from sexual exploitation. In her eyes the emancipation of women was an aim which required action on many different fronts. Even women's suffrage was a means, not an end, and she told an audience early in 1913, shortly before the anticipated votes on amendments to Asquith's reform bill, that if the suffrage was won it would be a beginning, not an end. 'The work', she pointed out, 'really would never come to an end. They should look on it as a journey, and be satisfied if they were making progress.'[1] Eighteen months later she told an open-air rally in Manchester that 'each generation must deal with the grievances of its own time'.[2] On the following day the Archduke Franz Ferdinand was shot in Sarajevo, and her words took on an ironic and unanticipated meaning.

Most of her other activities in the period were connected, often directly, with her suffrage work. This was particularly true of her writing, which could hardly have continued at the earlier pace, but which was remarkable given her punishing schedule of committee meetings, deputations, travelling and speaking engagements. She contributed articles to the daily and weekly press, including journals so various as the Conservative *Daily Mail* and *Morning Post*, the Liberal *Daily News* and *Nation*, and the Labour/socialist *Daily Citizen* and *New Statesman*. She also wrote for other journals at home and abroad[3] and for the suffrage press, particularly, from their inception in 1909, the *Common Cause* and *The Englishwoman*.

Much of her writing for the *Common Cause* dealt topically with the progress of the women's suffrage movement and presented current developments

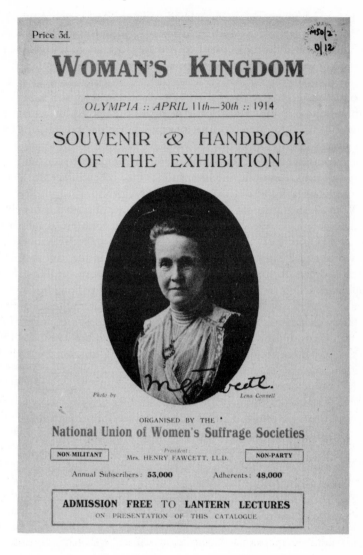

*Millicent Garrett Fawcett in 1914; the Woman's Kingdom Exhibition.*

in the most optimistic light possible. The fifteen articles which she wrote before the war for *The Englishwoman*, though often of greater length, were usually similar analyses of the contemporary suffrage scene. T*he Englishwoman* was a monthly intended to act as the 'literary-intellectual' equivalent[4] of such serious general monthlies as the *Contemporary Review* and other journals for which she had written many articles. Its editorial committee included several of her friends and colleagues, and the journal was the most authoritative expression of the views of constitutional suffragists.

Her most substantial article, published in the first number, was entitled ' "Men are men and women are women" '. It put forward trenchantly her familiar case that the differences between the sexes, far from justifying the exclusion of women as voters, were 'among the strongest and most irrefutable of the reasons for urging that no representative system is completely or truly national which entirely leaves out the representation of women'. She dealt with other shopsoiled arguments against women's suffrage equally unequivocally. Law in civilized communities, she pointed out, rested not on physical force but on justice. The argument that the women's vote was useful in municipal but not in national politics was meaningless, for a clear line between municipal and national affairs 'exists only in imagination'.[5] Like others of her articles this one was reprinted and sold as a pamphlet by the NUWSS.

With advancing age she was often asked to write obituaries of her elders and contemporaries in the women's movement. She contributed substantial accounts of Dorothea Beale and Elizabeth Blackwell to *The Times*, quoting Beale in words equally applicable to herself: 'I was born in the dark ages and have witnessed the Renaissance.'[6] She also wrote accounts of Rosa Morison, superintendent of women students at University College London, James Stuart, her co-worker of Cambridge days and Walter McLaren, the doughty parliamentary champion of women's suffrage.[7] She wrote two obituaries of W.T. Stead, who was drowned in the *Titanic* disaster in April 1912, and used the occasion of his death to press for the passage of the Criminal Law Amendment Bill, in danger of languishing in the House of Commons as an earlier bill had done until released by Stead's sensational journalism.[8] She contributed introductions to Helena Swanwick's *The Future of the Women's Movement* and to new editions of works by Elizabeth Blackwell and John Stuart Mill. She took a strikingly libertarian view of issues of freedom and censorship in her Mill introduction, condemning 'an oppressive yoke of uniformity of thought and practice' in terms which might appear to conflict with some of her past activity in the National Vigilance Association.[9]

She also found time amidst her other commitments to write a short history of *Women's Suffrage*. At the time of publication in 1912 it contained a good deal of information not easily available elsewhere. As with all her publications it was lucidly written, and it was also characteristic in the effectiveness of her jabs at anti-suffragists. H.N. Brailsford, to whom she sent a copy, told her that it was 'a triumph of compression, & even to people steeped in the subject it is full of new and suggestive things'.[10]

Her main 'other interest' in the period did not lead her away from women's suffrage. This was the international suffrage movement, established in Washington on a provisional basis in 1902. She was elected second vice-president at the inaugural congress in Berlin in 1904, which she did not attend, and first vice-president at the London congress in 1909.[11] Her international career would have begun much earlier had she accepted an invitation to become the president of the proposed International Council of

Women in 1888. She was later to be a vice-president of its British affiliate, the National Union of Women Workers, but she declined the international position offered her by the American organizer May Wright Sewall. Her reply was that it was 'to her mind "quite impossible that English and American women should have anything in common, the conditions of their lives and the purposes of their respective societies being so different" '.[12]

Though recollected and reported by Sewall in direct speech a quarter of a century later, this reply does have the authentic ring of the Fawcett who allegedly thought that the United States was 'on some other planet'.[13] It is also substantiated by the shrewd *Manchester Guardian* obituary: 'She tried hard to be nice to foreigners but remained completely foreign to them.'[14] If the 'foreignness' was mutual it was modified by the energy with which she pursued international contacts and attended the congresses of the International Woman Suffrage Alliance, at a time of severe transport and language difficulties. One British delegate, for example, reported that a speaker at the IWSA congress in Copenhagen in 1906 had 'made the delegates laugh heartily, but as she spoke in German I could not understand'.[15] She did not have the training or the flair for languages of a number of her younger colleagues, but she was not at the level of Lady Frances Balfour, who described herself in 1900 as 'insulated, isolated & insolent with regard to "foreign devils" '.[16]

The Copenhagen congress was the first she attended, and her role there seems to have been mainly ceremonial.[17] She was more active in subsequent congresses. She took a full part in Amsterdam in 1908, where she chaired some sessions and gave an officers' report. She was then still a strong advocate of suffragist harmony, and told the congress that different societies and methods benefited the British movement. The cause, she said, drew strength from the fact that 'there were suffragettes ready to go to prison and uneducated women who said that "it was unloidy-like to chine yourself to rilings" '.[18] By this time she had learned that militant methods were not the working-class contribution to the suffrage movement. Her state of mind at the time and the impact that the rejuvenated British movement had made on suffragists from other countries may have been illuminated by an unsigned note from a colleague. It told her that a German delegate had said 'how happy you look. I think she is quite right and there is nothing so good as success.'[19] Her state of mind and that of others may also have been illuminated by a note from the secretary, the American Rachel Foster Avery. This suggested that speakers should stand to speak on a trap door, be given a minute's warning, 'then a final tap of the bell, a touch of the button, and lo, the lady would disappear perorating!'[20]

However great the gulf between her and 'foreigners' Mrs Fawcett was in no doubt that an international dimension was valuable to the British movement. According to Ray Strachey, she was more enthusiastic about international links than the majority of her colleagues, whom she told that work

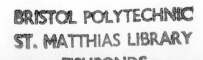

for women's suffrage in one country often brought success in another.[21] She invited the international alliance to meet in London in 1909, conscious of the fact that a gathering attended by women from twenty-one countries would result in extensive publicity and help to dispel the ignorance which she termed 'our chief foe'.[22] She was as president of the host society a dominant figure at the congress, presiding over several meetings including one at the Albert Hall, where a pageant of women's trades and professions made a striking impact.[23]

Her failure to attend the Stockholm congress in 1911 due to the joint suffrage march in London caused much distress to her Swedish colleagues, as noted above. She was, her correspondent told her, the British suffragist best known in Sweden.[24] In 1913 she addressed a public meeting in Vienna on her way to the huge congress in Budapest, where one of her responsibilities was to chair a meeting on the white slave traffic. She told a journalist at the congress that its most important aspect was to 'set the whole world almost to thinking and talking about the suffrage'.[25] She herself set the whole of the British delegation on a roar when an attempt was made by Carrie Chapman Catt, the IWSA president, to root out a delegate accused of 'living in sin'. But, it was claimed, there was more than one such delegate. Mrs Fawcett observed, 'with unsurpassable gravity', Maude Royden recalled, ' "My dear, none of us is safe." Anything more enchantingly comic from the leader, so sedate and beyond reproach, of the deputation all of whose members resembled her in this if in nothing else, could not be imagined.'[26]

The Budapest congress established a permanent headquarters in London, to which it moved its paper *Jus Suffragii*. Mary Sheepshanks, a British suffragist who spoke fluent French and German, became headquarters secretary and editor of the enlarged paper. An officers' meeting, also attended by a number of national presidents, was held in London in July 1914 to arrange the next congress, due to be held in Berlin in 1915. Instead, after the unimagined Great War, it was held in June 1920 in Geneva.[27] The outbreak of war and the fact that Mrs Catt was based in the United States meant that the London headquarters was to be the centre of the suffrage movement in the allied countries and Mrs Fawcett its leader.

A field in which international links were obviously crucial was the struggle against the white slave trade. She could not play as active a role as in the past, but she remained deeply concerned about this and related questions of public morality. She made frequent references to moral questions in her suffrage speeches, notably in addressing the rally in Hyde Park which ended the Pilgrimage in July 1913.[28] She was one of the speakers at the twenty-fifth anniversary celebration of the National Vigilance Association in 1910 and spoke with pride of her association with the NVA and of the change in public opinion towards its activities since the early days.[29] Shortly before taking to the road with the Pilgrimage she addressed an international congress convened by the NVA, where she was introduced by the Dean of

*Leaders of the International Woman Suffrage Alliance, 1914, including: Adela Stanton Coit (front row, left); Annie Furuhjelm, Marguerite de Witt Schlumberger, Carrie Chapman Catt, Millicent Garrett Fawcett (second row, from right); Chrystal Macmillan, Marie Stritt (third row, from left).*

Westminster as 'one whose name is well known throughout the world'. She was careful to link the traffic in women with the suffrage, pointing out that rising interest in both had taken place simultaneously, and that where women had been enfranchised their power to fight international prostitution had been greatly strengthened. So often characterized as lacking passion, she showed an appreciation of its importance in taking issue with the dean, who had warned that reformers should deal in 'a cold-blooded, dispassionate, and sensible manner' with the economic aspects of vice. In her view: 'Everything we can give is wanted; those who are warm-blooded should give their warm-bloodedness, and we may all give our reasoning faculties.'[30]

She had not lost her interest in women's higher education, though the pressure of her suffrage commitments had made it necessary to surrender her place on the Newnham council in 1909, thus ending her long institutional links with Cambridge. Closer at hand was the youthful London School of Economics where, as befitted an institution devoted to the social sciences, exceptional opportunities were offered to women both as staff and as students. The student paper, the *Clare Market Review*, reported her presence at the student union's annual dinner in February 1912, and later in the year that she had delivered her presidential address, 'a charming and witty discourse "In praise of gossip" ' to a large audience. The vote of thanks was moved by the school's director, William Pember Reeves, and seconded by Miss Brinton.[31]

Thereby hung a short but interesting tale. Miss Brinton was one of a small group of feminist students who decided that Mrs Fawcett should be elected honorary president. When A.J. Balfour, the union committee's first choice, declined to serve they fought off an attempt to elect the anti-suffragist Lord Avebury and secured Mrs Fawcett's election with only a single dissentient vote. She was a good choice, taking a more active role than was required of union presidents. Miss Brinton, who as Mary Stocks became a colleague and friend of Mrs Fawcett, and a feminist and educationist of distinction, worked with her as one of the union secretaries. In February 1913 she wrote to her future husband: 'It does seem rather queer that a person who worked with Mill and Fawcett and all those people whom I seem to regard as "history" should be leading the suffrage movement today and shouldn't seem at all old.'[32]

Mrs Fawcett also maintained her interest in India, where the problems of education and morality were strikingly related. In 1913 she wrote an article for the *Common Cause*, deploring the subordination of both British and Indian women in India, and stressing the abysmally low percentage of Indian girls and women who received a formal education.[33] The following year she became involved in an exceptionally unpleasant case which illustrated strikingly the helplessness of girls in the sub-continent. In 1911 H.B. McCormick, a British planter in Burma, purchased an 11-year-old Malayan girl named Aina for thirty rupees. The transaction was formally executed because, McCormick told the judicial committee of the Privy Council, when he had purchased Aina two years previously for ten rupees she had been returned to her mother. The affair was exposed in two articles in a Burmese paper by a British journalist named Channing Arnold, who in consequence was prosecuted for defamation and imprisoned for a year. The case aroused indignation among some of Arnold's fellow journalists and fury among feminists, including Mrs Fawcett, Chrystal Macmillan, Catherine Marshall and Maude Royden.[34]

Both Marshall's papers and the records of the India Office make clear the amount of time and energy which Mrs Fawcett devoted to the case despite her other commitments. She told David Alec Wilson, a writer and former Indian civil servant concerned to secure justice for Arnold, that she had been greatly 'stirred' by the case. Wilson, she acknowledged, was most disturbed about the wrong done to Arnold,

> while we feel most the intolerable degradation & ruin of childhood and the flimsy hypocrisy of passing 'White Slave Traffic' Acts here, while in British dominions in the East men are allowed to purchase openly and apparently without shame young children and behave to them as McCormick did to the child Aina.

She suggested a number of political and literary contacts and advocated a press campaign to do for Arnold what Zola had done for Dreyfus.[35]

She did not rest content with advice. She lobbied the India Office, where she had separate interviews with the secretary of state and the under-secretary. In a memorandum in June 1914 she claimed that the purchase of Aina meant not only ruin to the child herself but degradation of the British flag and the empire. If Indian children were not protected, she warned, 'racial poison' would spread and British rule be 'identified with sexual abominations lower than anything which either West or East had separately touched'.[36] However, she secured little satisfaction. With the outbreak of war the case appears to have been dropped, and Arnold himself was only narrowly saved from further prosecution.[37]

In general she did not express publicly her views on matters of contemporary political controversy in this life-and-death period of the suffrage campaign. One exception was her onslaught on Lloyd George in 1910, which exposed her anti-Liberal and anti-Celt prejudices with alarming candour.[38] Another was the highly controversial National Insurance Bill of 1911. She originally called the bill 'a great measure of constructive statesmanship',[39] but she soon modified this opinion. She joined twenty other women in a letter to the press which pointed out the bill's deficiencies and exclusions. Married women were not covered unless they worked for wages, and the contributions of a woman wage-earner were lost to her if she married and stopped work. There was no provision for women to be included in the act's administration, and the 30s maternity benefit was to be paid to the father. The signatories pointed out that the bill had been designed to benefit men and that its provisions would have been different if women had been able to vote.[40] Although the writers were mainly Unionists their criticisms were widely shared, notably by the Fabian Women's Group.[41]

Mrs Fawcett also denounced plans to assist families by periodic payments of the type later known as family allowances. Instead, a wife should have a legal claim to a share in her husband's income, increasing with the number of children.[42] In an article in *The Nation* in 1914, however, she accepted 'the most reasonable and moderate demands' of the Women's Co-operative Guild to establish municipal maternity centres, extend provisions for the notification of births, provide municipal midwives and raise maternity benefit (which after an amending act in 1913 was paid to the mother) to £7 10s 0d. 'The fact is clear', she wrote, 'that there is no adequate national care of maternity, and the nation is suffering from its want.' She pointed out that in Australia a maternity benefit of £5 was paid: 'But then, of course, in Australia women have the vote.'[43] In her view a benefit should not be paid in such a way that would allow the father to spend it in the public house. But she warmly approved provision for adequate maternity and infant care, even though paid in cash.

Although invited to join the Royal Commission on Venereal Disease in 1913 she declined to be distracted from her suffrage activities.[44] She did, however, write to Asquith emphasizing the importance of studying the causes of venereal disease, not merely its symptoms. Among these was an examination of prostitution and its links with inadequate working conditions and poor education.[45] Despite her own absorption in women's suffrage she encouraged Lady Frances Balfour to serve on the Royal Commission on Divorce in 1909. After initial reluctance she gave evidence to the commission in the midst of 'speaking engagements out of London [which] eat up nearly all my time'.[46]

In the event she gave her evidence in June 1910 on the day after leading a suffrage deputation to Asquith. She was greeted by the chairman of the commission, Lord Gorell, with the observation: 'You are so well known, Mrs Fawcett, that I need not ask who you are, as I have to ask some witnesses.'[47] It was to be expected that she should declare her belief in 'the permanence of the marriage tie as of the utmost importance both for the family and for the State'.[48] What may seem more surprising is the liberal and compassionate character of her evidence. Perhaps her most striking opinions were that cruelty was worse than adultery, and that in cases of permanent separation of the marriage partners, divorce should be available on grounds of mutual consent. The law, she maintained, 'should follow the fact. If the fact is that the marriage is dissolved and put an end to, and there is no hope of the two coming together again, then the possibility of relief should be given.' Asked if such a provision would not encourage collusion in obtaining divorce she replied: 'I should be inclined to face that.' Her attitude to sexual morality as represented in fiction and the theatre 'and in some degree in social life'[49] was not 'advanced' for her day, but in accepting divorce by consent she advocated a reform which parliament took nearly sixty years to enact.

Her aim, as Gorell put it to her, was 'to place the two sexes on an absolute equality'. The male standard of morality should be raised to the female. Parents should have equal rights of guardianship over their children, and men should be made legally responsible for the maintenance of their illegitimate children.[50] She was particularly anxious to assist the working-class woman: 'It cannot be right that there should be virtually one law for the rich and another for the poor.' Some witnesses had told the commission that there was no demand among the poor for divorce: 'You may as well say there is no demand among the poor for motor-cars or race-horses.' She did not express an opinion as to the best means of reducing the cost of divorce, but that it should be cheaper for the poor 'I have very little doubt whatever'. The economic value of a woman's work within the family should be recognized by entitling her to wages for housework or a certain proportion of her husband's wages. As the situation then existed, any savings which she made were her husband's: 'If she wants a postage stamp or a bootlace she has no money of her own to buy it.' If a married woman had a right to a share of her husband's wages she would be less likely to seek employment in a factory,[51] a point presumably intended to appeal to her male questioners.

Her liberal views resulted in severe questioning by Cosmo Gordon Lang, the Archbishop of York, and Sir Lewis Dibdin, a prominent ecclesiastical lawyer, who with a third commissioner filed a minority report. When the reports were published in 1912 Mrs Fawcett wrote to Frances Balfour, saying that she had not imagined that a commission containing such members would be able to produce a united report. She thought the minority 'absolutely hopeless and mistaking names & words for essential things'.[52] At one point Gorell had to intervene to stop Dibdin's aggressive questioning from turning into a quarrel. Her feminist convictions, her pragmatic acceptance of lesser evils so that greater ones could be ended and her lack of interest in theological detail did nothing to endear her to the commission's minority.[53]

She probably expected little from the Royal Commission, judging by her comment that divorce reform like other questions affecting women required 'something almost resembling a moral earthquake' if justice were to be done. The anti-suffrage Liberal James Bryce, she reminded Conservative readers, had wrongly predicted the imminent end of unequal access to divorce twenty years earlier.[54] 'This country is not governed by logic', she pointed out a little later: 'It is governed by Parliament.'[55] Its failure to act on the commission's relatively liberal reports is in consequence unlikely to have surprised her.

Despite her suffrage activities she managed to enjoy occasional long holidays, including 'a good long time' in Switzerland in the summer of 1908, a month in northern Italy in 1913 and some weeks in Wiltshire a year later.[56] Even on her speaking tours she slipped on her walking boots when the opportunity arose.[57] Conversely even when on holiday she was not always able to escape meetings. Visiting a friend in Algiers in February 1911 she held 'quite a successful little W.S. meeting . . . at the Presbyterian Church', she reported to Mrs Auerbach, enclosing a cheque for £1 2s 0d collected at the meeting.[58]

But this was not a period for writing travel articles, for spreading herself across many fields or for the combination of work and leisure which she most enjoyed. Militant guerrilla warfare, bringing women's suffrage to the forefront of politics, had suddenly interrupted the pattern of her life. As she drew up 'Our balance sheet' at the end of July 1914,[59] both her life and the life of the nation were about to be interrupted on a vastly greater and more tragic scale.

NOTES

1. *The Standard*, 18 January 1913 (JRL cuttings, vol. 10).
2. *MG*, 29 June 1914.
3. A letter survives which illustrates her tenacity in business matters. On 10 December 1912 she wrote to R.U. Johnson of the American *Century Magazine* asking 'if you are accustomed to receive articles without any fee to the writer?' She was subsequently paid £10 5s 9d for her article on 'Violence in the woman's suffrage movement' which had appeared in the magazine in November 1912 (MGF to Johnson, 10 December 1912 and 7 January 1913, Century Collection, New York Public Library).
4. David Doughan and Denise Sanchez (eds), *Feminist Periodicals 1855–1984* (Hemel Hempstead: Harvester Wheatsheaf, 1987), p. 28.
5. MGF, *The Englishwoman*, February 1909, pp. 21, 28, 30–1. She wrote 25 articles for the 144 numbers of the journal.
6. *The Times*, 10 November 1906 and 2 June 1910. She told Ray Strachey that she was the author of the Beale obituary in a letter dated 16 December 1927 (Strachey Papers, Oxford); the Blackwell obituary was identified on p. xv of her introduction to *Pioneer Work for Women* (note 9 below).
7. *CC*, 15 February, 11 July 1912, pp. 765, 228–9; 28 November 1913, p. 612.
8. MGF, 'In memoriam: W.T. Stead', *CC*, 25 April 1912, p. 37; 'W.T. Stead', *Contemporary Review*, May 1912, pp. 609–11; *The Standard*, 27 April 1912 (MAS, vol. 17); Frederic Whyte, *The Life of W.T. Stead*, vol. 1(1925), p. 163n.; vol. 2, pp. 349–51. An amended bill was passed late in 1912.
9. Helena Swanwick, *The Future of the Women's Movement* (1913); Elizabeth Blackwell, *Pioneer Work for Women* [1914 edn.]; John Stuart Mill, *On Liberty, Representative Government, The Subjection of Women* (1912 edn.), esp. pp. ix–xi.
10. H.N. Brailsford to MGF, 2 March [1912] (M50/2/1/356).
11. *Women's Suffrage Record*, June 1904, extra supplement; International Woman Suffrage Alliance, *Report of Fifth Conference and First Quinquennial* (1909), p. 45; Ida Husted Harper (ed.), *The History of Woman Suffrage*, vol. 6, 1900–1920 (1922), pp. 809–16.
12. May Wright Sewall (compiler), *Genesis of the International Council of Women* [?Indianapolis, n.p., 1914], pp. 20–4, 36–7.
13. See above, page 76.
14. *MG*, 5 August 1929.
15. *Report on the International Woman Suffrage Alliance Congress* (1906), p. 6 (M50/2/23/1).

16. Balfour to MGF, 14 March 1900 (FLALC, vol. 1bi).
17. *Report on the . . . Congress* (note 15 above), p. 11.
18. *Report of the Fourth Conference of the International Woman Suffrage Alliance* (1908), pp. 14–15, 17, 38.
19. Unidentified correspondent to MGF, undated (M50/2/23/7). The congress took place soon after the successful NUWSS demonstration on 13 June 1908.
20. Avery to *idem*, undated (M50/2/23/5).
21. MGF, 'The international aspects of women's suffrage', *The Englishwoman*, April 1909, pp. 273–4; *MGF*, pp. 241–4.
22. *Report of the Fourth Conference* (note 18 above), pp. 26–7.
23. *The Times*, 26–30 April, 1, 3, 4 May 1909; MGF in *CC*, 15 April 1909, pp. 7–8; Harper, pp. 835–6; Lisa Tickner, *The Spectacle of Women* (1987), pp. 100–4; IWSA, *Report of Fifth Conference* (note 11 above), pp. 25–56.
24. Signe Bergman to MGF, 16 May 1911 (see above, ch. 13, note 62).
25. Agnes Garrett to Clara Deneke, 14 June [1913] (Ms Eng. Letters, Bodleian Library); *Daily Chronicle*, 26 June 1913 (JRL cuttings, vol. 17); IWSA, *Report of Seventh Congress* (1913), pp. 52–3.
26. Maude Royden, 'A great experience' (FLA, box 224).
27. *Report of the Eighth Congress of the International Woman Suffrage Alliance 1920* (n.d.), pp. 27–8, 31, 35, 37.
28. *MG*, 28 July 1913.
29. W.A. Coote (ed.), *A Romance of Philanthropy* (1916), pp. 219–21. See above, page 90.
30. *Fifth International Congress for the Suppression of the White Slave Trade* [1913], pp. 162–5.
31. *Clare Market Review*, May 1912, p. 114; February 1913, p. 77.
32. London School of Economics Students' Union Committee minutes, 23 May, 14 June, 23 October 1912 (I owe this reference to Ms Maccoll of the BLPES); Mary Stocks, *My Commonplace Book* (1970) p. 91; Stocks, taped interview with Brian Harrison, 30 April 1974 (Fawcett Library).
33. *CC*, 12, 26 September, 3, 10 October 1913, pp. 383–4, 424, 444, 461.
34. D/Mar/3/30, on which this paragraph draws, is devoted to the Channing Arnold case. See also *CC*, 8 May, 10 July 1914, pp. 106–7, 296–7.
35. MGF to Wilson (copy), 13 May 1914 (D/Mar/3/30).
36. MGF, 'Considerations arising out of the Channing Arnold case' [June 1914] (Charles Henry Roberts Papers, India Office Library).
37. *CC*, 17 July 1914, p. 311.
38. See above, pages 184–5.
39. MGF, 'Women's suffrage', *The Englishwoman*, June 1911, p. 247.
40. *CC*, 13 July 1911, p. 256.
41. Jane Lewis, *Women in England 1870–1950* (1984), p. 48; Patricia Pugh, *Educate, Agitate, Organise* (Methuen, 1984), p. 114.
42. MGF, 'The woman's point of view', *Morning Post*, 19 April 1911.
43. MGF, 'The waste of life', *The Nation*, 4 April 1914, pp. 16–17.
44. MGF and Ethel M. Turner, *Josephine Butler* (1927), p. 135n.
45. MGF to Asquith, 13 September 1913 (copy, FLA, box 89 vol. 2).
46. Frances Balfour, *Ne Obliviscaris*, vol. 2 [1930], p. 424; Balfour to MGF, 16 December 1909; MGF to Balfour, 18 December 1909 and 29 May 1910 (FLALC, vols. 1g and 1hi).
47. Royal Commission on Divorce, *Evidence*, vol. II; P.P. 1912–13, vol. XIX, Cd. 6480, q. 21,729.
48. Cd. 6480, q. 21,732.
49. *ibid.*, qs 21,732; 21,736; 21,741; 21,791; 21,808; 21,863; 21,870; 21,879–80.

50. *ibid.*, qs 21,732–3; 21,749–57.
51. *ibid.*, qs 21,745; 21,758; 21,774–5.
52. MGF to Balfour, 11 February [1912] (FLALC, vol. 1jii).
53. Cd. 6480, qs 21,827–9; 21,837; 21,881–7.
54. MGF, 'Women and representative government', *Conservative and Unionist Women's Franchise Review*, October 1911, p. 149. She had used the phrase 'a moral earthquake' nearly twenty years earlier when discussing Stead's revelations of the 1880s. See above, page 91.
55. MGF, 'Our balance sheet', *The Englishwoman*, August 1914, p. 127. She later attributed the aphorism to Disraeli.
56. MGF to Philippa Strachey, 18 July 1908 (FLA, box 298); *CC*, 16 May 1913, p. 91; MGF to D.A. Wilson, 13 May 1914 (note 35 above). The trip to Italy was her first ' "real" holiday' for two years.
57. Her walks in the Scottish mountains with her sisters (p. 76 above) were cases in point.
58. MGF to Auerbach, 26 February [1911] (Fawcett Collection, IIAV); *CC*, 9 March 1911, pp. 779–80; 8 June 1917, p. 100.
59. See note 55 above.

# CHAPTER 16

## THE CATASTROPHE OF WAR 1914–15

As she considered the prospects of the suffrage movement at the end of July 1914, Mrs Fawcett detected hope primarily in the 'overwhelming evidence of the growing strength of the principle of women's suffrage in the country' and the continued alliance with the Labour party, to the defence of which she devoted a substantial part of her 'balance sheet'.[1] She produced no evidence to suggest that the Government, despite Asquith's apparently encouraging response to a deputation of working women led by Sylvia Pankhurst on 20 June, might be prepared to introduce a bill to enfranchise women. It was at this stage that the catastrophe of war suddenly intervened.

The *Common Cause* made the briefest of references on 31 July 1914 to the war which had already begun, though Britain was not yet a participant.[2] Three days later the executive committee of the National Union of Women's Suffrage Societies endorsed the decision already taken by Mrs Fawcett and Catherine Marshall (the other officers being away from London) to participate in a women's meeting called by a number of organizations representing women in the labour movement. The executive's decision was taken without opposition, but it was agreed that the union was uncommitted to any particular line of policy relating to the war. Each speaker should represent herself or her organization only.[3] So far the executive had committed itself to nothing very remarkable, but the resolution which it agreed to put to the meeting was an impressive feminist appeal for peace. 'In this terrible hour', it declared,

> when the outbreak of war in Europe is depending on decisions which women have no direct power to shape this meeting of women . . . deplore[s] . . . the outbreak of war in Europe as an unparalleled disaster. Women find themselves in the position of seeing all they most reverence and treasure, the home, the family, the race, subjected to irreparable injury, which they are powerless to avert . . . The women here assembled call upon the Governments of their several countries to support every effort made to restore peace.[4]

The resolution was agreed by the executive with a single abstention and no dissent. A similar resolution was agreed by the three officers of the International Woman Suffrage Alliance then in London and published as a manifesto. One of the three was Millicent Garrett Fawcett.[5]

The women's meeting was held at Kingsway Hall on 4 August, the day Britain entered the war. The shock was immense; it stunned educated feminists as it did the general public.[6] Most of the large audience at Kingsway Hall had come to attend a peace rally, and it was the opponents of war who were most warmly received. Speaking from the chair, however, Mrs Fawcett told the meeting that the time for a peace demonstration had passed. Europe was at war and Britain was to take part: 'We must therefore concentrate every effort on meeting the calamity, and try to alleviate the sufferings which must ensue.'[7] But whatever her own misgivings,[8] the enthusiasm of the audience and many of the speakers made the meeting into a demonstration for peace. Even such a close ally as Lord Robert Cecil wrote her an angry letter threatening to desert the suffrage camp and charging the national union with failing to speak for its fellow countrywomen.[9]

It was to war relief work that Mrs Fawcett was to turn her efforts in the months before the irrevocable split in the union's leadership took place. But before the night of war descended she wrote a front page article for *Jus Suffragii*, calling on her friends and associates in the international suffrage movement to hold the alliance together and to show that the power of justice and life was stronger than hatred and death. 'Indestructible links' bound international suffragists to each other: 'We have to show that what unites us is stronger than what separates us.'[10]

The issue of the *Common Cause* which reported the Kingsway Hall meeting with evident sympathy for the peacemakers contained a message from Mrs Fawcett to the members of the union. At its meeting on 3 August the executive had decided to 'suspend political propaganda during the next few months' and to use its organizational strength to relieve the victims of 'the economic and industrial dislocation caused by the war'.[11] Mrs Fawcett appealed to members, now that all hope of peace had disappeared, to use the framework of their suffrage societies to assist the national cause, and in particular women and children whom war would threaten with destitution: 'Now is the time for resolute effort and self-sacrifice on the part of every one of us to help our country . . . Let us show ourselves worthy of citizenship, whether our claim to it be recognised or not.'[12]

The executive decided at its meeting on 3 August to suspend the union's normal political work and ask member societies for their views on its role in time of war. By the time it next met on 6 August replies had already been received on behalf of over 200 of the 600 societies. All but two of the replies endorsed the executive's plan to undertake relief work, and it was to this activity that the union now turned energetically, both for its own sake and as an attempt to prevent members from taking part in other work which might lead to a collapse in its local organization.[13]

Mrs Fawcett's role in these early months of relief work remained that of standard bearer, as it had been in her suffrage activities.[14] The *Common Cause* wrote a month after the outbreak of war, with no apparent embarrassment, that she 'holds the Union together by an invisible bond of confidence and affection'.[15] Holding the union together and interpreting it to the outside world were in fact functions which none of its other leading figures could have performed so successfully. As early as September 1914 she was writing articles on the war work of the NUWSS, and several of them taken together give a picture in perspective of its activities in the early months.[16]

The union was approached 'from many quarters' to promote recruitment, she wrote in November 1914, a request declined on the grounds that it was not its function to lecture men on their duty but to encourage women to do theirs. Thinking that dislocation of employment would be a serious problem it kept all its staff and organizers in post, a wise precaution since in the first autumn of the war the percentage of unemployed women was well above its normal figure. Forty workshops were opened, and the London society was particularly active in training women in various aspects of engineering and related fields. Maternity centres and baby clinics were opened and efforts made to promote the conservation of essential food supplies. Assistance was provided to care for children, and through the medium of the IWSA many foreign women were repatriated or otherwise assisted. 'Since the outbreak of the war', she wrote as early as September 1914, 'thousands of offers of help and thousands of requests for assistance have passed through our office.'

Forty-five affiliated societies became Red Cross centres, and hospital units were assembled and despatched to France under the management of her niece Louisa Garrett Anderson and Flora Murray, her old opponents from the London society in pre-war days. Another important figure was Elsie Inglis, the Scottish doctor and suffragist who was to be the best-known British woman war doctor, and whose work was undertaken in close collaboration with the NUWSS. Given the demands for the reintroduction of the Contagious Diseases Acts in the context of large new army camps, the union societies were particularly sensitive to the questions of sexual morality which inevitably arose in wartime. They collaborated with other societies to open non-alcoholic refreshment rooms and supported efforts to prevent young girls from congregating around the camps, including such measures as a system of women's patrols. Suffragists perhaps more than other women quickly realized the importance of their activities in conditions of total war. Mrs Fawcett's unique prestige made her a powerful source of encouragement to the war work of her members, and her uncomplicated patriotism enabled her to carry out this function without doubts or hesitation. She wrote in December 1914: 'Our men have been heroes in the field. When they come back let them find that women have been doing work at home no less vital for the welfare of the nation.'

Even a lifelong feminist convinced of women's capacities could be surprised by the extent of their wartime achievements. A month after Britain's entry into the war she warned: 'The special work of women is on the same lines as their ordinary work.' This was in the fields of medicine and nursing,

*Women's war work* [margin annotation]

care and protection of factory and work girls, care of children, pregnant women and young mothers. Women doctors, she wrote, should do essential work at home rather than going to war: 'It may be more exciting and thrilling to try to get on the staff of a field hospital, but this is more especially men's work.'[17] It was counsel which she was soon to amend.

There is no reason to doubt that the first weeks of the war were a period of desperate sadness for Mrs Fawcett, as she was later to recall.[18] Yet they were in some respects also a period of hope. Organized feminists were unitedly engaged in work whose importance was increasingly recognized by the Government, and the case for women's suffrage was being advanced without being obviously advocated. She was able to warn against exaggerated pressure on men to join the army, and accounts of German atrocities which were shown to be untrue.[19] The full impact of the savage toll of war deaths which took twenty-nine lives in the Garrett and Fawcett families still lay in the future.[20] So too did the split in the national union itself, 'the only part of my work for Suffrage which I wish to forget', she wrote in 1918.[21]

The split, however, could not be long delayed. As Sandra Holton notes, it was impossible to prevent indefinitely the discussion of attitudes to the war.[22] The issues were too vast, convictions too strongly held, differences of opinion too great for attention to be long diverted to war relief work, however essential. Opposing views within the union, though fluid and confused, were based on different philosophies, both of which claimed to represent the deeper significance of the women's suffrage movement.[23] The opposing points of view were represented by Millicent Garrett Fawcett and Helena Swanwick, 'friends & colleagues for a good many years',[24] but soon to be divided by the most deep-rooted of principles.

Although many of the active members of the union were anxious to work for the restoration of peace, it is highly unlikely that the majority of members differed radically from the mass of the British population in their support for the war. Patriotism, the most powerful of political emotions, was stimulated by the German invasion of Belgium and France and the exaggerated press reports of atrocities. It required unusual conviction and strength of character at such a time for either men or women to defy popular sentiment. Like all successful leaders Mrs Fawcett's shared and articulated the convictions of her supporters, though many of them were undoubtedly influenced by her strong advocacy of the patriotic cause. She was, however, by no means among the most militaristic champions of the war in this early phase, as her colleague Alice Clark commented in November 1914.[25] Moreover, as Ann Wiltsher points out, in her eyes support for the suffrage implied support for the war. The British Empire, she claimed, was struggling for democracy, an aim in line with the union's own position as part of the democratic movement of the day.[26]

Helena Swanwick was unusual, though not unique, among opponents of the war in her education, her ability and her international connections.

There must have seemed nothing exceptional in her assertion to the Kingsway Hall meeting in August 1914: 'Woman was the guardian of the race. It was for her to replenish the earth when man had devastated it.'[27] But her words were meant as more than a rhetorical flourish. Two months later she tried unsuccessfully to persuade the union executive to call a special meeting of the council to determine its policy towards the war, a proposal characterized by Mrs Fawcett as 'premature and damaging to the Nation'. Mrs Swanwick's reply expressed her view both succinctly and effectively:

> She felt that the question of peace and war, involving as it did the question of the relations of reason and physical force, was at the basis of the whole Franchise movement and that therefore, to follow the line proposed by Mrs Fawcett would be to put the question of Women's Suffrage second.

Significantly she also told her colleagues that they must be prepared for the possibility of a split within the union.[28]

The months which followed were agonizing for the women who had laboured so effectively to build up the NUWSS and make it the leading expression of suffrage views. By the summer of 1915 Mrs Fawcett was divided politically from all her closest colleagues, a division which in certain cases led to permanent personal alienation.

It was a division which could lead to only one end, despite the galaxy of talent found on the losing side. There were three principal reasons for the inevitable result. The first was that Mrs Fawcett, the leading figure in the national union, trusted by her colleagues and members, echoed the patriotism of politicians and press and the public at large. Her advocacy of the patriotic line increased the difficulties of her opponents since many of them, notably Isabella O. Ford, were desperately anxious to avoid a quarrel with their leader.[29] Second, the patriots on the union executive were motivated by an uncomplicated belief in 'the sustaining of the vital strength of the nation', a phrase devised by Mrs Fawcett in November 1914[30] and repeated frequently thereafter. Her opponents were divided between pacifism, support for a negotiated peace and advocacy of propaganda campaigns to avoid future wars.[31] They were unable to act unitedly. Finally, women's suffrage would have lost a great deal of potential support had the national union condemned the war to which there was so little overt opposition. Feminist pacifists did not put pacifism before feminism. Rather, their conception of feminism had implications which put them at odds with many of their colleagues and most of the nation, and made them prefer peace to the early realization of votes for women.[32] This was not to their advantage within an organization dedicated to women's suffrage.

After Helena Swanwick's attempt in October 1914 to call a special NUWSS council had been defeated and hopes of a short war shown to be unrealistic, the issue became increasingly divisive within the leadership of the union. On 4 November the executive considered a resolution which Mrs Fawcett proposed for the agenda of the provincial council to be held the following week at Wallasey. A number of members indicated that they could not agree to a sentence explicitly supporting the British war effort, and it was dropped.[33] She made no attempt, however, to hide her sentiments. On the same day the press reported her lavish praise of Belgian resistance to the German invasion, 'an example of heroic courage and self-devotion which would rank with the very greatest deeds in history'.[34] As with her past opposition to Irish Home Rule, support from a respected figure not obviously tied to the government propaganda machine must have been worth any number of ministerial speeches or press exhortations.

A week later she told the delegates at Wallasey that service rather than criticism was demanded in the crisis of war. Five times within forty years, she declared, Germany had threatened to destroy France, and had stated that its next target was England. 'In the present war the moral sense of the civilised world stood with the Allies.' German intellectuals had extolled war as morally desirable. It was essential that 'our institutions should not be Prussianised'. The nation, she warned, was united in its support for the war. In contrast Maude Royden, editor of the *Common Cause*, claimed that the women's movement 'involved the assertion of spiritual force as greater than physical force, and the granting of the vote to women was a definite recognition of this'.[35] Opinion was fast becoming irreconcilable. Immediately after the end of the council Eleanor Rathbone, herself a passionate supporter of the war,[36] wrote to Catherine Marshall, expressing her alarm at the prospect of Marshall and others resigning from the executive: 'It would mean I feel the break up of the Union and also probably, the break up of Mrs Fawcett.' Although she had not attended the council the reports she had received 'confirm my fears for Mrs Fawcett. They all thought her so changed.' For the union to be broken up, 'with Mrs Fawcett on one side & all those of you on whom she has manifestly so leaned on the other' would be 'intolerable indecency'.[37]

The break which followed several months later, while probably unavoidable, was embittered by Mrs Fawcett's unwillingness to temper the expression of her views or to make any real effort to placate those of her colleagues with whom she disagreed. In December 1914 she reported to the executive that she had received a letter from Aletta Jacobs, the Dutch women's suffrage leader, proposing that a business congress of the IWSA be held in a neutral country in 1915. She made clear her own opposition to the proposal but could muster only one other member to support her.[38] Her patriotic fervour aroused, she was prepared to make full use of her unrivalled position in the suffrage movement and to take her case over the heads of her executive. Her position as president of the union and leader of the IWSA among the allied nations must also have reinforced her resolve not to accept the decision without a fight. Within a fortnight of the meeting she wrote to Carrie Chapman Catt, president of the IWSA, expressing her strong opposition to an international congress on the grounds that it would be almost certain to be disrupted by 'violent quarrels and fierce denunciations'. If a meeting were called she would refuse to attend it and if necessary would resign her position as first vice-president of the alliance.[39] Edited versions of this letter appeared in the *Common Cause* and *Jus Suffragii*, the latter following a New Year message of goodwill from Mrs Fawcett to IWSA members, beginning 'Hope all things, believe all things.'[40]

The annual council of the NUWSS, held early in February 1915, was an agonized and confusing event.[41] Many of the resolutions seemed to be victories for the advocates of peace, but they were, taken as a whole, sufficiently ambiguous to be 'interpreted in different ways by different groups of people', as Mrs Fawcett wrote later.[42] One expressed 'undying admiration of the heroism of those who are now serving this country in the defence of the Empire', and an editorial in the *Common Cause* noted that every reference to British troops was greeted by applause. Another endorsed the suspension of the suffrage campaign and the adoption of work aimed at 'the sustaining of the vital strength of the nation'. A resolution proposed by Mrs Fawcett expressed regret at the continuing disenfranchisement of women and advocated that at the post-war settlement the great powers should endorse women's suffrage. Other resolutions declared the council's belief in arbitration rather than war, sent 'friendly greetings to the women of all nations who are striving for the uplifting of their sex' and recommended the organization of education courses to study the causes and consequences of war and the means of preventing it in future. Yet another endorsed the executive's action in approaching Mrs Catt to ask her to convene a congress of the IWSA in a neutral country in 1915 or 'the earliest possible opportunity'. Mrs Fawcett was among the speakers against this resolution.[43]

Yet the advocates of peace retired from what might appear to have been an encouraging council in a bruised and shocked state. One reason was that the operative sentence of a resolution advocating a post-war settlement on lines laid down by Asquith was deleted. Committing the union's societies and members 'to work for the building up of public opinion' in support of the principles he had advocated, it was moved by Mrs Fawcett herself. The deletion of the sentence is unlikely to have distressed her greatly, but she played down its importance and it seems to have been taken with unnecessary seriousness by the overwrought advocates of peace.[44] Their alarm was increased by a ruling by the chair, Clara Rackham, that the resolutions passed were merely expressions of opinion which did not permit local secretaries to institute campaigns on their behalf.[45]

Equally distressing was Mrs Fawcett's own behaviour. Her opinions were well enough known and she had put them unmistakably before delegates in her presidential election address. It began: 'I am heart and soul for the cause of Great Britain in the present war.' It had been caused, she continued, by 'Prussian militarism' whose incompatibility with free institutions meant that if it triumphed women's suffrage would inevitably be dealt 'a searching blow'.[46] She made matters much worse by her speech from the chair at a public meeting held during the council. It effectively dismissed the resolutions and colleagues which sought a negotiated peace, an expression of international goodwill, or means of preventing future wars. Meaninglessly claiming to speak for herself alone, she asserted that 'the first national duty' was to ensure that Germany withdrew from occupied Belgium and France. Borrowing a phrase from the French theologian Paul Sabatier she declared: 'Until that is done I believe it is akin to treason to talk of peace.'[47]

The speech launched a period of internecine strife during which half the members of the union executive resigned. Mrs Fawcett's own uncomprehending and uncompromising behaviour was sharpened by the strains of wartime, the disruption of her world and the apparent collapse of her suffrage hopes. A hint of her mental and emotional state at this time is contained in the well-informed *Manchester Guardian* obituary, which commented that 'she could endure only by energetically willing to believe nothing but the best of her own "side".'[48] But the root of the difficulty lay in incompatible interpretations of the relationship between feminism and patriotism which the most emollient of colleagues could hardly have hoped to avoid.

The first to resign, on 18 February, was Maude Royden, who felt unable to continue as editor of the *Common Cause* primarily in consequence of the effective destruction of the so-called 'Asquith resolution'.[49] This was followed by the more important resignations of Kathleen Courtney and Catherine Marshall. As honorary secretary and parliamentary secretary of the union they had been essential to the formation and success of its policies. Mrs Fawcett told the executive when the resignations were presented on 4 March: 'Since the Union had grown the work had fallen on Miss Marshall and Miss Courtney, and she could not speak too highly of their work.'[50] The manner of their resignations outraged both her patriotism and her sense of personal propriety. Marshall's letter of explanation did not reach Mrs Fawcett before the meeting to which it was presented, causing deep offence and pain.[51] Courtney, as Mrs Fawcett and her friends thought, behaved in a deliberately wounding manner. The nature of her offence is not clear, but later letters between Mrs Fawcett and Helena Auerbach, who as NUWSS treasurer was her only ally among the honorary officers, show that both remained distressed and angry. Mrs Fawcett wrote: 'I had looked upon . . . Miss Courtney particularly as a close & intimate friend.'[52] Replying the same day Mrs Auerbach commented: 'For my part I shall *never* forget the pain which my friendship with & affection for Kathleen gave her the power to inflict.'[53]

Both Courtney and Marshall were also deeply wounded and both attempted without success to repair the breach with their former 'chief'. Courtney wrote to Chrystal Macmillan, another of the NUWSS peace party, in June 1915: 'Mrs F. seems quite unbalanced . . . She will not meet me, if she can help it, & will not even write to me civilly.'[54] An attempt to repair the breach the following year also failed.[55] Marshall, who had been 'My dear Catherine', was 'Dear Miss Marshall' in February 1918 when she wrote Mrs Fawcett a moving letter of congratulations on the success of the suffrage cause. The reply in her hour of triumph displayed no generosity of spirit. She rejected Marshall's plea for reconciliation and added a deeply-felt but insulting stricture on patriotism: 'My dearest wish, now and always through my 50 years of suffrage effort, has been so as to work as to help by any means within my power the cause of my country.'[56] Two days later she wrote to Ray Strachey, whom she described as 'also a worshipper at the rich shrine, the holy of holies, all that England stands for to her children and to the world'. Replying to Strachey's offensive comments about 'Catherine Marshall, & those other people', she proclaimed herself 'unforgiving to [England's] base & treacherous children who would fain stab her in the back in her moment of peril'.[57] This was the reality behind the startling assertion in the Fawcett seventieth-birthday number of the *Common Cause* that she was a leader with whom one could differ without forfeiting mutual friendship and affection.[58]

The resignations of Courtney and Marshall were soon followed by others. Mrs Catt, who relied heavily on her first vice-president and feared the disruption of the alliance, did nothing to encourage an international meeting and seems to have abandoned the idea with relief.[59] Its advocates, however, were not to be discouraged and plans to hold an independent international congress of women at The Hague came before the NUWSS executive on 18 March. If Mrs Fawcett's letter to Helena Auerbach may be believed, she was not only prepared to resign her presidency of the union if the congress was endorsed, but thought it 'very likely' that she would have to do so.[60] She led the opposition to taking part in the congress, and after an anguished discussion her position was endorsed by a majority of eleven to six.[61] It was also agreed that local societies should not be permitted to send delegates to The Hague. Her role was crucial, for there was a pro-peace majority on the union executive, but as previous experience had shown it was much easier to support the war without reservations than to devise an agreed pro–peace policy. The peace faction failed to muster its full strength because two of its number were absent and two others were unwilling to divide the union in pursuit of a policy which, they believed, neither the union council nor national sentiment supported.[62] In addition Clara Rackham, also an advocate of a negotiated peace, opposed the involvement of the national union in this type of non-suffrage activity.[63]

Even before the executive met Mrs Fawcett had written to the *New Statesman* to state as president of the NUWSS that it was wholly unconnected with the Hague Congress and that 'such of our members as are associated with it are so in their personal capacity and not as representatives of the National Union'.[64] Feelings had now become irreconcilable, and at the next meeting of the executive ten members resigned together with the head of the union's paid staff.[65] They included a number of her closest colleagues and personal friends, among them such leading figures as Maude Royden (whose earlier resignation had not included her membership of the executive), Helena Swanwick, Isabella Ford and Margaret Ashton. Some of their letters contained open or veiled attacks on Mrs Fawcett, and the quarrel necessarily intermingled personal with political factors. Maude Royden summarized the case of the departing members. The executive, she wrote, had 'at each meeting interpreted the resolutions of the Council more and more stringently in the sense that they were intended to have no operative intention whatever'. Lady Frances Balfour spoke for the patriots. The remaining members of the executive, she pointed out, 'did not consider that this was the right moment to work for peace. The very word "peace" put the Country in the wrong.'[66]

The week after the resignations Mrs Fawcett published two defences of her own position, one a letter to the officials of union societies, the other in the *Common Cause*. She did not make light of the loss of half her elected colleagues, but by calling attention to the personal attacks made on her she implicitly exaggerated their number and nature and sought to use her personal popularity to discredit the arguments of her opponents. 'The national task', she pointed out, accepted by 'the great majority of the nation', was to secure the evacuation of Belgium and France by the German armies. This was not the time to agitate for peace terms, she added, oversimplifying the motives of her opponents and the nature of the proposed congress, and the union council had not mandated the executive to do so. The issue of peace deeply divided the union, which as a body was agreed on a single object, women's suffrage. 'Let us . . . abstain . . . from those sectional activities which are perfectly certain to lead to disunion. This, I believe, is our only safe course.'[67]

It would be easy after a lapse of over seventy-five years to accept her position and regard the peace-seekers as unrealistic idealists whose prescriptions would have broken the union, antagonized public opinion and indefinitely delayed the achievement of women's suffrage. This was the attitude in 1915 of many members. Peace propaganda, one wrote to the *Common Cause*, would be impractical and dangerous. The union would be covered with derision and the suffrage cause harmed.[68] Even some like Clara Rackham and Chrystal Macmillan who sympathized with the cause of peace, disagreed with the sometimes confused and inconsistent conduct of its advocates. But the crisis in the union's affairs took place in the first year of an unprecedentedly horrifying war. As the critics feared, millions more were to die before it ended nearly three-and-a-half years later. Feminism to them had been symbolized before August 1914 by women's suffrage. Now it meant an effort to end the war or at the least to prohibit the conditions which could lead to another. Was the vote, some of the retiring members of the executive and their supporters asked, simply 'a political tool', or was it linked with 'the advocacy of the deeper principles, the consciousness of which has been the source of so much vigour and impassioned devotion to our workers'?[69] Votes for women, which in any case had been shelved since the outbreak of war, was now a matter of secondary importance.

The struggle for supremacy in the national union was fought out in the pages of the *Common Cause* in the weeks before the special council held in Birmingham on 17 and 18 June 1915. Mrs Fawcett's fullest contribution to the debate, however, was made in an article in *The Englishwoman*, which was controlled by her pro-war allies. Even readers who sympathized with her critics might have concluded that logic was on her side. In calling for a congress of the IWSA, she pointed out, the February council had not supported 'any international Congress, no matter on what subject, no matter under what conditions, no mattter by whom called'. The majority of IWSA officers had voted against holding a congress.[70] The NUWSS was a non-party organization. She would have been willing, she wrote with scant regard for her own past conduct, not to raise the question of the rights and wrongs of the war, but once it had been raised the union should decide its position. Her own view was that war, though horrible, was sometimes 'an imperative national duty'.[71]

The special council was a complete victory for the pro-war faction. A vote of confidence was passed in Mrs Fawcett and an ovation accorded her. The dissident members of the executive and their supporters did not stand for re-election and were replaced by a list which included Alys Russell, Margery Corbett Ashby, Mary Stocks and Ray Strachey, who was appointed to Catherine Marshall's former position as parliamentary secretary.[72] There is no doubt that Mrs Fawcett's prestige was an important factor in rallying support. But a more important reason for the result was the fact that the majority of the active members of the union were as unable to resist the patriotic appeal of the war as the majority of their fellow citizens. Loyalty to conventional values could be expressed as loyalty to their president. Appreciation was expressed of the work of the retiring members, especially Kathleen Courtney and Catherine Marshall,[73] but their example was not generally followed.

The executive was told at its meetings on 15 and 30 April that its decisions about the Hague Congress had been opposed by about thirty societies and federations and supported by nearly as many. This was hardly a striking vote of confidence, but when the executive met on 20 May it was told that the balance of society opinion was strongly in its favour, and further messages of support were reported to the meetings on 3 and 14 June. Mrs Fawcett herself was the object of many messages of loyalty and affection.[74] A significant development was the vote on 8 June in the large Manchester society, which had previously been at the forefront of the peace initiative. It now decided by a large majority to repudiate Margaret Ashton, its chairman and leading figure, and 'to endorse Mrs Fawcett's policy'. The new secretary reported the policy shift to Mrs Fawcett, who immediately replied: 'I am greatly delighted & cheered by your telegram received about 8.30 this morning. I believe that it represents the *N.U.* as a whole & that the retiring members of the Ex: Comm: have in reality a *very* small following.'[75] Vengeance must have been specially sweet since Margaret Ashton, like Kathleen Courtney, had particularly offended her when she resigned from the executive.[76] The report of the special council meeting in June 1915 was insufficiently detailed to analyze the nature and source of support for the various factions,[77] but the Manchester vote must qualify Ray Strachey's assertion, often accepted by historians, that the war party was strongest among the 'silent, inarticulate voters and the smaller country societies'. Kathleen Courtney's admission that the 'forward policy' had very little support is more likely to have represented the true situation.[78] A letter to Selina Cooper from her fellow NUWSS organizer Emilie Gardner must have spoken for many:

> What do you think of the present N.U. crisis? I am all on Mrs Fawcett's side . . . I am wholeheartedly for peace but I do think that the N.U. ought to stick to its guns about not mixing up with *any*thing else till we have the vote. What is the good of women holding congresses till they have the vote to make them effective.[79]

The new officers, Mrs Fawcett at their head, immediately repudiated the charge made by *The Standard* that their former colleagues were German or German-American 'tools'. 'No more unfounded assertion has probably ever found its way into a newspaper', they wrote.[80] She made light of the resignations in writing to Mrs Catt in July, professing herself unable to understand their cause: 'In my opinion a great deal was due to nerves and over work.'[81] She repeated the claim that the motives of the retiring members 'remain obscure' in an article published in 1924. But there was nothing obscure to her about the Hague Congress itself. It was 'a bit of German propaganda intended to weaken our powers of resistance'.[82]

As for Mrs Fawcett, the loss of friends and colleagues and the bitterness which surrounded their departure must have caused her severe distress. Firmly girt in the mantle of her passionate patriotism, it is unlikely that she thought seriously of resigning herself once she had secured her massive victory in June 1915. But a letter written a few months later to Helena Auerbach suggests that she had not emerged unscathed from the earlier quarrels. By October Clara Rackham had resigned from the NUWSS executive upon her appointment as a factory inspector, and Mrs Auerbach had written to say that she too intended to surrender her treasurer's post. Mrs Fawcett replied:

> Of course I have often thought of resigning myself and am only holding on with difficulty. The resignation of the 11 [actually 12] members in the spring, the recent loss of Mrs Rackham and the news in your letter of this morning

makes an accumulation of misfortunes almost more than I can bear. I do implore you to reconsider the whole matter and at any rate to stick to your post (which you have filled so admirably) until the end of the war . . . If you retire I feel I must do the same. I do entreat you not to abandon us.[83]

Faced with this appeal Mrs Auerbach did not retire.

As Jo Vellacott comments, the subsequent writings of both Mrs Fawcett and Ray Strachey ignored the contributions of their opponents of 1915 to the women's suffrage movement.[84] Until very recently they have been largely forgotten. Mrs Fawcett was not wholly unforgiving. Any coolness towards the devoted Isabella Ford was of short duration, and Ford was among the fourteen people, living and dead, to whom her book *The Women's Victory* (1920) was dedicated. She also remained on friendly terms with Helena Swanwick, and Maude Royden believed that she was responsible for inviting her to address the NUWSS victory rally in March 1918.[85]

Sybil Oldfield and Ann Wiltsher have recently pointed out that most prominent pre-war feminists were sympathetic to the attempts made in 1915 to achieve a negotiated peace.[86] Mrs Fawcett was one of very few leaders of the constitutional suffrage movement who supported the war wholeheartedly, but her support and her victory in 1915 were of critical importance. When electoral change again appeared on the political agenda in 1916 the NUWSS was in a strong position to claim that women should be included in any proposed reform bill. Whether the vote, preceded by war and schism, and followed by the decline of British feminism, was in these conditions worth winning, is a different question.

NOTES

1. MGF, 'Our balance sheet', *The Englishwoman*, August 1914, pp. 121–8.
2. *CC*, 31 July 1914, p. 351.
3. NUWSS, EC minutes, 3 August 1914 (M50/2/7/6).
4. *Ibid.*; published with minor amendments in *CC*, 7 August 1914, p. 377.
5. *Report of the Eighth Congress* (ch. 15, note 27 above), pp. 29–30; *Jus Suffragii*, 1 September 1914, p. 159.
6. Francesca Wilson, 'Dame Kathleen Courtney', typescript c. 1974 (FLA, box 458); Margery Corbett Ashby, typescript memoirs, ch. 5 (FLA, box 480); Helena Swanwick, *I Have Been Young* (1935), p. 239.
7. *CC*, 7 August 1914, p. 377.
8. Helena Swanwick's autobiography describes the change in the circumstances of the meeting as Britain's entry into the war was announced, together with other details not confirmed elsewhere, including Mrs Fawcett's 'very grave doubts' about the wisdom of holding the meeting (pp. 239–41). The doubts were probably recalled accurately, but Mrs Fawcett reported to the union's executive that the meeting had been 'very successful' (minutes, 6 August 1914).
9. The letter is reprinted in Sybil Oldfield, *Spinsters of this Parish* (1984), p. 179, and Jo Vellacott, 'Feminist Consciousness and the First World War', *History Workshop* (23, 1987), p. 88.
10. MGF, 'Message to the I.W.S.A.', *Jus Suffragii*, 1 September 1914, p. 159.

11. EC minutes, 3 August 1914.
12. *CC*, 7 August 1914, p. 376.
13. EC minutes, 3 and 6 August 1914.
14. *MGF*, p. 279.
15. *CC*, 4 September 1914, p. 418.
16. The next two paragraphs draw on the following MGF articles: 'What the National Union of Women's Suffrage Societies is doing', *The Queen*, 26 September 1914, p. 501; 'Women and the war', *Ladies' Field*, 21 November 1914 (supplement); 'Women's work in war time', *Contemporary Review*, December 1914, pp. 775–82; 'War relief and war service', *Quarterly Review*, January 1916, pp. 111–29; 'Scottish women's hospital for foreign service: war work of the N.U.W.S.S.' in A.M. de Beck (ed.), *Women of the Empire in War Time* (1916), pp. 24–7. There is also much relevant material in ch. 7 of her *The Women's Victory – and After* (1920).
17. *MG*, 4 September 1914.
18. Brian Harrison, *Prudent Revolutionaries* (1987), p. 27; *WIR*, pp. 221–2.
19. *MG*, 4 and 23 September 1914; *CC*, 25 September 1914, p. 453; *MGF*, pp. 279–80.
20. *MGF*, p. 282.
21. MGF to Catherine Marshall, 18 February 1918 (D/Mar/3/52).
22. Holton, *Feminism and Democracy* (1986), p. 135.
23. See Vellacott, pp. 88–9; Ann Wiltsher, *Most Dangerous Women* (1985), p. 67.
24. MGF to C. Sarolea, 21 January 1913 (above, ch. 13, note 7).
25. Alice Clark to Catherine Marshall, 15 November 1914 (D/Mar/3/39).
26. Wiltshire, p. 67; see also Holton, p. 135.
27. *CC*, 7 August 1914, p. 377.
28. NUWSS, EC minutes, 15 October 1914 (D/Mar/3/37).
29. Oldfield, pp. 309–10; Vellacott, p. 87.
30. EC minutes, 4 November 1914 (M50/2/7/8).
31. See Wiltsher, ch. 4; Holton, p. 135.
32. Here I follow Vellacott, p. 89, in preference to Oldfield, p. 189.
33. EC minutes, 4 November 1914.
34. *MG*, 4 November 1914.
35. NUWSS, minutes of provincial council meeting, Wallasey, 12 November 1914 (M50/2/6/1).
36. See Harrison, *Prudent Revolutionaries*, pp. 103, 118.
37. Rathbone to Marshall, 14 November 1914 (D/Mar/3/39); see also Wiltsher, pp. 67–8.
38. EC minutes, 3 December 1914 (M50/2/7/9). The Dutch proposal was also published in *Jus Suffragii* (Wiltsher, pp. 60–1).
39. MGF to Catt, 15 December 1914; printed in *MGF*, pp. 283–4, and Oldfield, pp. 190–1.
40. *CC*, 8 January 1915, p. 641; *Jus Suffragii*, 1 January 1915, pp. 216–17, 230.
41. See Wiltsher, pp. 70–2; Jo Vellacott, 'Anti-war suffragists', *History* (vol. 62, 1977), pp. 418–19.
42. *WL*, 25 July 1924, p. 208; Johanna Alberti, *Beyond Suffrage* (1989), p. 50.
43. *CC*, 12 February 1915, pp. 710–11; NUWSS, *Proceedings of the Annual Council*, 1915 (M50/2/6/2).
44. MGF in *MG*, 9 February 1915; MGF to George Armstrong (copy), 13 February 1915 (FLA, box 89 vol. 2); MGF to Catherine Marshall, 6 March 1915 (note 51 below); Wiltsher, pp. 73–4.
45. *Proceedings*, 1915 (note 43 above).
46. *ibid.*, election addresses (D/Mar/3/44).

47. *CC*, 12 February 1915, p. 712. Her notes for this speech (FLA, box 90a file 1) were couched in much more conciliatory terms, but she repeated her view that peace agitation was 'almost treachery' at the crucial meeting of the executive on 18 March (M50/2/7/13).

48. *MG*, 5 August 1929.

49. NUWSS, EC minutes, 18 February 1915 (M50/2/7/11).

50. *ibid.*, 4 March 1915 (M50/2/7/12).

51. Letters between the two women, dated 3 and 6 March 1915 and circulated to the NUWSS executive, are filed at D/Mar/3/45. See also Wiltsher, pp. 74–5.

52. MGF to Auerbach, 4 November 1916 (Fawcett Collection, IIAV).

53. Auerbach to MGF, 4 November 1916 (FLA, box 89 vol. 2).

54. [Kathleen Courtney] to Chrystal Macmillan (copy), 15 June 1915 (D/Mar/3/46).

55. Emily Leaf to MGF, 2 November 1916; MGF to Leaf (copy), 3 November 1916; Kathleen Courtney to MGF, 26 November 1916; MGF to Courtney, incomplete and undated draft (FLA, box 89 vol. 2).

56. Marshall to MGF, 7 February 1918 (FLALC, vol. 1m); MGF to Marshall, 18 February 1918 (D/Mar/3/52). Her reply to Courtney's congratulations took the form of a printed card (Courtney to Marshall, 5 March 1918; *ibid.*).

57. Strachey to MGF, 18 February 1918; MGF to Strachey, 20 February 1918 (Strachey Papers).

58. *CC*, 8 June 1917, p. 97.

59. Wiltsher, pp. 62–3; Catt to MGF and Adela Stanton Coit, 23, 29 November 1915 (M50/2/22/74). See also below, p 231.

60. MGF to Auerbach, 16 March [1915] (IIAV).

61. The minutes of this meeting (note 62 below) recorded a vote of eleven to five, but Mrs Fawcett's statements of the following month (note 67 below), giving the figures as eleven to six, are probably more accurate.

62. EC minutes, 18 March 1915 (M50/2/7/13, 14). Wiltsher, pp. 75–81, is essential reading for this episode and its aftermath.

63. Rackham to MGF, 19 April 1915 (FLA, box 89 vol. 2); files of the *Dictionary of National Biography* (Clara Rackham), University of Hull.

64. *New Statesman*, 20 March 1915, p. 589.

65. Chrystal Macmillan, a leading advocate of a negotiated peace, decided against resignation (*CC*, 25 June 1915, p. 163).

66. Maude Royden resignation letter, 15 April 1915 in D/Mar/3/45; other resignations and Frances Balfour comment in EC minutes, 15 April 1915 (M50/2/7/15).

67. *Mrs Fawcett's Letter Addressed to Secretaries of Federations and Societies*, 23 April 1915 (M50/2/9/45); MGF, 'The coming congress in Holland', *CC*, 23 April 1915, pp. 32–3.

68. 'A member of the N.U.W.S.S.', *CC*, 28 May 1915, p. 105.

69. Margaret Ashton and twelve others, 'Statement by retiring members and others', *ibid.*, 4 June 1915, pp. 121–2.

70. This ignored the fact that several officers had not been heard from (Wiltsher, p. 223).

71. MGF, 'The National Union of Women's Suffrage Societies and the Hague Congress', *The Englishwoman*, June 1915, pp. 193–200 (quotations, pp. 194–5).

72. *CC*, 25 June 1915, pp. 161–2; 14 January 1916, p. 543.

73. *ibid.*, 25 June 1915, p. 161.

74. M50/2/7/15, 16 (15, 30 April 1915); D/Mar/3/46 (20 May, 3 and 14 June).

75. Papers of the Manchester Society for Women's Suffrage; correspondence (M50/1/90, 92, 93, 96); *Annual Report*, 1915, pp. 13–17 (M50/1/4/45).

76. MGF to Helena Auerbach, 4 November 1916 (IIAV); *CC*, 25 June 1915, pp. 158–9; *WL*, 25 July 1924, p. 208.
77. NUWSS, *Proceedings of the Special and Half-Yearly Council*, June 1915 (M50/2/6/4).
78. *MGF*, p. 295; David Morgan, *Suffragists and Liberals* (1975), p. 136; Les Garner, *Stepping Stones to Women's Liberty* (1984), p. 24; Wiltsher, p. 80.
79. Emilie Gardner to Selina Cooper, 27 May [1915] (Cooper Papers, Lancashire County Record Office).
80. *CC*, 25 June 1915, p. 156.
81. MGF to Catt (copy), 21 July 1915 (FLALC, vol. 1l).
82. *WL*, 25 July 1924, p. 208.
83. MGF to Auerbach, 19 October 1915 (IIAV).
84. Vellacott, p. 82.
85. June Hannam, *Isabella Ford* (Oxford: Blackwell, 1989), pp. 172–3, 180; Swanwick to MGF, 19 December 1917 (FLALC, vol. 1l); Swanwick, p. 187; Sheila Fletcher, *Maude Royden* (Oxford: Blackwell 1989), p. 176 & n. See also Fletcher, p. 247.
86. Oldfield, p. 307; Wiltsher, pp. 82–3.

# CHAPTER 17

## VOTES FOR WOMEN 1915-18

Once the crisis was past, with some of the best-known dissidents taking up work for peace or adult suffrage,[1] the ranks of the National Union of Women's Suffrage Societies closed and it experienced surprisingly few echoes of the battles of 1915. This was partly because the departing members made no attempt to capture the organization, partly because most members accepted the inevitability of the war, but chiefly because the political ambience had changed. It is not clear how many local societies remained active, but the union may have lost about one in six of its societies and one in three of its members in the first two years of war.[2] But an active and vigorous membership was no longer so necessary since in the early years suffrage work was largely suspended and later it was conducted principally by writing and lobbying at national level. Public opinion was influenced without the meetings, marches and local propaganda of the pre-1914 years.

Mrs Fawcett's principal activities in the period fell into four parts. She remained first vice-president of the International Woman Suffrage Alliance, and with the divisions and difficulties of war became its leading figure. She was one of the leading publicists for women's employment, claiming that the achievements of women workers constituted a powerful reason for their enfranchisement. The struggle for an equal moral standard and for Indian women continued to occupy her attention and in war conditions became increasingly urgent. Above all she remained president of the NUWSS, and when suffrage work began again she led deputations and advocated votes for women with her old persuasiveness and lucidity, triumphantly leading to a successful conclusion the first phase of the campaign for the vote on equal terms with men.

It would have needed good luck, exceptional tact and exclusive devotion to the international suffrage cause to have conducted the IWSA without friction in a war involving many of its leading international affiliates. Mrs Fawcett had other preoccupations, and her IWSA work during the war was a record of using her prestige and geographical location to secure her ends with limited concern for the feelings of others.[3] Most suffragists, however, felt that the international movement should not be allowed to disappear, and

229

it may well have been the case that her 'minimalist' line, and particularly her opposition to using the IWSA machinery to advocate a negotiated peace, was the only method of keeping the alliance in existence during the Great War.

In Mary Sheepshanks, the IWSA secretary and editor of *Jus Suffragii*, she was pitted against a woman of many talents, strong convictions and an abrasive personality.[4] Until the autumn of 1915 *Jus* contained a number of articles in which discussion of the causes of the war and the means of preventing another could be interpreted by partisans as pacifist propaganda. Mrs Fawcett was one such partisan and another was Marguerite de Witt Schlumberger, president of the Union Française pour le Suffrage des Femmes and fourth vice-president of the IWSA. At the start of the war Schlumberger condemned it in forthright terms, but by November 1914 she had become a fervent advocate of the patriotic cause and an opponent of the internationalist approach which Mary Sheepshanks was attempting to follow in *Jus*.[5] Mrs Fawcett was her strong supporter, and through 1915 the two women, with the reluctant support of their IWSA colleagues and the new NUWSS executive, put increasing pressure on Sheepshanks to exclude controversial articles from the paper. This led to a period of severely strained relations with Mrs Fawcett. In June 1915 Emily Leaf, one of the NUWSS executive members who had resigned her position in the Hague Congress controversy, inaccurately reported to Catherine Marshall that Sheepshanks had resigned from *Jus* because of the 'tremendous scolding' that Mrs Fawcett had given her.[6] This quarrel was patched up, but relations remained strained until at least the end of 1915.[7]

In October Schlumberger and her colleagues in the Union Française wrote an open letter to Mrs Catt, the IWSA president, insisting in the pages of *Jus* that it must remain 'a *purely Suffragist* organ instead of becoming more and more a pacifist organ'.[8] The NUWSS executive agreed to endorse the protest, and its officers' letter conveying the decision took the opportunity to deplore the publication of five articles dealing with the general theme of war and peace which appeared in the October number.[9] This was too much even for some of the loyal members of the executive, particularly Mrs Fawcett's friend Caroline Osler of Birmingham, who pointed out that the October articles had considered issues of war and peace in the abstract rather than advocating an immediate end to the war. They were of the type which filled every serious journal: 'Indeed there is hardly any opening for writers in any other field at present.' Upon her initiative the executive agreed to a significant resolution opposing decisions on important policy questions being made by a small group at the end of long meetings.[10]

Mrs Fawcett again deplored the alleged 'articles on pacifism' and defended her conception of a sanitized *Jus* at this meeting, but her main effort was reserved for the IWSA itself. At a meeting of the headquarters committee in October attended by Mme Schlumberger it was decided that the paper should not publish articles on 'controversial political subjects'; pacifism was the only example specified.[11] Mrs Fawcett's lack of sentimentality and readiness to capitalize on the hesitations of others in forcing through this resolution show her as a political leader comparable in her own sphere to such contemporaries as Lloyd George and Lenin. Adela Stanton Coit, the German-born, London-based IWSA treasurer, and Annie Furuhjelm, the second vice-president and member of the Finnish Parliament, were among the members who accepted the resolution only to preserve unity within the alliance.[12] If pacifism was regarded as a controversial subject, Furuhjelm wrote, she was prepared to agree to its exclusion: 'I do this with regret. During the time of war Jus has seemed to me a refuge for the human point of view.' Moreover, the paper would be likely to be starved of copy if it were to be restricted to facts at the expense of views and ideas. On the envelope of this letter is a note by Mrs Fawcett: 'Letter from Miss Furuhjelm supporting resolution adopted by H.Q. com^ee Oct 9 1915'.[13]

Her next victim was Mrs Catt herself. The IWSA president was conscious of her distance from the European war and her London headquarters, anxious to keep the alliance together and clearly concerned to propitiate her famous first vice-president, her senior in years and prestige outside the United States. She was also sympathetic to discussion of peace, even though she had not been willing to take the controversial step of associating the alliance with the Hague Congress. Her reply to Mme Schlumberger's open letter, intended for publication in *Jus Suffragii*, stressed her belief that the international suffrage movement was 'inextricably bound up with the fate of movements looking to future permanent peace . . . Complete information concerning the Hague Congress and the peace work of its members must be not only of interest but necessary to all our auxiliaries.'[14]

Mrs Fawcett's attempt to amend or avert publication of this letter without a breach with Mrs Catt was skilfully conducted. Shortly before Christmas 1915 she set out her views at length, taking care to secure Mrs Coit's signature to a joint letter.[15] The authors, she wrote, 'venture most respectfully and affectionately to urge' that Mrs Catt's comments went well beyond agreed IWSA policy. The majority of members of the IWSA board had supported the resolution passed in October. 'We therefore earnestly beg you to rewrite your letter to Mme Schlumberger in the light of the foregoing facts.' Mrs Fawcett had asked Mary Sheepshanks to delay publication of the letter until Mrs Catt could be consulted, and this request had been 'readily agreed to'.[16]

Mrs Catt wrote again in January 1916, before this letter reached her, expressing her opposition to the October resolution of which she had apparently only recently learned, and asserting that the Schlumberger letter should have been sent to her as a private communication and not published. 'Do you think it is quite fair that JUS SUFFRAGII should print an open letter from the Vice-president to me without warning me that this was to be printed, and then suppress my reply?' But a few days later, after receiving the Fawcett–Coit letter she wrote again, withdrawing her opposition to the resolution and agreeing to the suppression of her reply to Mme Schlumberger.[17] She was bruised and offended by the incident, but further calm and friendly letters from Mrs Fawcett soon healed the breach.[18] Clearsightedness and tactful ruthlessness had achieved their ends. By the end of 1915 Mary Sheepshanks was restrained, *Jus Suffragii* muzzled and the IWSA quarantined from discussions of war and peace. Mrs Fawcett had triumphed almost single-handed over her doubtful or critical colleagues.

Her task was made easier by the fact that a number of them were pliable or inconsistent figures like Adela Coit, whose freedom of action must have been inhibited by her German birth. Musing regretfully over the Catt affair and a proposed move of the IWSA headquarters to Sweden, Mrs Coit wrote that she wanted to do what was best for the alliance, 'but I don't know my own mind about what *is* best!?'[19] This was a difficulty from which Mrs Fawcett did not suffer. Nothing, she told readers of *Jus*, was clearer to her than that the IWSA and its paper 'must be unsectarian and non-party, and must consequently avoid identifying themselves with any political propaganda on which Suffragists are divided'.[20]

During the remainder of the war years the IWSA was in general neither a controversial nor an influential body. Mrs Fawcett kept a firm eye on proceedings, chairing meetings, supervising Mary Sheepshanks and withholding promised financial support until she was satisfied that the October 1915 resolution was being carrried out.[21] The move to Sweden was fought off and a further Swedish proposal, that an IWSA congress should be held at the post-war peace negotiations with a memorial to the great powers drafted by Mrs Fawcett, was first agreed and then abandoned in face of French opposition to holding a meeting of women from both victorious and defeated powers. She continued to scrutinize *Jus Suffragii* to ensure that pacifism did not raise its head, and to reassure feminists in allied countries of her undivided support for the armed struggle (notably against the Austrian threat to her beloved Italy) and opposition to a negotiated peace.[22] As in other of her activities, however, her vigilance did not extend to the niceties of office administration. A letter from Mary Sheepshanks or an assistant to Mrs Coit in April 1918 discussed the organization of the IWSA headquarters, about which the writer had not consulted Mrs Fawcett: 'Office routine is not quite her line, and I did not think she would want to be troubled about it.'[23]

Mrs Fawcett's leadership of the IWSA during the war years was most notable for its unflinching determination to ensure that nothing the alliance said or did could be interpreted as expressing women's horror at the unprecedented carnage or their desire to hasten its end. An incident in April 1918, however, shows that hostility to Germany had not swept aside all other sentiments. Approached by the super-patriotic *Daily Mail* to resign from the IWSA board or dismiss its two German members she replied that she had no intention of doing either, even if the second request had been within her power. If she had the opportunity, she wrote, she would do what she could 'to stimulate the demand of German women for free, representative institutions'. Answering an enquiry from Mary Sheepshanks she referred to it as a 'silly, impertinent letter'.[24] She was ungenerous with those whose convictions differed from her own, but she needed no instructions on how to behave in accordance with her beliefs.

The war had not lasted long before she realized that the unprecedented economic activity of women, particularly in heavy industry, provided excellent ammunition for the attempt to improve their political and industrial status. Women's opportunities for industrial employment, previously hampered by the fourfold barrier of employers' tyranny, trade union hostility, government indifference and their own weakness had been significantly improved by wartime conditions. In January 1916 she wrote an article for *The Englishwoman* on themes which she was to elaborate in other articles and speeches. After taking the opportunity to tilt at the inclination of 'the "Intellectuals" ' to criticize support for the war she claimed that 'the matchless spirit, the undaunted courage and confidence' of men in the armed forces had been paralleled by the 'magnificent adaptability, the industrial efficiency, and the patriotism of women'. It had taken a European war to break down the old prejudices about the capacities of women – not least on the part of the Prime Minister, she pointed out in an earlier article.[25] Women were now 'pouring in thousands into trades and occupations from which hitherto they have been excluded', including the transport industry and above all munitions. She added to her account of new opportunities and achievements a demand that 'as far as possible' women should be paid the same wages as men for the same work, both for their own sake and so that the achievements of trade unions to which, she added uncharacteristically, 'the whole nation owes a deep debt of gratitude', should not be destroyed.[26]

The demand for equal pay was one with which she was henceforth to be identified, and was in sharp contrast to her previous views on the subject. If she was surprised to read in the *Manchester Guardian* in 1917 a letter quoting her opposition to equal pay in 1892,[27] she was not at a loss for a reply. 'One of the compensations for the sorrows and sufferings caused by the war', she wrote, had been higher wages for women. There were no longer large numbers of women earning wages below the level of subsistence; for the time they had 'tasted the sweets of a living wage'. Equal pay she termed 'a perfectly sound principle'.[28] Her changed stance was the result not only of observing the wartime achievements of women but also of her desire to ensure that their foothold in skilled industries would not be wiped out by men's demands after the war for their renewed exclusion. Moreover, if women were to be paid less than men for the same work the young movement for family allowances, to which she was unalterably opposed, would be greatly strengthened.[29] Equal pay was much to be preferred to state subsidy.

Her wartime and post-war writing on women's industrial gains have been criticized as distorted by nineteenth-century spectacles, rendering her view romantic and distorted.[30] These charges are not obviously unjust. After decades of painfully slow progress it was easy to exaggerate the importance of wartime change. But to accuse her of romanticism overlooks the fact that in her articles on women in industry she was exercizing the same propagandist function as in her suffrage speeches and writings. To claim: 'Women have shown their industrial capacity during the war in a way which has shattered many anti-feminist prejudices and preconceptions'[31] was arguably the best means of ensuring that wishes became facts.

Her most detailed wartime exposition of 'The position of women in economic life', published in 1917, was not susceptible to the charge of romanticism. She pointed with legitimate pride to women's unprecedented feats both as war doctors and nurses, and as industrial workers capable of surpassing the output of skilled men, but these passages were written in the context of women's continuing grievances and an attack on 'our national sin of wastefulness'. She again praised the achievements of trade unions. They were 'not only desirable but absolutely necessary', though their previous and some of their existing policies were misguided and tyrannous. By excluding women from skilled trades they had been responsible for reducing many of them to 'a position of virtual serfdom'. She also attacked the Government for paying grossly inadequate wages to women engaged in war production and excluding them from the higher grades of the civil service. Medicine was the only major profession to which they had gained admission, and in contrast to other countries 'women can hardly be said to have any commercial position at all'. The national interest dictated a change in women's economic role.[32]

Her articles repeatedly recounted 'wonderful tales of heroism and devotion' involving patriotic British men and women. But it was not merely a question of exhorting readers to 'lift up your hearts'. She pointed out in a reprinted lecture that pre-war British society had wasted the lives of infants and mothers. Drunkenness, immorality and sweated work also wasted life, as did the practice of keeping both men and women in occupations below their capabilities. The growth of a democratic society had made it possible for a relatively humbly-born figure like Asquith, then about to fall from office, to become Prime Minister. Now democracy was beginning to include women within its scope. The changes of war had revealed their capacities and concentrated attention on wages so low as to result in constant undernourishment.[33] These were her constant themes in her speeches and articles on women's work in wartime. They were only partly celebratory or romantic; their chief purpose was the practical one of building on what women had achieved to improve their conditions in the post-war years.

Although one of the compensations of the war had been a rise in the status of women, its impact was ambiguous. The sexual freedom of the war years shocked the conventional, and resulted in a number of measures designed to combat the alleged growth of prostitution, venereal disease and illegitimacy.[34] Such measures threatened women with the loss of rights widely accepted as permanent since the days of Josephine Butler. Mrs Fawcett objected to the compulsory notification of venereal disease in 1916 as a step towards reintroducing the principle of the Contagious Diseases Acts.[35] The following year a clause was introduced by the Home Secretary into a Criminal Law Amendment Bill then before Parliament which would have led to the detention in certain cases until the age of 19 of girls found soliciting, loitering or wandering in the streets. It led to vigorous protests in which she played a prominent part. She was also among the women who protested against parliamentary refusal to raise the age of consent to 17. In the event the bill was dropped, only to be resurrected after the war with similar objectionable clauses.[36]

She still maintained contact with her colleagues of 'white slavery' days. She chaired a conference in 1916 on the abolition of prostitution, which she regarded as a desirable rather than a practicable aim.[37] The Government, however, restricted its concern to consequences. Late in the war it attempted to prevent the spread of venereal disease by means of what she termed 'the abominable D.O.R.A. 40D'.[38] The Defence of the Realm Act, passed in 1914, was a catch-all measure which empowered the Government to act by regulation in many fields. Under regulation 40D, issued in March 1918, any woman suspected of infecting a serviceman with venereal disease could be pressured to undergo a medical examination and, if found to be infected, imprisoned for up to six months. The regulation at once met strong and widespread opposition.[39] Mrs Fawcett presided at a protest meeting held by fifty-four societies at the Queen's Hall a few days before the armistice, and declared that the regulations had 'no single redeeming feature'. It was iniquitous in the principle that women should be sexually subject to men, harmful and ineffective in practice. Maud Arncliffe-Sennett's lukewarm verdict was that she had spoken 'clearly and academically', but the meeting was followed by success; before the end of the month the regulation had been withdrawn.[40]

The ramifications of the war upon women were not limited to the European nations. Despite her other preoccupations Mrs Fawcett devoted a good deal of attention to India, particularly the education of women, and the relevant file in her papers makes clear her continuing concern. It also shows the trust and confidence with which she was held both by Indian women themselves and by British women in India.[41] In July 1915 she was the leading figure among a group of women who signed a memorial to Austen Chamberlain, Secretary of State for India, claiming that the small number of Indian girls being educated 'constitutes a grave danger to the social well-being of the Indian communities'. The memorial and a deputation which she led to Chamberlain the following October requested that a committee be established to give favourable consideration to proposals for reform. Chamberlain gave the deputation little encouragement,[42] but his successor Edwin Montagu was ostensibly more sympathetic. Mrs Fawcett wrote to him in October 1917 about the 'great and crying need for facilities for the education of the girls and women of India' and asked him to add two women to the commission recently appointed to enquire into Calcutta University. Although Montagu refused to do this, he assured her that he understood the importance of developing women's education, and the report of the commission in 1919, devoting a chapter to the education of women, offered further grounds for hope.[43]

The war also stimulated moves towards political emancipation in India. In 1917 Montagu promised steps towards Indian self-government, and Mrs Fawcett took up her pen to demand that Indian women should share in the growth of political power. She and the other NUWSS officers, none of whom had been in office at the outbreak of war, wrote to the imperial conference considering the question that to omit women from the antici-pated new electorates would be 'a national disaster which would go far to nullify the benefits which might otherwise be expected from the projected reforms'.[44] Montagu's reply was again sympathetic, but the opposition of Indian men and the apathy of women, reasons for inaction with which British suffragists had long been familiar, were widely regarded as obstacles.[45] She took much pleasure from the fact that by the time she wrote her autobiography in 1924, women had been enfranchised by their country-men in several parts of India.[46]

The crowning triumph of the war years was the grant of women's suf-frage to millions of British women. This was a development which would have been difficult to imagine in the summer of 1914, when suffragette militancy, prime ministerial disdain and the general hostility of the political classes seemed to have left the movement without hope of further advance. The National Union of Women's Suffrage Societies was too busy in its first year reorganizing itself on a war footing and purging its dissidents to advo-cate women's suffrage, which in any case had disappeared from the political scene with other domestic questions. In May 1915 the first wartime Coali-tion Government was formed, and Mrs Fawcett commented to Evelyn Atkinson, the union's new honorary secretary, that its creation meant that franchise reform would not be considered.[47]

In fact the balance of the new Government was more sympathetic to women's suffrage than its predecessor,[48] and the overt absence of party politics in the later years of the war was one of several factors which brought suffrage onto the political agenda. Despite Asquith's last-minute 'conver-sion' to apparent support for women's suffrage and Lloyd George's patent unreliability, the installation of the second coalition and a new prime minis-ter at the end of 1916 could only assist the suffragists. Politicians were in general agreement that the electoral register required revision to include voteless servicemen,[49] and Lloyd George understood more clearly than his predecessor that in coalition conditions more was to be gained than lost from recognizing women's claims at a time when electoral reform was pending. Moreover, while the vote was undoubtedly not given to women from gratitude for their war services, their widely-publicized achievements did lead to some genuine changes of mind and gave an opportunity to politicians to recant their anti-suffrage convictions without unacceptable loss of credibility.[50] Finally the NUWSS, shorn of its left-wing and pacifist leaders, and willing to wind down its Election Fighting Fund commitment to the Labour party,[51] worked for the first time with the political tide. Mrs Fawcett, still touring the country, writing articles and leading deputations, remained an admirable figurehead, while the non-party, patriotic Ray Strachey was undoubtedly a more acceptable parliamentary secretary than Catherine Marshall, who was now devoting her efforts to combating conscription. The granting of the vote to most women over 30 in 1918 was hailed as a great victory by feminists, but their share in its success was the result of working within the political system, not of forcing hostile political leaders to bow to the pressure of public opinion.

By the time of her sixty-ninth birthday in June 1916 Mrs Fawcett's early depression about the impact of war on the women's movement had lifted. Writing to thank her cousin Amy Badley for a birthday letter she observed that one of the blessings juxtaposed with the anguish and suffering of war was 'the increased sense of comradeship' between the sexes and the classes.[52] By the summer she was actively at work, though the NUWSS was committed only to the line that if a reform bill was introduced women should be included. In August 1916 she wrote to Evelyn Atkinson from Yorkshire that in a fortnight's absence from London she had met the committee of the Liverpool women's suffrage federation, spoken at a public meeting in Liverpool, written three articles, and visited London for a deputation to Conservative leaders and to attend an executive meeting of the union. That morning she had been asked to write an article for *The Englishwoman*: 'So I have not been entirely idle.'[53]

Even when one discounts the propaganda of the professional optimist, the *Englishwoman* article had a good deal to celebrate. In particular she acclaimed the mid-August recantation of *The Observer* on the suffrage issue, immediately followed by the apparent surrender of the Prime Minister, that 'barometer . . . of public opinion'.[54] Writing again to Evelyn Atkinson at the end of the month she expressed the view that Asquith could not 'altogether play us false now'. He had a changed public opinion to consider, and even if he attempted to wreck the women on the reef of adult suffrage, 'people are no longer terrified of it, as they used to be'.[55]

Mrs Fawcett must have been in a buoyant mood as she toured the NUWSS's south-western federation in October, followed by a visit to Lancashire.[56] She told the Manchester federation's annual meeting that 'they were bound to win before long',[57] and as she spoke the first stages in the campaign had finally begun. The most significant development was the appointment of the Speaker's Conference, an all-party committee intended to produce an agreed report on suffrage reform, of which votes for women was the most contentious issue. While the conference was meeting Lloyd George replaced Asquith as Prime Minister, a change of enormous potential to the women's cause. At the turn of the year Lady Frances Balfour received a letter from her friend Lord Balfour of Burleigh, which helped to explain why the recantations of the 'antis' seemed to be falling like autumn leaves. He remained in principle an opponent, but he wrote that 'the dice are loaded against those of us who even yet mistrust the change . . . MPs are afraid to vote against the possible new voters.'[58]

In January 1917 press speculation that the Speaker's Conference would not be recommending women's suffrage alarmed the NUWSS, and its officers wrote that the failure to include women in the new electorate would be 'disastrous for the British Empire of the future'.[59] The conference report published at the end of the month, however, recommended by a majority a form of women's suffrage which, though excluding youthful war workers, would enfranchise millions of women.[60] Jubilantly Mrs Fawcett told a rally three weeks later that 'though the [Speaker's Conference] brew seemed distinctly anti-Suffrage, when the tap was turned – Suffrage came out!'[61] The comment of *The Times*, another reluctant wartime convert, was that there was now little opposition in principle to the reform: 'Its advocates are almost forcing an open door.'[62]

The effort now begun by the NUWSS and about twenty sister organizations grouped in a consultative committee of women's suffrage societies was twofold. They had to persuade their supporters that the proposals of the Speaker's Conference, which included adult male suffrage, were sufficiently important, certain and final to abandon their cherished commitment to votes on equal terms for men and women. This was a greater challenge than it might have seemed, for belief in equal suffrage was strongly held, and support for votes for all adults had grown during the war years. They had also to secure sufficient parliamentary support to move from benevolent inaction to legislative reality. Even before the Speaker's Conference recommendations were published a sympathetic member, W.H. Dickinson, urged Mrs Fawcett to attempt to ensure that suffragists accepted its proposals, 'to avoid the risk of the government having an excuse' for inaction.[63] His advice was followed, indeed may hardly have been necessary. Mrs Fawcett, admitting that the proposals were not ideal, wrote to a colleague that there was 'a very real & imminent danger now that the Gov$^t$ may dissolve soon on the old register, and if so of course there is no chance of W.S.'. A parliamentary register with six million women would be 'a much safer position for the poorer industrial woman' than a register with none.[64] She assured Andrew Bonar Law and Walter Long, Conservative leaders and Cabinet ministers, that the societies of the consultative committee would accept the proposals of the Speaker's Conference 'as a reasonable compromise' if they were included in the government reform bill.[65]

This was indeed the general view. The NUWSS executive itself agreed with only a single dissentient to a motion of support for the conference proposals. It was moved by Ray Strachey and seconded by Mrs Fawcett.[66] Even Sylvia Pankhurst's Workers' Suffrage League was told by one of its officers in March 1917 that most suffragists felt that 'some measure is better than none', and a few days later it minuted its recognition that the Labour party conference's support for the limited proposals had 'knocked Adult Suffrage on the head for the present time'.[67]

The next stage was a letter from Mrs Fawcett to 'My dear Prime Minister' asking him to receive 'a Deputation of representative women' to put the case for including women in the forthcoming reform bill. Suffragists had 'considered the claims of their country before their own immediate demands', but this did not mean that the demand for women's suffrage had declined: 'We are convinced that the very reverse is the case.' Moreover, 'we know that you are our friend, as no previous Prime Minister has been.'[68]

This could not be called an artful letter concealing art, but Lloyd George had nothing to lose from the deputation and potentially much to gain, and he received it at the end of March. Mrs Fawcett led representatives of twenty-four women's suffrage societies and ten other organizations, in the judgement of *The Times* 'the largest and most picturesque deputation of women which has ever waited on a Prime Minister'.[69] It must certainly have been the case, as Ray Strachey told her mother, that it was 'no joke' to combine them into a coherent body.[70] Perhaps the most unusual representative was a Welshwoman who had been invited to address Lloyd George in Welsh. She recalled long afterwards her husband's pride that she had been 'commanded' by Mrs Fawcett to take part.[71] In her speech Mrs Fawcett did not neglect to point out that most women's suffrage societies supported the objective of equal voting rights, but added that she, like almost all the other delegates, much preferred 'an imperfect scheme that can pass to the most perfect scheme in the world that could not pass. We want the living child, and not the dead child.'[72] Lloyd George in his reply promised little, but the context had changed and his overt sympathy meant more than the empty promises of the past.[73]

From this point onwards the suffragists secured a string of victories. Mrs Fawcett patiently lobbied every member of the Government, and though her visits to the Midlands, the North and Scotland had to be curtailed by a rare bout of bronchitis, the reform bill progressed through the House of Commons, recording huge majorities for women's suffrage at second reading and in committee.[74] Ray Strachey, who as the union's parliamentary secretary, was well informed about shifts in parliamentary opinion, told her in May: 'The wave of feeling is really remarkable.'[75] In June Mrs Fawcett wrote to W.H. Dickinson, thanking him for his parliamentary support and hoping that the Commons majority 'will provide deep water enough to float us over the rocks of the House of Lords'.[76]

Shortly before she wrote this letter her seventieth birthday was celebrated with an outpouring of publicity and congratulations.[77] Characteristically she wrote to thank her cousin Amy Badley on the day itself:

> As you say these are wonderful & heroic times. The [March] Russian revolution, the coming in [to the war] of America, the march forward of freedom here and probably all over the world are great events indeed. I have had delightful letters & messages from my dear Suffragists: and I wish you could see my banks of flowers.[78]

She did not appear to her associates to be an old lady. An unsigned article in *Jus Suffragii* referred both to her intellectual alertness and her physical vigour:

> The present writer has lively recollections of walking behind the president of the National Union at breakneck speed from end to end of Victoria Street, gaining not an inch of ground; and to the present writer the existing Franchise Bill, by reason of its thirty years' age limit, will bring no more than a potential vote.[79]

The bill triumphantly concluded its passage through the House of Commons in December 1917, with the addition of an NUWSS-inspired amendment granting the local government vote to married women.[80] As time and the bill progressed Mrs Fawcett became a strong partisan of Lloyd George. She identified herself with his war policies, referring bluntly but privately to his parliamentary critics as 'little yapping curs' whom a speech by him had forced to 'retreat . . . to their kennels!'.[81] But his goodwill could not ensure an easy victory for women's suffrage in the House of Lords, and apprehensions remained strong. She prepared a carefully drafted statement to the peers published under the title 'A plea for peace'. Stressing the growth of suffragist sentiment among women themselves, the sweeping victories in the Commons and the need for women to participate in resolving problems of post-war reconstruction, she appealed to 'the wisdom of your Lordships not to provoke . . . needless storms'.[82]

It was this argument that the Lords would be unwise to challenge the overwhelming majority in the Commons which the anti-suffragist leader Lord Curzon used to signal his capitulation in the debate on 10 January 1918.[83] The result was a majority for the women's suffrage clause much larger than expected. Soon afterwards her old friend Kate Courtney, whose husband Leonard still represented in the Lords the Mill–Fawcett tradition of the 1860s, wrote in her diary: 'Mrs Fawcett was there [at the debate] too relieved & glad for words & she has deserved the success . . . I think we are safe now *at last*.'[84] This was an accurate judgement, though Mrs Fawcett feared until the end that victory might somehow be snatched away.[85] After the royal assent had finally been given her 'relief and joy', she wrote to a colleague, were 'intense. I feel as if I were in a dream.'[86]

# National Union of Women's Suffrage Societies.

## IN, CO-OPERATION WITH 17 OTHER SOCIETIES.

*Societies co-operating*

Actresses' Franchise League.

British Dominions Woman Suffrage Union.

Catholic Women's Suffrage Society.

Church League for Women's Suffrage.

Conservative and Unionist Women's Franchise Association.

Free Church League for Women's Suffrage.

Hastings and St. Leonards Women's Suffrage Propaganda League.

Irishwomen's Suffrage Federation.

Marchers' Qui Vive Corps.

Men's League for Women's Suffrage.

National Council for Adult Suffrage.

National Industrial and Professional Women's Suffrage Society.

New Constitutional Society for Women's Suffrage.

Scottish Churches' League for Women's Suffrage.

Scottish University Women's Suffrage Union.

United Suffragists.

Women's Freedom League.

# Women Suffragists' CELEBRATION

## QUEEN'S HALL, LANGHAM PLACE

(Sole Lessees   -   -   Messrs. CHAPPELL & CO.)

## Wednesday, March 13th, At 8 p.m.

## To Welcome the Extension of the Franchise to Women.

*Speakers :*

**Mrs. HENRY FAWCETT, LL.D.** (in the Chair)
**Rt. Hon. ARTHUR HENDERSON.**
**THE EARL OF LYTTON.**
**Rt. Hon. Sir JOHN SIMON.**

AND

**Miss MAUDE ROYDEN.**

*Music :*

### The London Symphony Orchestra & Full Choir

Conducted by Sir HUBERT PARRY

Tickets   -   -   21/-, 10/6, 5/-, 2/6 and 1/-.
Entertainment Tax in addition - 3/-   1/6   9d.   6d.   3d.

Admission Free (*Seats Unreserved*).

Apply to Mrs. Mackenzie, N.U.W.S.S., Room 7, 62, Oxford St., W.1.

Printed by HARRISON, JEHRING AND CO. LTD., 11-15, Emerald Street, London W.C.1

*Celebration of the suffrage victory, March 1918.*

The victory was incomplete and only in part the work of suffragists themselves, but they were naturally thrilled by the result so long awaited. A rally was held at the Queen's Hall, at which Sir Hubert Parry's music for Blake's 'Jerusalem' was played. Mrs Fawcett, who wrote to him that it should become 'the Women Voters' Hymn', believed that it had been written for the occasion, though the evidence of his biography suggests a different origin.[87] Whatever the truth there is no doubt that Parry had long been a suffragist and that he conducted the music for the celebration. He wrote in his diary: 'Lively uproar of joy when Mrs Fawcett went on platform. She spoke with sense & humour . . . The music went very well. The sound of "Jerusalem" when the audience joined in was tremendous.'[88]

Mrs Fawcett assessed the women's victory in a variety of interviews, speeches and articles, but perhaps her most reliable comment on the victory and her own work was made a year later to Amy Badley:

> You know how I have loved my work for W.S. and the uplift of women in other directions: how wonderful it has all been, during the war, instead of our work crumbling in our hands, it has been taken out of our hands by the tremendous movement for democracy.[89]

The war, she told her friend Lettice Fisher after the passage of her husband's Education Act, had been an agent of reform. It had 'changed men's minds so as to render Women's Suffrage, freedom for India, and a great step forward in national education not merely possible but actual facts'.[90]

She had too long been the professional optimist to cast doubt on the women's victory, but she was careful not to suggest that it was the end of their struggle. Even before the reform bill had received the royal assent she pointed out that without 'equal opportunities for the industrial women' the freedom conferred by the franchise was not secure.[91] In an interview with the weekly *National News* in March 1918 she acknowledged that the vote had been 'a very great victory', but she stressed the need for 'a good deal of legislation'. In industry women needed equal opportunities and equal pay. Discrimination against women in the civil service should be ended. Mothers should have equal guardianship rights with fathers, not merely the mockery of guardianship of illegitimate children. Even the winning of the vote had been an unsatisfactory compromise: 'A law which gives [an ex-soldier] of nineteen the vote and withholds it from a woman until she is thirty cannot be said to be a fair one.'[92]

The war years had put Mrs Fawcett's powers of leadership to a severe test. She had repeatedly displayed a lack of compassion and understanding of those who disagreed with her and an unwillingness to compromise, characteristics which could only have been strengthened by the adulation by which she had so long been surrounded. But she had kept the feminist flag flying during the war years. She had helped to preserve the existence of the international suffrage movement, championed the woman war worker and led British suffragists to a major victory. It was to her credit that after fifty years of struggle for women's suffrage, with millions more women enfranchised than she had demanded before the war, she recognized that their victory was incomplete. The end of the war was to raise many new problems and resurrect old ones, and women's gains were put under heavy pressure. The winning of the vote was no more than a start, and the 71-year-old leader was under no illusion that there were no more battles to fight.

NOTES

1. See Sylvia Pankhurst, *The Suffragette Movement* (1931), p. 600; Sandra Holton, *Feminism and Democracy* (1986), p. 146.
2. Figures given in *CC* varied, but the extremes were 602 societies in 1914 (14 August, p. 385) and 497 in 1916 (29 September, p. 316). The number of members, stated in the 1914 *Annual Report* (p. 10) as 54,592, was not subsequently reported. See also Holton, p. 133.
3. This conclusion is drawn especially from IWSA file M50/2/22.
4. See Sybil Oldfield, *Spinsters of this Parish* (1984), esp. ch. 9.
5. Marguerite de Witt Schlumberger to Carrie Chapman Catt (copy), 2 August 1914 (JRL, Women's Suffrage Collection, box 4); *idem* to 'Chère Madame', 25 November 1914 (M50/2/22/16). See also Ann Wiltsher, *Most Dangerous Women* (1985), pp. 58–9.
6. Emily Leaf to Catherine Marshall, 8 June 1915 (D/Mar/3/46).
7. The section of Mary Sheepshanks's unpublished autobiography preserved in the Fawcett Library is disappointingly uninformative about her relationship with Mrs Fawcett, but the strains are shown clearly in correspondence in M50/2/22.
8. *Jus Suffragii*, 1 October 1915, p. 7.
9. *ibid.*, 1 November 1915, p. 29.
10. NUWSS, EC minutes, 18 November 1915 (D/Mar/3/49).
11. M50/2/22/55, 77; *Report of the Eighth Congress* (ch. 15, note 27 above), p. 33.
12. Adela Stanton Coit, Annie Furuhjelm to MGF, 20, 29 November 1915, 1 March 1916 (M50/2/22/60, 64, 119).
13. M50/2/22/64.
14. Carrie Chapman Catt, open letter to Marguerite de Witt Schlumberger, 29 November 1915 (M50/2/22/76).
15. The drafts are in Mrs Fawcett's hand. Mrs Coit wrote to her on 27 December: 'On re-reading the letter I feel that you have said all that needs saying' (M50/2/22/79).
16. MGF and Coit to Catt (drafts), 22 December 1915 (M50/2/22/77, 78).
17. Catt to MGF and Coit 19, 24 January 1916 (M50/2/22/94, 96). See also *idem* to London officers, 10 April 1916 (M50/2/22/146).
18. *idem* to MGF, 24 January 1916; MGF to Catt, 3 (copy) and 11 (notes) February 1916 (M50/2/22/95, 97, 106).
19. Coit to MGF, 22 February, 1 March 1916 (M50/2/22/110, 119).
20. MGF in *Jus Suffragii*, 1 February 1916, p. 75.
21. MGF to Sheepshanks (copy), 11 January 1916; MGF to Coit (draft), 28 February 1916 (M50/2/22/87, 116).
22. M50/2/22/103–239, *passim*; *Jus Suffragii*, 1 October 1917, p. 14.
23. [?Mary Sheepshanks] to Adela Coit (copy), 18 April 1918 (JRL, IWSA Papers, box 1).

24. MGF to Sheepshanks, 2l April 1918 (*ibid.*, box 1); *MGF*, pp. 324–5.
25. MGF, 'The Prime Minister's discovery', *CC*, 12 November 1915, p. 400.
26. MGF, 'Lift up your hearts', *The Englishwoman*, January 1916, pp. 5–15 (quotations from pp. 7, 10, 13–14).
27. See above, page 103.
28. *MG*, 12, 16 October 1917; *The Times*, 27 August 1918.
29. MGF, 'Equal pay for equal work', *Economic Journal*, March 1918, pp. 1–6. See also Jane Lewis, *Women in England* (1984), pp. 201–3.
30. Gail Braybon, *Women Workers in the First World War* (Croom Helm, 1981), p. 204; Deborah Thom, 'The bundle of sticks' in Angela John (ed.), *Unequal Opportunities* (Oxford: Blackwell, 1986), p. 281.
31. MGF, 'The war's effect on woman's work', *War Illustrated*, 6 January 1917, p. 482.
32. MGF, 'The position of women in economic life', in William Harbutt Dawson (ed.), *After-War Problems* (1917), pp. 191–215 (quotations from pp. 191, 195, 207, 215).
33. MGF, 'The war conscience in time of peace', *The Englishwoman*, December 1916, pp. 196–209.
34. For a summary see Gail Braybon and Penny Summerfield, *Out of the Cage* (Pandora, 1987), pp. 107–13.
35. *CC*, 3 November 1916, p. 371.
36. *ibid.*, 20 April 1917, p. 12; *The Times*, 9, 16, 18 December 1920. The Criminal Law Amendment Act, finally passed in 1922, contained no new penal clauses of this type.
37. *The Shield*, April 1916, p. 67.
38. *Daily Chronicle*, 28 November 1918 (JRL, Women's Suffrage Collection, box 1).
39. NUWSS circular letter, November 1918 (MAS, vol. 28); *The Shield*, July 1918, pp. 2–4.
40. *CC*, 15, 29 November 1918, pp. 363, 383; MAS, vol. 28.
41. FLA, box 90 vol. 4.
42. *Memorial on the Education of Girls and Women in India*, July 1915 (Fawcett Library); M.E.A. Garrett to MGF, 12 June 1916 (FLA, box 90 vol. 4); *The Times*, 11 October 1915; *Times Educational Supplement*, 2 November 1915.
43. *CC*, 12 October 1917, p. 316; 15 August 1919, p. 222; also Fawcett–Montagu correspondence October 1917 in FLA, box 90 vol. 4.
44. *CC*, 5 and 19 July 1918, pp. 144, 178–9.
45. M50/2/22/257, 260–1; *WIR*, p. 255.
46. *WIR*, p. 256.
47. MGF to Evelyn Atkinson [?June 1915]; FLALC, vol. 1l; Martin Pugh, *Women's Suffrage* (1980), p. 33.
48. MGF, *The Women's Victory* (1920), pp. 124–5; *WIR*, p.231.
49. MGF, 'Progress of the women's movement in the United Kingdom' in Harper (ed.), pp. 742–3; *idem*, *The Women's Victory*, p. 121.
50. MGF, 'The council meeting', *CC*, 25 February 1916, pp. 614–15; *idem*, *The Women's Victory*, p. 133; Martin Pugh, 'Politicians and the woman's vote', *History* (vol. 59, 1974), pp. 366, 368, 373; David Close, 'The collapse of resistance to democracy', *Historical Journal* (vol. 20, 1977), pp. 899–905.
51. Holton, pp. 138–43. See also below, page 249.
52. MGF to Badley, 12 June 1916 (FLALC, vol. 14).
53. MGF to Atkinson, 9 August [1916] (FLALC, vol. 1l).
54. MGF, 'Nearing victory', *The Englishwoman*, September 1916, pp. 193–8. The quotation is from a letter from Ray Strachey to MGF, 16 August 1916 (Strachey Papers, Oxford).

55. MGF to Atkinson, 29 August 1916 (FLALC, vol. 1l).
56. *CC*, 27 October, 3, 10, 17 November 1916, pp. 365, 382, 398, 414; *MG*, 26, 30 October 1916.
57. *MG*, 30 October 1916.
58. Frances Balfour to MGF, 3 January 1917 (FLALC, vol. 1l); Martin Pugh, *Electoral Reform* (1978), pp. 151–2.
59. *The Times*, 19 January 1917; MGF, ' "An immense and significant advance" ', *The Englishwoman*, March 1917, p. 193.
60. MGF, *The Women's Victory*, pp. 140–1 & n.
61. *CC*, 2 March 1917, p. 623; Holton, p. 149.
62. *The Times*, 1 February 1917.
63. W.H. Dickinson to MGF, 19 January 191[7] (misdated 1916) (FLALC, vol. 1l).
64. MGF to Mrs Conway, 23 February 1917 (Girton Archives Cambridge).
65. PRO, Cab/24/6/1 (13 February 1917); Pugh, *Electoral Reform*, p. 142; NUWSS, EC minutes, 12 February 1917 (FLA, box 84/1).
66. NUWSS, EC minutes, 12 February 1917 (FLA, box 84/1).
67. Sylvia Pankhurst Papers, International Institute of Social History, files 14, 21; Pankhurst, pp. 603–5.
68. MGF to Lloyd George (copy) [March 1917] (FLALC, vol. 1l).
69. *The Times*, 30 March 1927.
70. Ray Strachey to [Mary Berenson] (copy), 1 April 1917 (Strachey Papers).
71. S.A. Edwards to Lloyd George, 25 October 1933 (Lloyd George Papers, House of Lords).
72. NUWSS, *Women's Suffrage Deputation to the Right Hon. David Lloyd George . . . 29 March 1917* (Women's Work Collection, Imperial War Museum), p. 5.
73. *ibid.*, pp. 20–30; Pugh, 'Politicians and the woman's vote', p. 374; Holton, p. 185 n. 70.
74. *CC*, 9, 23 March, 7 April, 4, 25 May, 1 June 1917, pp. 630, 666, 691, 42, 83, 95; *MGF*, pp. 312–15; MGF, *The Women's Victory* pp. 145–6.
75. Ray Strachey to MGF, May 1917 (Strachey Papers).
76. MGF to Dickinson, 22 June 1917 (Dickinson Papers, Greater London Record Office).
77. Some of the newspaper articles published in her honour may be found in JRL, Women's Suffrage Collection, box 1. The *CC* for 8 June was devoted to 'Our Mrs Fawcett birthday number'. See also *ibid.*, 15 June 1917, pp. 112–13.
78. MGF to Badley, 11 June 1917 (FLALC, vol. 14).
79. *Jus Suffragii*, 1 July 1917, p. 144.
80. *CC*, 5 October 1917, pp. 302–3; MGF, *The Women's Victory*, pp. 146–8.
81. MGF to Helena Auerbach, 20 November [1917] (Fawcett Collection, IIAV).
82. *CC*, 11 January 1918, pp. 501–2.
83. *Parl. Deb.* (Lords), 5th ser., 27, cols 522–3 (10 January 1918).
84. Kate Courtney's diary, 14 January 1918 (Courtney Papers, BLPES).
85. MGF to H.A.L. Fisher, 8 February 1918 (Fisher Papers, Bodleian Library).
86. MGF to Helen Fraser, 28 February 1918 (Fraser Papers, Museum of London).
87. *WIR*, pp. 250–1; Charles L. Graves, *Hubert Parry*, vol. 2, (1926), pp. 92–3, 174; *WL*, 28 May 1926, p. 143; *The Times*, 18 August 1927.
88. Parry diary, 13 March 1918 (Parry Papers, Shulbrede Priory).
89. MGF to Badley, 29 January 1919 (FLALC, vol. 14).
90. MGF to Lettice Fisher, 10 August 1918 (Fisher Papers).
91. *CC*, 8 February 1918, p. 561.
92. *National News*, 10 March 1918 (JRL, Women's Suffrage Collection, box 1).

# PART IV

## FINAL YEARS 1918–29

# CHAPTER 18

## THE AFTERMATH OF WAR 1918–21

When Lloyd George decided to push through the recommendations of the Speaker's Conference in 1917 his motive was unlikely to have been a lofty idealism. In the event the continuation of his Coalition Government into the post-war years meant that he had relatively little need to make a special appeal to women. Whether stimulated by gratitude or other considerations, however, women appear to have voted heavily for the coalition in the election of December 1918.[1] As for Mrs Fawcett, she could hardly have identified herself with the independent fragments of the Liberal party led by her old enemy Asquith or the now avowedly socialist Labour party against 'the man who won the war'. But Lloyd George's belated commitment to advocate women's suffrage with more than words ensured that her support would be active and uninhibited.

She did not renounce her previous sympathies with the Labour party. She wrote in friendly terms to Arthur Henderson after he was suddenly forced out of the Government in 1917, spoke warmly about Labour's record on women's suffrage in her *National News* interview in March 1918 and told the Election Fighting Fund committee that it must honour its existing commitments to the Labour party. It was thus possible to phase out the fund without a breach with Labour.[2] At its annual council meeting in March 1918 the National Union of Women's Suffrage Societies passed a vote of 'hearty thanks' to the Labour party for its past assistance. During the election campaign she wrote publicly to Henderson to extol the help which he had given to women's suffrage 'at every stage of our battle for representation'.[3] After the election Mrs Fawcett again wrote sympathetically about Labour. A leaflet dating from early 1920 warmly praised the party's wholehearted support on the suffrage issue, notwithstanding the middle-class nature of the women's movement. Contrasting the Labour attitude with that of Liberal statesmen like Winston Churchill and Reginald McKenna, both pre-war Home Secretaries, she dismissed outright 'recent criticisms [of] the supposed want of political foresight on the part of the Labour Party'.[4]

In her view, however, the general election of December 1918 belonged to Lloyd George. She told the pro-coalition *Daily Chronicle* in November

1918 that if she had twenty votes they would all be given to the Government. It was characteristic both of Mrs Fawcett herself and of the period that she should have put first his 'genius and insight' as a leader of the Allied war effort, but she did not neglect the Representation of the People Act. Its passage, she asserted, had made Britain 'for the first time a true democracy', a phrase which in other contexts she might have wished to qualify severely.[5]

Within a fortnight she had followed the newspaper article with an election rally for Lloyd George, taking the chair at a crowded women's meeting at Queen's Hall, where a few months earlier suffragists had celebrated their enfranchisement. She praised him lavishly. His 'strong and forceful personality . . . had made the women's cause his own. He did not wait and see', she continued with a jibe at Asquith which drew laughter and cheers, 'but he did . . . what others had been talking about for generations.'[6]

She was so adamant about her support for the coalition that when Sir John Simon, an Asquithian Liberal who had given outstanding assistance to suffragists in the final stages of the parliamentary struggle wrote to her in alarm about her support for Lloyd George, she flatly refused to assist him. She could not refer to any particular candidate in her Queen's Hall speech, she insisted, and ignored his plea for a letter of support. She claimed with little more candour than Asquith himself had habitually displayed that she never advised women how to vote, but she compared the record of the two leaders in Lloyd George's favour. In the existing national crisis, she stressed, she could not be guided by attitudes to women's questions alone. 'But I feel that the P.M.'s vigour, courage, insight and driving power have saved the country.'[7]

In practice she did not maintain this position in its full rigidity. Her message to Arthur Henderson quoted above amounted to an endorsement, and while she took the chair and spoke for Ray Strachey as an 'independent coalition' candidate, she also remained president of a national union which formally supported Mary Macarthur, the women's trade unionist who stood for Labour, and Margery Corbett Ashby, who was at once a leader of the NUWSS and a strong Asquithian Liberal.[8] She also issued with Jane, Lady Strachey, president of the Women's Local Government Society, a manifesto to women electors, asking them to support candidates of all parties who promised equality of employment, pay, morality, education and guardianship.[9]

The election was a walkover, though the coalition's number of seats greatly exaggerated its popular support. Mrs Fawcett, rejoicing in a letter to a colleague, commented that 'it surpassed every expectation'.[10] Among the defeated candidates were not only all the women apart from Constance Markiewicz in Dublin, but also such pro-suffrage male stalwarts as Simon and Henderson, Sir Willoughby Dickinson and Philip Snowden.[11] But by December 1918 the issue of women's suffrage was at best of secondary importance in the wake of the death and destruction of the recently ended war, and the daunting political and economic problems which awaited solution. The reaction of the Blathwayt family of suffragists in Somerset was perhaps indicative. Emily recorded in her diary how she had voted but did not think it worth mentioning that it had been her first vote. Mary, her daughter, was unqualified, though aged nearly 40. 'The General Election took place today', she wrote on 14 December. 'Women voted for the 1st time – I did not have a vote.'[12]

In the aftermath of the suffrage victory Mrs Fawcett was the recipient of a number of honours, whose award symbolized the peaceful ending of the fraught struggle for women's suffrage. Two were of special interest. On the day after the armistice she received a second doctorate of laws, this time from the University of Birmingham. The award was at the behest of the university's chancellor, Lord Robert Cecil, the old ally of the suffrage movement whose anger at the peace meeting in which the NUWSS had participated in August 1914 had long since been forgotten. She was referred to as 'a woman of scholarly attainments' and her leadership of the women's movement as 'honourable, sane and wholesome'.[13] It might have been added that she had long pursued unacceptable political goals by acceptable means. Both ends and means now received their reward.

After the passage in 1919 of a mutilated Sex Disqualification Removal Act the Government decided to appoint 'a limited number of representative women' to the position of magistrate.[14] The all-male composition of the magistracy had been a grievance of the women's movement for decades, and Mrs Fawcett was one of over 200 women, a number of them veterans of the suffrage campaign, appointed in the first batch in July 1920.[15] A few months later the National Union of Societies for Equal Citizenship, into which the NUWSS had been transformed the previous year, held a conference for women magistrates at which Mrs Fawcett took the chair. She told the meeting that she was ignorant of magistrates' work and hoped for enlightenment, and warned that women must not, as men had sometimes done in the past, favour their own sex unfairly.[16]

She was awarded the medal of Queen Elizabeth of Belgium in August 1920 in recognition of her services to Belgium during the war. Accepting the medal she coupled the work of the International Woman Suffrage Alliance with her own.[17] The women's movement itself gave her £500 as a New Year present in 1920, with the names of contributors beautifully lettered on vellum. The following year she and Agnes used the money to undertake their first visit to Palestine.[18] Another gift from women was the establishment of scholarships at Bedford College, London, of which she had long been a governor. Philippa, a former student, had redeemed early in 1918 a promise to give £100 to the college when women's suffrage was won. Soon afterwards an appeal was launched for funds to celebrate the victory and Mrs Fawcett's fifty years of work for the cause. A committee of titled and influential women was established, over £2,000 was raised within a short period, and Millicent Fawcett scholarships were regularly awarded in subsequent years.[19]

With the partial achievement of women's suffrage and the end of the war it did not take her long to decide to surrender her arduous official position. Early in January 1919 she announced that she would not stand for re-election to the presidency of the NUWSS or its executive committee at the annual council meeting in March. The reason she gave was her age, and this was undoubtedly accurate. It was also the case, however, that some of her colleagues were anxious to launch an immediate campaign to secure the vote for younger women and that she strongly opposed them.[20] She may have wished to leave her office before any clash took place, though in the absence of executive committee minutes for the relevant period there is no documentation of any formal discussion of the subject. In any event, her own view was undoubtedly the majority position, as she claimed in a letter to Helena Auerbach in August 1918: 'Almost all of us would feel it to be unwise immediately to raise the Suffrage question again until the country has had time to digest the bit they have already got.'[21] She told the *Manchester Guardian* that she wished to end her 'strenuous speaking tours' and the attendance at the 'exceedingly tiring' committee meetings, which our knowledge of them suggests would have tired a much younger woman.[22]

Before her retirement began she had a final official duty to undertake, to participate with other women from Allied countries in urging the case for improvement in women's conditions upon the peace negotiators meeting in Paris. This process began auspiciously in terms of her acceptability to the victorious powers, disastrously in terms of her later reputation. At the end of November 1918 she received a cable from Marie Stritt, president of the German women's suffrage association and her IWSA executive colleague. It asked her and other suffragists to use their influence to attempt to bring to an end the Allied blockade of Germany, whose continuation, she wrote, endangered the lives of millions of women and children.[23]

In May 1917 Mrs Fawcett had been among a large number of eminent men and women who signed a protest against the 'indiscriminate attack upon non-combatants' involved in the British bombing of Freiburg.[24] Eighteen months later she manifested no such quality of mercy. Her reply, published in *The Times*, was harshly unfeeling. It began with an outright refusal to appeal to the British Government to end the blockade. The world-wide food shortage, she wrote, had been aggravated by the unrestricted campaign of submarine warfare undertaken by Germany, which German public opinion had done nothing to impede. The British people, she declared, 'are not vindictive, but they have a strong sense of justice'. Almost all of them felt that the claims of Allied, liberated and neutral countries must be met before those of the enemy. In any event German food supplies had been described as adequate by the American food administrator Herbert Hoover.[25] She offered Frau Stritt as consolation only the view that if women had had a fair share of pre-war political power 'the criminal conspiracy of the autocratic rulers of Germany, which brought about the war, would have been an impossibility'.[26]

The extent of the subsequent famine in Germany makes this letter appear particularly shocking, and it did not represent the views of those feminists who had retained their international outlook during the war years. It caused Mary Sheepshanks severe agony, and finally she felt it her 'difficult duty' to write to the NUWSS executive to protest against what she regarded as their attitude of callous indifference to the problem of famine in Germany. 'You will not be in agreement with it', she wrote to Mrs Fawcett, 'but I felt called upon to write it. Even Foch now admits that Germany is on the verge of famine.'[27] The reply took the form of an old dodge. It was evident, Mrs Fawcett wrote, that Sheepshanks had considered Frau Stritt's telegram as an appeal to the NUWSS committee, 'whereas I treated it & considered it a personal communication to me, and I answered it in that sense'.[28] The reality was that Frau Stritt could have addressed her in no other capacity than that of the most influential leader of the British and international women's suffrage movement. The incident can only be regarded as a bleak example of the implacable side of her character, so often revealed when her patriotic convictions were involved.

Her credentials now established, she was ready to play her part in influencing the peace process. She arrived in Paris on 7 February 1919 with Ray Strachey and another NUWSS colleague for consultation with French, Belgian and other suffragists from Allied countries before constituting a deputation to lobby the government leaders then in the early stages of the peace conference. Their first visit was to President Woodrow Wilson, to whom they put the case for the appointing of an international commission of women to enquire into the conditions of women and children and the legislative provisions affecting them. Mrs Fawcett also urged that 'a people's peace' was the best safeguard against future wars and that it should be based on the votes of all the people. Wilson received the deputation sympathetically and promised to do what he could to further its aims before leaving for the United States a few days later. 'We came away very well satisfied', Mrs Fawcett wrote in the diary which she kept during her stay in Paris.[29]

In some respects she found the trip 'an extraordinar[il]y interesting time' in which she was glad to have participated, as she wrote to Mrs Catt upon her return to London. Interviews were obtained with many of the leading figures attending the conference, and the results were generally favourable. She was particularly impressed by Eleutherios Venizelos, the Greek leader, and she also recorded the comments of Georges Clemenceau, the French Prime Minister, and George Barnes, the former Labour leader who had remained with the Coalition Government in 1918. Clemenceau, she wrote, had no logical reason to oppose women's suffrage in principle, but regarded it as in essence a Protestant luxury. In Catholic countries, he maintained, women were too firmly under the control of the church to be awarded the vote. When she congratulated Barnes on his 'thumping majority' in the general election he replied: 'Well I had the women with me. They are dead against Bolshevism.'[30]

These interviews, arranged and led by Mrs Fawcett,[31] were generally heartening. So too was the evidence of the Allied victory, symbolized by a walk in Paris where she found that the statue of Strasbourg in the Place de la Concorde had lost the crepe veil which had covered it since the loss of the city to the Germans in the war of 1870.[32] One must accept, however, the word of Ray Strachey, her fellow delegate, intimate and biographer, that the ten days in Paris were an unhappy experience.[33] Mrs Fawcett was disturbed by the slow and desultory meetings of the conference of inter-Allied women and by the unrestrained atmosphere of post-war Paris, which she felt touched her own family. She warned her niece Gladys Wood, who was expecting a visit there from her son John, a 17-year-old midshipman, of the moral risks involved in 'just turning him out alone in Paris to look after himself. She did not much seem to have thought of this', the diary recorded.[34] Even nature turned against her on one occasion: 'It was a fearful night, deluges of rain & I took the opportunity of rolling in the mud just outside the Metro station. It did not improve my frock, but otherwise had no bad consequences.'[35] After the return to England of the three-woman delegation they were replaced by Margery Fry and Margery Corbett Ashby, whose feelings of frustration were even greater than their own.[36]

Her discontent with the international women's suffrage movement at this time was heightened by disagreements with her colleagues in the IWSA leadership. Despite her own strong nationalism she was less concerned to condemn Germany and more intent on preserving the IWSA itself than some of her colleagues in other victorious nations. In March 1919 she wrote to Marguerite de Witt Schlumberger to explain that although she sympathized entirely with 'your abhorrence of German brutalities', she had referred to Mrs Catt a letter to the *International Woman Suffrage News* (successor to *Jus Suffragii*) from French, Italian and Belgian suffragists containing a strong attack on Germany. The paper was, she pointed out, the joint property of the IWSA national affiliates and it had been agreed in 1914 that they should not attack each other in its pages. It was the mirror image of her censorship of Mrs Catt three years earlier, and the letter was not published.[37]

Much more irritating was Mrs Catt herself, who, unable to leave the United States during the final stages of the American suffrage struggle, sent contradictory advice and instructions. This was particulary vexing inasmuch as the IWSA was not officially involved in the inter-Allied women's lobby of the peace conference. One letter, Mrs Fawcett wrote to Mary Sheepshanks, made her feel inclined 'to resign my official position in the IWSA *at once*'.[38] Two months later Mrs Catt suggested that the IWSA headquarters committee based in London should present a memorial to the peace conference, which Mrs Fawcett strongly opposed as duplicating work already carried out by the inter-Allied group.[39]

She did not yield to the temptation to resign, and remained an active chairman of the headquarters committee of the IWSA and a prominent supporter of the international movement.[40] She wrote an article for its journal in December 1919 which strongly urged its continued existence to work for the enfranchisement of women wherever in the world they remained voteless.[41] She remained the IWSA first vice-president until wartime passions had cooled sufficiently to hold a congress in Geneva in June 1920, and continued her connection with the association in later years.

Although as already pointed out[42] it would be an exaggeration to suggest that Mrs Fawcett was constantly ill at ease among foreigners, she certainly had her moments of tribulation with them. Two such incidents took place in Paris at a later date and, in the view of her colleagues, said much about her character. 'Three enthusiastic representatives of a distant Latin race' asked if they could touch her hand. Her response was 'a mixture of kindly cordiality and deprecation which we find it impossible to describe', an observer recalled. On the following day she attended a service at the American church in Paris, where a patriotic hymn was played to the tune of the British national anthem. After the service Mrs Fawcett told a friend that she had sung the hymn, 'but . . . I sang my own words'.[43] Singing her own words was an activity of which she had never been afraid.

If the attempt to influence the peace congress in 1919 was a fraught and only partially successful undertaking, her participation in supporting the work of the League of Nations caused her no anxieties. She was an early believer in the league and was elected a vice-president of the League of Nations Unions soon after its formation at the end of 1918.[44] A year later she was the only woman among the eight British delegates to an international conference of League of Nations Unions held in Brussels.[45] At about the same time she chaired a meeting of representative women in London, and with Maude Royden was chosen as one of a committee of four to draw up a women's manifesto of support for the league.[46] The manifesto was published by the League of Nations Union in January 1920 and stressed the equal opportunities offered to women by the league's covenant. It also pointed out the importance of an informed and articulate public opinion as a force for peace. 'If women share this duty with men they will help to create a new force in the world which will strengthen the foundations of peace.'[47]

Her speeches and articles, strongly supporting the league and proclaiming that women were a potential force for peace,[48] were heavily influenced by her lifelong patriotism. She asserted in a draft probably written late in 1919 that a healthy nationalism was a prerequisite of a healthy internationalism.[49] In June 1920 she described the infant league as offering potential hope of avoiding another great European war. Yet, though its success would be 'the greatest triumph of internationalism which the world has yet seen', it would

be based on 'the fact of nationalism, and not the spurious, anaemic internationalism which produces patriots of every country but their own and
decries and belittles the love which ordinary healthy human beings bear to
their own land'.[50] Her model was the IWSA, which she pointed out had
developed into an important international movement from the patriotism of
women 'for their own dear motherlands'.[51]

Her forthright vocabulary recalls the wartime turmoil within the
NUWSS which undoubtedly inspired it, but in the context of the immediate post-war years it did not contradict a real desire that the work of the
league should grow and succeed. As usual her desire took a practical and
prominent form, though age and other commitments meant that she was
not among the more active figures in the LNU. The second anniversary of
the signing of the League of Nations covenant was celebrated in June 1921
with a march and rally in London. The *Woman's Leader*, successor to the
*Common Cause*, publicized the rally for several weeks, and afterwards reported Mrs Fawcett 'first on the field', walking at the head of the women's
contingent from the Embankment to Hyde Park at her customary brisk
pace. A year later she again attended the LNU demonstration on a cold, wet
June day and spoke from a platform in Hyde Park.[52]

Her commitment to internationalism was now so strong that she was one
of a small group of eminent women who wrote to the press in October
1921 to support Lloyd George on the eve of the Washington disarmanent
conference. 'He carries with him the passionate hopes of every woman.
Each woman who knows what war is wishes him God-speed in her heart.'
The signatories asked all girls and women aged 14 and over to send a
postcard of good wishes to Lloyd George, and a copy of their letter was
circulated to National Union of Societies for Equal Citizenship branches.[53]

Mrs Fawcett's last function as NUWSS president was carried out at its
1919 annual council, when the union bade her an emotional farewell,
adopted its new name and elected Eleanor Rathbone to succeed her. The
suffrage victory and the end of the war obviously closed an important
chapter of feminist history and a number of other veterans of the struggle
marked the occasion by their retirement, including Lady Frances Balfour
and Helena Auerbach, who had been the union's treasurer and Mrs
Fawcett's ally during the internal struggle in 1915.[54] By this time her
habitual optimism had become an irremovable mask. Her address to the
council rejected the feelings of anti-climax and disappointment which had
become noticeable within the union. The struggle to obtain the vote, she
declared, had been 'one of the most wonderful times in the whole history of
the world', while the future held 'nothing dismal . . . but . . . a real certain-
ty of a greater and better time to come'.[55] Interviewed at about the same
time by Harold Begbie, a prominent journalist, she rejected his pessimistic
pose and 'talked optimism, pure optimism, nothing but optimism . . . without truculence, without self-assertion'.[56]

It was undoubtedly useful to the movement that its best-known figure was so convinced of the moral and material progress of the modern world and women's role in it, and able to support her words with detailed evidence. But it was a stance increasingly at variance with the reality seen by other feminists. In November 1919 Eleanor Rathbone referred to the falling membership of many union societies, and the following month an article by Inez Ferguson, the NUSEC secretary, reinforced the conviction that the feminist tide had been reversed. 'The best optimist of us all cannot deny that feminist stock is low in Great Britain to-day', she wrote. There was little sympathy with women's aspirations and a general sentiment in favour of dismissing them from their wartime and even pre-war employments to make room for men.[57] Rathbone's presidential address to the NUSEC annual council in March 1921 was described by the *Manchester Guardian* as 'rather gloomy'. Public opinion, she declared, 'had definitely taken a step back'.[58] Even Mrs Fawcett admitted to Ray Strachey after a visit to Scotland that the press, which had previously improved, had reverted to treating women frivolously, making 'inane observations on the length of skirts or the shape of sleeves'.[59]

She was soon to experience for herself the depressing aftermath of the incomplete and ambiguous victory of 1918. Although she had now retired from the presidency of the NUWSS and reduced her commitments to the IWSA after spring 1919, she did not reduce the scale of her intellectual activity. By the summer of 1919, as if to justify her earlier claim that she was happiest with her books, she was hard at work on a sequel to her short history of women's suffrage published in 1912.[60] In December she signed a contract with Sidgwick & Jackson which gave her a 10 per cent royalty on the first 5,000 copies of the book in both cloth and paper editions.[61] Despite a vexatious injury to her foot which became sufficiently serious for an operation to be carried out by a woman surgeon in February 1920, she completed her proofs and returned them in time for the book to be published the following month.[62] Entitled *The Women's Victory – and After: Personal reminiscences 1911–1918*, it was the most important of her several contributions to the history of the suffrage struggle. Though personally reticent it was written in lively style and spiced at the publisher's suggestion with cartoons from *Punch*.[63] It remains an indispensable account of the events it describes as well as an important biographical source.

Before the end of April, however, Frank Sidgwick wrote to her to say that sales had been poor, despite generally favourable press notices, and that it would be necessary to obtain support from NUSEC and other friendly organizations if the book was to be saved from commercial failure.[64] NUSEC and the *Woman's Leader* each took a thousand copies and Mrs Fawcett herself a further hundred.[65] None the less, Sidgwick wrote two years later that it had 'fallen quite flat, and it is fairly clear that the people who were interested in the movement while it was a movement, lost all interest in its history as soon as the main object was gained.'[66] A striking passage in Ray Strachey's review of the book half admitted that this decline of interest had taken place and offered an explanation:

> It is impossible to read this book through without a sigh for the days that are gone. For it was all so straightforward, and it was all so simple. The old arguments . . . were so easy to answer, and we knew our way so well. And then, how picturesque it was! The Pilgrimage: the Banners: the Processions: Hyde Park on a Sunday, and the rotten eggs at street corners! Gone are all these pleasures, and in their place – the vote.[67]

The author herself, however, refused to admit discouragement. Her publisher had requested a chapter on the work which still lay ahead of organized feminism, and she complied in part. She listed the current NUSEC demands and criticized the Government for substituting its own Sex Disqualification Removal Bill in place of a more sweeping measure introduced by the Labour party. But these passages appeared in a chapter entitled 'The difference the vote has made'. Only two important acts affecting women had been passed between 1902 and 1914, she wrote, while no fewer than seven had been carried through both Houses of Parliament in the brief period since the passage of the Reform Act in 1918: 'Already the practical results of women's suffrage have surpassed our expectations.'[68]

Her final article for *The Englishwoman*, published in January 1920, had a similar title and a similar theme. A comparison of legislation before and after 1918 made abundantly plain 'to every open mind' the difference made by women's suffrage: 'The astonishing thing is that any one with an ounce of political experience should ever have doubted it.'[69] Younger or less optimistic colleagues might note sadly that organized feminism had already begun to unravel, and the parliamentary machine move in low gear, but she continued to insist with a good deal of evidence that the condition of women made steady progress.[70]

The process of ageing is seldom a happy one, but for Mrs Fawcett it appeared to make little difference. She remained in full possession of her faculties. Freed from wearying speaking tours and fraught committee meetings she remained much in demand as a speaker, to chair meetings and lectures, write introductions and lend her name to a variety of good causes. When Venizelos visited Britain in October 1919 she held a reception for him at which leaders of many aspects of the women's movement were present. At the end of 1920 she took the chair at a mass meeting held in Central Hall Westminister to celebrate the women's suffrage victory in the United States and welcome Mrs Catt to England. The following May she played a prominent part at the celebration dinner at the Midland Hotel in Manchester which commemorated the centenary of the *Guardian* and C.P. Scott's fifty years as its editor.[71]

But her announced intention to continue her work for 'the development of women's freedom'[72] was not confined to ceremonial appearances. In

February 1920 she presided over the inauguration of a new women's paper. The *Common Cause*, house organ of the NUWSS, had inevitably concentrated on the detailed development of the suffrage struggle, and it was hoped that there were many potential readers of a more general feminist weekly. The *Woman's Leader*, close to NUSEC, but not its official publication, was launched with a board of directors consisting of six women and a man. Mrs Fawcett chaired the board, and among the other directors were Eleanor Rathbone, Mary Stocks and Ray Strachey. The day before publication Mrs Fawcett, nursing her injured foot, held a reception for women journalists at her London home. Subsequently share capital of £15,000 was advertised to the readership.[73] It was a brave venture, and the paper's survival in the inhospitable climate of the 1920s was a considerable achievement. She continued to hold the post of chairman until 1925.[74]

Her opposition to launching an immediate campaign to enfranchise younger women was probably influenced by a desire not to add to the problems of the Lloyd George Government. But it seemed to her more urgent in the aftermath of war to concentrate feminist efforts on combating attempts to push women out of their wartime jobs, noticeable well before the onset of economic depression in 1920. In her retirement speech to the NUWSS she pointed to the pressing need to protect the 'industrial freedom' of women.[75] In a letter to *The Times* in June 1919 she deplored the redistribution of Pre-war Practices Bill and asked that trade union restrictions should not be extended to post-war occupations: 'It does not seem as if the pledges need bear so wide and so ruinous an interpretation, or that because women were not allowed to build ships before the war it must be illegal for them to build aeroplanes to-day.'[76] Later she told a London audience that the struggle for industrial freedom must continue, aided by the victories already won: 'We cannot be half free and half serf.'[77]

Other causes with which she was involved in the period included a successful attempt to ward off a discriminatory Criminal Law Amendment Act, support for equal treatment for women jurors,[78] and a new and prolonged effort to secure degrees for women at Cambridge, thirty years after Philippa's academic triumph. Among the replies she received was one from the historian G.M. Trevelyan, who wrote that he was 'honoured by getting a "whip" ' from her, and another from the former Dean of Salisbury, who told her that at 85 he was too old to travel from the Isle of Wight to vote.[79] The decision to give women 'titular degrees' but refuse them even limited membership of the university was a bitter blow and was followed by an undergraduate riot in which the gates of Newnham were damaged. In a letter to *The Times* Mrs Fawcett commented acidly that if a fund was established to compensate the college for the damage the Newnham council should 'accept the gift and then pass it on to the county lunatic asylum'.[80]

Women's suffrage was for the moment quiescent, but the inveterate optimist was still engaged on several other aspects of the women's cause.

Her continued observation and participation in events, however, did not prevent her from reducing her commitments, and the activities of the national union no longer had an exclusive claim on her time. She had dropped none of her interests, and a new part of the world now beckoned. Early in 1921 she and Agnes set out on their first visit to Palestine, and a new dimension was added to her life.

NOTES

1. Martin Pugh, *The Making of Modern British Politics 1867–1939* (Oxford: Blackwell, 1982), pp. 197–8.
2. MGF to Arthur Henderson (copy), 23 August 1917 (FLALC, vol. 1l); *National News*, 10 March 1918; EFF committee minutes, 19 February 1917 (filed, with correspondence, in FLA, box 89 vol. 3); *MGF*, pp. 298–300; Sandra Holton, *Feminism and Democracy* (1986), pp. 142–3, 183–4.
3. *CC*, 22 March 1918, p. 660; *Daily News*, 6 December 1918 (JRL, Women's Suffrage Collection, box 1).
4. MGF, *Would Labour Help the Middle Classes?*, leaflet proof dated in manuscript February 1920 (M/50/8/8).
5. *Daily Chronicle*, 28 November 1918 (JRL, Women's Suffrage Collection, box 1). See also MGF, 'The coming general election', *The Englishwoman*, December 1918, pp. 97–100.
6. *The Times*, 10 December 1918.
7. Simon to MGF, 8 December 1918; MGF to Simon (copy), 9 December 1918 (FLA, box 89 vol. 3). See also *MGF*, pp. 328–9.
8. *CC*, 29 November, 13 December 1918, pp. 390, 415–6. Election leaflets in the Strachey Papers advertise Ray as candidate and speaker in Brentford and Chiswick on 4 and 6 December, with 'Mrs Henry Fawcett, LL. D.' in the chair.
9. *To Women – and especially to Women Electors*, 25 November 1918 (Women's Work Collection, Imperial War Museum).
10. MGF to Helen Fraser, 12 January 1919 (Fraser Papers, Museum of London).
11. *CC*, 3 January 1919, pp. 449, 455.
12. Diaries of Emily and Mary Blathwayt, 14 December 1918. Another suffragist, Kate Courtney, found her choice of candidates too uninspiring to justify voting. See her *Extracts from a Diary During the War* (privately printed 1917), p. 175.
13. Birmingham University, Programme of Installation of Chancellor, 12 November 1918 (FLA, box 89 vol. 3); *CC*, 22 November 1918, p. 369; Lord Cecil, *A Great Experiment* (Cape, 1941), p. 62.
14. *MG*, 20 July 1920.
15. *ibid.*; *The Times*, 20 July 1920.
16. *The Times*, 1 December 1920; *WL*, 3 December 1920, p. 948.
17. FLA, box 90a file 7.
18. *ibid.*, box 90c file 3; MGF, *Six Weeks in Palestine* (1921), introduction; *MGF*, p. 340.
19. *Evening News*, 18 February 1918; *CC*, 22 February, 15 March, 19 April, 5 July 1918; pp. 590, 636, 6, 152; Margaret Tuke, *A History of Bedford College for Women* (London: Oxford University Press, 1939), pp. 235–6.
20. *CC*, 10 January 1919, pp. 462, 467; *WL*, 15 November 1929, p. 316; George G. Armstrong, *Memories* (Unwin Bros, 1949), p. 170.
21. MGF to Auerbach, 27 August [1918] (Fawcett Collection, IIAV).

22. *MG*, 11 January 1919. See above, pages 171–3.

23. *The Times*, 2 December 1918.

24. *Goodwill*, 23 June 1917, p. 209.

25. I have been unable to corroborate this claim. Hoover had said that European food supplies would soon improve, and press reports before and after she wrote insisted that German fears of famine were exaggerated (*MG*, 23, 29 November 1918; *The Times*, *Daily Telegraph*, 25 November, 2 December 1918; *Morning Post*, 25, 27 November 1918).

26. *The Times*, 2 December 1918. See also Irene Cooper Willis, *How We Came Out of the War* (Bradford: International Bookshops, 1921), pp. 40–5, for press and political support for the blockade.

27. Adela Coit to Mary Sheepshanks, 6 December 1918; Sheepshanks to Coit and to MGF (copies), 20 January 1919 (JRL, IWSA Papers, box 1); *idem*, duplicated letter to NUWSS executive committee, 18 January 1919 (FLA, box 90 vol. 4).

28. MGF to Sheepshanks, 21 January 1919 (IWSA Papers, box 1).

29. MGF's Paris diary, 7–15 February 1919 (FLA, box 90 vol. 5); *CC*, 21 February 1919, p. 540; *International Woman Suffrage News*, March 1919, pp. 71–3; MGF, 'In Paris', *The Englishwoman*, April 1919, pp. 1–3; *WIR*, pp. 253–5.

30. As note 29; also MGF to Carrie Chapman Catt (copy), 19 February 1919 (FLA, box 90 vol. 5).

31. *MGF*, p. 331.

32. MGF diary (note 29 above), 13 February [1919].

33. *MGF*, pp. 331–2.

34. MGF diary, 9, 10, 12 February.

35. *ibid.*, 15 February.

36. Letters and copies in FLA, box 90 vol. 5 from both women to MGF and Eva Hubback written in March and April 1919 make plain their frustration, only partly mitigated by a glowing account from Corbett Ashby on 13 April of another deputation to Woodrow Wilson.

37. MGF draft letter to Marguerite de Witt Schlumberger, 7 March 1919 (FLA, box 90 vol. 5). See above, pages 231–2.

38. MGF to Sheepshanks, 27 February 1919; Sheepshanks to MGF (copies), 7 February, 3 March 1919; *idem* to Chrystal Macmillan (copy), 4 March 1919 (IWSA Papers, boxes 1 and 2).

39. Sheepshanks to Adela Coit (copy), 22 April 1919 (*ibid.*, box 1).

40. MGF letters to Mary Sheepshanks and Elizabeth Abbott, 1918–20, and IWSA headquarters committee minutes, 6, 23 January, 6, 16, 18 February 1920 (IWSA Papers, boxes 1 and 2); MGF, 'A welcome to the I.W.S.A.', *WL*, 26 November 1920, p. 917.

41. MGF, 'The future of the I.W.S.A.', *International Woman Suffrage News*, December 1919, p. 35.

42. See above, page 203.

43. 'Biography', *WL*, 19 June 1931, p. 155. The incidents are there undated, but Mary Stocks (*My Commonplace Book* (1970), pp. 71–2) assigns the second one to the international congress of 1927 (i.e. 1926).

44. *League of Nations Journal*, February 1919, p. 73.

45. *CC*, 5 December 1919, p. 437; *International Woman Suffrage News*, December 1919, p. 34.

46. League of Nations Union, *Annual Report*, 1920, p. 31; *To-day and To-morrow*, January 1920, p. 62.

47. *Women's Support of the League of Nations* (n.d.) (British Library), reprinted in *The League*, February 1920, pp. 171–2; *The Times*, 5 January 1920.

48. A typical speech was reported in the *MG*, 4 October 1920. A more reflective article had appeared in the wake of alarming election meetings, at which women 'roared for the Kaiser's blood as loudly as the men' (' "Still in thy right hand carry gentle peace" ', *CC*, 20 December 1918, p. 427).

49. MGF, 'Nationalism and internationalism', undated draft in IWSA Papers, box 1; *MGF*, p. 326.

50. MGF, 'Internationalism', *WL*, 11 June 1920, p. 429. For similar sentiments see MGF, 'Women and internationalism', *Time and Tide*, 5 and 12 March 1926, pp. 227–8, 252.

51. *WL*, 10 December 1920, p. 968.

52. *ibid.*, 1 July 1921, p. 335; 30 June 1922, p. 171; Johanna Alberti, *Beyond Suffrage* (1989), p. 197.

53. *The Times* 26 October 1921; *WL*, 4 November 1921, p. 502.

54. *CC*, 14, 21 March 1919, pp. 583, 591, 606, 609–10.

55. *ibid.*, 21 March 1919, p. 606; NUWSS, *Annual Report*, 1918, p. 25.

56. *Daily Chronicle*, 18 February 1919 (JRL, Women's Suffrage Collection, box 1).

57. *CC*, 28 November 1919, p. 432; *International Woman Suffrage News*, December 1919, p. 40.

58. *MG*, *The Times*, 9 March 1921; Mary Stocks, *Eleanor Rathbone* (1949), pp. 107–8.

59. Quoted in Brian Harrison, *Prudent Revolutionaries* (1987), p. 21. The letter was dated 4 September 1921.

60. Isabella Ford to MGF, 10 August 1919 (FLALC, vol. 1m). See above, page 73.

61. Sidgwick & Jackson to MGF (copies), 4 November, 12 December 1919 (Sidgwick & Jackson letter-book, Bodleian Library).

62. MGF to Elizabeth Abbott, 21 January [1920], 31 January, 12 February 1920; to Chrystal Macmillan (copy), 1 February 1920 (IWSA Papers, box 1); to Amy Badley, 14 February 1920 (FLALC, vol. 14); Sidgwick & Jackson letter-book, 19, 24, 30 January, 9, 18 March 1920.

63. Sidgwick & Jackson letter-book, 4 November 1919.

64. *ibid.*, 26 April 1920.

65. *ibid.*, 4 May 1920.

66. *ibid.*, 3 May 1922.

67. *WL*, 19 March 1920, p. 158.

68. Sidgwick & Jackson letter-book, 4 November 1919; MGF, *The Women's Victory* (1920), ch. 10 (quotation, p. 157).

69. MGF, 'The difference suffrage has made', *The Englishwoman*, January 1920, p. 7.

70. I have borrowed these metaphors from Harrison, *Prudent Revolutionaries*, p. 7, and Stocks, *Eleanor Rathbone*, p. 112. See below, page 264.

71. *CC*, 24 October 1919, p. 343; *WL*, 3 December 1920, p. 948; *MG*, 4 May 1921.

72. MGF to Emily Murgatroyd and Selina Cooper, 12 January 1919 (Cooper Papers, Lancashire County Record Office).

73. *The Times*, 6 February 1920; *WL*, 19 March, 16 April 1920, pp. 163, 256.

74. *WL*, 10 April 1925, p. 84.

75. *CC*, 21 March 1919, p. 606.

76. *The Times*, 20 June 1919.

77. *CC*, 26 December 1919, p. 487.

78. *The Times*, 16 December 1920; 1 February 1921.

79. Trevelyan, W. Page Roberts to MGF, 27, 29 November 1920 (M50/3/1/44–5).

80. *The Times*, 21, 27 October 1921; Rita McWilliams-Tullberg, *Women at Cambridge* (1975), chs 9–10.

# CHAPTER 19

———————— • ————————

## A VIGOROUS RETIREMENT 1921–5

The travellers began in Cairo, which Mrs Fawcett had last visited nearly a
quarter of a century earlier, and then spent six weeks in Palestine. The trip
was a huge success, as she wrote to Amy Badley upon their return: 'We have
had a most delightful and interesting time. Palestine surpasses all we had
expected in the way of interest & beauty.'[1] They enjoyed the trip so much
that they repeated it in March 1922. Still enthusiastic, they made further
visits in 1927 and in 1928, when both sisters were in their eighties. As usual
they showed the qualities of indefatigability expected by their friends. They
were accompanied on the final visit by Louisa Garrett Anderson, who
recalled after her aunt Millicent's death an attempt to visit Gerash, 'an
inaccessible place in Transjordania', when their car stuck in a snowdrift as
darkness approached: 'The discomfort and danger were considerable, and I
may say that the only members of the party who were not in the least
disturbed were my aunts.'[2]

Mrs Fawcett wrote articles for the *Woman's Leader* on all her visits except
in 1922. After the earlier expeditions she wrote for private circulation *Six
Weeks in Palestine* (1921) and *Our Second Visit to Palestine* (1922). They were
serialized in the *Woman's Leader* in 1924–5 and, slightly revised, published
commercially as *Easter in Palestine, 1921–1922* in 1926. Her views of the
condition of women, relations between Arabs and Jews and the problems of
colonial administration thus received repeated exposure, and she also wrote
enthusiastic traveller's accounts of visits to sites and monuments.

Her bias, not unnaturally, was towards the Jews, especially the women
educationists of British nationality among them. She found their attitude to
representative government much more acceptable than that of the Arabs,
but she suggested on several occasions that Muslim opinion towards the
education of women was becoming more liberal. She was reserved about
Zionism as a creed and insisted that it was possible to create a Jewish national
home without infringing the rights of the non-Jewish population. Only
25,000 Jews had emigrated to Palestine under British administration since
the end of the war, she wrote in 1922. She was enthusiastic about Sir
Herbert Samuel's report on his five years as high commissioner, particularly

263

his encouragement of the Palestinian Women's Council and appointment of a woman government inspector and social worker. A *Times Literary Supplement* reviewer noted her tenderness towards 'administrative susceptibilities', her favourable view of progress under British administration, and her anxiety to record details of improved relations between Muslims and Jews. When Christian, Jew and Muslim were brought into contact, she wrote in 1926, they gradually learned to work in harmony. This was 'the best sign of all for the future of Palestine'.[3] Undoubtedly she described the relations of the various religions and ethnic groups more optimistically than was justified, but she could not have anticipated the catastrophes which subsequent decades were to bring.

Although she had surrendered the presidency of the National Union of Women's Suffrage Societies when it became the National Union of Societies for Equal Citizenship in 1919, it remained central to her hopes and concerns for women. She attended the annual council meeting in 1920 and played an active part from a prominent position on the platform. It was, she and other delegates commented, 'like the old days back again', and the *Woman's Leader* observed contentedly that in electing Eleanor Rathbone as president the union had not lost Mrs Fawcett.[4] She missed the council meetings in 1921 and 1922 because of her visits to Palestine, but she unexpectedly attended a NUSEC conference in July 1921, where Rathbone generously described her as 'spiritually still our President'.[5] One wonders how happy the new president was that her successor continued her activities within the union, particularly when the two women became embroiled in argument over family endowment a few years later.[6]

In 1922 she wrote a four-page leaflet published by NUSEC on 'What the vote has done'. It brought up to date her earlier publications on the subject and was in turn revised and expanded in later years, but it was not simply a celebration of the women's vote. She pointed out that women's position in the civil service was still far from satisfactory, although she exaggerated as 'a notable Parliamentary victory' the Government's apparent acceptance of equal access to the civil service, about which Philippa Strachey had written jubilantly to her.[7] She also listed the parliamentary vote for younger women, equal guardianship of infants and legislation to improve the rights of married women as urgent requirements.[8] In a letter to *The Times* published shortly before the publication of the leaflet she strongly criticized the Government's half-hearted observance of its own Sex Disqualification Removal Act. Cuts in expenditure which had adversely affected women police, and the blocking of Lady Rhondda's attempt to take her claimed seat in the House of Lords were among her targets. Women electors, she asserted, asked what the act meant in practice. 'Does it not resemble the razors at the fair, which were made to sell and not to cut?'[9]

Political developments provided modest encouragement for feminists. In September 1921 Margaret Wintringham was returned as a Liberal in a by-election in Louth, joining the Conservative Nancy Astor elected two years previously. Mrs Fawcett wrote a letter of support for Mrs Wintringham and was 'overjoyed' by the result. It should, she added, encourage the Government to pass a long-awaited Criminal Law Amendment Act, and the act duly followed in 1922.[10]

Despite her criticisms of the Lloyd George Government she was distressed by indications that it was falling apart, and particularly by Conservative attacks on Lloyd George himself. Lord Robert Cecil, her associate in women's suffrage and the League of Nations Union, wrote to her at length in May 1922, defending himself against criticisms which she had made of him in a letter to Ray Strachey.[11] She replied that he was injuring himself by his attacks on Lloyd George, who was 'making the struggle of his life to establish the Peace of Europe on sound lines, to bring Germany & Russia once more into the European comity'. She remembered the attacks made by Lord Salisbury, Cecil's father, on Disraeli in the 1860s, she wrote. Both Disraeli and Lloyd George were 'men of genius, erratic perhaps but each did great national service . . . your father came to a different frame of mind after a few years and so I very earnestly trust will you.'[12]

Enough Conservatives agreed with Cecil for the coalition to break up and Lloyd George to fall from power in October 1922. At the election which followed shortly afterwards the number of women candidates was nearly double that of 1918, but though Lady Astor and Mrs Wintringham kept their seats feminists were disappointed that they remained the only women in the House of Commons.[13] After the results were announced Mrs Fawcett wrote an article for the *Woman's Leader* urging readers not to feel discouraged. Lady Astor and Mrs Wintringham had amassed large majorities and Ray Strachey, standing for a second time in the same constituency had greatly increased her vote. Other women candidates had polled well and several of them had been fairly close to victory. Four years was a short period for women to make their mark in the House of Commons, and future prospects were bright.[14]

None the less, the mood of pessimism endured. Early in 1923 the *Woman's Leader* called attention to the inequalities in women's condition which remained to be combated by a diminished band of feminists.[15] After the NUSEC annual council two months later an anonymous report offered a shrewd though incomplete explanation. The council meetings had been very vigorous, the report observed,

> though it is very different from the crowded councils of pre-war days, when fares were lower, domestic servants available, when there was still a leisured class, and when the glaring injustice of an unenfranchised sex with the thrills of periodic heresy hunts drew crowds to London.

Many NUSEC delegates were engaged in practical professional work. 'The professional feminist has now almost disappeared.'[16]

What might be thought a symbolic comment on the recession of the feminist tide was made some months later with the report of an all-male committee appointed by the Government to examine conditions of service and employment in the civil service. It opposed equal pay for women and recommended salary reductions for certain categories of women employees. The committee was chaired by Elizabeth's son Alan Garrett Anderson, whose upbringing and family ties were of little avail against post-war anxiety to preserve male domination and return to the comforting certainties of the past.[17]

Yet as Mrs Fawcett persisted in pointing out both publicly and privately, events in the early 1920s made reality of some longstanding feminist aspirations. She wrote to Amy Badley in June 1923 in delight when, in large part due to NUSEC lobbying,[18] the scandal of unequal access to divorce was at last rectified:

> Every year's experience of the voting power of women brings home to me the tremendous value of what we won in 1918. The passage of the equal divorce law last Friday by that immense majority is evidence enough in itself of why we struggled so long and unceasingly for the right of self protection through representation. It is a wonderful piece of good fortune for me to have lived to see my dream come true.[19]

Another cause for rejoicing in 1923 was the result of the general election, which returned eight women to the House of Commons, but another election within a year cut their number in half; Mrs Wintringham was among those who lost their seats.[20]

Although no longer an officer of the International Woman Suffrage Alliance Mrs Fawcett did not lose her interest in its operations. In a speech to the NUSEC annual council in March 1923 she called attention to the IWSA congress to be held in Rome the following May. 'British women were not really free themselves', she declared, 'as long as women in other countries did not share their freedom.' She also spoke hopefully about the political and educational enfranchisement of Muslim Palestinian women.[21] At the Rome congress Carrie Chapman Catt stepped down after nearly twenty years as IWSA president and was succeeded by Margery Corbett Ashby. Soon afterwards Mrs Fawcett was appointed a member of the headquarters committee, a body whose diminished importance involved much less commitment of time and energy than in earlier years.[22]

To modern readers the delay before women were granted the vote on equal terms with men may seem insignificant and their eventual victory inevitable. This was by no means the case, though bills for granting votes to younger women were introduced in almost every year after 1918, and 222 Members of Parliament signed a memorial for equal citizenship in 1922.[23] In the early 1920s Mrs Fawcett renewed her public concern for women's suffrage, though the changed conditions of the period meant that mass campaigns were no longer in vogue. It was time to intervene, for the youthful 'flappers' of the period were the subject of widespread comment and disapproval, even on the part of some suffragists. In a debate at the London School of Economics in March 1924 Lady Frances Balfour spoke longingly of the young woman of the past, whom she asserted had been deeply concerned with political and religious life. Her successor of the 1920s did her best to imitate the courtesan, 'her face a mass of powder, her red lips gashed out of all human resemblance'.[24]

Mrs Fawcett was soon to emerge as the champion of the 'modern girl', but what brought her into the suffrage controversy once more was a series of claims on the part of Conservative MPs that the suffrage issue had been settled in 1918 for an agreed period of at least ten years. She replied at length with her usual detailed references, pointing out that suffragists had accepted the 1918 measure as a compromise and quoting Lord Curzon, who had referred in the House of Lords to the age limit of thirty as 'arbitrary, artificial, and illogical'. In fact, she wrote, 'we had never hauled down our flag'.[25] Chances of achieving the goal of equal suffrage now seemed good, with a Labour Government in office and such suffrage champions as Philip Snowden and Arthur Henderson in leading positions. But the Government prevaricated, and its sudden fall in October 1924 came too soon for Henderson's half promises to be put to the test.[26]

As she grew into old age she naturally suffered the death of associates, friends and family, and the added burden of writing their obituaries and speaking at memorial services. Among the most prominent was Emily Davies, whom she had disliked in youth, but to whom she grew somewhat closer late in life. She wrote a graceful letter to Margaret Llewelyn Davies, Emily's niece and Bertrand Russell's confidante in the adult suffrage controversy within the NUWSS before the war, praising her aunt's services to the women's movement from its beginnings, and explaining that her duties as a magistrate had prevented her from attending the funeral.[27] She wrote about Isabella Ford, who had loved 'dearest Millie' so long and unselfishly, in warm and relatively unguarded terms, and spoke at her memorial service.[28] Sam, Alice and Josephine, three of her remaining siblings, died betwen 1923 and 1925. She described Alice in the year before her death as 'a great dear' in a letter to Ray Strachey,[29] but Sam's death in 1923 was a harder blow. He had been a suffragist, from his strategic position as a prominent solicitor a leading supporter of women's entry to the legal profession, and a much loved brother. 'In our big family', she wrote to Philippa Strachey, 'he came next to me & we were always close friends & comrades. I miss him more than I can say.'[30] Harry's sister Maria Fawcett, with whom Millicent had remained on affectionate terms during her years of widowhood, died in the same year, at the age of 93, and was also much missed. [31]

It was in 1923 that she was finally persuaded to write her memoirs, not an easy task despite her felicity with words, for she had a rooted objection to writing about herself.[32] The book, printed in instalments in the *Woman's*

*Leader*, was published in 1924 as *What I Remember*. Contemporaries criticized her reticence about herself, while historians have termed it 'bland' and
'disappointing'.[33] The criticisms are reasonable. Though it could not be
expected that she would write uninhibitedly about living people, the book
is pallid beside Sylvia Pankhurst's riveting *The Suffragette Movement* (1931),
and a far less valuable record than Ray Strachey's *The Cause*, published in
1928. A section about the wartime conflict within the NUWSS published
in the *Woman's Leader* was not bland, but it was blatantly unfair and was
fortunately omitted from the book.[34]

None the less, there is a good deal of information to be gathered or
inferred from a book of 'charming memories',[35] and its account of her early
life made a considerable contribution to social history. For those who
searched, the book contained revealing 'incidents and touches of character'.
Reviewers had no difficulty in discerning that she was 'a truly happy warrior', and that her combined 'national' and individual qualities made her an
appropriate and outstanding leader, despite her lack of personal magne-
tism.[36] Moreover, it was no easy task to write in a manner which satisfied
the curiosity of contemporaries or a later age in which reticence is a vice.
Ray Strachey criticized the book trenchantly though affectionately in both a
private letter and a published review. 'If the thing was "what I remember
about you" it would be so very different', she told the author.[37] Yet when
she had her opportunity she wrote a biography of Mrs Fawcett which was to
be criticized for its 'almost baffling reserve'.[38]

By the mid-1920s many of Mrs Fawcett's commitments were largely
ceremonial. She returned to the London Society for Women's Service
(formerly Suffrage) executive in 1923 when she succeeded her daughter
Philippa as president.[39] A happy occasion was the jubilee dinner of the
London School of Medicine for Women in 1924, at which the pioneering
work of her sister Elizabeth was praised and she received an ovation when
she rose to reply to the toast to 'women's work'.[40] Another was the public
celebration of the return of an unprecedented number of women to the
House of Commons in 1923, at which she was a principal speaker.[41]

But the fact that she had become something of a living legend did not
prevent her from remaining an influential voice in demanding reforms in
women's conditions abroad and at home. In February 1922, for example,
she led a deputation to Lord Lytton, a staunch ally in the pre-war suffrage
struggle and now the recently appointed governor of Bengal, to ask for
political and educational reforms for Bengalese women. Lytton's sister Lady
Constance Lytton, who as a militant had written to Mrs Fawcett a decade
earlier to deplore her criticisms of the Women's Social and Political Union ,
now wrote to express thanks 'for having spoken exactly in the right spirit –
my brother felt overcome and sincerely grateful to you'.[42] In July 1925 she
addressed an international conference of women in science and industry at
the Empire Exhibition at Wembley in unusually sombre mood. Women's

lowly position in industry she termed 'one of the disappointments of my life'. During the war women had done 'such wonderful things, things that surprised everybody . . . Where is all that gone now?'[43] On a less public level she remained chairman of the East Anglian Sanatorium, in whose affairs she was much more than a figurehead. Detailed notes survive from the mid-1920s in which she manifested her concern about domestic and financial arrangements.[44]

The progress of a graceful old age, in which she was treated with almost universal acclamation, was rudely interrupted by differences of opinion which gradually became irreconcilable. The wartime growth of government, the development of the Labour party and the onset of economic slump had had profound repercussions on the women's movement. Moreover, in Eleanor Rathbone the movement had elected a leader with radical views of the future of feminism, as firm in her convictions and unwilling to compromise as Mrs Fawcett herself, as she had shown in the pre-war controversy over the Election Fighting Fund.[45] In consequence Mrs Fawcett's most serious battle in the 1920s was fought not against external social and legal constraints on women, but over differing interpretations within the feminist movement of their needs and rights.

The issue was family endowment, or allowances, which as an enduring advocate of *laissez-faire* economics she had opposed since she had first encountered suggestions of 'subsidising motherhood'. An early example was a review of *The Woman Socialist* (1907), which the author, Ethel Snowden, had probably forgotten when she referred publicly to Mrs Fawcett in 1925 as 'my beloved friend'.[46] The review expressed alarm at the prospect of the ideal socialist society depicted by Mrs Snowden in which the state would assume a major share of responsibility for the cost of child care: 'To some this is a dream; to others, and probably a majority, it is a nightmare.' Most men and women associated with 'this Socialist nightmare of abolishing the ordinary responsibilities of marriage and substituting for them State salaries for mothers' were childless, she observed snidely. If the state were to guarantee comfort for all it would have to control marriage and the number of children born, 'a remedy worse than the disease it is intended to remove'.[47]

The movement for family endowment, stimulated by the wartime payment of separation allowances to servicemen's wives and children, took its first organized form in 1917, when Rathbone founded the Family Endowment Committee. Four of its seven members were or had been among the leaders of the NUWSS.[48] It is not necessaray to discuss in detail a controversy which has spawned a large literature,[49] but the issue became increasingly prominent in the 1920s, dividing NUSEC in 1925 and contributing to a serious split in the union two years later. The protagonists were inspired by opposing visions of the meaning of women's equality, but battle lines were not symmetrical either within or outside the women's movement, as illustrated by divisions within the Labour party on the issue.[50]

Rathbone's continuing advocacy of family endowment in the wider political world gradually became highly controversial within NUSEC. Mrs Fawcett wrote to the *Woman's Leader* in 1922 to express her strong opposition to the scheme. It would, she claimed, be a major disincentive to the willingness of parents to bear the responsibility of caring for their children.[51] The rebirth of the original committee, subsequently council, as the Family Endowment Society and the publication of Rathbone's influential book *The Disinherited Family* in 1924 brought the incipient conflict within NUSEC closer to an open breach. 'A man has no right', she wrote in answer to Mrs Fawcett, 'to want to keep half the world in purgatory, because he enjoys playing redeemer to his own wife and children.'[52]

NUSEC annual councils discussed family endowment on several occasions from 1919, but it was not until 1925 that an open breach developed. By this time Mrs Fawcett was heavily involved with the issue. She explained herself at length in an article in the *Woman's Leader* and more briefly in *The Vote*. Her principal argument remained the question of family responsibility. If parents were relieved of their legal burden to support their children, she wrote, 'one of the very strongest inducements to submit to the drudgery of daily toil would be withdrawn'. Family endowment was altogether different from the provision of hospitals, schools and parks at public expense, for such subsidies did not undermine parental responsibility. It would also attack the English principle of self-government and deprive wage-earners of the power to decide how to spend their wages. A scheme for family endowment would be a capital levy under another name, a vast amount of money which would necessarily reduce capital available for investment in trade and industry. 'We are already the most heavily taxed people in the world.' She claimed that the nation had made 'immense' physical and moral progress since the end of the eighteenth century. It was much more sensible to continue in the same manner than 'to upset the whole fabric of domestic life'. With a reference to a famous essay by Charles Lamb she commented: 'It is bad economics to burn down your house to roast your pig.'[53]

Eleanor Rathbone's commitment to family endowment may demonstrate her primary commitment to social reform rather than feminism.[54] It seems more accurate, however, to accept her own distinction between what she termed 'the old and the new feminism'. The world of the 1920s had changed but the changes had been disappointingly incomplete. Most women now voted, but their progress in the professions had been limited and in industry retrograde since the end of the war. Women's leaders, she told the NUSEC annual council in March 1925, felt 'baffled and rather helpless' in the face of 'deep-rooted economic causes'. The answer, she suggested, lay in social reforms of a type particularly beneficial to women: 'The achievement of freedom is a much bigger thing than the breaking off of shackles.'[55] Family endowment lay at the centre of her vision of feminist social reform.

The issue was fought out at the NUSEC annual council in March 1925. Mrs Fawcett, newly created a dame, received an ovation when she rose to move a resolution to urge the Government to establish without delay a proposed all-party conference on equal suffrage. The following day she led the opposition to a motion moved by Eleanor Rathbone to commit NUSEC to the principle of family allowances. Her speech took her audience through the arguments she had published in the *Woman's Leader* a few weeks earlier. Family allowances would weaken parental responsibility and cripple productive industry, and were unnecessary in view of the steady improvement in social conditions in the past century. It would be a much better alternative to give the wife a specified share of her husband's income. The paper reported that her speech was delivered with 'great moderation relieved by many characteristic touches of humour and racy and apposite anecdotes'.

The debate was an echo of the divisions on war and peace which had split the NUWSS a decade earlier, and the battle lines presented an interesting contrast to those of 1915. Mrs Fawcett's supporters included Chrystal Macmillan, a leading internationalist during the war years. Among her opponents were not only Eleanor Rathbone and Mary Stocks, who had been strong advocates of the patriotic line, but Kathleen Courtney, who now found herself in the majority against her old leader and antagonist. The amendment to delay a decision was defeated by 122 to 45; the motion of support passed by 111 to 42. It was a convincing and unprecedented vote against the union's former leader and most revered figure. It was also a rebuff which might have endangered the periodic anonymous gifts of £1,000 made via Mrs Fawcett to the NUSEC and the LSWS. Some at least of these gifts had been made by a wealthy supporter named Sarah Clegg, most recently in recognition of her creation as dame at the start of the year.[56]

The NUSEC council was followed not only by her resignation as chairman of the board of directors of the *Woman's Leader*, but as an individual member of NUSEC itself.[57] It was, however, an unusual kind of resignation. Several months earlier she had written to Eleanor Rathbone that 'no difference of opinion will ever break our affectionate friendship', and her resignation letter published in the *Woman's Leader* was equally generous.[58] She remained a NUSEC vice-president, and her serialized account of her visits to Palestine in 1921 and 1922 continued to be published in the paper. Her letters, articles and reviews continued to appear periodically in its pages, and she remained in close contact with the NUSEC leaders, particularly in support of the campaign for equal franchise. A greater contrast with the bitter split of 1915 could hardly be imagined.

Her appointment as Dame Grand Cross of the British Empire was made possible by the creation in 1917 of the Order of the British Empire, which admitted women to membership from its inception. For some time there had been complaints that she had been unjustly excluded from the honours list. *The Observer*, for example, criticized her omission from the list submitted by Stanley Baldwin when he resigned as Prime Minister early in 1924: 'Her position is unique. Recognition would have been universally applauded.'[59] A few months later press reports suggested that she was to be honoured, but it was not until the New Year honours of 1925 that the award was finally made. Henceforth she was known as Dame Millicent Fawcett.[60]

The pleasure within the women's movement was tempered by the fact that the award was not a more prestigious one. The *Manchester Guardian's* London correspondent wrote that women had long wished to see Mrs Fawcett's name in an honours list, but they had hoped that she would receive 'the coveted Order of Merit'. The following day the paper published a letter from Florence Underwood of the Women's Freedom League, suggesting that she would have 'rendered invaluable service' in the House of Lords.[61] But if there was disappointment in some quarters it did not stand in the way of enthusiastic celebrations.

The new dame was warmly received at the annual meeting of the Council for the Representation of Women in the League of Nations a fortnight after receiving her honour. The president commented appropriately that recognition had been made of her 'great life work for women and for the Empire'.[62] The following month a formal reception was held at Claridge's Hotel to honour the three new dames: Mrs Fawcett, the actress Ellen Terry and the surgeon Louisa Aldrich-Blake. Three little girls, representing social service, drama and science, laid wreaths at their feet, and each woman received a white vellum album embroidered with gold from Princess Helena Victoria.[63] 'Dame Millicent Fawcett's elegant curtsey as she received the book', the *Manchester Guardian* reported, 'was much admired.' It also noted the presence of the faithful Agnes, her resemblance to her sister so great that she received frequent congratulations from well-wishers.[64]

A reception for Mrs Fawcett and other guests of honour, which she told Amy Badley had been 'most successful', was held at the NUSEC council in March 1925,[65] but the union's principal celebration was delayed until July because of the death of her sisters Alice and Josephine. It took the form of a garden party at Aubrey House, formerly the home of the suffragists Clementia and Peter Taylor, where the young Millicent Garrett had first attracted the attention of Henry Fawcett in 1865.[66] It was a moving occasion, and the album which she received included hundreds of signatures of friends and admirers, many of which contained affecting messages.[67] The *Woman's Leader* noted the presence of a number of former NUWSS colleagues, including Kathleen Courtney and Margaret Ashton, another former colleague and antagonist. It also noted the absence of Catherine Marshall, present, 'one hoped . . . in spirit'. There were also former militants and many active workers for women, some of them under 30 and hence voteless.[68] Although

*The three new dames, February 1925; seated from right: Louisa Aldrich-Blake, Ellen Terry, Millicent Garrett Fawcett.*

Mrs Fawcett was a symbol not only of what had been achieved but of what remained to be achieved, her honour was evidence that her type of feminism was acceptable to the nation's political and social leaders. This was emphasized by a message from Lord Cecil of Chelwood, formerly Lord Robert Cecil, describing her as 'one of the outstanding figures of her time, who had always stood for what was right nationally and internationally'. Mrs Fawcett too struck a patriotic note by commenting that the same women who had worked for the suffrage later became organizers of women's war work.[69]

Though now aged 78 she maintained a lively interest in travel, books and the women's cause. Her closing years were to be marked by continued activity and by celebrations of women's achievements. Her enthusiasm is easy to understand if one considers the growth of women's freedom since she began her public work nearly sixty years earlier. There was, for a woman approaching her eightieth birthday, much to celebrate.

NOTES

1. MGF to Badley, 16 April 1921 (FLALC, vol. 14).
2. Louisa Garrett Anderson in *WL*, 15 November 1929, p. 315.
3. This paragraph draws on the books cited; MGF articles in the *WL*, 11 March, 15 April, 13 May 1921, pp. 87, 165–6, 226; 14 July 1922, p. 188; 18 March, 8 April, 6, 13 May 1927, pp. 44, 73, 105, 113; 30 March, 6 April 1928, pp. 64, 71–2; and *The Times Literary Supplement* review of *Easter in Palestine*, 18 March 1926, p. 192.
4. *WL*, 19 March 1920, pp. 162–3.
5. *ibid.*, 22 July 1921, p. 378.
6. See above pages 269–71.
7. Philippa Strachey to MGF [August 1921]; MGF to Philippa Strachey, 12 August 1921 (FLALC, vol. 2e). For the authoritative account of women's unequal position in the inter-war civil service see Meta Zimmeck, 'Strategies and stratagems for the employment of women in the British Civil Service, 1919–1939', *Historical Journal* (vol. 17, 1984), pp. 901–24.
8. MGF, *What the Vote has Done* (1922).
9. *The Times*, 14 June 1922.
10. *WL*, 23, 30 September 1921, pp. 454, 462; MGF, *What the Vote has Done*.
11. Lord Robert Cecil to MGF (copy), 31 May 1922 (Cecil of Chelwood Papers, BL Add. Mss).
12. MGF to Cecil, 2 June 1922 (*ibid.*).
13. *WL*, 24 November 1922, pp. 338–9.
14. *ibid.*, p. 337. In fact, while Lady Astor's majority was comfortable, Mrs Wintringham's was insecure, as was shown in 1924.
15. *ibid.*, 5 January 1923, p. 390.
16. *ibid.*, 16 March 1923, p. 51. In February 1915 Dorothea Rackham had led the polling for the executive with 473 votes (NUWSS, *Annual Council Proceedings*; M50/2/6/2); in March 1923 Mary Stocks was in the same position with 135 votes (*WL*, 16 March 1923, p. 55).
17. *The Times*, 7, 11, 18, 22 September 1923; *WL*, 14 September 1923, p. 257.
18. Mary Stocks, *Eleanor Rathbone* (1949), p. 112.

19. MGF to Badley, 11 June 1923 (FLALC, vol. 14). The third reading of the Matrimonial Causes Act passed the House of Commons on 8 June by 257 votes to 26.
20. *WL*, 14 December 1923, p. 371; 7 November 1924, p. 326.
21. *MG*, 9 March 1923.
22. International Alliance of Women for Suffrage and Equal Citizenship, *Report of Tenth Congress* (1926), pp. 46, 53.
23. MGF, *What the Vote has Done* (1924, 1927 edns); *MG*, 28 June, 3 August 1922.
24. *The Times*, 19 March 1924.
25. *ibid.*, 6 June 1924.
26. *MG*, 30 May, 5 August 1924.
27. MGF to Margaret Llewelyn Davies, 20 July 1921 (Girton Archives, Cambridge). Her obituary notice appeared in the *WL*, 22 July 1921, p. 372.
28. *WL*, 25 July, 1 August 1924, pp. 208–9, 218.
29. MGF to Ray Strachey, 27 February 1924 (Strachey Papers, Oxford).
30. MGF to Philippa Strachey, 31 May 1923 (FLALC, vol. 8); *MGF*, p. 355.
31. *MGF*, p. 355.
32. *ibid.*, p. 343.
33. *Westminster Gazette*, 4 December 1924; *The Times*, 5 December 1924 (Fawcett Library biographical cuttings); Martin Pugh, *Women's Suffrage* (1980), p. 40; Brian Harrison, *Prudent Revolutionaries* (1987), p. 326.
34. *WL*, 25 July 1924, p. 208. This was the only section of the serialized version not published in the book. See above, page 224.
35. *Time and Tide*, 5 December 1924, p. 1190.
36. *New Statesman*, 14 February 1925, p. 542; *Evening Standard*, 1 January 1925; (Fawcett Library cuttings); *International Woman Suffrage News*, January 1925, p. 61.
37. Ray Strachey to MGF, 30 May 1924 (Strachey Papers); *WL*, 5 December 1924, p. 361.
38. *WL*, 19 June 1931, p. 155.
39. LSWS, *Annual Reports* (Fawcett Library).
40. *The Times*, 27 October 1924; *WL*, 31 October 1924.
41. *The Times*, 8 December 1923.
42. Constance Lytton to MGF, 22 February 1912 (M50/2/1/353), 17 March 1922 (FLA, box 90 vol. 6); *Catholic Citizen*, 15 March 1922, p. 19.
43. *Woman Engineer*, September 1925, pp. 60–1.
44. General Secretary's correspondence, East Anglian Sanatorium Company, c. 1925 (Jane Walker Hospital Records, Bury St Edmunds).
45. See above, pages 194–5.
46. As note 43.
47. MGF, review of *The Woman Socialist*, *Economic Journal*, September 1907, pp. 376–8. Cp. p. 52 above.
48. Stocks, *Eleanor Rathbone*, p. 84.
49. A minimum list includes Jane Lewis's two articles: 'Beyond suffrage: English feminism in the 1920s', *Maryland Historian* (vol. 6, 1973), pp. 1–17; and 'The English movement for family allowances, 1917–1945', *Histoire Sociale–Social History* (vol. 11, 1978), pp. 441–59; John Macnicol, *The Movement for Family Allowances, 1918–45* (Heinemann, 1980); Carol Dyhouse, *Feminism and the Family in England 1880–1939* (1989), pp. 92–104; and Hilary Land, 'Eleanor Rathbone and the economy of the family' in Harold Smith (ed.), *British Feminism in the Twentieth Century* (1990), pp. 104–23.
50. Stocks, *Eleanor Rathbone*, pp. 95–6, 101, 144–5.
51. *WL*, 22 September 1922, p. 271.

52. Eleanor Rathbone, *The Disinherited Family* (Allen & Unwin, 1924), p. 272.
53. MGF, 'The case against family endowment', *WL*, 30 January 1925, pp. 3–5; MGF, 'Family endowment', *The Vote*, 12 June 1925, p. 189.
54. As suggested by her contemporary Crystal Eastman (Blanche Wiesen Cook (ed.), *Crystal Eastman on Women and Revolution* (New York: Oxford University Press, 1978), pp. 228–9); and by Lewis, 'Beyond suffrage', pp. 11–14.
55. *WL*, 13 March 1925, pp. 51–2. For discussion of the old and new feminism see Stocks, *Eleanor Rathbone*, ch. 9; Lewis, 'Beyond Suffrage'; Johanna Alberti, *Beyond Suffrage* (1989), chs. 6–7.
56. The previous two paragraphs draw on the *MG*, 21 February, 12 and 13 March 1925; *The Times*, 13 March 1925; *WL*, 9 January, 20 March 1925, pp. 403, 61–2. For Sarah Clegg's gifts see also *MGF*, pp. 226, 336, 345, 354; FLALC, vol. 1m (MGF note on telegram dated 1 November 1923 and Philippa Strachey to MGF, 19 November 1926); and *WL*, 26 December 1930, p. 354.
57. *WL*, 10 April 1925, p. 84; Cook (ed.), p. 229; *MGF*, p. 335.
58. Stocks, *Eleanor Rathbone*, p. 118; *WL*, 10 April 1925, p. 84.
59. *The Observer*, 10 February 1924. See also *Time and Tide*, 15 February 1924, pp. 147–9.
60. *MGF*, p. 345. It was commonly observed that it would be difficult to call her anything other than Mrs Fawcett. The difficulty will not be resisted here.
61. *MG*, 1 and 2 January 1925. The Order of Merit, instituted in 1902, was awarded to Florence Nightingale in 1907, then to no other woman until 1965. Women were first admitted to the House of Lords with the creation of life peerages in 1958.
62. *WL*, 23 January 1925, p. 419.
63. Mrs Fawcett's is preserved in FLA, box 90c file 4.
64. *MG*, 11 February 1925.
65. MGF to Badley, 12 March 1925 (FLALC, vol. 14); *WL*, 20 March 1925, p. 62.
66. See above, pages 11 and 12 n. 41.
67. It is preserved in FLA, box 90c file 5.
68. *WL*, 31 July 1925, p. 213; *Time and Tide*, 31 July 1925, pp. 739–40.
69. *The Times*, 24 July 1925.

# CHAPTER 20

————— · —————

## STILL CAMPAIGNING 1925–9

Millicent Garrett Fawcett was not among those women who, according to Brian Harrison's entertaining anecdotes, led inter-war feminism with their dresses inside out and their hats the wrong way round.[1] Yet like other upper-middle-class feminists she was little concerned by convenience or comfort. Ann Wiltsher's account, drawn from a reminiscence by Rosika Schwimmer, of her reluctance to travel by taxi in August 1914 to appeal for peace at the various national embassies was overlaid by bitter political differences, but it carries the ring of truth.[2] Mrs Fawcett did not possess a telephone, she wrote her own letters, she travelled by bus even when over 80, with little regard to her own safety.[3] Her agility was demonstrated by her visits to the author Gwen John, whom she did not meet until she was 80, travelling by foot or bus and climbing five flights of stairs to John's flat.[4]

An appealing account was given in 1960 to Jo Manton, biographer of her sister Elizabeth, by an elderly woman who had, presumably briefly, been Mrs Fawcett's resident secretary at her Gower Street home. The events described, though they probably took place before the 1920s, were typical of her behaviour towards her correspondents and her younger associates. 'All letters were answered the same day. [The secretary] sat at her post, but Millicent said "It does not seem altogether courteous to answer a letter by typewriter", and wrote herself.' As midnight approached she told the young woman that her parents would not wish her to be out so late, and with a 'Good night, my dear', she went out herself in time for the last postal collection.[5]

A report of a meeting in December 1927 which she entertained with anecdotes about her travels by bus appeared below the heading: 'Mrs Fawcett Tries a Cocktail. Praise of the Modern Girl. Good Legs and Good Manners.'[6] By this time she had become a prominent champion of 'the blessed young', a term which she had borrowed from Sir Hubert Parry.[7] Youth was a cause which she could endorse uninhibitedly, involving her professional optimism, concern to win the battle for equal franchise and her own convictions. In a letter to *The Times* in April 1926 she had defended the behaviour and manners of the young, praising their independence, sincerity and frankness.[8] She told the December 1927 meeting that she thought modern girls 'perfectly splendid', picking out their pink silk stockings for particular praise: 'I like their legs and I like their short petticoats. There is nothing wrong with their legs; they are perfectly beautiful. Such nice straight legs are a credit to us.'[9]

The spectacle of a woman of 80 praising the legs of the young was not without its comic aspect, as *Punch* realized. It published a flaccid poem intended to be gently mocking, calling attention to her recommendation of coloured stockings for both sexes as protection against traffic.[10] Nothing daunted, Mrs Fawcett retorted that it had been her good fortune to have her championship of the young celebrated in this manner, 'a distinction of which I am very proud'. It had encouraged her, she wrote, to continue to collect facts which showed the young in a good light.[11]

She was similarly concerned to show that attitudes to women and morality in Britain had improved since the previous century. This was an easy task. In April 1929 she sent Ray Strachey a cutting from *The Times* reproducing a report published a century earlier, suggesting that a wife who had committed adultery might find her only solace in death. Two months later, only weeks before her death, she sent another cutting for possible use in a radio programme: 'The difference between then & now is very remarkable, & *now* is so much more wholesome than *then*.'[12]

Her introduction to the cocktail in 1926 was perhaps an exception to the wholesomeness of 'now'. In a speech to a public meeting staged by the National Union of Societies for Equal Citizenship she strongly defended the modern girl, notably from the charge that she was 'a constant imbiber of cocktails'. Soon afterwards she was brought 'a bottle of "cocktail" ' contributed by donors, most of them abstainers, and members of NUSEC and other women's organizations. The bottle was kept for a Sunday evening treat, she recalled, but with less than total success: 'I had certainly tasted worse things, but my sister said she was sure she never had.'[13]

One aspect of 'now' about which there could be no ambiguity was the final grant of votes to women aged between 21 and 30, as well as certain previously disqualified categories of older women. NUSEC had by this time drifted away from its earlier close links with the Labour party[14] and it was left to Stanley Baldwin's Conservatives, in office between 1924 and 1929, to gain the credit for the final political emancipation of women. Mrs Fawcett took part in a NUSEC rally at Central Hall, Westminster, on 26 February 1926, and in an open-air demonstration in London the following July. This was 'probably the nearest approach to one of the great suffrage demonstrations of pre-war days that the present generation is likely to see', the *Manchester Guardian* commented.[15] Mrs Fawcett, Mrs Pankhurst and Mrs Despard all took part, the last-named joining the march despite the handicap of 82 years. 'One saw people running to the platform when Dame Millicent Fawcett, on rising to speak, was greeted with the truthful but incongruous assurance that she was a jolly good fellow.'[16]

Her case for votes for younger women rested on two main arguments. The first was that Britain was alone in discriminating against them. Not only the white dominions but also Burma had introduced the vote on equal terms, and Norway had done so six years after the partial enfranchisement of women in 1907. The second was that the country needed the voice of the young, and they should be given their opportunity: 'They will grow old quickly enough; but let us benefit from their youth as long as it lasts for helping on the right solution of the great problems that lie before us.'[17] One young woman whose voice had been heard was Barbara Wootton, in 1926 principal of Morley College. She was a member of the Committee on National Debt and Taxation appointed by the Labour Government in 1924 when she was only 26 and hence unable to vote. 'It is not a good thing in any country to maintain a law which is flagrantly at variance with common-sense and justice.'[18]

Even in early 1927 the Conservative Government hesitated about whether or not to introduce the 'flapper' vote.[19] The *Manchester Guardian* reported opposition within both the Cabinet and the Conservative party in Parliament.[20] The King's speech early in 1927 made no reference to the subject and Lord Salisbury told the House of Lords that it was still being considered.[21] On 28 January twenty-two prominent women, Mrs Fawcett among them, wrote to *The Times* to ask that the previous undertakings of Conservative ministers be honoured. The 'great majority of industrial and professional women' were excluded from the vote, they claimed.[22] Subsequently, at the behest of Philippa Strachey, she sent a telegram to every member of the Cabinet and then signed a letter to *The Times* which had been drafted by Eleanor Rathbone. It pointed out that the Government had been committed to introduce equal franchise by a statement made by the Home Secretary in 1925.[23] After a long debate in Cabinet Baldwin announced in the House of Commons on 13 April that the measure would be introduced into the next session of Parliament.[24]

Although the Commons endorsed the bill overwhelmingly, suffragists had many anxieties before they were able to celebrate their final victory in July 1928. Mrs Fawcett took advantage of her semi-retired status to visit Palestine for a fourth time early in 1928, but she took some part in the public campaign for the vote, speaking at a meeting in Trafalgar Square in July 1927 and writing at length to *The Times* the following October.[25]

The bill itself was reassuring. Writing to Alys Russell from Jerusalem in March 1928 she commented that it was 'just perfect'. She had feared that it would have disqualified recipients of the 'dole', thus risking the loss of Labour party support.[26] Replying to her letter of thanks after its passage Stanley Baldwin told her: 'We have had our difficulties with the Bill but I never doubted we should get it through in the simple and complete form it ultimately assumed.'[27] The articles which she wrote after its passage were unremarkable, but it is worth noting that in her moment of final triumph she acknowledged the enormous contribution of the militant suffrage campaign and of Mrs Pankhurst, who had died in June 1928.[28] At a celebration at Cliveden, the Astor country house, she was reported as 'looking so ridiculously young that it was impossible to believe that she has lived through the whole Parliamentary movement'.[29]

The previous year she had celebrated her eightieth birthday. About 200 friends and admirers marked the occasion by raising £1,000 to endow a Dame Millicent Fawcett study bedroom in Crosby Hall, a fifteenth-century mansion in Chelsea which had been reconstructed and enlarged, and opened as an international hall of residence for university women.[30] Its associations with More and Erasmus made it of particular importance in her eyes. The generous *Manchester Guardian* report commented that she remained 'happily vigorous in mind and body', a view supported by her letter of thanks which called attention to the paper's exaggeration of her contribution to the infant suffrage movement of the 1860s.[31] She also pointed out to Philippa and Ray Strachey a misprint in Ray's history of the London and National Society for Women's Service which they had given her.[32] Among the messages of congratulation which she received was a felicitously worded telegram from her old colleague and sparring partner Carrie Chapman Catt: 'Congratulations upon your long life your leadership your achievements your host of friends. You have made this a different world for women.'[33]

Despite her supposed dislike of public speaking she continued to appear on platforms until shortly before her death. It was Mrs Fawcett who was asked to propose the toast at the silver wedding of Emmeline and Frederick Pethick-Lawrence in October 1926, a significant choice in view of their pre-war quarrels over militancy, and the fact that Fred was now a Labour Member of Parliament. As usual she appears to have found the right words, since Emmeline told the gathering that she had been 'deeply moved' by her speech.[34] In June of the same year, taking the place of Maude Royden, she was a principal speaker at a rally in Hyde Park which marked the end of the Women's Peace Pilgrimage, a large-scale event modelled on the NUWSS Pilgrimage of 1913.[35] She had recently returned from the International Woman Suffrage Association congress in Paris, and told her listeners that it had been a demonstration for peace through the League of Nations as well as for women. She appealed for 'a finer, saner spirit' which would avoid future wars, a spirit which did not conflict with the brightly burning fire of her own patriotism.[36]

Her visits to Palestine in 1927 and 1928 had taken place at the time of the NUSEC annual councils, but she attended the 1929 council, where her appearance and reception provided further evidence that her resignation from the union in 1925 had been more nominal than real. She moved the first resolution, celebrating the passage of the equal franchise act and calling the attention of delegates to the need to concentrate on the future development of feminism. They must work, she said, to achieve equal opportunity for all women and to educate women to use their vote to best advantage.[37] Some weeks later she laid the foundation stone for the new headquarters of the London and National Society for Women's Service, with whose predecessor bodies she had so long been connected, and of which she remained honorary president. She reminisced about her sixty-one years in the movement and the friends she had made, and again called attention to the rights and opportunities which still remained to be gained if the equality of the sexes were to be realized. Even now, a few weeks before her eighty-second birthday, the press commented on her youthful appearance as well as her obvious happiness.[38]

Like her speaking appearances, her writing continued until her death. She sent articles, travel notes, reviews, obituary notices and useful cuttings to the *Woman's Leader*, and her last article, found among her papers, was a review duly published after her death.[39] But even at 80 she did not rest content with ephemeral articles, and at the end of 1927 she published a biography of Josephine Butler, written jointly with Ethel M. Turner, secretary of the committee established to commemorate the Butler centenary in 1928. Among the committee's functions was a London meeting in April at which Mrs Fawcett was one of the speakers to an audience of 2,500 people.[40] An obituary in *The Shield*, the journal of the Association for Moral and Social Hygiene, successor to Josephine Butler's Ladies' National Association, presents a graphic picture of her near the close of her life: 'Till within a few weeks of her death she was in the habit of climbing our fifty odd stairs, arriving at the top without visible effort or fatigue. It is, indeed, almost impossible to imagine her flustered or out of breath.'

Although she was a vice-president of the association, it was not until the Butler centenary that she became well-known in its office: 'The manuscript of her book was typed in the office and it frequently happened that the whole staff would engage in an attempt to elucidate her handwriting!'[41]

The result would sometimes be 'lamentable' and Mrs Fawcett joined the laughter when a blunder was exposed:

> But our affection and admiration had its roots in something deeper than appreciation of her friendliness and infectious gaiety . . . No leader of a great movement was ever so completely regardless of the prestige which such a position gives as Dame Millicent; no great lady was ever more simply courteous than she, or could more easily establish an equal human relationship with those whom she met. An hour spent in her company was a delightful experience. She would tell, in vivid language, story after story of bygone days and dead heroes, bringing both to life with the sure touch of genius.[42]

As this passage suggests, the bulk of the book appears to have been the work of Mrs Fawcett. She told Ray Strachey that she had found her impressions of Josephine Butler 'not easy to transfer into print',[43] and it cannot be claimed that the finished product was an outstanding contribution to scholarship. It suffered even more than some of her other books from oversimplification and lack of analysis of conflicting points of view. Even the friendly *Shield* remarked that it might have been improved by a touch of the 'mordant style' of Lytton Strachey.[44] In her first sentence she proclaimed her belief that Josephine Butler was 'the most distinguished Englishwoman of the nineteenth century', and at the end, casting round for a possible fault in the heroine she could cite only an extravagant gesture in filling a prostitute's grave with camelias.[45] The book was firmly based on contemporary sources, however, and the autobiographical touches by the principal author added to its interest.

It was perhaps typical that one of her longest journeys, made early in 1929, should have been her last. She and Agnes sailed to Ceylon where they met their niece Louisa Garrett Anderson, then on her way home from Australia. The two old ladies enjoyed the opportunity to relax and enjoy winter sunshine, though Millicent's reading made no concession to the passage of years, and she appears to have tired of their enforced leisure.[46] Her arrival in Colombo on 26 January on board the Orient Line's *Otranto* was a considerable local event, and the *Ceylon Daily News* published an interview with her on its front page. Asked why she had come to Ceylon she replied that she had wished to visit the East, 'and as I heard that the women's suffrage movement is making some advance in Ceylon, I decided to come here'. Women's suffrage, she told her interviewer, was appropriate in the East as well as the West. Soon afterwards, at a hall in Colombo, she addressed her final women's suffrage meeting. After a full programme of sightseeing the sisters sailed home on another Orient Line ship on 7 February.[47]

Although these final years were full of opportunities 'to stand and stare',[48] to indulge her passions for reading and listening to music and to enjoy the homage of her colleagues in the women's movement, they were not free from controversy. To the last she continued to make clear her opposition to important aspects of the 'new feminism'. In June 1926 she wrote at length to *The Times*, opposing family allowances on the old ground that they would reduce parental responsibility and result in higher taxes in an already overburdened country. She also pointed out that had family allowances already been in existence the state would have in effect helped to finance the General Strike the previous month. The strike had been defeated, she added gratuitously, 'mainly owing to the initiative and activity of large numbers of young men and women of all classes [who had] carried the gratitude of the country as a whole'.[49]

Eleanor Rathbone was among those stung to reply to this letter. Margery Corbett Ashby and two colleagues also wrote, maintaining that adequate parental care could not be provided without adequate income. Another correspondent argued that it was inconsistent to oppose family allowances for married men while simultaneously supporting the case for equal pay for men and women. Nothing daunted, Mrs Fawcett wrote the following month to reiterate her case and to deny the supposed inconsistency in her position. Moreover, whatever shortcomings there had been in protecting the nation's children, their health had improved, for infant mortality had fallen by half since the beginning of the century.[50]

The development of the new feminism brought about a division within the ranks of the national union executive which did not involve Mrs Fawcett directly but which raised issues with which she was deeply concerned. In consequence of decisions taken at the council meeting in March 1927 eleven members of the executive resigned, leaving a bare majority of the members elected the previous year. The principal point at issue was the weakening of the union's attitude to protective legislation affecting only women, but other issues of social reform were also involved, including family allowances and birth control.[51] Like the 1925 controversy this new division involved a number of women who had taken part in the 1915 schism, though alliances had changed, and among the 'new' feminists were a number of the executive's older members.[52] Mrs Fawcett wrote soon afterwards to Ray Strachey: 'I agree with you in believing that the fundamental cause of the split was the adoption by the N.U. of all kinds of objects which many of us believe to be either useless or mischievous or both.'[53] It was fortunate for the union that this ill-timed and somewhat reckless debate did not prevent the Government from announcing a month after the split its intention to legislate for equal franchise.

At 80 even Mrs Fawcett was too old to be leading campaigns, but she was a participant in the movement to oppose restrictive legislation until the end of her life. In November 1926 she was among twenty-eight women who signed a protest against a parliamentary bill intended to forbid women from employment which involved the use of lead paint. A bill which treated women as non-adults, the signatories wrote, which denied them the right of self-decision, was 'a retrograde measure', inspired by 'a false humanitarianism [and] doubtful facts'. Although the bill was passed the fight was not abandoned.[54] A further clash between opposing views occurred when she was visiting Ceylon early in 1929,[55] but a few days after her death her name was among the signatories of a letter to *The Times* which opposed suggestions of new restrictions on women's employment. In a postscript to the letter her former IWSA colleague Elizabeth Abbott, the leader of the movement against restrictions, wrote that she had studied the letter with care, suggested a minor alteration, signed it and asked for a fair copy.[56] Two days later her final illness began.

Her other interests at the end of her life were less controversial but no less characteristic. Late in 1927 she wrote the final revision of her NUSEC leaflet, *What the Vote has Done*, which now extended to eight pages. A final note commented on the improvement of parliamentary behaviour since women had obtained the vote in 1918: 'Democracy is a great teacher of manners.'[57] In the autumn of 1928 she wrote a series of articles for the

*Woman's Leader* on the first Queen Elizabeth, drawing on a recent biography by Gwen John.[58] The articles, with their mixture of patriotism and feminism, notably their praise of monarchs and Cecils, hardly needed an author's by-line, and they followed successful efforts by both writers to restore the contemporary statue of the Queen outside the church of St Dunstan in the West, Fleet Street. Money was raised and Mrs Fawcett unveiled the statue at the end of July 1928. In a letter to Ray Strachey a few days later she wrote: 'I have had a sheaf of nice newspapers cuttings about Queen Elizabeth. She has had quite a good press. I hope it will promote the sale of Miss Gwen John's book.'[59] She was also the moving spirit in a successful effort to secure legal prohibition of marriage below the age of 16, and her enduring interest in India was nicely symbolized by the fact that her final, posthumous article in the *Woman's Leader* was a review of a biography of Saroj Nalini, an Indian feminist.[60]

She remained active until her final weeks. In May 1929 she stayed in an old inn in Canterbury which, she noted, had been recommended by the French ambassador in the reign of the English Henry IV.[61] In June she visited Brighton, having received, she wrote, 'an invitation from my husband's old constituency' to visit a school;[62] Harry had died fifty-five years previously. She was delighted in the same month by the appointment of the first woman Cabinet minister, Margaret Bondfield, who was made Minister of Labour in Ramsay MacDonald's second Labour Government. 'The Rt. Hon. Margaret is such a nice title isn't it', she observed to Amy Badley. Bondfield herself, replying to Mrs Fawcett's letter of congratulations, wrote: 'Yes, my official title is "The Right Honourable Margaret", but I am the same as usual.'[63]

On 18 July, sixty years and a day after her first suffrage speech, she was a guest of honour at a NUSEC lunch given to celebrate the new Cabinet minister and the thirteen other women returned to the House of Commons.[64] It was her final public appearance. Three days later she fell ill, her worsening condition causing such widespread concern that a medical bulletin had to be posted outside her Bloomsbury home.[65] She died peacefully in the early morning of 5 August, nearly two months after her eighty-second birthday. As Mary Stocks recalled, she had died after celebrating a feminist victory, but had missed the worst of the economic depression and the onset of the international catastrophes of the 1930s. The account continued with an appropriately old-fashioned touch: 'The President of the Immortals behaved with great consideration when he led her gently away at this particular moment.'[66]

An unabated zeal for public causes and the care which she devoted to travel, music and literature had not prevented her from ensuring that her financial affairs remained buoyant. (In this respect also the date of her death was fortuitous.) A file in the Fawcett Library contains details of forty-six shareholdings which she purchased at various dates between 1896 and June

1929. They included government and local authority stocks and shares in such a variety of companies and causes as Bryant and May, the Orient Steam Navigation Company, the Bank of Egypt, the Buenos Ayres Pacific Railway, the Aldeburgh Gas Company, Artisans' and Labourers' Dwellings, Ladies' Residential Chambers, the First Garden City Ltd and the East Anglian Sanatorium Company, which she willed to its medical superintendent, her friend Jane Walker.[67] Her estate was valued at £23,045 6s 7d, which, even allowing for the change in the value of money since 1884, was considerably more than the £9,535 7s 2d left by Henry Fawcett.[68] Apart from £1,000 left to Philippa Strachey and an annuity of £500 to her sister Agnes the remainder of her estate was left to her daughter Philippa.[69]

Her death was marked by long obituaries in a variety of publications, from the daily and weekly press to feminist journals. Less expected notices appeared in *The Draughtsman*, the *Vaccination Inquirer*, which recalled her opposition to compulsory vaccination at the end of the nineteenth century, and the *Catholic Herald*, attacking her as 'one of the most bitter enemies of Irish freedom' and 'exceedingly anti-Catholic'.[70] Her funeral took place at Golders Green Crematorium, and on 19 November a memorial service was held in Westminster Abbey, attended by 'all the grandees in the world', Ray Strachey told her mother.[71] Five Cabinet ministers including 'the Rt Hon Margaret' and fifty Members of Parliament were in attendance. Among them were Arthur Henderson, now Foreign Secretary, Stanley Baldwin and Lloyd George, three of the less unreliable friends of the women's suffrage movement among contemporary politicians.[72] There were also representatives of over eighty women's national organizations of all kinds, among them nurses, teachers, civil servants, engineers and doctors. 'And then', Ray Strachey told a radio audience, 'there were hundreds and hundreds of her colleagues of the days of the suffrage fight.'[73]

It is difficult and probably inappropriate to estimate the nature of the contribution made by Millicent Garrett Fawcett to women's freedom. The reason is partly that her life melts into the history of the women's movement itself; she was not a charismatic leader sufficiently dominant to shape it to her own wishes. Her personality, Ray Strachey complained to her mother and daughter, was quiet, reasonable and unsensational.[74] Moreover, it is difficult not to compare her with Emmeline Pankhurst, in contrast to whom almost all other contemporaries appear colourless, and whose career as suffrage leader was marked by so many incidents of the type easily remembered by careless posterity. Brian Harrison quotes an interesting comparison between the two women written by Vera Brittain when the Pankhurst statue was unveiled in 1930. Mrs Pankhurst's memorial service had been characterized by passion and emotion, she wrote, while Mrs Fawcett's was 'official and impersonal'. This verdict might have been challenged by those of the Westminster Abbey congregation of November 1929 who had been in tears, but it is difficult to disagree with

Brittain's comment: 'Humanity reserves its plaudits for those who have stirred its imagination.'[75]

Modern readers inhabit a different world from that of the feminist whose imagination was most deeply stirred by the sexual exploitation of defenceless women and by an inflexible and unattractive form of patriotism. It is difficult to warm to a woman who suddenly consigned friends and colleagues to oblivion because their reactions to a catastrophic war differed from her own. Yet she may well stand as a symbol of the different world which women had succeeded in creating for themselves in her lifetime. Alone among her contemporaries she worked for over sixty years for the emancipation of her sex, touching virtually every aspect of feminist aspirations and inspiring the devotion and loyalty of large numbers of women. Moreover, despite her concentration on women's suffrage and her professional optimism she was in no doubt that feminism could not come to an end once women were finally enfranchised on equal terms with men.

Students of the turbulent history of the modern world have rightly assigned a leading position to militant movements whose dynamic leaders have swayed populations by their oratory and their determination. But pressure groups working on democratic lines and engaged in long-term campaigns to move public and political opinion have an importance often disguised by their habitual lack of glamour. It is in this sphere that most aspects of the feminist movement have operated, achieving significant though agonizingly delayed reforms. Millicent Garrett Fawcett was the most important figure produced by British constitutional feminism. Two generations after her death, as her successors campaign for modern versions of the goals which preoccupied her, the vision, realism and unwearying enthusiasm which she brought to the struggle have not lost their relevance.

NOTES

1. Harrison, *Prudent Revolutionaries* (1987) , esp. pp. 100, 153, 168–9, 206, 286, 289–90, 319.
2. Wiltsher, *Most Dangerous Women* (1985) pp. 15–16.
3. *MG*, 2 December 1927; A.H.W. (Helen Ward), obituary notice in *International Woman Suffrage News*, October 1929, pp 1–2; *MGF*, pp. 228, 338.
4. *WL*, 15 November: 1929, p. 318.
5. Jo Manton to author, 14 September 1986, 16 October 1929. Other accounts (note 3 above) state that she did not employ a secretary.
6. *MG*, 2 December 1927.
7. *WL*, 2 July 1926, p. 200; Charles L. Graves, *Hubert Parry*, vol. 1 (1926), pp. 365–6, 375.
8. *The Times*, 7 April 1926. Her intimate friend Jane Walker was among those who thought that 'the pendulum had swung too far' and that greater reticence was 'much needed' on the part of the young (*WL*, 13 April 1928, p. 81).
9. As note 6.

10. *Punch*, 25 January 1928, p. 90.
11. *WL*, 13 April 1928, p. 82.
12. MGF to Ray Strachey undated (but April 1929) and 6 June 1929 (Strachey Papers, Oxford). The second cutting has not survived.
13. *WL*, 12 March 1926, p. 59; *Daily Telegraph*, 9 April 1926 (Fawcett Library cuttings); *MG*, 2 December 1927.
14. Harold Smith, 'Sex vs class: British feminists and the Labour movement, 1919–1929', *The Historian* (vol. 22, 1984), esp. pp. 32–3; Johanna Alberti, *Beyond Suffrage* (1989), pp. 180–4.
15. *WL*, 5 March 1926, p. 49; *MG*, 2 July 1926.
16. *MG*, 5 July 1926.
17. *WL*, 26 February, 2 July 1926, pp. 37, 200.
18. *MGF*, 'Votes for brides', *John Bull*, 6 November 1926, p. 28.
19. David Close, 'The collapse of resistance to democracy' (1977), pp. 916–18.
20. *MG*, 22 February, 13 April 1927.
21. *Parl. Deb.* (Lords), 5th ser., 66, cols 1-3, 34 (8 February 1927).
22. *The Times*, 28 January 1927.
23. *ibid.*, 13 April 1927 (see *Parl. Deb.*, 5th ser., 180, col. 1504, 20 February 1925); Diana Hopkinson, *Family Inheritance* (Staples Press, 1954), p. 92.
24. *Parl. Deb.*, 5th ser., 205, col. 358 (13 April 1927); Close, pp. 916–17.
25. *MG*, 18 July 1927; *WL*, 22 July 1927, p. 192; *The Times*, 4 October 1927.
26. MGF to Alys Russell, 14 March 1928 (Strachey Papers).
27. Stanley Baldwin to MGF, 5 August 1928 (FLALC, vol. 1m).
28. *MG*, 15 June 1928; *WL*, 20 April, 6 July 1928, pp. 87–8, 175. See also *MGF*, pp. 348–9.
29. *WL*, 27 July 1928, p. 205.
30. *ibid*, 12 November 1926, pp. 359–60.
31. *MG*, 13, 21 June 1927.
32. MGF to Philippa and Ray Strachey, 2 August 1927 (FLALC, vol. 1m). The society had previously been known as, among other titles, the London Society for Women's Suffrage. It is now the Fawcett Society.
33. Carrie Chapman Catt to MGF, 9 June 1927 (*ibid.*).
34. *The Vote*, 15 October 1926, p. 325.
35. Jill Liddington, *Selina Cooper* (1984), pp. 406–7.
36. *MG*, 21 June 1926. In January 1928 she planned to print on her own notepaper a passage from Robert Browning's 'Home thoughts from the sea', which included lines she had often quoted: ' "Here and here did England help me: how can I help England?" – say' (MGF to Christopher Strachey, 2 January [1928], Strachey Papers).
37. *MG*, *The Times*, 7 March 1929; *WL*, 15 March 1929, p. 44.
38. *The Times*, 25 April 1929; *MG*, 26 April 1929.
39. *WL*, 9, 16 August 1929, pp. 210, 218, 219.
40. *The Shield*, September 1928, pp. 219–20.
41. Her handwriting, previously almost as lucid as her prose style, deteriorated towards the end of her life.
42. *The Shield*, September 1929, p. 268.
43. MGF to Ray Strachey, 2 January 1928 (Strachey Papers).
44. *The Shield*, September 1928, p. 203.
45. MGF and Turner, *Josephine Butler* (1927), pp. 1, 152.
46. MGF to Ray Strachey, 21 January 1929 (Strachey Papers); *MGF*, pp. 357–8. Her reading included a life of Lord Curzon in three volumes by Lord Ronaldshay and a short article for the *WL* on Curzon's changing attitude to feminist causes (1 March 1929, p. 29).

47. *Ceylon Daily News*, 26, 28, 30 January 1929; *Times of Ceylon*, 26 January, 7 February 1929.
48. *MGF*, p. 339.
49. *The Times*, 24 June 1926.
50. *ibid.*, 26 June–19 July 1926, *passim*. Her second letter was published on 15 July.
51. *WL*, 11 March 1927, pp. 36–8. For a recent perspective see Harold L. Smith, 'British feminism in the 1920s' in Smith (ed.), *British Feminism in the Twentieth Century* (1990), esp. pp. 58–9.
52. *MG*, 7 March 1927; Jane Lewis, 'Beyond Suffrage' (1978), pp. 12–13.
53. MGF to Ray Strachey, 9 April 1927 (Strachey Papers).
54. *The Times*, 11 November 1926, 16 November 1927.
55. *ibid.*, 1, 11 February 1929; Harrison, *Prudent Revolutionaries*, p. 148.
56. *The Times*, 9 August 1929.
57. MGF, *What the Vote has Done* (1927 edn.), p. 8.
58. *WL*, 28 September, 5, 12 October 1928, pp. 261, 269, 276.
59. *MGF*, pp. 352–3; MGF to Ray Strachey, 9 August [1928].
60. *WL*, 16 August, 15 November 1929, pp. 219, 316; *MGF*, pp. 353–4.
61. MGF to Ray Strachey, 18 May 1929 (Strachey Papers).
62. MGF to Miss Ward, 18 June 1929 (FLALC, vol. 1m).
63. MGF to Badley, 22 June 1929 (FLALC, vol. 14); Bondfield to MGF, 18 June 1929 (*ibid.*, vol. 1m); *MGF*, p. 359.
64. *MGF*, p. 360; *WL*, 9 August 1929, p. 209.
65. *MG*, *Evening Standard*, 31 July 1929 (Fawcett Library cuttings).
66. Stocks, *Eleanor Rathbone* (1949), pp. 128–9.
67. FLA, box 599.
68. Probate Registry Calendars, 1884 and 1929 (Somerset House).
69. Will of Millicent Garrett Fawcett (Somerset House); MGF to Philippa Strachey, 10 May 1929 (FLALC, vol. 8f).
70. *The Draughtsman*, 8 August 1929; *Vaccination Inquirer*, 2 September 1929 (scrapbook acquired by Fawcett Library, September 1988); *Catholic Herald*, 24 August 1929 (Fawcett Library cuttings). She had, however, worked harmoniously with Catholic suffragists for many years, and the *Catholic Citizen* wrote warmly of her: 'We shall ever remember with gratitude her noble work for women' (15 September 1929, p. 71).
71. Ray Strachey to Mary Berenson, 21 November 1929 (Strachey Papers).
72. *MG*, 20 November 1929.
73. Reprinted in abridged form in *WL*, 22 November 1929, p. 324.
74. Harrison, *Prudent Revolutionaries*, p. 42; Barbara Strachey Halpern in conversation with author, 17 October 1986.
75. Harrison, *Prudent Revolutionaries*, p. 42; *MG*, 5 March 1930.

# BIBLIOGRAPHY

### ARCHIVES

Where another scholar has provided research assistance her name is indicated in brackets.

*British Library Add. Mss*
    Auckland Papers
    Cecil of Chelwood Papers
    Dilke Papers
    Edmund Garrett Papers
    Mary Gladstone Papers
    Macmillan Archive
    C.P. Scott Diaries and Letters
    Maud Arncliffe-Sennett Collection

*British Library of Political and Economic Science*
    Courtney Papers
    Lansbury Collection
    LSE Student Union Minutes
    Mill–Taylor Collection

*University of Cambridge*
    Churchill College Archives: W.T. Stead Papers
    Girton College Archives
    Newnham College Archives
    Trinity College Archives
    Trinity Hall Archives: Leslie Stephen Ms biography of Henry Fawcett

*Cumbria Record Office*
    Catherine Marshall Papers

*Dyrham Park, Somerset*
    Blathwayt Diaries

*University of Edinburgh*
    Sarolea Collection

*Fawcett Library*
    Biographical Cuttings File
    Josephine Butler Letter Collection
    Fawcett Library Archives
    Fawcett Library Autograph Letter Collection
    MGF Scrapbook

*Greater London Record Office*
  W.H. Dickinson Papers
  London County Council: Minutes of Technical Education Board
  Microfilm Marriage Register, St Mary Bryanston Square
  School Board for London: Minutes and Annual Reports
  Women's Local Government Society Papers
*Holborn Public Library*
  MGF Letters
*House of Lords Record Office*
  Lloyd George Papers
*University of Hull*
  Records of the *Dictionary of Labour Biography*: Clara Dorothea Rackham
  Union of Democratic Control Papers
*Imperial War Museum*
  Women's Work Collection
*India Office Library*
  Charles Henry Roberts Papers
*Indianapolis Public Library*
  May Wright Sewall Papers (Gail Malmgreen)
*International Information Centre and Archives for the Women's Movement,*
  *Amsterdam*
  Fawcett Collection
*International Institute of Social History, Amsterdam*
  Sylvia Pankhurst Papers
*Iowa State Historical Society, Rossetti Collection*
  Philippa Fawcett Letter
*Johns Hopkins University*
  J.S. Mill Letters
*Kent County Record Office*
  Stanhope Mss
*King's College London: Department for Ladies*
  Archives (Jane Platt)
*Lancashire County Record Office*
  Selina Cooper Papers
*Library of Congress*
  Carrie Chapman Catt Papers (Gail Malmgreen)
*University of Liverpool*
  Rathbone Collection
*McMaster University, Hamilton, Ontario*
  Bertrand Russell Papers (Sheila Turcon)
*Manchester Public Library*
  Manchester Society for Women's Suffrage Papers
  MGF Papers
*University of Manchester, John Rylands Library*
  IWSA Papers
  IWSA, Women's Suffrage Collection
  C.P. Scott Papers
  Women's Suffrage Press Cuttings
*Mitchell Library, Glasgow*
  Glasgow and West of Scotland Association for Women's Suffrage: Letter Book
    and Minutes (Leah Leneman)
*Museum of London*
  Helen Fraser Papers

*National Museum of Labour History, Manchester*
   Labour Party Archives
*New York Public Library*
   Century Collection (Gail Malmgreen)
*Oxford:*
   *Bodleian Library*
   H.A.L. Fisher Papers
   Sidney Lee Correspondence
   Ms Eng. Letters
   C.H. Pearson Papers
   Sidgwick & Jackson Letter Book
   *Strachey Papers* (then in possession of Barbara Strachey Halpern; MGF letters from
      this collection now in Fawcett Library)
*Public Record Office*
   Cabinet Papers
   Home Office Papers
   J.R. MacDonald Papers
   War Office Papers (Susan Sutton)
*Queen's College London*
   Archives
*University of Reading*
   Macmillan Archive
*St Brelade, Jersey*
   Elizabeth Garrett Anderson Papers
*Scottish Record Office*
   Frances Balfour Papers (Joan Huffman and Leah Leneman)
*University of Sheffield*
   A.J. Mundella Papers
*Shulbrede Priory, Lynchmere, Surrey*
   Parry Papers
*Somerset House*
   Wills, Probate Registries
*Suffolk County Record Office*
   *Lowestoft*
   Microfilm Marriage Register, St Peter and St Paul, Aldeburgh
*Bury St Edmunds*
   Jane Walker Hospital Records
*Surrey County Record Office*
   Quarter Sessions Records (Susan Sutton)
*University of Texas*
   Richard Garnett Collection
*Working Men's College, London*
   Journal, Annual Reports, Correspondence
*Yale University* (Gail Malmgreen)
   J.S. Mill Papers
   Fawcett Letters

## PUBLICATIONS BY MILLICENT GARRETT FAWCETT

Each is listed once only, even if published in various versions.

*Books*
(published in London)

*Political Economy for Beginners* (Macmillan, 1870), pp. 200.

(with Henry Fawcett) *Essays and Lectures on Social and Political Subjects* (Macmillan, 1872), pp. 368.

*Tales in Political Economy* (Macmillan, 1874), pp. 104.

*Janet Doncaster* (Smith Elder, 1875), pp. 314.

*Some Eminent Women of our Times: Short biographical sketches* (Macmillan, 1889), pp. 231.

*Life of Her Majesty Queen Victoria* (W.H. Allen, 1895), pp. 262.

*Life of the Right Hon. Sir William Molesworth, Bart., M.P., F.R.S.* (Macmillan, 1901), pp. 346.

*Five Famous French Women* (Cassell, 1905), pp. 304.

*Women's Suffrage: A short history of a great movement* (T.C. & E.C. Jack [1912]), pp. 94.

*The Women's Victory – and After: Personal reminiscences, 1911–1918* (Sidgwick & Jackson, 1920), pp. 176.

*What I Remember* (T. Fisher Unwin, 1924), pp. 272.

*\*Easter in Palestine, 1921–1922* (T. Fisher Unwin, 1926), pp. 188.

(with Ethel M. Turner) *Josephine Butler: Her work and principles and their meaning for the twentieth century* (Association for Moral and Social Hygiene, 1927), pp. 164.

\*First privately published as: *Six Weeks in Palestine: Spring, 1921* [1921], pp. 72; and *Our Second Visit to Palestine: Spring, 1922* [1922], pp. 78.


## Pamphlets

(published in London unless otherwise indicated)

*Mrs Fawcett on Women's Suffrage* (Birmingham: reprinted from *Birmingham Morning News* [?1872]), pp. 8.

(with Henry Fawcett and Thomas Bazley) *Factory Acts Amendment Bill* (Macmillan, 1873), pp. 40.

*Mr Fitzjames Stephen on the Position of Women* (Macmillan, 1873), pp. 15.

*The Martyrs of Turkish Misrule* (Cassell Petter & Galpin, 1877), pp. 24.

(with Henry Fawcett) *Free Education in its Relation to the Social Condition of the People* (Women's Printing Society [1890]), pp. 16.

*A Reply to the Letter of Mr Samuel Smith, M.P. on Women's Suffrage* (Central Committee of NSWS, 1892), pp. 11.

*Home and Politics* (Women's Printing Society [1894]), pp. 8.

*Speech* [to the National Union of Women Workers] *on the New Rules for Dealing with the Sanitary Condition of the British Army in India* (Women's Printing Society [?1897]), pp. 24.

*Women's Suffrage: An address delivered at the junior constitutional club* (n.p., 1897), pp. 18.

(with C.W. Radcliffe Cooke, MP) *Women's Suffrage in Parliament* (NUWSS, 1898), pp. 11.

*Extract from a Private Letter . . . about the Forthcoming International Congress* (n.p., [1899]), pp. 4.

*International Congress. The White Slave Trade: its causes, and the best means of preventing it* (n.p., 1899), pp. 8.

*Women's Suffrage: A speech delivered to the women's debating society, the Owens College, Manchester* (Manchester: North of England Society for Women's Suffrage, 1899), pp. 15.

(and others) *Helen Blackburn: Memoir & notices* (John Bale Sons & Danielsson, 1903), pp. 23.

*Speech by Mrs Henry Fawcett: Chairman at the dinner of the Women's Local Government Society, November 29th, 1905* (WLGS [?1905]), pp. 2.

*Debate Between Mrs Humphry Ward and Mrs Henry Fawcett, LL. D.* (n.p. [1909]), pp. 30.
*Wanted: a Statesman* (Glasgow n.p., 1909), pp. 11.
*Would Labour Help the Middle Classes?* (n.p. [1920]), proof (M50/8/8).
*What the Vote Has Done* (NUSEC, 1922), pp. 4; (1924 edn), pp. 4; (1925 edn), pp. 6; (1926 edn), pp. 6; (1927 edn), pp. 8.


## Articles

An attempt, inevitably arbitrary, has been made to exclude letters, reviews, NUWSS statements and reports of speeches.
*Common Cause*
  15 April 1909, pp. 7–8
  22 July 1909, p. 196
  30 June 1910, p. 179
  7 July 1910, p. 199
  1 December 1910, p. 552
  2 November 1911, p. 515
  7 December 1911, pp. 612–13
  8 February 1912, p. 749
  15 February 1912, p. 765
  29 February 1912, p. 802
  28 March 1912, p. 863
  4 April 1912, p. 880
  25 April 1912, p. 37
  2 May 1912, p. 51
  23 May 1912, p. 100
  30 May 1912, p. 117
  25 July 1912, p. 265
  29 November 1912, pp. 584–5
  13 December 1912, pp. 615–16
  17 January 1913, p. 700
  24 January 1913, p. 715
  31 January 1913, p. 735
  28 February 1913, pp. 800–1
  7 March 1913, p. 817
  9 May 1913, p. 67
  11 July 1913, p. 227
  12 September 1913, pp. 383–4
  14 November 1913, pp. 574–6
  28 November 1913, p. 612
  23 January 1914, p. 784
  7 August 1914, p. 376
  23 April 1915, pp. 32–3
  2 July 1915, pp. 174–5
  30 July 1915, p. 225
  6 August 1915, pp. 234–5
  1 October 1915, p. 313
  5 November 1915, p. 380
  12 November 1915, p. 400
  25 February 1916, pp. 614–15
  19 May 1916, p. 82
  7 July 1916, pp. 166–7

14 July 1916, pp. 178–9
29 December 1916, p. 504
9 February 1917, pp. 578–9
7 April 1917, pp. 686–7
13 April 1917, pp. 4–5
22 June 1917, p. 125
5 October 1917, pp. 302–3
16 November 1917, pp. 382–3
7 December 1917, pp. 428–9
4 January 1918, pp. 484–5
11 January 1918, pp. 501–2
18 January 1918, pp. 516–17
15 February 1918, p. 572
15 March 1918, pp. 632–3
10 May 1918, pp. 38–40
17 May 1918, p. 51
24 May 1918, pp. 62–3
5 July 1918, p. 144
4 October 1918, p. 282
5 November 1918, p. 358
20 December 1918, p. 427
24 January 1919, p. 487
21 March 1919, p. 606
25 April 1919, p. 14
30 May 1919, p. 72
26 December 1919, p. 496
23 January 1920, p. 532

*The Englishwoman*
1909:   February, pp. 17–31
        April, pp. 271–80
        December, pp. 144–51
1910:   July, pp. 243–7
        pp. 273–84
1911:   January, pp. 1–7
        June, pp. 241–7
1912:   January, pp. 1–9
        February, pp. 127–8
        March, pp. 241–3
        June, pp. 241–5
1913:   January, pp. 1–6
        February, p. 121
1914:   January, pp. 1–4
        August, pp. 121–8
        November, pp. 96–100
1915:   June, pp. 193–200
1916:   January, pp. 5–15
        September, pp. 193–8
        December, pp. 196–209
1917:   March, pp. 193–7
1918:   March, pp. 163–8
        December, pp. 97–100
1919:   April, pp. 1–3
1920:   January, pp. 1–7

*Woman's Leader*
  6 February 1920, p. 4
  11 June 1920, p. 429
  20 August 1920, p. 637
  26 November 1920, p. 917
  11 March 1921, p. 87
  15 April 1921, pp. 165–6
  13 May 1921, p. 226
  22 July 1921, p. 372
  7 April 1922, p. 76
  14 July 1922, p. 188
  24 November 1922, p. 337
  27 July 1923, p. 205
  17 August 1923, p. 229
  30 November 1923, p. 352
  25 July 1924, pp. 208–9
  31 October 1924, p. 318
  26 December 1924, p. 384
  30 January 1925, pp. 3–5
  28 August 1925, p. 244
  26 February 1926, p. 37
  2 July 1926, p. 200
  18 March 1927, p. 44
  8 April 1927, p. 73
  6 May 1927, p. 105
  13 May 1927, p. 113
  29 July 1927, p. 200
  9 December 1927, p. 353
  23 December 1927, p. 365
  30 March 1928, p. 64
  6 April 1928, pp. 71–2
  20 April 1928, pp. 87–8
  6 July 1928, p. 175
  13 July 1928, p. 184
  28 September 1928, p. 261
  5 October 1928, p. 269
  12 October 1928, p. 276
  7 December 1928, p. 338
  21 December 1928, p. 356
  25 January 1929, p. 397
  1 February 1929, p. 403
  1 March 1929, p. 29
  10 May 1929, p. 110
  24 May 1929, p. 126

*What I Remember* was serialized from 14 September 1923 until 29 August 1924. *Two Spring Visits to Palestine, 1921–1922* (later *Easter in Palestine*) was serialized from 3 October 1924 until 31 July 1925.

*Other articles, chapters and introductions*

*Alexandra College Magazine* (Dublin), June 1904, pp. 3–9; 'Women and politics'.
*The Arrow*, 4 May 1888, pp. 103–5; 'For home and country'.

de Beck, A.M. (ed.), *Women of the Empire in War Time* (Dominion of Canada News Co., 1916), pp. 24–7; 'Scottish women's hospital for foreign service: war work of the N.U.W.S.S.'.

Blackwell, Elizabeth, *Pioneer Work for Women* [J.M. Dent, 1914], pp. vii–xv; Introduction.

*Century Magazine* (New York), November 1912, pp. 148–9; 'Violence in the woman's suffrage movement'.

*Chambers's Encyclopaedia* (1889 edn), vol. 4, pp. 567–8; 'Henry Fawcett'.

*Cheltenham Ladies' College Magazine*, spring 1894, pp. 5–24; 'The story of the opening of university education to women'.

*The Congregationalist*, January 1873, pp. 15–20; 'Edmond About's social economy'.

*Conservative and Unionist Women's Franchise Review*
    October 1911, pp. 148–9; 'Women and representative government'.
    October–December 1915, p. 41; 'Life's cost'.

*Contemporary Review*
    September 1885, pp. 326–31; 'The protection of girls. I. Speech or silence'.
    November 1886, pp. 719–27; 'The use of higher education to women: address to the students of Bedford College'.
    May 1887, pp. 639–53; 'Holes in the education net'.
    December 1889, pp. 822–9; 'The employment of children in theatres'.
    November 1890, pp. 712–20; 'Infant marriage in India'.
    June 1892, pp. 761–8; 'The women's suffrage question'.
    March 1894, pp. 433–7; 'New Zealand under female franchise'.
    May 1895, pp. 625–31; 'The woman who did'.
    March 1896, pp. 347–56; 'Degrees for women at Oxford'.
    March 1899, pp. 328–42; 'The Vaccination Act of 1902'.
    November 1903, pp. 635–55; 'Impressions of South Africa, 1901 and 1903'.
    December 1906, pp. 820–6; 'The prisoners of hope in Holloway Gaol'.
    May 1912, pp. 609–11; 'W.T. Stead'.
    December 1914, pp. 775–82; 'Women's work in war time'.
    July 1916, pp. 40–6; 'The new parliamentary register and votes for women'.
    March 1917, pp. 312–18; 'The speaker's conference on electoral reform'.
    October 1918, pp. 387–90; 'Equal pay for equal value'.
    November 1919, pp. 518–22; 'Cambridge and women's university education'.
    April 1928, pp. 442–6; 'Josephine Butler 1828–1928'.

*Daily Chronicle*, 28 November 1918; 'Why I support Mr Lloyd George and the coalition programme'.

*Daily Citizen*, 4 November 1912; ' "Who's for us? For him are we" '.

*Daily Graphic*, 23 January 1890; 'Women's suffrage in America and in England'.

*Daily Mail*, 20 November 1906; 'Why we women want votes'.

*Daily News*
    26 April 1884; 'Examinations for women at Oxford'.
    3 June 1884; 'Women's suffrage and the new reform bill'.
    9 March 1912; 'Broken windows – and after'.
    3 August 1916; 'The women's claim'.
    15 April 1918; 'New women voters: the responsibility of citizenship.'
    23 October 1918; 'Women Members of Parliament'.

Dawson, William Harbutt (ed.), *After-War Problems* (Allen & Unwin, 1917), pp. 191–215; 'The position of women in economic life'.

*The Echo*
    'The employment of children in theatres'
    10 December 1888; 'How the factory acts and education act have worked'.
    12 December 1888; 'What the teachers of the children say'.

15 December 1888; 'What theatrical people say'.

18 December 1888; 'The economic difficulty'.

*Economic Journal*

March 1892, pp. 173–6; 'Mr Sidney Webb's article on women's wages'.

March 1918, pp. 1–6; 'Equal pay for equal work'.

*Encyclopaedia Britannica*

(9th edn, 1877), vol. 6, pp. 211–19; 'Communism'.

(12th edn, New York, 1922), vol. 31, pp. 1034–9, 'Woman suffrage'.

*English Review*, March 1918, pp. 260–6; 'War and reconstruction: women and their use of the vote'.

*Evening News*, 11 January 1918; 'Votes for women: the end of my desire'.

*Examiner*

5 April 1873, p. 351; 'The government and the bank act'.

17 May 1873, pp. 515–17; '[John Stuart Mill's] influence as a practical politician'.

10 July 1875, pp. 769–70; 'Professor Cairnes'.

*Fortnightly Review*

November 1868, pp. 554–71; 'The medical and general education of women'.

May 1870, pp. 622–32; 'The electoral disabilities of women'.

April 1889, pp. 555–67; 'The women's suffrage bill. I. The enfranchisement of women'.

July 1889, pp. 123–31; 'Women's suffrage: a reply'.

November 1891, pp. 673–85; 'The emancipation of women'.

*Forum* (New York), December 1892, pp. 453–64; 'Women in English politics'.

*Fraser's Magazine*, February 1872, pp. 234–41; 'An American on representation'.

Gates, G. Evelyn (ed.), *The Woman's Year Book 1923–1924* (Women Publishers [1923]), pp. 15–21; 'Historical survey'.

*Good Words*, November 1878, pp. 853–60; 'The old and the new ideals of women's education'.

Harper, Ida Husted (ed.), *The History of Woman Suffrage vol. 6, 1900–1920* (National American Woman Suffrage Association, New York, 1922) pp. 725–51; 'Progress of the women's movement in the United Kingdom. 1900–1920.'

*The Humanitarian*, July 1893, pp. 43–9; 'Politics in the home'.

*Imperial Colonist*, March 1904, pp. 28–30; 'Openings for women in South Africa. I. Gardening'.

*John Bull*, 6 November 1926, p. 28; 'Votes for brides'.

*Jus Suffragii* and *International Woman Suffrage News*

1 September 1914, p. 159; 'Message to the IWSA'.

1 January 1915, pp. 216–17; 'A New Year's message to all the countries in the IWSA', p. 230; 'Ought there to be an international congress of women in the near future'.

1 April 1915, pp. 262–3; 'Women's suffrage and a European congress after the war'.

1 November 1915, p. 20; 'The women's movement in India'.

December 1918, p. 26; 'To women of all nations'.

December 1919, p. 35; 'The future of the IWSA'.

*Ladies' Field*, 21 November 1914 (supplement), pp. 7–8; 'Women and the war'.

*Leeds Mercury*, 8 May 1894, 'A living wage'.

*Liberal Unionist*, 3 August 1887, pp. 1–2; 'Mr Fawcett and the formation of a non-party political association'.

*Liberty Annual*, 1893, pp. 3–7; 'Liberty for women'.

Loftie, W.J. (ed.), *Orient Line Guide* (Sampson Low):

2nd edn, 1885, pp. 140–53, 'Italy'; pp. 154–78, 'European cities';

3rd edn, 1888, pp. 77–98; 'Naples'; pp. 99–114, 'Cities of Italy'; pp. 115–22, 'Germany';

4th edn, 1890 (as third edition);

5th edn, 1894, pp. 61–74, 'From Gibraltar to Naples' (part);

6th edn [1901], pp. 49–60, 'London to Marseilles and Naples' (part); pp. 92–6, 'Cairo'.

*London Pupil Teachers' Association Record*, September 1887, p. 1; no title.

*Macmillan's Magazine*

April 1868, pp. 511–17; 'The education of women of the middle and upper classes'.

September 1870, pp. 376–82; 'Proportional representation'.

April 1871, pp. 481–7; 'A short explanation of Mr Hare's scheme of representation'.

January 1872, pp. 180–9; 'National debts and national prosperity'.

*Magazine of Art*

October 1884, pp. 1–8; 'The New Forest. I. Picturesque'.

November 1884, pp. 45–52; 'The New Forest. II. Historical'.

September 1885, pp. 485–92; 'Burnham Beeches'.

*Manchester Examiner and Times*, 1 March 1889; 'Women's suffrage'.

*Manchester Guardian*, 6 July 1928; 'Equal franchise. Victory after sixty years'.

Marchant, James (ed.), *Public Morals* (Morgan and Scott [1902]), pp. 242–5; 'Words of encouragement'.

Mill, J.S., *On Liberty, Representative Government, The Subjection of Women* (Oxford University Press, 1912 edn), pp. v–xviii; Introduction.

*Morning Post*, 19 April 1911; 'The Divorce Commission Evidence. The woman's point of view'.

Morten, Honnor, *Questions for Women (and Men)* (A. & C. Black, 1899), pp. 1–13; Introduction.

*The Nation*

4 April 1914, pp. 16–17; 'The waste of life'.

27 February 1915, pp. 679–80; '1815 and 1915–16'.

*National Review*, March 1888, pp. 44–61; 'Women's suffrage: a reply'.

National Union of Women Workers, Annual Reports:

1891, pp. 210–16; 'Valedictory address'.

1892 (appendix), pp. 3–12; 'Amendments required in the Criminal Law Amendment Act 1885'.

1895, pp. 72–80; 'The probable effect on the position of women of granting them the parliamentary suffrage'.

1900, pp. 58–61; 'The work of women as government officials and on public boards'.

1906, pp. 81–3; 'Women's suffrage'.

*New Review*, November 1890, pp. 450–4; 'Indian child marriage'.

*New Statesman*, 1 November 1913 (supplement), pp. viii–x; 'The remedy of political emancipation'.

*Nineteenth Century*

August 1878, pp. 347–57; 'The future of Englishwomen: a reply'.

August 1883, pp. 285–91; 'Women and representative government'.

May 1886, pp. 740–8; 'Women's suffrage: a reply'.

July 1889, pp. 86–96; 'The appeal against female suffrage: a reply'.

*Pall Mall Gazette*

14 January 1884; 'Women's suffrage and the franchise bill'.

1 March 1886; 'The second reading of the women's suffrage bill'.

12 February 1887; 'The Travellers' Aid Society'.

*Quarterly Review*, January 1916, pp. 111–29; 'War relief and war service'.

*The Queen*, 26 September 1914, p. 501; 'What the National Union of Women's Suffrage Societies is doing'.

*Review of Reviews*
    September 1913, pp. 196–7; 'Votes for women: a reply to Mr Lloyd George'.
    July 1918, pp. 30–1; 'The new women voters'.
*Review of the Churches*, July 1895, pp. 204–6; 'On the separate education of the sexes'.
*St James's Gazette*, 7 January 1889; 'For women's suffrage'.
Stanton, Theodore (ed.), *The Woman Question in Europe: A series of original essays* (Sampson Low, 1884), pp. 1–30; 'England. I. The women's suffrage movement'.
*Sunday Magazine*, February 1890, pp. 124–8; 'Theatre children: or, ought Christians to patronise performances by young children?'
Swanwick, Helena, *The Future of the Women's Movement* (Bell, 1913), pp. xi–xiv; Introduction.
*Time*, May 1888, pp. 528–32; 'Altissima Peto. An address to high school pupils'.
*Time and Tide*, 5, 12 March 1926, pp. 227–8, 252; 'Women and internationalism'.
*The Times*
    10 November 1906; obituary of Dorothea Beale.
    2 June 1910; obituary of Elizabeth Blackwell.
    26 August 1916; 'Helping the refugees. National Union of Women's Suffrage Societies.'
*Times of India*, 24 August 1929; 'Can women influence international policy?'
*Universal Review*, November 1888, pp. 289–94; 'The progress of woman. I. In political education'.
*Vigilance Record*
    January 1890, pp. 138–9; 'Infant marriage in India'.
    February 1893, p. 4; 'Workers wanted' (with Mary Bunting).
*The Vote*, 12 June 1925, p. 189; 'Family endowment'.
*War Illustrated*, 6 January 1917, pp. 482, 484; 'The war's effect on woman's work'.
*Westminster Gazette*
    17 May 1897; 'The report of the Cambridge Syndicate on women's degrees'.
    4 July 1901; 'The concentration camps in South Africa'.
    1 August 1916; 'The government and the question of registration and franchise reform'.
Wollstonecraft, Mary, *A Vindication of the Rights of Woman* (1792; T. Fisher Unwin, 1891), pp. 1–30; Introduction.
*Woman at Home*, (?January) 1907, pp. 568–9; 'Ought women to have the suffrage?'
*Woman's World*, November 1888, pp. 9–12; 'Women's suffrage'.
*Women's Franchise*
    27 February 1908, p. 397; 'Next Friday in the House of Commons'.
    29 October 1908, p. 196; 'The National Union by-election policy'.
    19 November 1908, p. 237; 'National Union manifesto'.
    10 December 1908, p. 284; 'The Chancellor of the Exchequer at the Albert Hall meeting'.

OTHER SOURCES (SELECTED)

(Books published in London unless otherwise indicated)
Anderson, Louisa Garrett, *Elizabeth Garrett Anderson 1836–1917* (Faber, 1939).
Alberti, Johanna, *Beyond Suffrage: Feminists in war and peace, 1914–28* (Basingstoke: Macmillan, 1989).
Bahlman, Dudley W.R. (ed.), *The Diary of Sir Edward Walter Hamilton 1880–1885*, two volumes (Oxford University Press, 1972).
Balfour, Frances, *Ne Obliviscaris: Dinna forget*, volume 2 (Hodder & Stoughton [1930]).

Billington, Rosamund, 'Women, politics and local liberalism: from "female suffrage" to "votes for women" ', *Journal of Regional and Local Studies* (vol. 5, 1985), pp. 1–14.

Billington, Rosamund, 'The women's education and suffrage movements', 1850–1914: innovation and institutionalisation' (unpublished doctoral thesis, University of Hull, 1976).

Blackburn, Helen, *Women's suffrage: A record of the women's suffrage movement in the British Isles with biographical sketches of Miss Becker* (Williams & Norgate, 1902).

Bland, Lucy, 'The married woman, the "new woman" and the feminist: sexual politics of the 1890s' in Jane Rendall (ed.), *Equal or Different: Women's politics 1800–1914* (Oxford: Blackwell, 1987), pp. 141–64, 267–70.

Caine, Barbara, 'John Stuart Mill and the English women's movement', *Historical Studies* (vol. 18, 1978), pp. 52–67.

Close, David, 'The collapse of resistance to democracy: conservatives, adult suffrage, and second chamber reform, 1911–1928', *Historical Journal* (vol. 20, 1977), pp. 893–918.

Coote, W.A. (ed.), *A Romance of Philanthropy: Being a record of some of the principal incidents connected with the exceptionally successful thirty years' work of the National Vigilance Association* (NVA, 1916).

Davidoff, Leonore and Hall, Catherine, *Family Fortunes: Men and women of the English middle class 1780–1850* (Hutchinson, 1987).

Davis, Tracy C., 'The employment of children in the Victorian theatre', *New Theatre Quarterly* (vol. 2, 1986), pp. 116–35.

Dobbie, B.M. Willmott, *A Nest of Suffragettes in Somerset: Eagle House, Batheaston* (n.p., 1979).

Dyhouse, Carol, *Feminism and the Family in England 1880–1939* (Oxford: Blackwell, 1989).

Garner, Les, *Stepping Stones to Women's Liberty: Feminist ideas in the women's suffrage movement 1900–1918* (Heinemann, 1984).

Goldman, Lawrence (ed.), *The Blind Victorian: Henry Fawcett and British liberalism* (Cambridge: Cambridge University Press, 1989).

Graves, Charles L., *Hubert Parry: His life and works*, two volumes (Macmillan, 1926).

Gwynn, Stephen and Tuckwell, Gertrude M., *The Life of The Rt. Hon. Sir Charles W. Dilke, Bart., M.P.*, two volumes (John Murray, 1917).

Harrison, Brian, *Prudent Revolutionaries: Portraits of British feminists between the wars* (Oxford: Clarendon Press, 1987).

Harrison, Brian, *Separate Spheres: The opposition to women's suffrage in Britain* (Croom Helm, 1978).

Harrison, Brian, 'Women's suffrage at Westminster 1866–1928', in Michael Bentley and John Stevenson (eds), *High and Low Politics in Modern Britain* (Oxford: Clarendon Press, 1983), pp. 80–122.

Harvie, Christopher, *The Lights of Liberalism: University liberals and the challenge of democracy 1860–86* (Allen Lane, 1976).

Hobhouse, Emily, *The Brunt of the War: And where it fell* (Methuen, 1902).

Hollis, Patricia, *Ladies Elect: Women in English local government 1865–1914* (Oxford: Clarendon Press, 1987).

Holton, Sandra Stanley, *Feminism and Democracy: Women's suffrage and reform politics in Britain, 1900–1918* (Cambridge: Cambridge University Press, 1986).

Hume, Leslie Parker, *The National Union of Women's Suffrage Societies* (New York: Garland, 1982).

Jalland, Pat, *Women, Marriage and Politics 1860–1914* (Oxford: Clarendon Press, 1986).

Kamm, Josephine, *John Stuart Mill in Love* (Gordon & Cremonesi, 1977).

Kent, Susan Kingsley, *Sex and Suffrage in Britain, 1860–1914* (Princeton: Princeton University Press, 1987).

Leventhal, F.M., *The Last Dissenter: H.N. Brailsford and his world* (Oxford: Clarendon Press, 1985).

Levine, Philippa, *Victorian Feminism 1850–1900* (Hutchinson, 1987).

Lewis, Jane (ed.), *Before the Vote was Won: Arguments for and against women's suffrage* (Routledge & Kegan Paul, 1987).

Lewis, Jane, 'Beyond suffrage: English feminism in the 1920s', *Maryland Historian* (vol. 6, 1973), pp. 1–17.

Lewis, Jane, *Women in England 1870–1950: Sexual divisions and social change* (Brighton: Wheatsheaf, 1984).

Liddington, Jill, *The Life and Times of a Respectable Rebel: Selina Cooper (1864–1946)* (Virago, 1984).

Liddington, Jill and Norris, Jill, *One Hand Tied Behind Us: The rise of the women's suffrage movement* (Virago, 1978).

McCrone, Kathleen E., *Playing the Game: Sport and the physical emancipation of English women, 1870–1914* (Lexington: University Press of Kentucky, 1988).

McWilliams-Tullberg, Rita, *Women at Cambridge: A men's university – though of a mixed type* (Gollancz, 1975).

Manton, Jo, *Elizabeth Garrett Anderson* (Methuen, 1965).

Mineka, Francis E. and Lindley, Dwight N. (eds) *The Later Letters of John Stuart Mill 1849–1873*, vols 2–4 (Toronto: University of Toronto Press, 1972).

Morgan, David, *Suffragists and Liberals: The politics of woman suffrage in England* (Oxford: Blackwell, 1975).

Oakley, Ann, 'Millicent Garrett Fawcett: duty and determination (1847–1929)' in Dale Spender (ed.), *Feminist Theorists: Three centuries of women's intellectual traditions* (Women's Press, 1983), pp. 184–202.

Oldfield, Sybil, *Spinsters of this Parish: The life and times of F.M. Mayor and Mary Sheepshanks* (Virago, 1984).

Pankhurst, E. Sylvia, *The Suffragette Movement: An intimate account of persons and ideals* (Longmans, Green, 1931).

Pugh, Martin, *Electoral Reform in War and Peace, 1906–18* (Routledge & Kegan Paul, 1978).

Pugh, Martin, 'Labour and women's suffrage' in Kenneth D. Brown (ed.), *The First Labour Party 1906–1914* (Croom Helm, 1985), pp. 233–53.

Pugh, Martin, 'Politicians and the woman's vote 1914–1918', *History* (vol. 59, 1974), pp. 358–74.

Pugh, Martin, *Women's Suffrage in Britain 1867–1928* (Historical Association, 1980).

Ramelson, Marian, *The Petticoat Rebellion: A century of struggle for women's rights* (Lawrence and Wishart, 1967).

Rempel, Richard A., Brink, Andrew and Moran, Margaret (eds), *The Collected Papers of Bertrand Russell, volume 12: Contemplation and action, 1902–14* (Allen & Unwin, 1985).

Robson, A.P.W., 'The founding of the National Society for Women's Suffrage 1866–1867', *Canadian Journal of History* (vol. 8, 1973), pp. 1–22.

Rosen, Andrew, 'Emily Davies and the women's movement, 1862–1867', *Journal of British Studies* (vol. 19, 1979), pp. 101–21.

Rosen, Andrew, *Rise Up, Women!: The militant campaign of the Women's Social and Political Union 1903–1914* (Routledge & Kegan Paul, 1974).

Rover, Constance, *Love, Morals and the Feminists* (Routledge & Kegan Paul, 1970).

Rover, Constance, *Women's Suffrage and Party Politics in Britain 1866–1914* (Routledge & Kegan Paul, 1967).

Rubinstein, David, *Before the Suffragettes: Women's emancipation in the 1890s* (Hemel Hempstead: Harvester Wheatsheaf, 1986).

Rubinstein, David, *School Attendance in London 1870–1904: A social history* (Hull, University of Hull, 1969).

St Helier, Mary (Lady), *Memories of Fifty Years* (Arnold, 1909).

Sharp, Evelyn, *Unfinished Adventure: Selected reminiscences from an Englishwoman's life* (John Lane the Bodley Head, 1933).

Sidgwick, Arthur and Sidgwick, Eleanor Mildred, *Henry Sidgwick: A memoir* (Macmillan, 1906).

Smith, Harold (ed.), *British Feminism in the Twentieth Century* (Aldershot: Edward Elgar, 1990).

Smyth, Ethel, *Impressions that Remained: Memoirs*, volume 2 (Longmans, Green, 1919).

Stephen, Barbara, *Emily Davies and Girton College* (Constable, 1927).

Stephen, Leslie, *Life of Henry Fawcett* (Smith, Elder, 1885).

Stocks, Mary, *Eleanor Rathbone: A biography* (Gollancz, 1949).

Stocks, Mary, *My Commonplace Book* (Peter Davies, 1970).

Strachey, Ray, *Millicent Garrett Fawcett* (John Murray, 1931).

Swanwick, Helena, *I Have Been Young* (Gollancz, 1935).

Tickner, Lisa, *The Spectacle of Women: Imagery of the suffrage campaign 1907–14* (Chatto & Windus, 1987).

Vellacott, Jo, 'Feminist consciousness and the First World War', *History Workshop* (23, 1987), pp. 81–101.

Walker, Linda, 'Party political women: a comparative study of Liberal women and the Primrose League, 1890–1914' in Jane Rendall (ed.), *Equal or Different: Women's politics 1800–1914* (Oxford: Blackwell, 1987), pp. 165–91, 270–5.

Whyte, Frederic, *The Life of W.T. Stead*, two volumes (Cape, 1925).

Wiltsher, Ann, *Most Dangerous Women: Feminist peace campaigners of the great war* (Pandora, 1985).

# INDEX

Note: Titles such as Dame, Lady, Lord and Sir are supplied only where relevant to the text. The relationship to MGF of Dunnells and Garretts with identical forenames is indicated in brackets. For initials see list at front of book.